SCOTT, FORESMAN AND COMPANY
EXPLORING MATHEMATICS ®

AUTHORS

L. Carey Bolster
Coordinator of Mathematics
Baltimore County Public Schools
Towson, Maryland

Clem Boyer
Coordinator of Mathematics, K-12
District School Board of Seminole
County
Sanford, Florida

Thomas Butts
Associate Professor, Mathematics
Education
University of Texas at Dallas
Richardson, Texas

Mary Cavanagh
Math/Science Coordinator
Solana Beach School District
Solana Beach, California

Marea W. Channel
Mathematics Resource Teacher
Los Angeles Unified School District
Los Angeles, California

Warren D. Crown
Associate Professor of Mathematics
Education
Rutgers, The State University of
New Jersey
New Brunswick, New Jersey

Jan Fair
Mathematics Department
Allan Hancock College
Santa Maria, California

Robert Y. Hamada
District Elementary Mathematics
Specialist
Los Angeles Unified School District
Los Angeles, California

Margaret G. (Peggy) Kelly
Associate Professor
California State University, Fresno
Fresno, California

Miriam Leiva
Professor of Mathematics
University of North Carolina at
Charlotte
Charlotte, North Carolina

**Mary Montgomery
Lindquist**
Callaway Professor of Mathematics
Education
Columbus College
Columbus, Georgia

William B. Nibbelink
Professor, Division of Early
Childhood and Elementary
Education
University of Iowa
Iowa City, Iowa

Linda Proudfit
University Professor of Mathematics
and Computer Education
Governors State University
University Park, Illinois

Cathy Rahlfs
Mathematics Coordinator
Humble Independent School District
Humble, Texas

Rosie Ramirez
Assistant Principal
Charles Rice Elementary School
Dallas, Texas

Jeanne F. Ramos
Mathematics Adviser
Los Angeles Unified School District
Los Angeles, California

Gail Robinette
Elementary Mathematics
Coordinator
Fresno Unified School District
Fresno, California

David Robitaille
Head, Department of Mathematics
and Science Education
University of British Columbia
Vancouver, British Columbia,
Canada

James E. Schultz
Associate Professor of Mathematics
The Ohio State University
Columbus, Ohio

Richard Shepardson
Professor, Division of Early
Childhood and Elementary
Education
University of Iowa
Iowa City, Iowa

Jane Swafford
Professor of Mathematics
Illinois State University
Normal, Illinois

Benny Tucker
Professor of Education; Chairman,
Education Department
Union University
Jackson, Tennessee

John Van de Walle
Associate Professor of Education
Virginia Commonwealth University
Richmond, Virginia

David E. Williams
Former Director of Mathematics
Education
School District of Philadelphia
Philadelphia, Pennsylvania

Robert J. Wisner
Professor of Mathematics
New Mexico State University
Las Cruces, New Mexico

Editorial Offices: Glenview, Illinois
Regional Offices: Sunnyvale, California • Tucker, Georgia
Glenview, Illinois • Oakland, New Jersey • Dallas, Texas

CONTRIBUTING AUTHOR

Janet K. Scheer
Director of Field Services
    for Mathematics
Scott, Foresman and Company
Glenview, Illinois

CONSULTANTS

Reading
Robert A. Pavlik
Professor and Chairperson,
Reading/Language Arts
    Department
Cardinal Stritch College
Milwaukee, Wisconsin

At-Risk Students
Edgar G. Epps
Marshall Field
Professor of Urban Education
Department of Education
University of Chicago
Chicago, Illinois

**Limited-English-Proficient
Students**
Walter Secada
Department of Curriculum
    and Instruction
University of Wisconsin
Madison, Wisconsin

Mainstreaming
Roxie Smith
Associate Provost
Northwestern University
Evanston, Illinois

Gifted Students
Christine Kuehn Ebert
Assistant Professor of Education
University of South Carolina
Columbia, South Carolina

CRITIC READERS

Tony Barajas
Grace M. Nicholson School
Montgomery, Illinois

Jean (Bagley) Brennan
Johnson School
Nahant, Massachusetts

Jonathan Brinkerhoff
Shell Beach Elementary School
Pismo Beach, California

Leonor Esquivel Chavera
Zavala Special Emphasis
    Elementary School
Corpus Christi, Texas

Howard Cohn
Lone Star Elementary School
Jacksonville, Florida

Beverly Ireland
Loomis School
Loomis, California

Mary Jaramillo
Goliad Elementary School
Odessa, Texas

Lin Jennings
Longoria Elementary School
Brownsville, Texas

Robert Leyva
Hellbeck Elementary School
Pueblo, Colorado

Rosemary Marich
Youngstown City Schools
Youngstown, Ohio

Feliciano Mendoza
Miles Avenue School
Huntington Park, California

Ann Marie O'Leary
Peter Muschal School
Bordentown, New Jersey

Vincent F. Rozen
Norwood Avenue Elementary
    School
Cranston, Rhode Island

Jan Sands
Western Oaks Elementary
    School
Bethany, Oklahoma

Diane C. Yee
Jefferson Year Round School
Oakland, California

ISBN: 0–673–33103–2

Copyright © 1991 Scott,
Foresman and Company,
Glenview, Illinois
All Rights Reserved.
Printed in the United States of
America.

56789-RRW-97969594939291

ACKNOWLEDGMENTS
Design
Cover and Special Features:
SHELDON COTLER + ASSOCIATES

Art Direction and Production/
    Core Lessons: Taurins Design
    Associates, Inc./NYC

Scott, Foresman Staff and
    Rosa + Wesley Design
    Associates

Editorial Development
Scott, Foresman Staff and
    Falletta Associates

Photographs
Cover: Richard Chesnut xi (tl):
Lawrence Migdale xi (bl):
Lawrence Migdale xi (c): Tony
Freeman, PhotoEdit xi (tr):
Lawrence Migdale xii (bc):
Lawrence Migdale xiii (t):
Stephen Frisch, Stock Boston
xiv–xv: Courtesy International
Business Machines Corporation
xvii (tl): David R. Frazier xviii (tr):
Jan Doyle, PhotoEdit xix (tr):
Scott, Berner, The Picture Cube
1 (tl): Alan Oddie, PhotoEdit 1
(br): Mary Kate Denny, PhotoEdit
Scott, Foresman photographs by:
Richard Chesnut 17, 34–35, 50,
104, 105, 130, 131, 163,
218–219, 248, 249, 252–253,
269, 311, 402, 403, 406–407,
418, 452, 453, 470–471, 485,
497, 517; Arie deZanger 16,
72–73, 87, 228, 294–295, 310,
379, 485; Fred Schenk 2–3,
108–109, 148–149, 184–185,
311, 328–329, 340, 341,
358–359, 463; unless otherwise
acknowledged, all photographs
are the property of Scott,
Foresman and Company. Clare
Aich: 62, 74, 75, 76, 77, 110,
128, 156, 188, 189, 190, 202,
234, 258, 277, 302, 303, 314,
315, 342, 416, 417, 420, 421,
428, 440, 481, 509, 511, 512,
530 Peter Arnold, Inc.: Keith
Scott Morton 148–149; Erica
Stone 218–219 Woodfin Camp &
Associates, Inc.: Craig Aurness
438–439; John Ficara 218–219
Comstock: 184–185 Judy
Gurovitz: 118, 377 Richard
Hutchings: 18, 32, 37, 52, 53,
92, 112, 126, 127, 132, 133,
170, 192, 196, 202, 230, 238,
246, 272, 296, 300, 301, 330,
338, 349, 364, 366, 420, 426,
446, 479, 521 The Image Bank:

(Continued on page 572)

Contents

Chapter **3** Two-Digit Addition and Subtraction

Chapter **4** Three- and Four-Digit Addition and Subtraction

Chapter 5 Time, Measurement, and Geometry

Chapter 6 Multiplication Concepts

Chapter 7 Multiplication Facts

Chapter 8 Geometry and Measurement

Chapter 9   Division Concepts

Chapter 10   Division Facts

Chapter **11** Fractions and Decimals

Chapter **12** Time and Money

Chapter 13 Multiplication Computation

Chapter 14 Statistics, Graphing, and Probability

Chapter 15 Division Computation

WELCOME TO
EXPLORING
MATHEMATICS

Mathematics is valuable and interesting. The next ten pages describe some of the ways your book will help you explore and discover more of the wonders of mathematics.

Your book will help you build your

Math Power

Build your math power by doing
Problem Solving and Critical Thinking

You will use math to solve problems all your life. When you solve problems in your book, you will do more than find answers. You will learn how to think mathematically.

In Chapter 1, tell the page numbers where you first find these.

1 "Problem-Solving Guide"
- Understand
- Plan and Solve
- Look Back

2 "Tips for Problem Solvers"

3 An exercise called "Critical Thinking"

Build your math power by looking for

Connections

Your book will help you explore connections. You will see connections between math and the real world.

In Chapter 2, tell the page numbers where you first find these headings.

4 Consumer Connection

5 Science Connection

6 Career Connection

7 Social Studies Connection

*Build your math power
by working on*

Number Sense and Using Data

You want your work with numbers to make sense. You need to be able to understand numbers, estimate, and do mental math. To read and use data, you will gather, organize, display, and study data.

1 Find a chapter that begins with a Number Sense Project about school lunches. Then find where this project is continued. (Hint: Find the Problem-Solving Workshop within the chapter.) On what page is the project continued?

2 On page 92, what kind of estimation is used?

3 On what page is the Data File that you'll use with Exercise 7 on page 96?

Scott, Fores

NUME

SENS

WORKSHOP

Build your math power by using
Calculators and Computers

Calculators and computers can help you solve problems and learn mathematics. It's important to know when calculators can help you and when they are not needed.

4 On page 24, what math topic does a calculator help you learn?

5 On page 229, what math topics does a computer help you learn?

6 In Chapter 9, which page asks you to "Explore with a Calculator" to complete number sentences by picking a number and a math sign?

7 Which exercises on page 143 ask you to tell whether or not you would use a calculator?

Use your book to help you
Do Your Best

To do your best,
Expect to Succeed

When you want to learn something, it helps to believe in yourself. Whether you are learning a sport, a musical instrument, or mathematics, a positive attitude can make a big difference.

To do your best,
Build Your Understanding

When you understand what you're doing, you do it better and remember it longer. So it pays to study the "Build Understanding" part of the lessons.

1 On page 18, why is it easy to see what new math words are being taught?

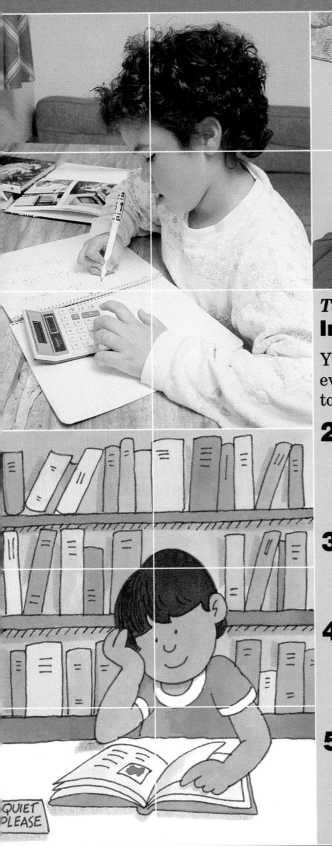

To do your best, learn ways to do
Independent Study

You can learn how to study math even when a teacher is not there to help.

2 On page 4, look to the right of the words "Check Understanding." On what page can you find another example for that lesson?

3 On page 5, look to the right of the word "Practice." On what page can you find more practice for that lesson?

4 There is an Independent Study Handbook in the back of your book. On what page does the "Math Study Skills" section begin?

5 Name the first and last words defined in the glossary on page 563.

Your book will help you through
Active Learning

You'll learn math by doing
Math Activities

Activities help you understand math. Some activities use materials that help you show numbers, measure objects, do experiments, explore shapes, or solve problems.

1 What materials are used in the activity on page 36?

2 Use your "Math Sketcher" or a ruler to draw a picture that shows two equal parts of a rectangle.

Doing math includes
Reading, Writing, Talking, Listening

Reading, writing, talking, and listening in math class will help you think mathematically.

3 In Chapter 1, tell the page number where these first occur.

"Talk About Math"

"Write About Math"

"Reading Math"

A good way to learn is by
Working in Groups

In real life and in math class, people can often solve problems better by working together.

4 How many students should work together in a group to do the "Building Hundreds" activity on page 36?

5 In the "Explore As a Team" on page 163, what is the "Tip for Working Together"?

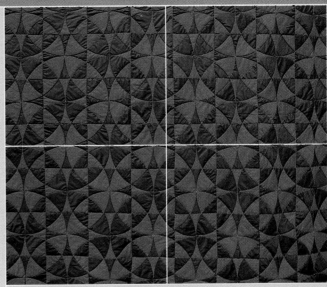

To have a math adventure, catch the spirit of
Exploration

Be a Math Explorer and discover new things. Look for patterns. Check out your hunches, and try different ways to solve problems.

6 On what pages in Chapter 2 do you explore patterns in numbers with a number chart?

7 In "Explore Math" on page 47, what are you asked to do in problems 20–21?

A key ingredient to learning math is
Enjoying Math

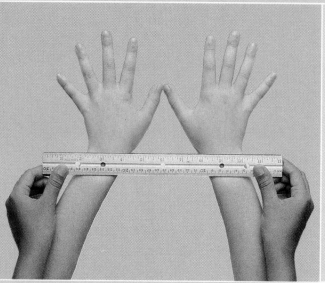

Your book will help you
Enjoy Math at School

The explorations in your book will help you discover and enjoy mathematics.

1 In Chapter 8, what pages ask you to explore folding and cutting paper?

2 Fold a sheet of paper in half. Cut half of an apple with scissors or by tearing. Unfold the paper. Do you have a whole apple?

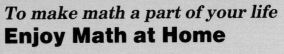

To make math a part of your life
Enjoy Math at Home

Outside of school, share math ideas with others and continue to explore math your whole life.

3 In the Math-at-Home Activity on page 131, how many dry beans are used?

4 Play this estimation game with someone at home. Choose items such as light switches. Guess how many are in your house. The player with the closest estimate scores 1 point. Repeat this with 4 other items. The player with the most points wins.

Using Basic Facts

Did You Know: In 1961, 1 out of 4 children in the U.S. were firstborn. In the 1980's, about 1 in 2 were firstborn.

Number-Sense Project

Estimate
Estimate how many children in your class are the oldest child in their family.

Gather Data
Write down your estimate. Then take a class count to see how many children actually are the oldest in their families.

Analyze and Report
Was your estimate too high or too low? Compare with other students.

Number Sense

Build Understanding

Numbers can be used in many ways.

A. Numbers are used to *count*. There are 8 apples in Mrs. Lindsay's shopping cart.

B. Numbers are used to *label*. Mrs. Lindsay is looking for cereal in aisle 4.

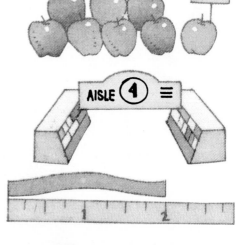

C. Numbers are used to *measure*. Mrs. Lindsay bought a piece of ribbon that is 2 feet long.

D. Numbers are used to tell the *order* of things. Mrs. Lindsay is 3rd in line at the checkout.

 Talk About Math   What are some other examples of how numbers are used?

Check Understanding

For another example, see Set A, pages 28–29.

For each picture, tell if the number is used to count, to label, to measure, or to tell order.

1.

2.

3.

4. **5.** **6.**

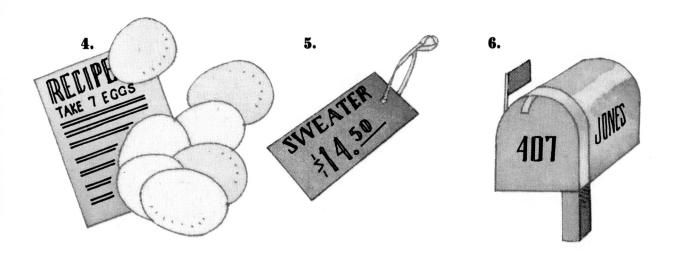

Practice

For More Practice, see Set A, pages 30–31.

Read each sentence. Tell if the number is used
to count, to label, to measure, or to tell order.

7. There are 37 cars in the
parking lot.

8. The hockey game was in
the 2nd period of play.

9. Glenda weighed 87 pounds.

10. The airplane was a
747 jet.

11. There are 27 students in
Ms. Blake's class.

12. It is 6 miles to Grandma's
house.

13. Paula was 3rd in line for
dessert.

14. The package was tagged
"Inspected by No. 148."

15. Jane lives at 77 East
Mulberry Street.

16. "I'm going to see my uncle
on Sunday, May 9."

Problem Solving

Solve each problem.

Mrs. Lindsay bought theater tickets.

17. How many different
numbers are used on the tickets?

18. How is each number used?

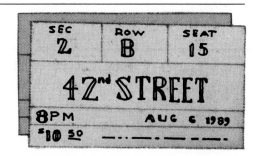

5

Addition and Subtraction

Build Understanding

 More or Less

Materials: Small objects for counting

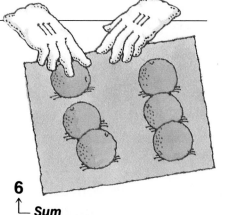

A.a. Show 3 objects.
Show 3 more.
How many objects are there in all?

b. Write the basic fact.   **3 + 3 = 6**

Addends ⎸————⎸   ⎸— Sum

c. Make a table to record your work.

d. Show a number of objects.
Show 3 more.
Record the total in the table.

e. Repeat *d* 2 more times using a different number of objects each time.

	+3
3	6

B.a. Show 10 objects.
Take 4 away.
How many objects are left?

b. Write the basic fact.   **10 − 4 = 6**

⎸— Difference

c. Make a table to record your work.

d. Show a number of objects.
Take 4 away.
Record the difference in the table.

e. Repeat *d* 2 more times using a different number of objects each time.

	−4
10	6

■ **Write About Math** Write a word problem using one of the facts you completed in Example A or B.

Check Understanding

For another example, see Set B, pages 28–29.

Tell the rule for each table in Exercises 1–3. Use the rule to complete the table for Exercises 4–7.

1.

6	14
2	10
8	16
9	17

2.

10	3
8	1
14	7
7	0

3.

1	3
3	5
5	7
7	9

		−4
4.	11	
5.	4	
6.	13	
7.	6	

Practice

For More Practice, see Set B, pages 30–31

Use the rule given. Find the missing numbers.

		+5
8.	6	
9.	8	
10.	0	
11.	2	

		−2
12.	5	
13.	9	
14.	4	
15.	2	

		+6
16.	6	
17.	8	
18.		13
19.		9

		−7
20.	14	
21.		1
22.		8
23.	7	

Problem Solving

Follow the arrows. Find the missing number for each circle.

24.
$$⑨ \to +5 \to ○$$
$$\uparrow \qquad \qquad \downarrow$$
$$-1 \qquad \qquad -7$$
$$\uparrow \qquad \qquad \downarrow$$
$$○ \leftarrow +3 \leftarrow ○$$

25.
$$④ \to +3 \to ○$$
$$\uparrow \qquad \qquad \downarrow$$
$$-2 \qquad \qquad +8$$
$$\uparrow \qquad \qquad \downarrow$$
$$○ \leftarrow -9 \leftarrow ○$$

26.
$$⑩ \to -2 \to ○$$
$$\uparrow \qquad \qquad \downarrow$$
$$+3 \qquad \qquad -4$$
$$\uparrow \qquad \qquad \downarrow$$
$$○ \leftarrow +3 \leftarrow ○$$

Operation Sense

Build Understanding

The Case of the Sticky Cover-up!
Materials: Objects of the same size

Sticky Fingers stuck stickers on numbers and symbols. Help Mathy Sleuth solve the case.

A. What number is under the 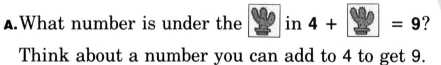 in 4 + 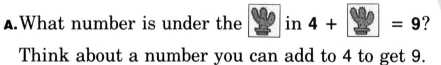 = 9?

Think about a number you can add to 4 to get 9.

a. Arrange 4 objects in a row. In another row, add one object at a time until there are 9 objects altogether.

b. Count the objects in the second row.

4 + 5 = 9

B. What symbol is under the in 5 3 = 2?

a. Use 5 objects. Add 3 objects. Do you get 2?

b. Take away 3 objects. Do you get 2?

5 − 3 = 2

c. What combinations of numbers *are the same as* 7?

7 is the same as 1 plus 6.   5 and 2 are 7.
3 + 4 = 7   16 − 9 = 7

■ **Write About Math**   Look at Example C. Write 5 more number combinations that are the same as 7.

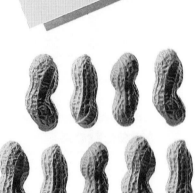

Check Understanding

For another example, see Set C, pages 28–29.

Use your objects to tell what number or symbol is under each sticker in Exercises 1–3.

1. 8 − 🍦 = 6

2. 7 🍐 5 = 12

3. 10 = 5 🌳 5

4. What word means "is the same as"?

Practice

For More Practice, see Set C, pages 30–31.

Tell what number or symbol is under each sticker.

5. 1 = 9 − 🕯️

6. 0 🌙 4 − 4

7. 🌷 − 2 = 8

8. 6 = 🖌️ + 5

9. 11 = 3 👩 8

10. 6 + 🍀 = 6

11. 7 = 7 − ⚓

12. 8 🏠 6 + 2

13. 4 = 4 🐸 0

Problem Solving

Write a number sentence using all of the given numbers and symbols. **Remember** that the values on each side of the "=" sign must be the same.

14. 1, 5, 6, −, =

15. 3, 9, 6, −, =

16. 12, 5, 7, +, =

Explore ——————— Math

17. Suppose 👁️ + 🎼 = 8. What could be under the stickers?

18. Suppose 🍐 − 🌳 = 5. What could be under the stickers?

19. Can there be more than one answer for Problems 17 and 18? Why or why not?

Using a Problem Solving Guide

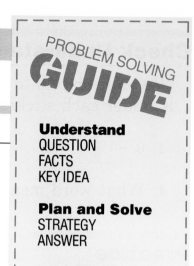

Build Understanding

Solving a problem is like taking a trip. There may be more than one way to get an answer. Sometimes you need to start over. The Problem-Solving Guide is like a map that can help you find your way.

Mr. Barker teaches gym. He is taking stock of his gym equipment. Of 8 mats, 3 are old. How many are new?

Understand
QUESTION
FACTS
KEY IDEA

Plan and Solve
STRATEGY
ANSWER

Look Back
SENSIBLE ANSWER
ALTERNATE APPROACH

Understand

QUESTION _____
What are you asked to find?

FACTS _____
What facts are given?

KEY IDEA _____
How are the facts
and question related?

Plan and Solve _____

STRATEGY
What can you do to solve
the problem?

ANSWER _____
Give the answer in a sentence.

Look Back _____

SENSIBLE ANSWER
Did you check your work?

ALTERNATE APPROACH _____
Is there another way to get
the same answer?

Understand

QUESTION   How many mats are new?

FACTS   8 mats in all. 3 are old.

KEY IDEA   The other mats are new.

Plan and Solve

STRATEGY   Subtract to find how
many are new.

$$\begin{array}{r} 8 \\ -3 \\ \hline 5 \end{array}$$

ANSWER   There are 5 new gym
mats.

Look Back

SENSIBLE ANSWER   Use addition to check
your answer. 5 + 3 = 8

■ **Talk About Math**   Can you think of
a different way to solve the problem?

Check Understanding

1. What are the three steps of the Problem-Solving Guide?

Answer each question about the problem at the right.

2. What are you asked to find?

3. What unit label will you use for the answer?

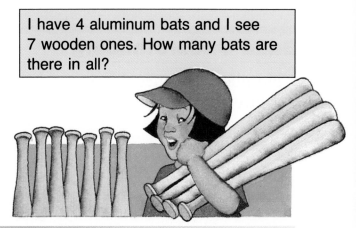

I have 4 aluminum bats and I see 7 wooden ones. How many bats are there in all?

Practice

Answer each question about the problem at the right.

4. What facts are given?

5. Rewrite the problem in your own words.

6. The answer is 5. Give this answer in a sentence.

7. Complete this sentence. "I know that the answer to Question 6 makes sense for this problem because . . ."

There are only 7 basketballs. I need 12 for use in the gym. How many do I need to buy?

Solve each problem. Use the Problem-Solving Guide to help you.

8. Of the 14 soccer balls, 5 needed to be inflated. How many had enough air?

9. Mr. Barker had a dozen volleyball nets. He lent 3 of them to another school. How many nets did he have left?

Families of Facts

Build Understanding

Number sentences that are
related make up a *family of facts.*

A.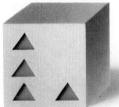

One family of facts is:
5 + 4 = 9
4 + 5 = 9
9 − 5 = 4
9 − 4 = 5

B.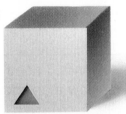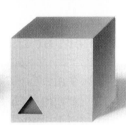

One family of facts is:
1 + 1 = 2
2 − 1 = 1

c.Mental Math   Use families of facts to
help you remember basic facts. If you
know that 4 + 2 = 6, you can use the
family of facts to recall that 2 + 4 = 6,
6 − 2 = 4, and 6 − 4 = 2.

■ **Write About Math**   Write 3 other
families of facts like the one in Example B.
What is special about these families?

Check Understanding

For another example, see Set D, pages 28–29.

Write the family of facts for each picture.

1.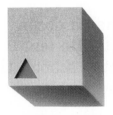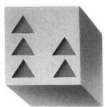

2.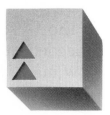

3. Write the family of facts for 5, 5, 10.

Number Sense Suppose that two
numbers of a family of facts are 7 and 1.

4. Name a number that could
be the third number in that
family of facts.

5. What other number could
the third number be?

Practice

For More Practice, see Set D, pages 30–31.

Write the family of facts for each picture.

6.

7.

8.

9.

Copy and complete each number sentence.

10. $9 + 6 = $ ▦

$15 - 6 = $ ▦

$6 + 9 = $ ▦

$15 - $ ▦ $ = 6$

11. $3 + 7 = $ ▦

$10 - 7 = $ ▦

$10 - 3 = $ ▦

▦ $ + 3 = 10$

12. $8 + 0 = $ ▦

$8 - 8 = $ ▦

$8 - 0 = $ ▦

▦ $ + 8 = 8$

Write the family of facts for the numbers in each exercise.

13. 2, 4, 6

14. 3, 5, 8

15. 4, 7, 11

16. 2, 9, 11

17. 14, 8, 6

18. 1, 7, 6

19. 9, 3, 6

20. 8, 0, 8

21. 5, 0, 5

22. 3, 3, 6

23. 5, 5, 10

24. 12, 7, 19

Copy. Then write each answer. Circle the fact that does not belong to the family.

25. $12 - 5$	**26.** $9 - 4$	**27.** $16 - 7$	**28.** $15 - 8$
$5 + 8$	$5 + 4$	$9 - 7$	$8 + 7$
$13 - 5$	$4 + 5$	$7 + 9$	$15 - 9$
$8 + 5$	$9 - 5$	$16 - 9$	$7 + 8$
$13 - 8$	$5 + 5$	$9 + 7$	$15 - 7$

Mixed Practice Find each answer. **Remember** to watch the signs.

29. $\begin{array}{r} 5 \\ +7 \\ \hline \end{array}$	**30.** $\begin{array}{r} 8 \\ -2 \\ \hline \end{array}$	**31.** $\begin{array}{r} 12 \\ -\ 4 \\ \hline \end{array}$	**32.** $\begin{array}{r} 16 \\ -\ 8 \\ \hline \end{array}$	**33.** $\begin{array}{r} 9 \\ +3 \\ \hline \end{array}$	**34.** $\begin{array}{r} 6 \\ +6 \\ \hline \end{array}$
35. $\begin{array}{r} 13 \\ -\ 6 \\ \hline \end{array}$	**36.** $\begin{array}{r} 1 \\ +9 \\ \hline \end{array}$	**37.** $\begin{array}{r} 10 \\ -\ 2 \\ \hline \end{array}$	**38.** $\begin{array}{r} 4 \\ +6 \\ \hline \end{array}$	**39.** $\begin{array}{r} 17 \\ +\ 7 \\ \hline \end{array}$	**40.** $\begin{array}{r} 7 \\ -3 \\ \hline \end{array}$

Problem Solving

Solve each problem.

41. Use one of the facts you wrote for Exercises 13–24 to write a word problem.

TIPS FOR PROBLEM SOLVERS

Be confident so you can do your best.

Critical Thinking
Find the missing numbers.

42. I am the largest number in my family of facts. The other two numbers are 3 and 5. Who am I?

43. Use Data On page 4, Mrs. Lindsay has apples in her cart. Look at the way the apples are arranged. Write a family of facts for the picture.

44. There are only two different numbers in my family of facts. The largest number is 8. Who are we?

For each picture, tell if the numbers are used
to count, to label, to measure, or to tell order.

1.

2.

3.

Find each answer.

| **4.** 8
+2 | **5.** 12
− 4 | **6.** 9
−3 | **7.** 5
+8 | **8.** 18
− 9 |

Tell what number or symbol is under each sticker.

9. [brush] + 5 = 6   **10.** 2 [glasses] 8 = 10   **11.** 4 = [frog] − 7

Solve each problem.

12. There were 6 new
baseballs and 4 used ones.
How many baseballs were
there in all?

13. There are 7 fielder's
gloves and 3 catcher's
mitts. How many more
fielder's gloves than
catcher's mitts are there?

Write the family of facts for these numbers.
14. 3, 9, 12   **15.** 1, 6, 5   **16.** 0, 3, 3

Explore as a Team

1. Use 36 white cards. Write each of the numbers 1–9 on a separate card. There will be 4 sets. Mix well and make a pile face down on the table.

2. Use 17 pink cards. Write each of the numbers 2–18 on separate cards. Each team member gets 4 of these and places them face up on the table.

TIPS FOR WORKING TOGETHER

Help keep your group on task.

3. Then each member draws white cards in turn trying to make an addition basic fact for the numbered pink cards he or she has. Once played, the white cards cannot be moved.

4. When one member has made facts for all 4 numbers, talk about which facts were easiest to make. Which were the hardest?

5. Repeat the process and see if your statements for Exercise 4 are still correct.

Explore with a Computer

Use the *Graphing and Probability Workshop Project* with this activity.

1. Look around your classroom. Count the number of circles, rectangles, and triangles you find. For example, a book looks like a rectangle. Write how many of each shape you find.

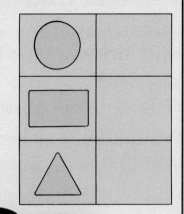

2. At the computer, type the number of each shape in the table.

3. Select the **Bar graph** option. What does the graph show?

Number-Sense Project

Look back at pages 2–3. Choose the number sentence from those below that best describes each family pictured on pages 2–3. Explain why.

1. $4 + 1 = 5$ **2.** $2 + 2 = 4$
3. $2 + 3 = 5$ **4.** $1 + 3 = 4$

Critical Thinking Activity

Place the numbers 1–9 in the squares to make sums of 15. The sum of each row, column and diagonal must be 15.

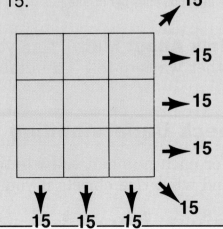

15
15
15
15
15 15 15 15

Even and Odd

Build Understanding

That's Odd!

Materials: Small objects for counting

What makes a number even or odd?

An assembly line can produce more than 500 cans per minute.

a. Take 6 objects. Try to separate them into 2 equal piles.

b. Take 9 objects. Try to separate them into 2 equal piles.

c. Repeat a and b using 4, 5, 7, 8, 10, 11, 12, and 13 objects.

d. Which numbers can make two even piles with none left over?

These are called **even numbers.**

e. Which numbers must have one left over?

These are called **odd numbers.**

■ **Talk About Math** Can you think of any other ways to tell if a number is even or odd?

Check Understanding

For another example, see Set E, pages 28–29.

For each number, tell whether it is even or odd and why. Use objects if you need them.

1. 8   **2.** 5   **3.** 17   **4.** 54   **5.** 33   **6.** 50

18

Practice

For More Practice, see Set E, pages 30–31.

Tell if each number is odd or even.

7. 23   **8.** 42   **9.** 98   **10.** 701   **11.** 114   **12.** 85

13. 234   **14.** 467   **15.** 105   **16.** 76   **17.** 67   **18.** 77

Mental Math   Find each sum.

19. 4 + 2   **20.** 6 + 8   **21.** 2 + 6   **22.** 4 + 8   **23.** 8 + 2

24. 1 + 5   **25.** 7 + 9   **26.** 7 + 5   **27.** 3 + 1   **28.** 9 + 1

29. 9 + 4   **30.** 6 + 7   **31.** 3 + 8   **32.** 6 + 9   **33.** 8 + 5

Problem Solving

Number Sense   Use Exercises 19–33. Tell if the sum is odd or even. What is the sum of

34. two even numbers?   **35.** two odd numbers?

36. an even and an odd number?

Calculator   Use a calculator to see if the answers you gave for Problems 34–36 are true for these numbers:

37. 327 + 659   **38.** 108 + 214   **39.** 1,357 + 2,468

Skills _____ Review   pages 4–5

Write a sentence using the numbers and words in each exercise.

1. 6 days   **2.** 5th day   **3.** 21 cents   **4.** size 10

5. 18 miles   **6.** July 4   **7.** 1st place   **8.** 3 o'clock

---

Use Data from a Picture

Build Understanding

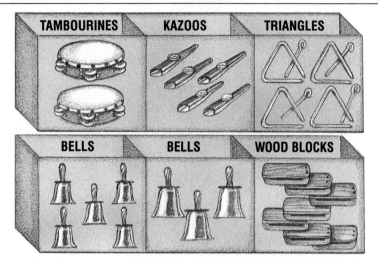

The music room has many different instruments. How many bells are in the boxes?

Understand   QUESTION   How many bells are there?

FACTS   Two boxes have bells. One box has 5 bells. The other box has 3 bells.

KEY IDEA   To find how many bells there are in all, you can add.

Plan and Solve

$5 + 3 = 8$

There are 8 bells in the boxes.

Look Back   You can also find the answer by counting the bells in the two boxes.

■ **Talk About Math**   If each student can ring two bells, how many students are needed to ring the bells?

RECORDERS

Check Understanding

Use the pictures on page 20 to solve the problem.

Are there more wood blocks or recorders?

1. How many recorders are there?

2. How many wood blocks are there?

3. Are there more recorders or wood blocks?

4. Do you need to tell how many more?

Practice

Use the pictures on page 20 and below to solve the problems.

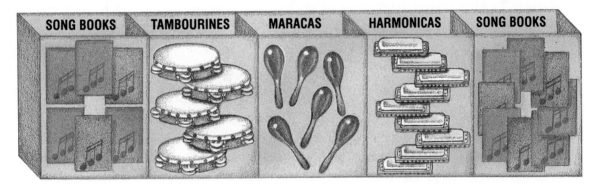

5. How many song books are there in all?

6. How many tambourines are there in all?

7. How many more harmonicas are there than recorders?

8. Are there more maracas or kazoos?

What is the total number of instruments that can be played by

9. blowing them?   10. shaking them?   11. tapping them?

12. How many more instruments are made of wood only than are made of metal only?

13. How many instruments are made of both wood and metal?

Ordering Events

Build Understanding

Betsy drew these 4 pictures showing how she and some friends made a snowman. She dropped them on the floor. Tell how she can put them back in order.

Which is the first picture? Why?

Which is the second picture? Why?

Which is the third picture? Why?

Which is the last picture? Why?

When the pictures are *in order*, they show a *sequence* of events.

■ **Write About Math**   List some of the things you do each day. Be sure you put them in order.

What kinds of things can you do in the snow?

Check Understanding

For another example, see Set F, pages 28–29.

Put each set of pictures in order.

1.

2.

Practice

For More Practice, see Set F, pages 30–31.

Order the following according to the rule.

3. Put in alphabetical order: carrot, apple, potato, celery

4. Put in numerical order from least to greatest: 8, 1, 5, 3, 6

5. Put in order by height, shortest first: puppy, goat, gorilla, giraffe

6. Put in order by age, youngest first: teenager, toddler, senior citizen, infant.

Problem Solving

Critical Thinking Write these sentences in the correct order.

7. Jack shoveled the snow.
It snowed a lot.
Jack put on his boots to go out.
It was beginning to snow.

8. Marti left for school.
Marti ate breakfast in the kitchen.
Marti woke up.
Marti got out of bed.

Reading ———— Math

If the events are in order, write *yes*. If they are not, write the sentences in order.

1. Mickey put on his shoes.
Mickey put on his socks.

2. John opened the door.
John entered the room.

3. Tricia dried her wet hands.
Tricia washed her hands.

4. Nadia put the envelope in the mailbox.
Nadia sealed the envelope.

Find a Pattern

Build Understanding

Have you ever played a game using a calculator?

On his calculator, Pablo entered 4. Then he pushed three other keys which he called his secret key sequence. This is what the display showed.

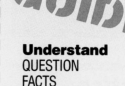

PROBLEM SOLVING
GUIDE

Understand
QUESTION
FACTS
KEY IDEA

||||➡ **Plan and Solve**
STRATEGY
ANSWER

Look Back
SENSIBLE ANSWER
ALTERNATE APPROACH

Here you see other numbers Pablo entered along with this secret key sequence. The display for each is shown. Can you tell what Pablo's secret key sequence is?

Enter	Display
4	7
7	10
3	6
0	3

Understand   The secret key sequence does the same thing to each number keyed in.

||||➡ **Plan and Solve**   STRATEGY   Look for a pattern. Each display is 3 more than the number keyed in.

$$4 + 3 = 7$$
$$7 + 3 = 10$$
$$3 + 3 = 6$$
$$0 + 3 = 3$$

ANSWER   Pablo is using the sequence $+$ 3 $=$.

Look Back   Use addition to check the key sequence with each number given. Do your answers match the display numbers?

■ **Write About Math** Try Pablo's key sequence with 3 other numbers. Is the display always 3 greater than the number you keyed in?

Check Understanding

Answer each question.

1. Rachel's secret sequence is $+$ 9 $=$. What display will she get if she enters 3? 5? 7? 9?

2. Amy's secret key sequence is $-$ 5 $=$. What display will she get is she enters 5? 8? 10? 14?

Practice

Tell what key sequence was used.

3. 5   13
    9   17
    11   19
    2   10

4. 2   1
    5   4
    3   2
    8   7

5. 7   5
    5   3
    11   9
    6   4

6. 0   6
    2   8
    5   11
    7   13

7. 6   1
    12   7
    17   12
    5   0

8. 7   16
    5   14
    0   9
    6   15

9. **Critical Thinking** Mary said, "Pablo could key in this sequence and still get a number that is 3 more than 4." Why does this work?

4 $+$ 6 $-$ 6 $+$ 3 $=$

Choose a ⬛ Strategy

10. Use + or − in each ▦ to make the number sentence correct.   3 ▦ 4 ▦ 5 ▦ 6 ▦ 7 ▦ 8 = 9

Solve each problem.

1. What number am I? Begin with 5. Add 5. Subtract 2. Subtract 4. Then add 3.

2. Write a sentence using the numbers and words: toys, 5, 3 days.

3. The pages fell out of this baby book. Put them in order to tell a story.

4. Use the picture to answer. If 3 people enter the cafeteria, and each takes a different kind of sandwich, how many sandwiches will be left?

5. Dexter bought 3 notebooks, 6 pencils, and 2 erasers. How many school supplies did he buy?

6. **Data File** Use data from pages 104-105. Which teams scored the most runs? How many more runs did the Mets score than the Pirates?

7. **Make a Data File** Look through a newspaper or magazine. Find and cut out pictures or sentences that show the different ways numbers are used (to label, to count, to measure, to tell order). Paste on paper and label.

Problem Solving REVIEW

Number Scramble Game

1. In a game of Number Scramble, Marcy has these game tiles on her rack.

She can use the numbers and signs only once to make the display shown on her card.

Display $\boxed{14}$

This is the sequence she keyed into her calculator.

$8 \boxed{+} 6 \boxed{=}$

Was there another sequence she could have used?

---

2. Play Number Scramble. The rack of game tiles and the display card are given for each exercise.

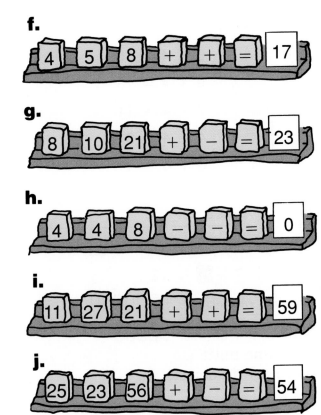

a. 9 8 + = 17

b. 11 7 − = 4

c. 12 13 + = 25

d. 23 7 − = 16

e. 37 55 + = 92

f. 4 5 8 + + = 17

g. 8 10 21 + − = 23

h. 4 4 8 − − = 0

i. 11 27 21 + + = 59

j. 25 23 56 + − = 54

Reteaching

Set A pages 4–5

Numbers are used in many ways.

To count:
There are 4 boys and 4 girls.

To label:
We live on Third Street.

To measure:
The car is 8 feet long.

To tell the order of things:
The Cubs came in 1st.

Remember that a number, such as a date, can be used in more than one way.

Read each sentence. Tell if the number is used to count, to label, to measure, or to tell order.

1. We stayed in room 837 at the Peabody Hotel.

2. I was born on October 17.

Set B pages 6–7

The rule in this table says: "add 4."

Find the missing numbers.

	+4
6	▦
9	▦
7	▦
4	▦
▦	4

$6 + 4 = 10$
$9 + 4 = 13$
$7 + 4 = 11$
$4 + 4 = 8$
$0 + 4 = 4$

Remember that the addends are the numbers used to find the sum.

Use the rule given. Find the missing numbers.

1.

	+7
2	▦
8	▦
▦	13
5	▦

2.

	+6
4	▦
9	▦
7	▦
▦	12

Set C pages 8–9

What number is under the ■?

$$7 + ■ = 12$$

Show 7 objects.   ▢▢▢▢▢▢▢

Now add 1 object   ▢▢▢▢▢
at a time until
there are 12 objects.

The second row has 5 objects. So
$$7 + 5 = 12.$$

Remember that there are several combinations of numbers that name the same number.

Tell what number is under each sticker.

1. $4 + ■ = 13$

2. $■ + 9 = 16$

Set D pages 12–14

Here is the family of facts for 4, 6, and 10.

6 + 4 = 10
4 + 6 = 10
10 − 6 = 4
10 − 4 = 6

If you know the basic fact, you can use it to write the other facts.

Remember that you can use families of facts to help you remember basic facts.

Write the family of facts for each picture.

1.   2.

Set E pages 18–19

Which groups of objects can be separated into 2 equal parts?

4

5

6

7

Numbers that can make 2 equal parts are even numbers. Numbers that cannot are odd numbers.

Remember that you can make an even number into an odd number by adding one to the even number.

Tell if each number is odd or even.

1. 11   **2.** 20   **3.** 22   **4.** 49

5. 33   **6.** 64   **7.** 109   **8.** 240

Set F pages 22–23

Write the names of the following states in alphabetical order.

Massachusetts
Texas
California
Florida

Now write the names in order according to the number of letters from least to greatest.

Remember that there are things you do that must be done in a certain order. Other events are put in an order according to a rule.

Order the following according to the rule.

1. Put in alphabetical order: banana, onion, cucumber

2. Put the items in Exercise 1 in order according to the number of letters from least to greatest.

More Practice

Set A   pages 4–5

Read each sentence. Tell if the number is used
to count, to label, to measure, or to tell order.

1. He is over 6 feet tall.

2. It is 5 miles to the mall.

3. The parking lot can hold 380 cars.

4. They were moved to room 218.

5. José hit a home run in the eighth inning.

6. Alice has a ticket for the game on September 28.

7. She scored 20 points in the game.

8. She has grown 2 inches this year.

Set B   pages 6–7

Use the rule given. Find the missing numbers.

	+4				−6				+8				−8
1.	3	▒	**6.**	▒	2	**11.**	5	▒	**16.**	12	▒
2.	8	▒	**7.**	9	▒	**12.**	8	▒	**17.**	▒	3
3.	7	▒	**8.**	6	▒	**13.**	6	▒	**18.**	▒	2
4.	▒	4	**9.**	7	▒	**14.**	▒	10	**19.**	14	▒
5.	5	▒	**10.**	8	▒	**15.**	▒	8	**20.**	8	▒

Set C   pages 8–9

Tell what number or symbol is under each
sticker.

1. $3 = 7 - \blacksquare$

2. $9 = 7 \,\blacksquare\, 2$

3. $\blacksquare + 3 = 8$

4. $7 \,\blacksquare\, 8 - 1$

5. $4 + \blacksquare = 4$

6. $6 - \blacksquare = 0$

7. $\blacksquare - 2 = 9$

8. $8 = \blacksquare + 5$

9. $9 = 6 + \blacksquare$

10. $4 + 5 \,\blacksquare\, 9$

11. $3 - \blacksquare = 0$

12. $4 + 4 = \blacksquare$

Set D pages 12–14

Write the family of facts for each picture.

1.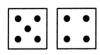

2. (dice image)

Copy and complete each number sentence.

3. 6 + 7 = ▦
    13 − 6 = ▦
    7 + 6 = ▦
    13 − ▦ = 6

4. 7 + 4 = ▦
    11 − 4 = ▦
    11 − 7 = ▦
    ▦ + 7 = 11

5. 8 + 5 = ▦
    13 − 8 = ▦
    13 − 5 = ▦
    ▦ + 8 = 13

Copy and write each answer. Circle the fact that does not belong to the family.

6. 13 − 6 =
    6 + 5 =
    11 − 5 =
    11 − 6 =
    5 + 6 =

7. 8 − 5 =
    5 − 3 =
    8 − 3 =
    5 + 3 =
    3 + 5 =

8. 6 + 8 =
    14 − 8 =
    14 − 6 =
    8 − 6 =
    8 + 6 =

9. 12 − 9 =
    12 − 3 =
    9 − 3 =
    3 + 9 =
    9 + 3 =

Mixed Practice Find each answer.

10. 6
       +7

11. 9
       −2

12. 12
       −3

13. 4
       +9

14. 16
       −7

15. 9
       +9

Set E pages 18–19

Tell if each number is odd or even.

1. 17   **2.** 36   **3.** 84   **4.** 91   **5.** 68   **6.** 120

Mental Math Find each sum.

7. 2 + 7   **8.** 8 + 7   **9.** 4 + 9   **10.** 7 + 3   **11.** 6 + 5

Set F pages 22–23

Order the following according to the rule.

1. Put in numerical order from least to greatest: 9, 4, 7, 2, 6.

2. Put in alphabetical order: goat, donkey, tiger, elk.

Enrichment

Missing Sums and Addends

Complete this addition table.
To find the missing addend for Exercise 25, use subtraction.

8 is the sum of 3 plus what?
12 is the sum of 7 plus what?
10 is the sum of 5 plus what?

All three answers should be the same. If not, check your subtraction.

	+	3	7	5	9	6	8
1.–6.	6						
7.–12.	8						
13.–18.	7						
19.–24.	9						
25.–28.		8	12	10			
29.–34.	4						

Find the correct sums or addends for this addition table.

	+			3			
35.–40.							
41.–47.							13
48.–53.			12			11	
54.–59.	5	9					
60.–65.		8			9		
66.–70.	8			15		16	
71.–77.				9			
78.–83.						17	15

Chapter 1 Review/Test

1. Tell if the number in the picture is used to count, to label, to measure, or to tell order.

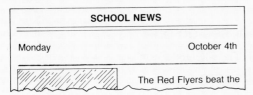

2. Use the rule + 4. Find the missing number.

	+ 4
7	11
4	
2	6

Add or subtract.

3. 9
  +5

4. 10
  − 6

5. 7
  +8

Tell what sign belongs in each box.

6. 8 ▦ 5 + 3

7. 16 ▦ 7 = 9

8. Which fact does not belong to the family?

  6 + 8 = 14
  14 − 6 = 8
  8 − 6 = 2
  8 + 6 = 14
  14 − 8 = 6

Tell if each number is odd or even.

9. 57

10. 238

11. 99

12. How many more squares are there than triangles?

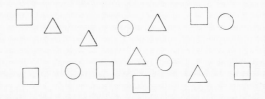

13. Put in order from the beginning of the day: lunch, supper, afternoon snack, breakfast.

14. Look at the numbers in the top row. Tell what pattern was used to get the numbers in the bottom row.

8	1	7	10	25
12	5	11	14	29

Read this problem. Then answer the questions below.

A school owns 9 microscopes. It will need 9 for the new school year. How many must it buy?

15. What facts are given?

16. The answer is 0. Write this answer in a sentence.

17. ■ **Write About Math** In Exercise 8, tell *why* the fact you chose does not belong to that family.

Place Value

Did You Know: Sometimes, all the houses on one side of the street have odd numbers. All the houses on the other side of the street have even numbers.

Number-Sense Project

Estimate

Predict the address of the buildings closest to the home or apartment you live in.

Gather Data

Draw a picture of your house or apartment. Also draw the 2 nearest neighbors on your side of the street. Put your street number under your house. Predict the house numbers for your 2 neighbors. Check to see what they are when you go home.

Analyze and Report

Did you know your house or apartment number? Did you predict the house numbers of your neighbors correctly? Correct the numbers in your drawing. Put the pictures up for others to see.

Understanding Hundreds

Build Understanding

ACTIVITY

Building Hundreds
Materials: Place-value materials
(hundreds, tens, and ones)
Groups: 3–5 students

Do you think there are really
hundreds of fish in this
aquarium? It is hard to tell.

TROPICAL PET LAND
BIG FISH SALE
We have hundreds of fish!

Use place-value materials to help you
see one hundred.

a. How many tens can you cover with ones?

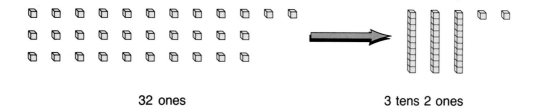

32 ones   3 tens 2 ones

b. How many tens do 56 ones cover?

c. How many hundreds can you cover with tens?

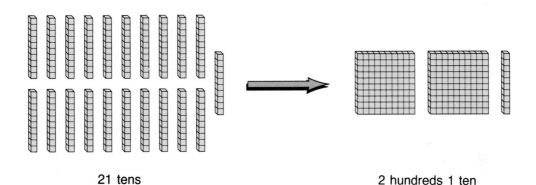

21 tens   2 hundreds 1 ten

d. How many hundreds do
43 tens cover?

■ **Talk About Math**
Explain why 138 ones is
equal to 1 hundred,
3 tens, and 8 ones.

For another example, see Set A, pages 66–67.

Check Understanding

Use your place-value materials to make as many tens as you can. Then use I and • to record your work.

1. 30 ones   **2.** 34 ones   **3.** 41 ones   **4.** 18 ones

5. 50 ones   **6.** 12 ones   **7.** 35 ones   **8.** 27 ones

9. Look at Exercises 1 and 2. How are they different?

Use your place-value materials to make as many hundreds as you can. Then use □ and I to record your work.

10. 30 tens   **11.** 33 tens   **12.** 19 tens   **13.** 45 tens

14. 26 tens   **15.** 50 tens   **16.** 43 tens   **17.** 24 tens

18. Look at exercises 10 and 11. How are they different?

Practice

For More Practice, see Set A, pages 68–69.

Use your place-value materials to make as many tens as you can. Use I and • to record your work.

19. 20 ones   **20.** 50 ones

21. 30 ones   **22.** 42 ones

23. 37 ones   **24.** 40 ones

25. 24 ones   **26.** 13 ones

27. 44 ones   **28.** 35 ones

29. 10 ones   **30.** 28 ones

Use your place-value materials to make as
many hundreds as you can. Use □, I, and •
to record your work.

31. 40 tens   **32.** 20 tens   **33.** 30 tens   **34.** 13 tens

35. 48 tens   **36.** 26 tens   **37.** 39 tens   **38.** 50 tens

39. 34 tens   **40.** 42 tens   **41.** 15 tens   **42.** 37 tens

43. 23 tens   **44.** 18 tens   **45.** 44 tens   **46.** 16 tens

47. 39 tens 42 ones

48. 27 tens 38 ones

Problem Solving

Mental Math   Solve each problem.

49. The pet store wants no more than 5 fish in each small fish bowl. One small bowl has 13 fish in it. How many fish should be taken out of the bowl?

50. Julio will give Juan 7 tropical fish for his birthday. Juan already has 9 tropical fish. How many tropical fish will Juan have after Julio gives him his birthday present?

Reading ———— Math

Numbers and Symbols   Write each sentence using numbers and symbols.

1. three plus five is eight   **2.** four plus nine is thirteen

3. fifteen minus nine is six   **4.** two plus seven is nine

5. five minus four is one   **6.** nine minus seven is two

7. seven plus eight is fifteen   **8.** nine minus zero is nine

9. six plus seven is thirteen   **10.** twelve minus six is six

Hundreds, Tens, and Ones

Build Understanding

The Spring Carnival Committee at Moss School sold tickets for rides. There were rolls of one hundred tickets, strips of ten tickets, and single tickets.

The third graders bought 4 rolls, 3 strips, and 2 singles. How many tickets did they buy?

CARNIVAL TICKETS BOUGHT

Grade	Rolls	Strips	Singles
Third	4	3	2
Fourth	3	8	7
Fifth	0	9	3

What do you like to do at a carnival?

4 hundreds	3 tens	2 ones

Expanded form ⟶ **400** + **30** + **2**

Standard form ⟶ **432**

four hundred thirty-two

The third graders bought 432 tickets.

■ **Talk About Math** Can the value of the digit in the tens place ever be greater than the value of the digit in the hundreds place? Explain.

40

Check Understanding

For another example, see Set B, pages 66–67.

Use □, I, and • to draw the hundreds, tens, and ones.

1. 200 + 40 + 5   **2.** 327   **3.** four hundred seven

4. 300 + 40   **5.** 508   **6.** two hundred thirty

Practice

For More Practice, see Set B, pages 68–69.

Tell how many hundreds, tens, and ones.
Then write the number in standard form.

7. 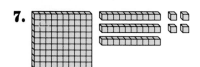   **8.** 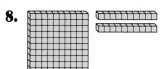   **9.**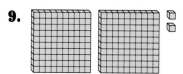

10. two hundred eleven   **11.** one hundred sixty   **12.** seventy-nine

Number Sense   In the following exercises,
tell whether the 3 is the hundreds digit, the
tens digit, or the ones digit.

13. 734   **14.** 386   **15.** 473   **16.** 230   **17.** 703

18. 301   **19.** 238   **20.** 235   **21.** 394   **22.** 123

23. Write Exercises 18–22 in expanded form.

Problem Solving

Solve the problem.

24. The parents of the sixth graders
bought 4 single tickets and 7 rolls.
How many tickets did they buy?

TIPS FOR
PROBLEM SOLVERS

Organize your work
to help you think clearly.

Comparing Numbers

Build Understanding

This chart shows the heaviest fish ever caught.

Which fish was heavier, the Atlantic Tuna or the Halibut?

Find the information in the table. Compare the two numbers.

Fish Records	
Type of Fish	Weight
Atlantic Tuna	375 pounds
Blue Shark	437 pounds
Halibut	350 pounds
Pacific Tuna	435 pounds
Striped Marlin	494 pounds
Sturgeon	468 pounds

Show: Atlantic Tuna 375 pounds

Halibut 350 pounds

Think: 375 ⬚ 350   The hundreds digits are the same.

375 ⬚ 350   The tens digits are not the same.
7 tens is more than 5 tens.
So 375 is more than 350.

Write: **375 > 350**   or   **350 < 375**

The Atlantic Tuna is heavier than the Halibut.

■ **Talk About Math** How do you think a sentence using < could be changed to a sentence using >? Explain your answer.

Remember:
> means "greater than."
< means "less than."

42

Check Understanding

For another example, see Set C, pages 66–67.

Replace ⬡ with < or >. For each exercise, tell which digits you have to compare.

1. 298 ⬡ 476   **2.** 246 ⬡ 229   **3.** 421 ⬡ 429   **4.** 598 ⬡ 601

5. Suppose you see this headline in the newspaper. It is torn. Can you still tell if the weight of this fish is a record? Explain how you know. (Hint: use the chart on page 42.)

GIANT STRIPED MARLIN CAUGHT!
Fish Weighed 4□3 Pounds!

Practice

For More Practice, see Set C, pages 68–69.

Replace ⬡ with < or >.

6. 495 ⬡ 476   **7.** 702 ⬡ 698   **8.** 89 ⬡ 203   **9.** 573 ⬡ 578

10. 286 ⬡ 276   **11.** 437 ⬡ 582   **12.** 27 ⬡ 502   **13.** 9 ⬡ 85

14. 58 ⬡ 580   **15.** 272 ⬡ 227   **16.** 36 ⬡ 630   **17.** 252 ⬡ 225

18. 62 ⬡ 107   **19.** 332 ⬡ 323   **20.** 56 ⬡ 65   **21.** 607 ⬡ 670

Problem Solving

Use the chart on page 42. Tell which fish is heavier.

22. Sturgeon or Atlantic Tuna   **23.** Blue Shark or Pacific Tuna

Critical Thinking Find each answer.

24. What is the least three-digit number with a 2 in the tens place? Explain your answer.

25. Write a 3-digit number whose tens digit is 4 and whose ones and hundreds digits add up to 2.

Ordering Three-Digit Numbers

Build Understanding

The four third-grade classes at Campbell School sold candles shaped like dinosaurs to raise money. Make a list of the classes in order from most sold to least sold.

Third Grade Candles Sold

Class	Number Sold
Miss Méndez's	238
Mrs. Jackson's	106
Mr. Kubiak's	346
Mrs. Huang's	142

An apatosaurus could weigh as much as 70,000 pounds.

3 hundreds **2 hundreds** **1 hundred**

346 238 142
106

Use the hundreds digits to order. If the hundreds digits are the same, compare the tens.

142 ⠿ 106

4 > 0   4 is greater than 0.

142 > 106   So 142 is greater than 106.

The numbers from greatest to least are 346, 238, 142, and 106.

So the classes in order are Mr. Kubiak's, Miss Méndez's, Mrs. Huang's, and Mrs. Jackson's.

■ **Write About Math** Write 128, 120, and 123 from least to greatest. Describe what you do when the hundreds digits and the tens digits in each number are the same.

Check Understanding

For another example, see Set D, pages 66–67.

Write the numbers between

1. 125 and 129.   **2.** 831 and 837.   **3.** 97 and 104.

Number Sense The list at the right got smudged. Explain how you can find each answer anyway.

Which class sold more candles?

4. Mrs. Winger's or Mr. Kling's

5. Mr. Kling's or Miss Jay's

Fourth Grade Candles Sold

Class	Number Sold
Mrs. Winger's	3▧6
Mr. Kling's	2▧4
Miss Jay's	296

Practice

For More Practice, see Set D, pages 68–69.

Write the numbers between

6. 821 and 827.   **7.** 457 and 462.   **8.** 194 and 202.

Write these numbers in order from least to greatest.

9. 783   79   830   832   **10.** 307   370   703   730

11. 60   72   136   156   **12.** 543   453   545   455

13. 136   163   135   168   **14.** 93   309   390   319

15. 584   504   575   540   **16.** 630   639   936   976

Skills ——— Review   pages 12–15

Write the family of facts for the numbers in each exercise.
1. 8, 5, 13   **2.** 16, 7, 9   **3.** 0, 5, 5   **4.** 8, 8, 16

Patterns in Numbers

Build Understanding

Nimble Numbers
Groups: Partners

Number charts can help you see patterns in numbers. Imagine crossing out each of these counting numbers in a hundreds number chart. What patterns do you see?

a. Start with 3. Count by fives.

b. Start with 12. Count by twos.

c. Start with 27. Count by tens.

NUMBER CHART

1	2	3	4	5	6	7	8	9	10
11	12	13	14	15	16	17	18	19	20
21	22	23	24	25	26	27	28	29	30
31	32	33	34	35	36	37	38	39	40
41	42	43	44	45	46	47	48	49	50
51	52	53	54	55	56	57	58	59	60
61	62	63	64	65	66	67	68	69	70
71	72	73	74	75	76	77	78	79	80
81	82	83	84	85	86	87	88	89	90
91	92	93	94	95	96	97	98	99	100

■ **Talk About Math** Tell why you think it might be useful to count in ways other than counting just one thing at a time.

Check Understanding

For another example, see Set E, pages 66–67.

Explain how you can use the number chart to find a number that is

1. 10 less than 37.   **2.** 5 less than 28.   **3.** 2 less than 75.

4. Pick any number in the chart less than 91. Compare it to the number just below it. What can you say about the two numbers?

Practice

For More Practice, see Set E, pages 68–69.

Count by twos.

5. Begin at 14. Count to 24.   **6.** Begin at 6. Count to 12.

7. Begin at 9. Count to 19.   **8.** Begin at 26. Count to 38.

Count by fives.

9. Begin at 15. Count to 40.   **10.** Begin at 25. Count to 55.

11. Begin at 4. Count to 34.   **12.** Begin at 8. Count to 43.

Count by tens.

13. Begin at 30. Count to 100.   **14.** Begin at 12. Count to 42.

Describe each pattern. Then find the missing numbers.

15. 6, 11, 16, 21, ▦, ▦,   **16.** 17, 19, 21, ▦, ▦,

17. 39, 49, 59, 69, ▦, ▦,   **18.** 83, 87, 93, 97, ▦, ▦,

Problem Solving

Explore ———— Math

Count to 20 first by 2s and then by 5s.
What numbers do you say both times you count?

19. Write down the numbers from 1 to 20.

20. Start with 2. Count by 2s. Circle each number.

21. Start with 5. Count by 5s. Put a square around each number.

22. Which numbers have a square *and* and a circle?

Rounding to Tens and Hundreds

Build Understanding

A. In this model train display, the distance from the water tower to the train station is 271 centimeters.

A **rounded number** tells about how many. Round 271 to the nearest hundred.

Think of the number line as a roller coaster. The hundreds are at the bottoms of the hills.

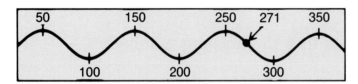

Imagine a marble at 271. It would roll forward to 300. 271 rounded to the **nearest hundred** is 300. The water tower is about 300 centimeters from the station.

B. Round 271 to the nearest ten.

Think of the number line as a roller coaster again. Now all of the tens are at the bottoms of the hills.

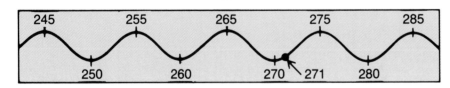

If you put a marble at 271, it would roll back to 270. 271 rounded to the **nearest ten** is 270.

■ **Talk About Math** Explain when you might round 283 to the nearest ten and when you might round 283 to the nearest hundred. Why were the situations different?

Check Understanding

For another example, see Set F, pages 66–67.

Find each answer.

1. Use the hundreds roller coaster to round 121 to the nearest hundred.

2. Make a tens roller coaster. Begin at 175 and end at 225. Use your roller coaster to round 192 to the nearest ten.

Round each number to the nearest ten.

3. 48   **4.** 72   **5.** 327   **6.** 491   **7.** 348   **8.** 961

Practice

For More Practice, see Set F, pages 68–69.

Round each number to the nearest hundred.

9. 299   **10.** 116   **11.** 529   **12.** 904   **13.** 672

14. 416   **15.** 790   **16.** 149   **17.** 151   **18.** 89

Round each number to the nearest ten.

19. 724   **20.** 116   **21.** 299   **22.** 71   **23.** 613

24. 19   **25.** 403   **26.** 368   **27.** 399   **28.** 2

Midchapter Checkup

Find each answer.

1. Give the missing number:
   40 ones = ⬚ tens

2. Tell what the 5 means in 586.

3. Replace ⬚ with < or >:
   402 ⬚ 204

4. Write 123, 321, and 312 in order from least to greatest.

5. Count by twos. Begin at 62. Count to 74.

6. Round 437 to the nearest hundred.

Explore as a Team

1. You may count up to only 10 beans. Estimate the number of beans in each picture.

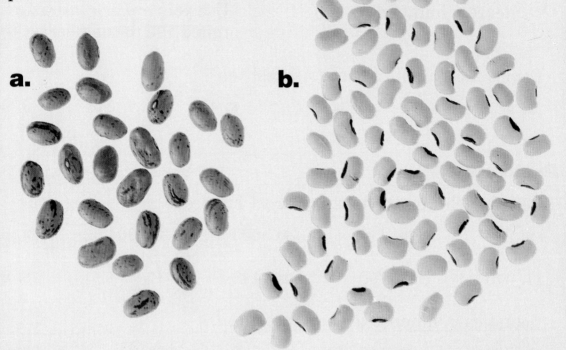

a.

b.

2. Each person in the group should reach into a bowl of beans and take out a handful.

3. Estimate the number of beans in each handful. Find the actual number to check your estimates.

TIPS FOR **WORKING TOGETHER**

Remember, you can disagree without being disagreeable.

Real-Life Decision Making

You are paying for a toy with 40 pennies. You want to make it easy for the clerk to count the pennies to see that they are all there. How will you arrange them on the counter?

Number-Sense Project

Look back at pages 34-35.
In the pictures below, some buildings do not have house numbers.
What could they be? Write your prediction.

1.

279   281   287

2.

18   For Sale   26

Visual Thinking Activity

1. How many ducks are in the pond?

2. How many ducks are inside the fence?

3. How many ducks are inside the fence and in the pond?

51

Use Logical Reasoning

Build Understanding

Ms. Rucker, a photographer, took pictures of the students. One picture was of Dan, May, and Carl. The numbers on their shirts made a three-digit number.

The hundreds digit was the sum of the tens and ones digits. The ones digit was double the tens digit.

PROBLEM SOLVING
GUIDE

Understand
QUESTION
FACTS
KEY IDEA

➤ **Plan and Solve**
STRATEGY
ANSWER

Look Back
SENSIBLE ANSWER
ALTERNATE APPROACH

CARL
2

DAN
6

SUE
5

AMY
3

MAY
4

SAM
7

In what order did they appear in the picture?

Understand Who stood first, second, and third in the picture? You can work with the digits 6, 4, and 2 to find the three-digit number that fits the clues.

➤ **Plan and Solve** STRATEGY Use logical reasoning.

6 is the sum of 4 and 2. It must be the hundreds digit. 2 doubled is 4. It must be the ones digit. The number is 624.

ANSWER The order is Dan, Carl, and May.

Look Back Check again to see that the number fits all of the clues.

■ **Talk About Math** Explain why you should check the number to see if the digits fit all the clues.

Check Understanding

Carl, Sue, and Sam posed for a different picture. Their shirts made a three-digit number that was less than 500. The tens digit was the sum of the hundreds and ones digits. In what order did they appear in the picture?

1. What are Carl's, Sue's, and Sam's numbers?

2. Which digit should be the sum of the other two?

3. Which of the student's numbers is the sum of the other two?

4. What two three-digit numbers can you write using 7 as the tens digit?

5. Which of the two numbers you wrote is less than 500?

6. How were the students lined up?

Practice

These groups of students also posed for pictures. How were they lined up?

7. The number made by Carl, Amy, and Sue was more than 400. The ones digit was more than the tens.

8. The number made by Sam, Amy, and Sue was less than 400. The ones digit was 2 less than the tens digit.

Two groups of three students covered their faces and posed for mystery pictures. Name the students in the order in which they appeared in each picture.

9. The number they made was between 500 and 600. The tens digit was 3 more than the ones digit.

10. The number they made was between 200 and 300. The ones digit was 4 less than the tens.

Understanding Thousands

Build Understanding

A. Building Thousands
Materials: Place-value materials (hundreds, tens, and ones)
Groups: 3–5 students

Ten boxes of pencils are packed in each case. How many pencils are there in each case?

a. Each box holds 100 pencils. Use a hundred square for each box. How many hundreds do you need to show?

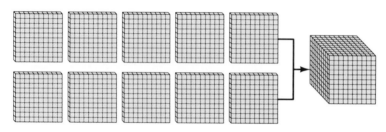

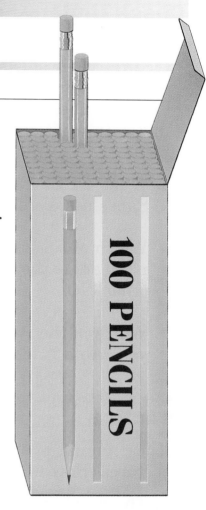

100 PENCILS

10 hundreds make 1 thousand.
There are 1 thousand pencils in each case.

| 100 pencils | 100 pencils | | 100 pencils | 100 pencils |
| 100 pencils | 100 pencils | 100 pencils | 100 pencils | 100 pencils |

b. How many thousands can you make?

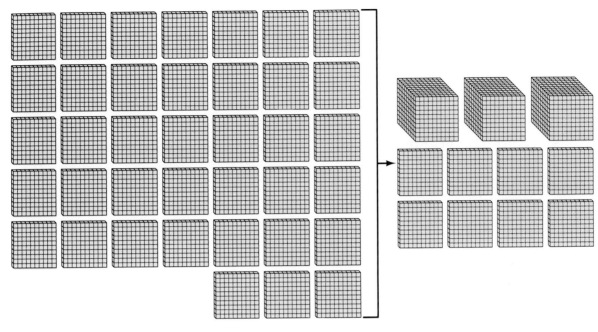

38 hundreds   3 thousands 8 hundreds

c. How many thousands can you make from 43 hundreds?

B. Write this number in standard form.

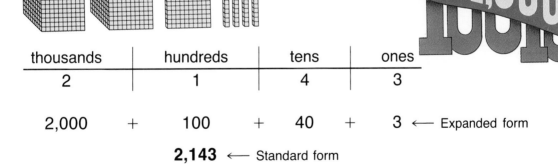

thousands	hundreds	tens	ones
2	1	4	3

2,000   +   100   +   40   +   3   ← Expanded form

2,143   ← Standard form

two thousand, one hundred forty-three

■ **Talk About Math** Explain what 0 means in 4,902.

Check Understanding

For another example, see Set G, pages 66–67.

Write the word that will complete each sentence.

1. 10 tens = 1 ___?___

2. 10 ones = 1 ___?___

3. 10 hundreds = 1 ___?___

4. 20 tens = 2 ___?___

5. Write the standard form.

6. Draw a picture to show 3,046. Describe how the 0 affects your drawing.

Practice

For More Practice, see Set G, pages 68–69.

Write the word or words that will complete each sentence.

7. 90 ones = 9 ___?___

8. 90 tens = 9 ___?___

9. 90 hundreds = 9 ___?___

10. 68 hundreds = ___?___

Write the standard form.

11.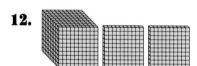

12.

13.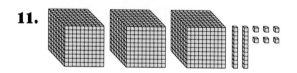

14.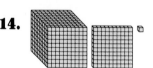

15. 4,000 + 900 + 20 + 6

16. 8,000 + 30 + 7

17. 7,000 + 100 + 9

18. 5,000 + 200 + 60 + 3

19. eight thousand, seven

20. three thousand, five hundred eleven

Write the digit that is in the

21. hundreds place of 5,402. **22.** thousands place of 9,003.

23. tens place of 6,207. **24.** thousands place of 4,996.

25. ones place of 7,348. **26.** hundreds place of 3,475.

Calculator Write the answer you think a calculator would give. Then use a calculator to check your answers.

27. 2000 ⊕ 300 ⊕ 70 ⊕ 5 ⊜

28. 8000 ⊕ 200 ⊕ 10 ⊕ 3 ⊜

29. 4000 ⊕ 60 ⊕ 9 ⊜

30. 5000 ⊕ 800 ⊕ 6 ⊜

31. 7000 ⊕ 70 ⊜

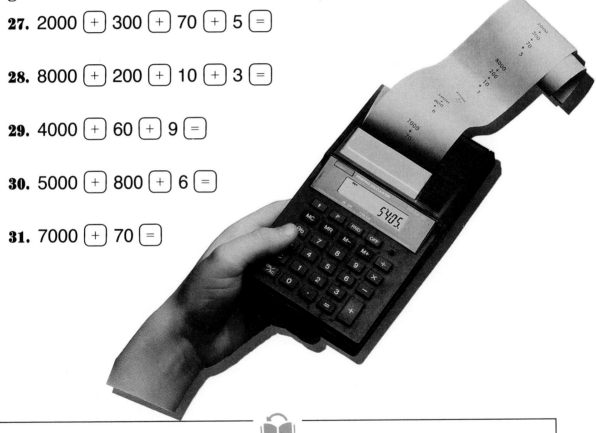

Skills ___ **Review** pages 6–7

Write the number that is one less.
1. 46 **2.** 18 **3.** 51 **4.** 22 **5.** 30 **6.** 80

Mental Math Add or subtract.

7. 3	**8.** 7	**9.** 5	**10.** 11	**11.** 7	**12.** 9
+1	−1	+4	− 8	−5	+6

Comparing and Ordering Numbers

Build Understanding

A. Mary lives in Los Angeles. Students in her class have pen pals in all of the cities in this chart. Mary decided to find out whose pen pal lives farthest away.

Which city is farther from Los Angeles, Atlanta or Cincinnati?

Distance from Los Angeles	
Atlanta	2,182 miles
Chicago	2,054 miles
Cincinnati	2,179 miles
New Orleans	1,883 miles
Minneapolis	1,889 miles
San Francisco	387 miles

Show: Atlanta

Cincinnati

Think:

2,182 ⬚ 2,179   The thousands digits are the same.

2,182 ⬚ 2,179   The hundreds digits are the same.

2,182 ⬚ 2,179   The tens digits are not the same.
8 tens is greater than 7 tens.
So, 2,182 is greater than 2,179.

Write: 2,182 > 2,179   or   2,179 < 2,182

Atlanta is farther from Los Angeles than Cincinnati is.

B. Find the distances from Los Angeles for New Orleans, Minneapolis, and San Francisco. List them in order from greatest to least.

■ **Talk About Math** Describe how you can order the numbers in Example B from least to greatest.

1,889   1,883   387

58

Check Understanding

For another example, see Set H, pages 66–67.

Replace ▓ with < or >. For each exercise, tell which digits you have to compare.

1. 5,148 ▓ 4,185
2. 3,456 ▓ 3,459

3. 7,041 ▓ 7,401

4. In Example B, which digits did you have to look at to tell whether New Orleans or Minneapolis was farther away from Los Angeles?

Practice

For More Practice, see Set H, pages 68–69.

Replace ▓ with < or >.

5. 6,450 ▓ 6,504
6. 9,205 ▓ 9,250
7. 5,079 ▓ 5,709

8. 5,398 ▓ 6,000
9. 5,298 ▓ 928
10. 4,398 ▓ 4,397

11. 6,239 ▓ 6,293
12. 3,079 ▓ 3,709
13. 7,001 ▓ 6,999

Mixed Practice Write these numbers in order from least to greatest.

14. 6,705 6,075 6,507 675
15. 498 4,972 49 489

16. 4,279 7,942 4,297 987
17. 56 506 6,052 6,502

Problem Solving

Solve each problem.

18. **Critical Thinking** Use the digits 8, 3, 9, and 5. Write the greatest four-digit number you can.

19. **Use Data** Look at the chart on page 42. Which is heavier, the Atlantic Tuna or the Pacific Tuna?

Ten-Thousands and Hundred-Thousands

Build Understanding

A. The Helfmans have had their car for five years. Look at the odometer and find how many miles the car has been driven.

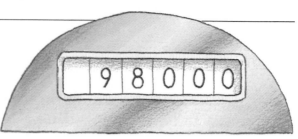

ten-thousands	thousands	hundreds	tens	ones
9	8	0	0	0

Think: The digits 9 and 8 show how many thousands.
Read: ninety-eight thousand
Write: 98,000

The car has been driven 98,000 miles.

B. What number is 1,000 more than 99,000?

Think: One more thousand makes 100 thousand.
Read: one hundred thousand
Write: 100,000

C. Write 431,756 in words.
Think about a place-value chart.

hundred-thousands	ten-thousands	thousands	hundreds	tens	ones
4	3	1	7	5	6

four hundred thirty-one thousand, seven hundred fifty-six

■ **Write About Math** Write a sentence telling the meaning of 0 in the numbers 508,161 and 580,161. Write a second sentence telling the difference in those meanings.

Check Understanding

For another example, see Set I, pages 66–67.

Find each answer.

1. 41,000 means ▦ thousands.

2. What number is 1,000 more than 23,000?

3. Write ninety thousand in standard form.

For Exercises 4–7, write the numbers in words.
Then read each number aloud.

4. 423,156   **5.** 237,095   **6.** 409,127   **7.** 813,006

Practice

For More Practice, see Set I, pages 68–69.

Number Sense   Tell what the 1 means in each number.

8. 31,000   **9.** 49,618   **10.** 12,425   **11.** 88,291

12. 137,772   **13.** 220,891   **14.** 314,842   **15.** 100,008

Write each number in standard form.

16. seventeen thousand, three hundred twelve

17. two hundred seventy-three thousand, five hundred sixty-nine

18. five hundred sixty thousand

19. four hundred forty thousand, seven

20. three hundred forty-two thousand, one hundred five

21. fifty thousand, one hundred twelve

22. nine hundred thousand, twenty-eight

23. twenty-eight hundred

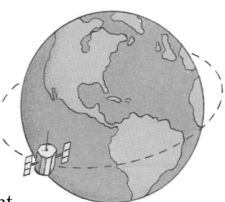

Give Sensible Answers

Build Understanding

Johnny is a third grader at Lincoln School. His hobby is collecting baseball cards.

Johnny had just 75 cents. He bought a pack of cards. How much money did he have left?

50 cents   75 cents   1 dollar

Understand   Johnny had just 75 cents to begin with.

Plan and Solve   You know that Johnny must end up with less money than he started with.

Look Back   SENSIBLE ANSWER   Look at the answer choices to see which one makes the best sense. 75 cents is the same amount Johnny started with. 1 dollar is more than Johnny had at the beginning. 50 cents is the only answer choice that is less than 75 cents.

ALTERNATE APPROACH   You could model the problem using play money.

PROBLEM SOLVING GUIDE

Understand
QUESTION
FACTS
KEY IDEA

Plan and Solve
STRATEGY
ANSWER

Look Back
SENSIBLE ANSWER
ALTERNATE APPROACH

■ **Talk About Math**   The students rode in a school bus to the baseball game. Naomi guessed there were about 400 students on each bus. Explain why this is not a reasonable answer.

Check Understanding

Johnny plays baseball almost every day with his friends. About how many hours does he play baseball each week?

1 hour   10 hours   100 hours

Answer these exercises to help you choose a sensible answer.

1. How many days are in a week?

2. Guess how many hours Johnny plays baseball each day.

3. If Johnny plays that much each day, how many hours would he play all week?

4. Which of the answer choices is closest to your guess?

Practice

Choose the most sensible answer.

5. Johnny has 423 cards in his collection. His friend, Luis, has many more. How many cards does Luis have?

373   425   480

6. In a Little League game, Johnny's team scored 7 runs but lost. How many runs did the other team score?

5   7   9

7. Johnny once saw his favorite player, Eric Davis, hit a home run. How far did it go?

4 feet   400 feet   40,000 feet

8. Johnny's younger brother, James, likes to look at the card collection. How old is James?

6   10   13

Problem-Solving Review

Solve each problem.

1. Together Karen and Elaine have 13 seashells. Elaine has 1 more than Karen. How many shells does each girl have?

2. Nikki and her brother walked to the movie they saw and then walked home again. How long were they gone?

15 minutes
1 hour
3 hours

3. Look for a pattern. Write the next line of numbers.

4. I am an even number. In money, I am greater than 2 dimes but less than a quarter. You can make me with 4 coins. What am I?

5. Sonia counted her mother's savings coupons. There were three $1-off coupons, five 10¢-off coupons, and an 8¢-off coupon. If Sonia's mother uses all the coupons, how much will she save?

6. **Data File**
Use data from pages 104-105. List the golf scores from the lowest score to the highest score.

7. **Make a Data File**
Look through newspapers and magazines for stories or charts that show numbers in the ten-thousands or hundred-thousands. Which are easier to find? Do most of the numbers name money, distance, population, sports scores, or something else?

Problem Solving REVIEW

Explore with a Calculator

How Much Will it Cost?

1. Mrs. Smith had a gardener trim some bushes. The initial cost to come was $3. Then it cost $7 for every bush. The total cost was $31. How many bushes did he trim?

You can use a key sequence like this:
3 ⊞ 7 ⊞ 7 ⊞ . . .
until the display shows 31.

Use a key sequence like the one above to

a. count by fives from 12 to 42.

c. count by twos from 5 to 23.

b. count by tens from 23 to 83.

d. count by threes from 16 to 34.

Solve these problems using a key sequence like the one above.

2. The fee for repairing a computer was $15 plus $12 for every hour of work. The total cost was $63. How many hours did the repair take?

3. The car repair bill was $157. If parts were $37 and the hourly rate was $40, how many hours did the repair take?

4. It is $6 an hour to rent a bike plus a service charge of $12. How much will it cost to ride for 5 hours?

Reteaching

Set A   pages 36–39

Cover 2 tens with 21 ones.
You will have 1 one left over.

21 ones   2 tens   1 one

Remember that it takes 10 ones to make 1 ten and 10 tens to make 1 hundred.

Make as many tens as you can. Use l and • to record your work.

1. 33 ones   **2.** 52 ones

Set B   pages 40–41

How many hundreds, tens, and ones are in this number? Write this number in standard form.

three hundred   forty-five
3 hundreds   4 tens 5 ones

300   +   40 + 5

345 ← Standard form

Remember that the value of the tens digit cannot be greater than the value of the hundreds digit.

Tell how many hundreds, tens, and ones. Then write the number in standard form.

1. Eighty-two **2.** Six hundred nine

Set C   pages 42–43

Replace ⬚ with < or >.

436 ⬚ 429

The hundreds digits are the same. The tens digits are not the same. Since 3 tens is more than 2 tens,

436 > 429 or 429 < 436.

Remember that the symbol > or < points to the smaller number. Replace ⬚ with < or >.

1. 375 ⬚ 362   **2.** 88 ⬚ 141

3. 418 ⬚ 425   **4.** 695 ⬚ 702

Set D   pages 44–45

Write these numbers in order from least to greatest.

683   429   432   517

Use the hundreds   683   517   429
digits to order.   432
Compare the tens: 429 ⬚ 432.
Since 2 < 3, 429 < 432.
Order: 429   432   517   683

Remember to compare the tens if the hundreds digits are the same. Write these numbers in order from least to greatest.

1. 481   396   224   368

2. 80   45   181   165

Set E pages 46–47

Describe this pattern. Then find the missing numbers.

3, 7, 11, 15, ▦, ▦, ▦,

Begin with 3. Then count by 4s. The missing numbers are 19, 23, and 27.

Remember that finding a pattern can make counting easier.

Describe the pattern. Then find the missing numbers.

1. 4, 7, 10, 13, ▦, ▦

Set F pages 48–49

Round 436 to the nearest ten.

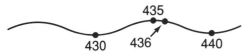

If you put a marble at 436, it would roll forward to 440.

Remember that the tens are at the bottom of the hills when you round to the nearest ten.

Round each to the nearest ten.

1. 34   **2.** 119   **3.** 342

Set G pages 54–57

Write 3,000 + 100 + 20 + 2 in standard form.

3,122 ◄─────── Standard form

Remember that it takes 10 hundreds to make 1 thousand. Write the standard form.

1. 5,000 + 300 + 40 **2.** 9,000 + 4

Set H pages 58–59

Compare 4,286 and 4,276.

The thousands digits and the hundreds digits are the same.

Since 8 > 7, 4,286 > 4,276

Remember that > means greater than and < means less than.

Replace ▦ with < or >.

1. 8,362 ▦ 8,371   **2.** 6,459 ▦ 6,549

Set I pages 60–61

Write 618,432 in words.

Hundred thousands	Ten thousands	Thousands	Hundreds	Tens	Ones
6	1	8	4	3	2

six hundred eighteen thousand, four hundred thirty-two

Remember to think about a place-value chart when you read a number. Write the number in standard form.

1. four hundred sixty thousand, two hundred twenty-seven

More Practice

Set A pages 36–39

Use your place-value materials to make as
many tens as you can. Then use **l** and • to
record your work. See margin for place value work.

1. 43 ones   **2.** 50 ones   **3.** 16 ones   **4.** 36 ones

Use your place-value materials to make as
many hundreds as you can. Use ☐, **l**, and •
to record your work. See margin for place value work.

5. 30 tens   **6.** 10 tens   **7.** 24 tens   **8.** 44 tens

Set B pages 40–41

Tell how many hundreds, tens, and ones.
Then write the number in standard form.

1. six hundred two   **2.** nine hundred fifty   **3.** ninety-eight

Number Sense In the following exercises,
tell whether the 4 is the hundreds digit, the
tens digit, or the ones digit.

4. 864   **5.** 249   **6.** 461   **7.** 947   **8.** 804

Set C pages 42–43

Replace ⁂ with $<$ or $>$.

1. 542 ⁂ 536   **2.** 409 ⁂ 381   **3.** 368 ⁂ 386   **4.** 78 ⁂ 219

5. 127 ⁂ 172   **6.** 62 ⁂ 620   **7.** 501 ⁂ 510   **8.** 82 ⁂ 28

Set D pages 44–45

Write the numbers between

1. 432 and 438.   **2.** 346 and 351.   **3.** 296 and 304.

Write the numbers in order from least to greatest.

4. 640 82 721 726   **5.** 60 81 123 103

6. 402 390 405 309   **7.** 841 826 796 791

Set E pages 46–47

1. Begin at 9. Count by twos. Count to 21.

2. Begin at 6. Count by fives. Count to 31.

Describe each pattern. Then find the missing numbers.

3. 11, 15, 19, 23, ▦, ▦   **4.** 23, 28, 33, 38, ▦, ▦

Set F pages 48–49

Round each number to the nearest hundred.

1. 377   **2.** 212   **3.** 664   **4.** 706   **5.** 539

For Exercises 6–10, round Exercises 1–5 to the nearest ten.

Set G pages 54–57

Write the standard form.

1. 6,000 + 400 + 30 + 5   **2.** 7,000 + 90 + 6

3. 2,000 + 300 + 9   **4.** six thousand, eighty-nine

Write the digit that is in the

5. hundreds place of 8,304.   **6.** tens place of 7,408.

Set H pages 58–59

Replace ▦ with < or >.

1. 3,841 ▦ 3,481   **2.** 2,084 ▦ 2,048   **3.** 9,642 ▦ 9,643

Set I pages 60–61

Number Sense   Tell what the 3 means in each number.

1. 42,739   **2.** 38,149   **3.** 53,904   **4.** 87,423

Write each number in standard form.

5. nineteen thousand, five hundred sixteen

6. one hundred thirty-two thousand, eight hundred six

Enrichment

Millions and Billions

About two hundred forty-four million, six hundred thousand people live in the United States.

How would you write that number in standard form?

millions			thousands			ones		
hundred-millions	ten-millions	millions	hundred-thousands	ten-thousands	thousands	hundreds	tens	ones
2	4	4	6	0	0	0	0	0

Write: **244,600,000** ⟵ Standard form
Use commas to separate
each set of 3 digits.

Start at the right.
The first set of 3 digits tells how many ones.
The second set of 3 digits tells how many thousands.
The third set of 3 digits tells how many **millions.**

Write each number in standard form.

1. Four hundred sixty-one
million, seven hundred forty
thousand, six hundred

2. Seven hundred eighty-one
million, five hundred fifty-
two thousand, seventeen

3. Eight hundred seven million,
four hundred thousand, eight
hundred ninety-four

4. Nine hundred seventy
million, three hundred
thousand, forty-six

The next set of 3 digits greater than millions is **billions.**
Write each number in standard form.

5. One hundred four billion,
four hundred fifty-one
thousand

6. Three billion, twenty million,
one hundred thirty thousand

Chapter 2 Review/Test

Use □, I, and • to show how many hundreds, tens, and ones are in

1. 62 ones.   **2.** 78 tens.

3. Write the standard form for nine thousand, eight hundred forty-one

In 357,801, which number is in

4. the hundreds place?

5. the hundred-thousands place?

6. the ten-thousands place?

Replace each ⊞ with < or >.

7. 427 ⊞ 348

8. 2,976 ⊞ 3,951

9. Write the numbers in order from least to greatest.

  581   642   539

10. Write the numbers as you count by twos from 66 to 74.

11. Round 76 to the nearest ten.

12. Round 542 to the nearest hundred.

13. Write a three-digit number using the digits 3, 6, and 9. The hundreds digit is the sum of the tens and ones digits. The ones digit is greater than the tens digit.

14. Anna's team scored 5 goals and won. Choose the most sensible answer for the number of goals the other team scored.

  3 goals   5 goals   7 goals

Read this problem. Then answer the question below.

Gil weighs 72 pounds. His sister Tammy weighs 58 pounds. Which of them weighs more?

15. Choose the question that has the same meaning as the question in the problem.

  a. How much more does Gil weigh than Tammy?

  b. Does Gil weigh more than 60 pounds?

  c. Who weighs more, Gil or Tammy?

16. ■ **Write About Math**
Explain what the 0 means in 591,048.

Two-Digit Addition and Subtraction

3

Did You Know: During your lifetime you eat about 60,000 pounds of food. This is the equivalent in weight of six elephants.

Number-Sense Project

Estimate
The sandwiches shown are tuna, hamburger, pita, peanut butter with jelly, and turkey sub. Estimate how many of each sandwich your classmates would choose for lunch.

Gather Data
Write down your estimates. Then take a count of your classmates to see how many would choose each sandwich.

Analyze and Report
Were your estimates accurate? What information might have helped you make more accurate estimates?

Choose an Operation

PROBLEM SOLVING
GUIDE

Understand
QUESTION
FACTS
KEY IDEA

➤ **Plan and Solve**
STRATEGY
ANSWER

Look Back
SENSIBLE ANSWER
ALTERNATE APPROACH

Build Understanding

Nishi and John both made yarn dolls at the fair. Nishi made 16 dolls and John made 9. How many more did Nishi make than John?

Understand   To find out how many more dolls Nishi made than John, you need to compare.

➤ **Plan and Solve**   STRATEGY   Choose an operation. To find out how much greater 16 is than 9, you should subtract.

$$16 - 9 = 7$$

ANSWER   Nishi made 7 more dolls than John.

Look Back   You can check the answer by adding.

$$9 + 7 = 16$$

■ **Talk About Math**   How can drawing a picture help you decide whether to use addition or subtraction?

Check Understanding

Solve the problem by answering Exercises 1–4.

On Monday, Tommy made 8 potholders. On Tuesday, he made 2 more than he made on Monday. How many potholders did Tommy make on Tuesday?

1. How many potholders did Tommy make on Monday?

2. What do you know about how many potholders Tommy made on Tuesday?

3. Should you add or subtract? Why?

4. How many potholders did Tommy make on Tuesday?

Practice

Solve each problem.

5. Chim and Jonathan made 14 candles in all. 8 of them were red. The rest were blue. How many blue candles did they make?

6. If Kuri could have made just 3 more paper roses, she would have had 10. How many roses did Kuri make?

7. Chisako made 12 origami swans. She sold 9 of them at the fair. How many swans did she have left?

8. Jane made 8 key cases. Nan made 3 more than Jane. How many key cases did Nan make?

Choose a Strategy

Which One Won?

9. In a race, Jeff finished last. Mark finished behind Christine and in front of Juanita. Who won the race?

Renaming for Addition and Subtraction

Build Understanding

Fill the Baskets
Materials: Place-value materials (tens and ones)
Groups: 3–5 students

A. Judy fills baskets at her family's apple orchard. She puts 10 apples in each basket.

Show her work with place-value materials, using a ten for each basket and a one for each apple.

a. Suppose Judy has 27 apples. Think about putting them in baskets. Show the different ways Judy can group these apples. Then write your results.

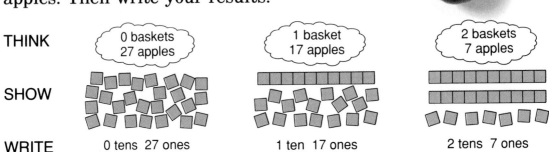

THINK	0 baskets 27 apples	1 basket 17 apples	2 baskets 7 apples
SHOW			
WRITE	0 tens 27 ones	1 ten 17 ones	2 tens 7 ones

b. Suppose Judy has 2 baskets of apples. Think about taking the apples out of the baskets. Show what happens when you empty each basket. Then write the results.

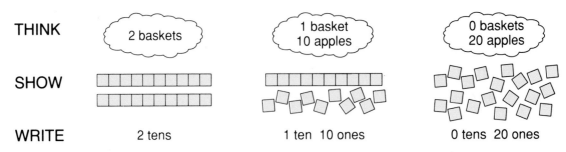

THINK	2 baskets	1 basket 10 apples	0 baskets 20 apples
SHOW			
WRITE	2 tens	1 ten 10 ones	0 tens 20 ones

B. At one point on Monday, Judy had filled 7 baskets and had 13 more apples. How many full baskets did she have when she was all finished? Use place-value materials to show her work.

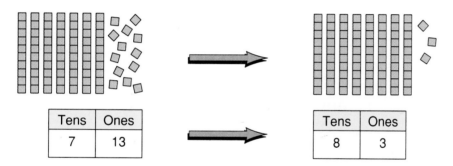

Tens	Ones
7	13

Tens	Ones
8	3

C. On Tuesday, Judy filled 6 baskets and had 7 apples left. Then her dog, Applesauce, knocked over one of the baskets. How many full baskets and single apples did she have then?

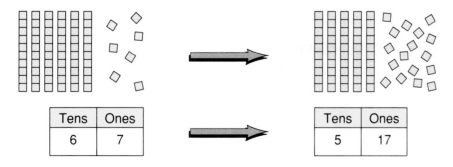

Tens	Ones
6	7

Tens	Ones
5	17

■ **Talk About Math** Look again at the numbers in Examples B and C. What happened to the number of tens in each example? What happened to the number of ones?

77

Check Understanding

For another example, see Set A, pages 98–99.

Number Sense   Use your place-value materials to answer these questions. Then draw a picture to show how you got your answer.

1. How many tens can you make from 14 ones? How many ones are left over?

2. How many ones do you have when you take apart a ten?

Copy and complete each sentence. Use place-value materials if you need them.

2 tens 16 ones is the same as

3. ▦ tens 6 ones.   **4.** 1 ten ▦ ones.   **5.** ▦ tens 36 ones.

Practice

For More Practice, see Set A, pages 100–101.

Use your place-value materials. Make all the new tens you can. How many tens and ones do you have now?

6. Tens	Ones
6	12

7. Tens	Ones
4	16

8. Tens	Ones
5	10

9. 3 tens 14 ones   **10.** 7 tens 23 ones   **11.** 2 tens 20 ones

Use your place-value materials. Trade 1 ten for 10 ones. How many tens and ones do you have now?

12. Tens	Ones
7	3

13. Tens	Ones
6	2

14. Tens	Ones
2	9

15. 5 tens 4 ones   **16.** 9 tens 0 ones   **17.** 1 ten 5 ones

Mixed Practice   Add or subtract.

18. $9 + 8$ **19.** $15 - 7$ **20.** $12 - 5$ **21.** $6 + 7$ **22.** $8 + 7$

23. $7 + 3$ **24.** $6 + 6$ **25.** $10 - 6$ **26.** $16 - 9$ **27.** $18 - 9$

Problem Solving

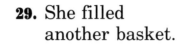

Judy and her brother, Brian, went to gather apples. Judy started with 5 full baskets and 7 single apples. How many baskets and apples did she have after the event in each problem occurred? Draw a picture to show what is happening each time.

28. Brian gave her 6 more apples.

Tens	Ones
5	?

29. She filled another basket.

Tens	Ones
?	?

30. Brian gave her 6 more apples.

Tens	Ones
?	?

31. A customer bought 2 baskets.

Tens	Ones
?	?

32. Applesauce ate 2 apples.

Tens	Ones
?	?

33. Brian gave her 5 more apples.

Tens	Ones
?	?

Skills 📖 **Review**   page 541

Write the numbers in order. Start with the least number.

1. 87 84 86 85 **2.** 13 16 14 15 **3.** 45 75 95 25

Write the numbers in order. Start with the greatest number.

4. 97 94 96 95 **5.** 36 34 35 37 **6.** 18 20 21 19

Two-Digit Addition

Build Understanding

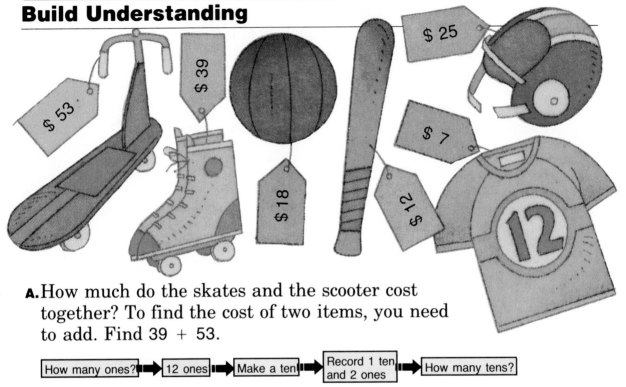

A. How much do the skates and the scooter cost together? To find the cost of two items, you need to add. Find 39 + 53.

| How many ones? | ➡ | 12 ones | ➡ | Make a ten | ➡ | Record 1 ten and 2 ones | ➡ | How many tens? |

$$\begin{array}{r} 39 \\ +53 \\ \end{array}$$

$$\begin{array}{r} {\scriptstyle 1} \\ 39 \\ +53 \\ \hline 2 \end{array}$$

$$\begin{array}{r} {\scriptstyle 1} \\ 39 \\ +53 \\ \hline 92 \end{array}$$

The skates and scooter cost $92.

B. Find 12 + 25.

| How many ones? | ➡ | 7 ones |

| Record 7 ones. | ➡ | How many tens? |

Cannot make a ten.

$$\begin{array}{r} 12 \\ +25 \\ \end{array}$$

$$\begin{array}{r} 12 \\ +25 \\ \hline 7 \end{array}$$

$$\begin{array}{r} 12 \\ +25 \\ \hline 37 \end{array}$$

■ **Talk About Math** How was what you did in Example A different from what you did in Example B?

Check Understanding

For another example, see Set B, pages 98–99.

Use Examples A and B to answer each question.

1. How can you tell whether you will need to make a ten?

2. Would you need to make a ten to figure the cost of the basketball and the scooter?

Copy the exercises. Circle the ones for which you will have to make an extra ten. Then find the sums.
Remember to draw a picture if it will help you.

3. 62 + 27   **4.** 74 + 8   **5.** 56 + 46   **6.** 7 + 81   **7.** 84 + 16

Practice

For More Practice, see Set B, pages 100–101.

Find the sums.

8. 63 + 29	**9.** 48 + 51	**10.** 53 + 28	**11.** 70 + 16	**12.** 26 + 18
13. 42 + 39	**14.** 85 + 12	**15.** 45 + 45	**16.** 27 + 38	**17.** 87 + 5

18. 4 + 17   **19.** 54 + 3   **20.** 32 + 65   **21.** 34 + 47   **22.** 17 + 39

Problem Solving

Solve each problem.

23. How much would the basketball and jersey cost together?

24. Scott's mom spent $57 in the store. What 2 things did she buy?

TIPS FOR PROBLEM SOLVERS

Compare problems to help you relate new problems to ones you've solved before.

Addition: Mental Math

Build Understanding

Mrs. Delgrado's class has a mental math contest every week. The students who are best at addition each do it differently.

A. To find 35 + 23, Mary uses place value. She breaks apart both numbers.

$$30 + 20 = 50$$
$$5 + 3 = 8$$
$$50 + 8 = 58$$

B. Bobby also uses place value to find 35 + 23. He breaks apart only the second number.

$$35 + 20 + 3 =$$
$$55 + 3 = 58$$

C. Carlos thinks about a part of the hundred number chart.

31	32	33	34	35	36	37	38	39	40
41	42	43	44	45	46	47	48	49	50
51	52	53	54	55	56	57	58	59	60

D. Alice is great with problems like 39 + 25.

39 is 1 less than 40.
$$40 + 25 = 65$$
1 Less than 65 is 64.

■ **Talk About Math** Which method do you like best? Why? Can you think of another way to add mentally?

Check Understanding

For another example, see Set C, pages 98–99.

Number Sense Use the examples. Answer each question.

1. Explain how Carlos's method works. How does he know how far to go down and over?

2. Explain how Alice's method works. For what kinds of exercises would it work best?

Which method would you use to find

3. 27 + 19? **4.** 67 + 32? **5.** 28 + 49? **6.** 36 + 42? **7.** 49 + 12?

Practice

For More Practice, see Set C, pages 100–101.

Find each sum mentally. Write which method you used.

8. 52 + 30 **9.** 37 + 20 **10.** 43 + 40 **11.** 65 + 19 **12.** 26 + 13

13. 25 + 43 **14.** 63 + 28 **15.** 57 + 29 **16.** 22 + 56 **17.** 65 + 43

18. 67 + 19 **19.** 39 + 58 **20.** 27 + 12 **21.** 19 + 74 **22.** 39 + 24

Explore ———— Math

Find each missing number. **Remember** to use mental math strategies to help you.

23. 37 + ▦ = 67   How many more tens are needed?

24. ▦ + 17 = 19   How many more ones are needed?

25. ▦ + 35 = 39   **26.** 34 + ▦ = 94   **27.** 72 + ▦ = 92

28. ▦ + 42 = 49   **29.** 48 + ▦ = 88   **30.** ▦ + 29 = 79

31. ▦ + 55 = 58   **32.** 27 + ▦ = 57   **33.** 16 + ▦ = 95

Three or More Addends

Build Understanding

This treasure map was shown in a book about Redbeard the Pirate's secret island.

How many steps is it from the dock to the anchor using the stone path?

Since there are 3 sections to the stone path, add the amounts together. Find 15 + 25 + 32.

What would a map from your home to school look like?

| Think: How many ones? | ▸ | Record 1 ten and 2 ones. | ▸ | Think: How many tens? | ▸ | Record 7 tens. |

$$
\begin{array}{r}
1\,5 \\
2\,5 \\
+3\,2 \\
\end{array}
\qquad
\begin{array}{r}
^{1} \\
1\,5 \\
2\,5 \\
+3\,2 \\
\hline
2 \\
\end{array}
\qquad
\begin{array}{r}
^{1} \\
1\,5 \\
2\,5 \\
+3\,2 \\
\hline
2 \\
\end{array}
\qquad
\begin{array}{r}
^{1} \\
1\,5 \\
2\,5 \\
+3\,2 \\
\hline
7\,2 \\
\end{array}
$$

There are 72 steps from the dock to the anchor along the stone path.

■ **Talk About Math** Can you add the ones by starting at the bottom? Can you do the same with the tens?

84

Check Understanding

For another example, see Set D, pages 98–99.

Find each answer.

1. **Number Sense** Show how you would write 25 + 7 + 39. Explain why it is important to line up the digits correctly. Then add.

2. 56 + 18 + 17   **3.** 49 + 24 + 8   **4.** 29 + 6 + 22 + 25

Practice

For More Practice, see Set D, pages 100–101.

Find these sums.

5. 47 + 23 + 14   **6.** 52 + 28 + 12   **7.** 9 + 35 + 28

8. 65 + 8 + 21   **9.** 37 + 46 + 13   **10.** 26 + 6 + 32

11. 44 + 35 + 4   **12.** 39 + 7 + 43   **13.** 6 + 34 + 23 + 8

14. 27 + 55 + 9   **15.** 8 + 42 + 16   **16.** 14 + 3 + 19 + 5 + 20

Midchapter ———— Checkup

Solve each problem.

1. Jaime had 9 marbles. Bob had 6. How many more marbles did Jaime have than Bob?

2. Mark had 4 model cars at home and 5 at school. How many did he have in all?

Find the missing number.
3. 6 tens 8 ones = 5 tens ▦ ones

Add. **Remember** to line up the digits correctly.
4. 16 + 8   **5.** 35 + 35   **6.** 17 + 39 + 4   **7.** 6 + 23 + 34

8. Use mental math to find 29 + 34.

Real-Life Decision Making

Here is a treasure map. The map shows a ■, a drawing, and the name of a landmark where treasures are buried. You may pick up one treasure from each landmark you visit.

1. What is the fewest number of steps to the crossbar from Start? (Each θ is one step.)

2. If you took the fewest steps from Start to the flower, how many treasures could you pick up?

3. You may take up to 100 steps to collect treasures. Decide which landmarks you will visit.

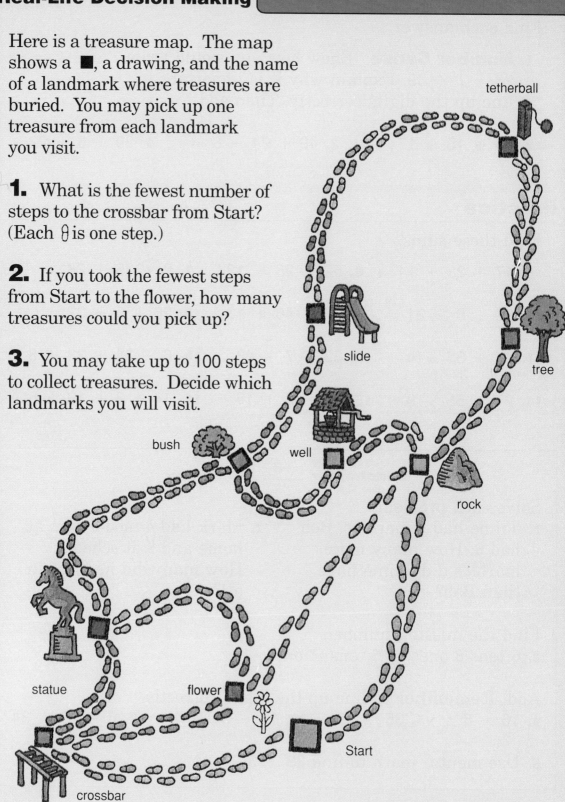

Number-Sense Project

Look back at pages 72-73.
The counts for sandwiches ordered by two grades are shown in this chart.

Sandwich Count		
Sandwich	Grade 3	Grade 4
Hamburger	13	14
Tuna	8	7
Pita	11	10
Peanut Butter with Jelly	6	9
Turkey sub	5	7

1. How many tuna sandwiches were ordered by both grades?

2. Suppose there are 60 students in each grade. Use that information and this chart to show how many students brought their own lunches that day.

3. What was the most popular sandwich? The least popular sandwich?

Explore with a Computer

Use the *Spreadsheet Workshop Project* for this activity. Find out how many boys and girls are in classes in your school. Enter the information into a spreadsheet form. The spreadsheet form will show the sum of the data you type. Think about the totals the spreadsheet form shows. Are the totals reasonable?

Number of Boys and Girls			
Class	Boys	Girls	Total

Two-Digit Subtraction

Build Understanding

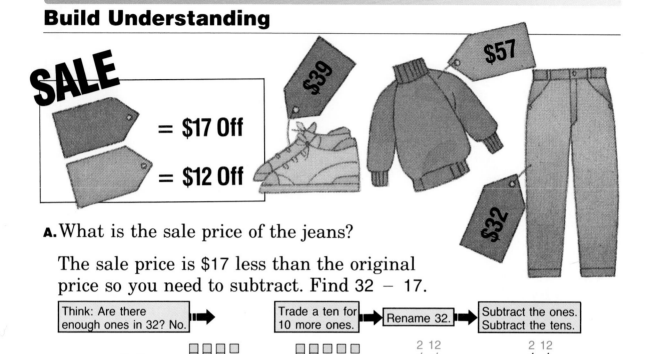

SALE

= $17 Off

= $12 Off

A. What is the sale price of the jeans?

The sale price is $17 less than the original price so you need to subtract. Find 32 − 17.

| Think: Are there enough ones in 32? No. | Trade a ten for 10 more ones. | Rename 32. | Subtract the ones. Subtract the tens. |

```
 3 2          3 2          2 12          2 12
-1 7         -1 7          3̸ 2̸          3̸ 2̸
                          -1 7          -1 7
                                        1 5
```

The sale price of the jeans is $15.

B. Find 57 − 12. You can use addition to check your answer.

| Are there enough ones in 57? Yes. | Subtract the ones. | Subtract the tens. |

Check by adding.

```
 5 7          5 7          5 7 ←── These two          1 2
-1 2         -1 2         -1 2      numbers should   +4 5
                5           4 5      be the same. ──→   5 7
```

■ **Talk About Math** Explain how you can use addition to check subtraction. Then tell how you might use subtraction to check addition.

Check Understanding

For another example, see Set E, pages 98–99.

Use Examples A and B to answer each question.

1. Would you need to rename the first number to find the sale price of the coat?

2. What is the sale price of the dress?

Copy the exercises. Circle the ones for which you will have to rename the first number. Then find each difference. **Remember** that you can draw a picture to help you.

3. 75 − 36   **4.** 34 − 21   **5.** 78 − 36   **6.** 82 − 59   **7.** 37 − 25

Practice

For More Practice, see Set E, pages 100–101.

Find each difference.

8. 92	**9.** 99	**10.** 81	**11.** 86	**12.** 40
− 29	− 48	− 28	− 70	− 39

13. 81	**14.** 57	**15.** 70	**16.** 75	**17.** 92
− 39	− 12	− 45	− 28	− 5

18. 89 − 43   **19.** 93 − 7   **20.** 40 − 39   **21.** 63 − 8   **22.** 74 − 16

Problem Solving

Use the picture on page 88. What is the sale price of the

23. shoes?   **24.** sweater?   **25.** jeans and sweater?

26. Use Data Use the data on page 80 to find how much more the ball costs than the bat.

27. 🖩 **Calculator** What 3-digit number and 2-digit number have a sum of 161 and a difference of 109?

Subtraction: Mental Math

Build Understanding

The students in Mrs. Delgrado's class who are best at mental addition are also good at mental subtraction.

A. To solve 57 − 23, both Mary and Bobby use place value. They break apart the second number.

$$57 - 20 = 37$$
$$37 - 3 = 34$$

B. Carlos thinks about a part of the hundred number chart.

31 32 33 34 35 36 37 38 39 40
41 42 43 44 45 46 47 48 49 50
51 52 53 54 55 56 57 58 59 60

C. Alice is great with problems like 56 − 19.

19 is 1 less than 20.
$$56 - 20 = 36$$
1 more than 36 is 37.

■ **Talk About Math** Which method do you like best? Why? Can you think of another way to subtract mentally?

Check Understanding

For another example, see Set F, pages 98–99.

Number Sense Use the examples to answer each question.

1. Explain how Carlos's method works. How does he know how far to go up and over?

2. Explain how Alice's method works. For what kinds of problems would it work best?

Find the difference mentally. Write which method you used.

3. $57 - 30$ **4.** $96 - 40$ **5.** $57 - 18$ **6.** $35 - 19$ **7.** $25 - 19$

Practice

For More Practice, see Set F, pages 100–101.

Find each difference mentally. Write which method you used.

8. $63 - 20$ **9.** $56 - 30$ **10.** $83 - 40$ **11.** $38 - 23$ **12.** $84 - 23$

13. $54 - 31$ **14.** $57 - 29$ **15.** $42 - 26$ **16.** $53 - 38$ **17.** $82 - 14$

18. $48 - 11$ **19.** $74 - 19$ **20.** $28 - 9$ **21.** $42 - 27$ **22.** $34 - 15$

Problem Solving

Tell whether you would use mental math or paper and pencil to solve each problem. Then find the answer.

23. Mark had 48 counters. He used 19 of them. How many did he have left?

24. Jan has 28 blue counters, 92 yellow counters, and 55 red counters. How many counters does she have in all?

Critical Thinking Replace each ▦ with the digit 2, 3, 6, or 8 to make the given sum or difference. Do not use any digit more than once in any exercise.

25.
```
  ▦ ▦
- ▦ ▦
─────
  4 5
```

26.
```
  ▦ ▦
+ ▦ ▦
─────
  9 1
```

27.
```
  ▦ ▦
+ ▦ ▦
─────
  6 4
```

28.
```
  ▦ ▦
- ▦ ▦
─────
    8
```

Estimation

Build Understanding

A. Jiro is a reporter for the local newspaper. He often estimates the attendance at PTA meetings for his articles.

He used front-end estimation to report attendance for the first two meetings.

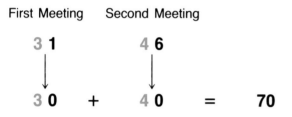

First Meeting   Second Meeting

3 **1**   4 **6**
↓   ↓
3 **0**   +   4 **0**   =   **70**

Jiro reported that more than 70 people attended those meetings.

B. The editor at the newspaper estimated the attendance by increasing the first digit of each number by 1.

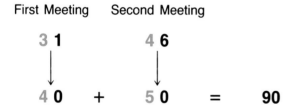

First Meeting   Second Meeting

3 **1**   4 **6**
↓   ↓
4 **0**   +   5 **0**   =   **90**

She wrote that fewer than 90 people attended the meetings.

c. Estimate 51 − 39.

51 − 39

50 − 30 = 20

PTA Attendance
First meeting:
31
Second meeting:
46

The PTA (Parent-Teacher Association) was started in 1897 to help school children.

■ **Talk About Math** In Examples A and B, tell why the actual attendance must fall between 70 and 90.

Check Understanding

For another example, see Set G, pages 98–99.

Answer each question.

1. Do you think a front-end estimate for an addition exercise will always be less than the actual sum?

2. Is your estimate in Example C more or less than the actual difference?

3. Use front-end estimation to estimate 49 − 31. Is your estimate more or less than the actual difference?

4. Why can a front-end estimate for a subtraction exercise be more or less than the actual answer?

Estimate each answer.

5. 85 − 27   6. 16 + 38   7. 67 + 85   8. 39 − 22   9. 12 + 49

Practice

For More Practice, see Set G, pages 100–101.

Estimate each answer.

10. 98 − 42   11. 76 − 15   12. 35 + 39   13. 58 + 19   14. 27 − 11

15. 72 − 46   16. 44 + 52   17. 84 − 19   18. 27 + 32   19. 38 + 29

Tell whether the sum will be greater than or less than 100.

20. 36 + 55   21. 44 + 44   22. 16 + 98   23. 24 + 39   24. 78 + 25

Reading ———— Math

Vocabulary The actual attendance in Examples A and B falls between 70 and 90. This is called the *range.*

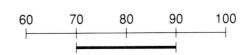

For Exercises 12, 13, 16, 18, and 19 above, find the range.

Deciding When an Estimate Is Enough

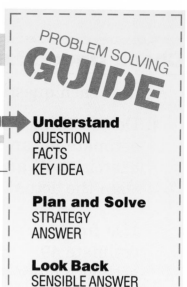
PROBLEM SOLVING
GUIDE

Understand
QUESTION
FACTS
KEY IDEA

Plan and Solve
STRATEGY
ANSWER

Look Back
SENSIBLE ANSWER
ALTERNATE APPROACH

Build Understanding

Suppose you have 50¢. You need paper and crayons. Will you have enough money?

Understand   QUESTION   Do you have enough money to buy paper and crayons?

FACTS   Paper costs 38¢. Crayons cost 21¢. You have 50¢.

KEY IDEA   To see if you have enough money, you don't have to find the exact amount. You can estimate the cost of the paper and crayons. Then compare to see if your estimate is greater than or less than 50¢.

Plan and Solve   Estimate the cost by rounding.

$$
\begin{array}{r}
3\,8 \quad \text{rounds to} \rightarrow \quad 4\,0 \\
+2\,1 \quad \text{rounds to} \rightarrow \quad +2\,0 \\
\hline
6\,0
\end{array}
$$

The estimated cost is about 60¢. You do not have enough money to buy both paper and crayons.

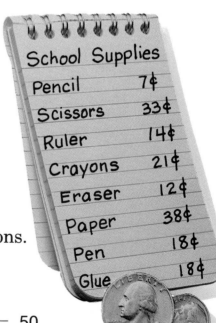

School Supplies

Pencil	7¢
Scissors	33¢
Ruler	14¢
Crayons	21¢
Eraser	12¢
Paper	38¢
Pen	18¢
Glue	18¢

Look Back   You can also use front-end estimation.

$$
\begin{array}{ccc}
38 & + & 21 \\
\downarrow & & \downarrow \\
30 & + & 20 = 50
\end{array}
$$

The actual cost will be more than 50¢.

■ **Talk About Math**   Do you think front-end estimation will always be helpful in estimating whether or not you have enough money? Why or why not?

Check Understanding

Suppose you have 30¢.

1. Do you have enough money to buy glue and a pen? How did you decide?

2. You need to buy a pen. Do you have enough money to buy more items? What ones?

Practice

Suppose you have 25¢. Do you have enough money to buy the following items? Tell how you know.

3. Pen and eraser

4. Ruler and glue

5. Pencil and eraser

6. Glue and eraser

Choose as many items as possible that you can buy for

7. 37¢.   **8.** 48¢.   **9.** 98¢.   **10.** 75¢   **11.** 89¢.   **12.** $1.

Choose a _____ Strategy

Betty's Blocks
13. Betty stacked all her blocks in the shape of a staircase. The highest step was 8 blocks high. How many blocks did she use?

Problem Solving REVIEW

Solve each problem.

1. Write the next 3 numbers in the pattern.
    1,268   1,278   1,288

2. The number on Jake's soccer-team shirt is 18. Jake was the 4th player out of the locker room for the team's 2-mile practice run. Tell whether each number is used to count, measure, or show order.

3. Mrs. Archer gave the cashier at the supermarket coupons for 25¢, 39¢, and 20¢. How much did she save by using those coupons?

4. The Pilgrim puppet costs one dollar more than the difference between the prices of the other two puppets. How much does the Pilgrim puppet cost?

5. Write a word problem for the number sentence. $11 - 6 = 5$.

6. Every person whose ticket had a 7 in the tens place, and 8 in the hundreds place, and a 5 in the ones place won a prize at the Arts and Crafts Fair. Which of these tickets were winners?

7. **Data File** Use data from pages 104-105. What is the difference between the high temperature in Seattle and the high temperature in Atlanta?

8. **Make a Data File** Find a supermarket advertising flier. Cut out all the coupons. Estimate how much you would save if you bought all those products.

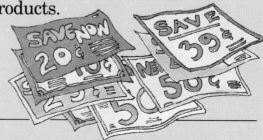

Explore with a Calculator

What's the address?

1. Sam gave Darian this set of directions to get to his house on Elm Street. The final display is Sam's address. What is Sam's address?

a. Start with 76 in the display.

b. Add 9 tens.

c. Add 67.

d. Add 3 tens and 2 ones.

e. Subtract 5 tens and 8 ones.

f. Add 204.

g. Subtract 6 tens and 7 ones.

h. Add 2 hundreds, 3 tens, and 1 one.

i. What is Sam's address?

2. Darian made a similar set of directions for discovering his address on Carpenter Lane. What is his address?

a. Start with 7 tens and 4 ones.

b. Add 401.

c. Subtract 210.

d. Add 6 tens and 2 ones.

e. Add 491.

f. Subtract 1 hundred and 7 tens.

g. Subtract 87.

h. Add 38.

i. What is Darian's address?

Reteaching

Set A pages 76–79

You have 2 tens and 5 ones. You can trade 1 ten for 10 ones.

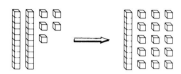

So 2 tens 5 ones = 1 ten 15 ones.

Remember that you can trade ones for tens if you have 10 or more ones. Trade 1 ten for 10 ones. How many tens and how many ones do you have now?

1.	Tens	Ones
	5	2

2.	Tens	Ones
	3	4

Set B pages 80–81

Find 34 + 17.
Add the ones: 7 + 4 = 11. Trade the 11 ones for 1 ten and 1 one. Then add the tens.

```
  34            1 ←——— 1 ten
+ 17    ⇨       34
              + 17
                51 ←——— 1 one
```

Remember that adding the ones will tell you whether you need to make a ten.

Find the sums.

1.	**2.**	**3.**
46	34	58
+ 25	+ 45	+ 25

Set C pages 82–83

Find 38 + 34. Use place value. Break apart both numbers.

```
  38  ⇨  30   8  ⇨   60
+ 34   + 30 + 4    + 12
         60  12      72
```

Remember to use the method you like when you add mentally.

Find each sum mentally.

1. 47 + 40   **2.** 35 + 57

Set D pages 84–85

Find 12 + 25 + 36.
Add the ones: 2 + 5 + 6 = 13

Record 13 ones as
1 ten 3 ones

```
  1
  12
  25
+ 36
   3
```

Now add the tens.

```
  1
  12
  25
+ 36
  73
```

Remember to line up the digits correctly.

Find these sums.

1. 26 + 7 + 30   **2.** 32 + 37 + 14

3. 43 + 18 + 24   **4.** 29 + 8 + 42

Independent Study RETEACHING

Set E   pages 88–89

Find $43 - 15$.
You cannot subtract the ones.

Trade 1 ten for 10 ones.

43 ———→3 tens   13 ones

3 13

$$\begin{array}{r} 43 \\ - 15 \\ \hline \end{array}$$

$$\begin{array}{r} 4\overset{3}{\cancel{4}}3 \\ - 15 \\ \hline 28 \end{array}$$

Remember to use addition to check your answer.

Find each difference.

1. $\begin{array}{r} 83 \\ - 44 \\ \hline \end{array}$ 2. $\begin{array}{r} 76 \\ - 35 \\ \hline \end{array}$ 3. $\begin{array}{r} 52 \\ - 20 \\ \hline \end{array}$

4. $\begin{array}{r} 50 \\ - 28 \\ \hline \end{array}$ 5. $\begin{array}{r} 37 \\ - 16 \\ \hline \end{array}$ 6. $\begin{array}{r} 30 \\ - 19 \\ \hline \end{array}$

Set F   pages 90–91

Find $56 - 28$ mentally.
Think: It is easy to subtract 30.

$$\begin{array}{r} 56 \\ - 28 \\ \hline \end{array} \implies \begin{array}{r} 56 \\ - 30 \\ \hline 26 \end{array}$$

Since 30 is 2 more than 28, the actual difference will be 2 more than 26. 2 more than 26 is 28.
So $56 - 28 = 28$.

Remember that if you subtract more at the beginning, you have to add more to find the actual difference.

Find each difference mentally.

1. $\begin{array}{r} 47 \\ - 30 \\ \hline \end{array}$ 2. $\begin{array}{r} 83 \\ - 50 \\ \hline \end{array}$ 3. $\begin{array}{r} 29 \\ - 18 \\ \hline \end{array}$

4. $\begin{array}{r} 56 \\ - 33 \\ \hline \end{array}$ 5. $\begin{array}{r} 36 \\ - 28 \\ \hline \end{array}$ 6. $\begin{array}{r} 34 \\ - 18 \\ \hline \end{array}$

Set G   pages 92–93

Estimate the sum by using front-end estimation.

$$\begin{array}{r} 36 \\ + 47 \\ \hline \end{array} \implies \begin{array}{r} 30 \\ + 40 \\ \hline 70 \end{array}$$

Now estimate the sum by increasing the first digit of each number by 1.

$$\begin{array}{r} 36 \\ + 47 \\ \hline \end{array} \implies \begin{array}{r} 40 \\ + 50 \\ \hline 90 \end{array}$$

The actual sum is between 70 and 90.

Remember that an estimated sum will always be less than the actual sum when you use front-end estimation.

Estimate each answer.

1. $\begin{array}{r} 46 \\ + 32 \\ \hline \end{array}$ 2. $\begin{array}{r} 68 \\ + 25 \\ \hline \end{array}$ 3. $\begin{array}{r} 29 \\ + 27 \\ \hline \end{array}$

4. $\begin{array}{r} 89 \\ + 12 \\ \hline \end{array}$ 5. $\begin{array}{r} 31 \\ + 48 \\ \hline \end{array}$ 6. $\begin{array}{r} 76 \\ + 25 \\ \hline \end{array}$

More Practice

Set A pages 76–79

Use your place-value materials. Make all the new tens
you can. How many tens and ones do you have now?

1.	Tens	Ones
	3	11

2.	Tens	Ones
	7	14

3.	Tens	Ones
	6	18

4. 4 tens 13 ones **5.** 5 tens 24 ones **6.** 6 tens 30 ones

Use your place-value materials. Trade 1 ten
for 10 ones. How many tens and ones do you have now?

7.	Tens	Ones
	4	6

8.	Tens	Ones
	8	4

9.	Tens	Ones
	9	7

10. 6 tens 3 ones **11.** 5 tens 8 ones **12.** 3 tens 5 ones

Mixed Practice Add or subtract.

13. 6 + 9 **14.** 17 − 9 **15.** 11 − 6 **16.** 4 + 7 **17.** 7 + 7

18. 8 + 6 **19.** 16 − 7 **20.** 17 − 8 **21.** 15 − 6 **22.** 8 − 8

Set B pages 80–81

Find the sums.

	1.	2.	3.	4.	5.
	36	71	64	27	60
	+26	+17	+29	+19	+13

6. 5 + 19 **7.** 67 + 2 **8.** 43 + 36 **9.** 56 + 19 **10.** 46 + 45

Set C pages 82–83

Find each sum mentally. Write which method you used.

	1.	2.	3.	4.	5.
	38	49	34	52	64
	+20	+40	+27	+36	+29

	6.	7.	8.	9.	10.
	48	38	81	78	46
	+17	+21	+16	+15	+26

Set D pages 84–85

Find these sums.

1. 28 + 6 + 20   2. 44 + 26 + 13   3. 27 + 32 + 7

4. 56 + 9 + 32   5. 24 + 39 + 14   6. 36 + 8 + 23

7. 6 + 39 + 52   8. 33 + 55 + 10   9. 47 + 24 + 12

Set E pages 88–89

Find each difference.

1. 74 − 47	2. 66 − 52	3. 32 − 19	4. 50 − 22	5. 73 − 30
6. 41 − 28	7. 75 − 15	8. 56 − 29	9. 60 − 35	10. 46 − 9

11. 76 − 41   12. 80 − 34   13. 84 − 8   14. 33 − 4   15. 72 − 38

Set F pages 90–91

Find each difference mentally. Write which
method you used.

1. 38 − 20	2. 86 − 40	3. 46 − 21	4. 87 − 34	5. 92 − 50
6. 63 − 22	7. 48 − 19	8. 34 − 28	9. 84 − 17	10. 56 − 39

Set G pages 92–93

Estimate each answer.

1. 68 − 24	2. 84 − 32	3. 46 + 36	4. 39 + 26	5. 39 − 14
6. 53 − 37	7. 68 − 49	8. 33 + 63	9. 34 + 45	10. 46 + 36

Tell whether the sum will be greater than or less than 100.

11. 48 + 39   12. 96 + 21   13. 66 + 32   14. 34 + 42   15. 52 + 39

Enrichment

Missing Digits

Lupita's wet puppy shook himself and got water drops on her math homework. Help her find each digit covered by the water drops. Look for number clues.

$$\begin{array}{r} 3\,5 \\ -\,1\,\text{\scriptsize⬤} \\ \hline 1\,9 \end{array}$$

CLUE: Look at the ones column.
5 ones − ones = 9 ones
5 ones − = 9 doesn't seem possible.

THINK: Maybe the top number was renamed and the was subtracted from 15 ones.

15 ones − ones = 9 ones
15 − = 9

TRY: Try 6. It works!

$$\begin{array}{r} 3\,5 \\ -\,1\,6 \\ \hline 1\,9 \end{array}$$

Complete each exercise. **Remember** to look for number clues.

1.
$$\begin{array}{r} 5\text{▦} \\ -\,2\,3 \\ \hline 3\,5 \end{array}$$

2.
$$\begin{array}{r} 3\,9 \\ +\,2\text{▦} \\ \hline 6\,2 \end{array}$$

3.
$$\begin{array}{r} 7\,4 \\ -\,\text{▦}7 \\ \hline 2\,7 \end{array}$$

4.
$$\begin{array}{r} 5\text{▦} \\ +\,3\,8 \\ \hline 9\,3 \end{array}$$

5.
$$\begin{array}{r} 2\,7 \\ -\,\text{▦}8 \\ \hline 9 \end{array}$$

6.
$$\begin{array}{r} 3\text{▦} \\ +\,\text{▦}4 \\ \hline 8\,2 \end{array}$$

7.
$$\begin{array}{r} 2\text{▦} \\ -\,1\,6 \\ \hline 7 \end{array}$$

8.
$$\begin{array}{r} 7\,6 \\ +\,\text{▦}1 \\ \hline 9\text{▦} \end{array}$$

9.
$$\begin{array}{r} 3\,9 \\ +\,2\text{▦} \\ \hline 6\,2 \end{array}$$

10.
$$\begin{array}{r} \text{▦}6 \\ -\,2\text{▦} \\ \hline 4\,9 \end{array}$$

11.
$$\begin{array}{r} 7\text{▦} \\ -\,3\,4 \\ \hline \text{▦}0 \end{array}$$

12.
$$\begin{array}{r} \text{▦}2 \\ -\,2\,7 \\ \hline 6\text{▦} \end{array}$$

Chapter 3 Review/Test

Rename. Make all the new tens you can.

1.

Tens	Ones
2	18

2.

Tens	Ones
7	10

Rename. Trade 1 ten for 10 ones.

3.

Tens	Ones
3	8

4.

Tens	Ones
5	2

Add.

5.
$$65 + 17$$

6.
$$26 + 24$$

7.
$$19 + 19$$

8. Add 28 + 41 mentally. Write which method you used.

Add.

9. 45 + 13 + 12

10. 32 + 20 + 19 + 6

Subtract.

11.
$$83 - 59$$

12.
$$61 - 24$$

13.
$$27 - 9$$

Find each difference mentally. Write which method you used.

14. 74 − 19   **15.** 55 − 37

Estimate each sum or difference.

16. 68 + 27   **17.** 51 − 32

18. Mr. Cruz baked 24 muffins. He baked 11 more rolls than muffins. How many rolls did Mr. Cruz bake?

19. You have 75¢. Can you buy a 45¢ pad and a 49¢ pen?

Read this problem. Then answer the question below.

Ella had 37 crayons. She gave 16 of them to Cal. How many crayons did she have left?

20. Choose the sentence that correctly answers the problem.

a. Ella has 21 more crayons than Cal.

b. Ella has 21 crayons left.

c. Together, Ella and Cal have 37 crayons.

21. ■ **Write About Math**
Explain the method you used to estimate in Exercise 17.

DATA FILE

American League
Indians 1, White Sox 0
Red Sox 5, Brewers 1
Tigers 5, Yankees 3
Orioles 7, Blue Jays 5
Angels 4, Rangers 3
Athletics 4, Royals 3
Mariners 3, Twins 1

National League
Cubs 5, Cardinals 1
Phillies 5, Expos 3
Mets 7, Pirates 3
Astros 3, Reds 0
Padres 3, Giants 0
Dodgers 3, Braves 1

1. Baseball Scores

1. Chart
Baseball scores
for October 1, 1989.

2. Chart
The best score in a game of
golf is the lowest score.

3. Weather Map
The high temperature
and low temperature is
recorded for each city.
The first number is the
high temperature. The
second number is the low
temperature.

4. Bar Graph
The graph shows the
number of hours the
computers are used
each day.

The British Open 1989

Past Champs		
Year	Winner	Score
1980	Tom Watson	271
1981	Bill Rogers	276
1982	Tom Watson	284
1983	Tom Watson	275
1984	Seve Ballesteros	276
1985	Sandy Lyle	282
1986	Greg Norman	280
1987	Nick Faldo	270
1988	Seve Ballesteros	273

2. Golf Champs

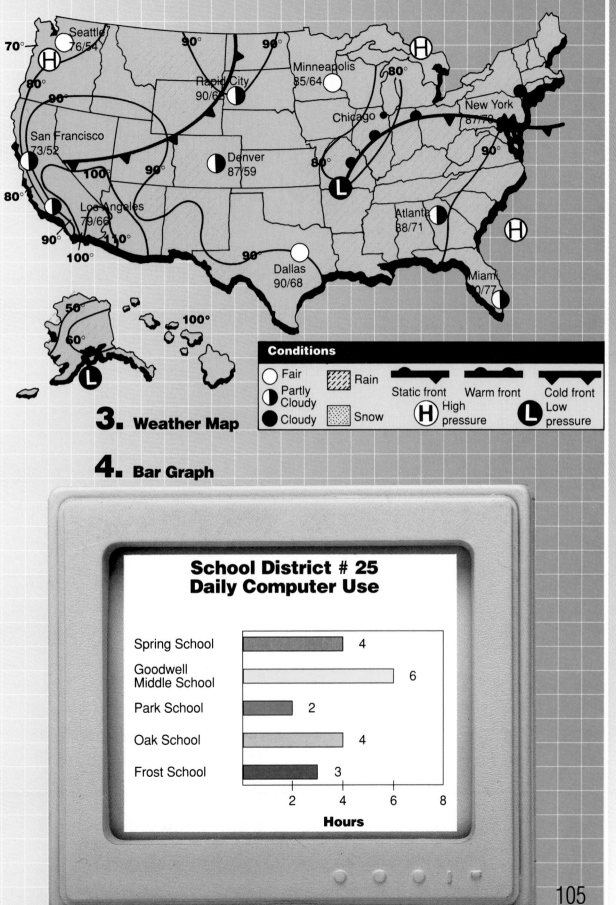

Seattle
76/54
70°
H
80°
90°
San Francisco
73/52
80°
90°
100°
Los Angeles
79/66
90°
110°
100°

90°
90°
Rapid City
90/65
Minneapolis
85/64
80°
Chicago
Denver
87/59
80°
90°
L
90°
Dallas
90/68
Atlanta
88/71
H
New York
87/78
90°
H
Miami
90/77

50°
60°
100°
L

3. **Weather Map**

Conditions

○ Fair ▨ Rain ▬ Static front ◖ Warm front ◣ Cold front
◐ Partly Cloudy ▦ Snow Ⓗ High pressure Ⓛ Low pressure
● Cloudy

4. **Bar Graph**

School District # 25
Daily Computer Use

School	Hours
Spring School	4
Goodwell Middle School	6
Park School	2
Oak School	4
Frost School	3

Hours: 2 4 6 8

Cumulative Review/Test, Chapters 1-3

Give the letter for the correct answer.

1. Tell what number or sign belongs in the box.

8 = 8 − ▨

A 1   **B** 0   **C** 8   **D** 16

2. Add.

  7
+3

A 4
B 11
C 9
D 10

3. Add.

  9
+8

A 17
B 16
C 15
D 1

4. Subtract.

 15
− 6

A 11
B 8
C 9
D 7

5. Which fact does not belong to the family?

A 9 + 5 = 14   **B** 14 − 5 = 9
C 9 − 5 = 4   **D** 14 − 9 = 5

6. Which numbers are written in order from least to greatest?

A 11	12	10	14	13
B 10	11	12	13	14
C 12	11	10	14	13
D 14	13	12	11	10

7. Which is the hundreds digit in 627?

A 6   **B** 7   **C** 2

8. Which number sentence is true?

A 562 < 332   **C** 562 > 432
B 562 = 432   **D** 532 < 432

9. Which numbers are written in order from least to greatest?

A 563	702	519	681
B 681	563	702	519
C 702	681	563	519
D 519	563	681	702

10. What is the next number when counting by fives?

50   55   60   65   ▨

A 70   **B** 67   **C** 66   **D** 75

11. Arrange these numbers to match the directions.

6   4   2

The ones digit is the sum of the hundreds and tens digits. The hundreds digit is twice as big as the tens digit.

A 246   **C** 642
B 426   **D** 624

12. Which is the thousands digit in 6,789?

A 7   **B** 8   **C** 9   **D** 6

13. What is the standard form?

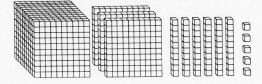

A 136   **C** 1,365
B 365   **D** 3,165

14. Which is the ten-thousands digit in 387,029?

A 8   **B** 7   **C** 2   **D** 9

15. Choose the most sensible answer.

Macky is 9 years old. His sister is just entering first grade. What is her age?

A 9 years   **C** 12 years
B 6 years   **D** 3 years

16. Solve the problem.

Monday Carl practiced violin for 47 minutes. Tuesday he practiced for 52 minutes. How much longer did he practice on Tuesday than on Monday?

A 77 minutes   **C** 15 minutes
B 5 minutes   **D** 25 minutes

17. Add.

$$58$$
$$+\,34$$

A 83
B 82
C 94
D 92

18. Add.

$$17$$
$$26$$
$$+\,44$$

A 86
B 87
C 77
D 98

19. Subtract.

$$82$$
$$-\,14$$

A 72
B 78
C 68
D 62

Read the problem below. Then answer the question.

Ned has a flock of chickens. He has 21 Rhode Island Reds and 8 Plymouth Rocks. How many more Rhode Island Reds than Plymouth Rocks are there?

20. Which number sentence would you choose to solve the problem?

A $21 - 8 = $ ▦
B $21 + 8 = $ ▦
C $29 - 8 = $ ▦
D $29 - 21 = $ ▦

Three- and Four-Digit Addition and Subtraction

4

Did You Know: Domino toppling was popular in the 1980s. Some people have set up dominoes 12 hours a day for a whole month just to topple them down.

Number-Sense Project

Estimate
Estimate the number of dominoes in this picture.

Gather Data
Count the number of each color. Add these numbers together to find how many in all.

Analyze and Report
Compare your count with your estimate.

Using Money to Rename

Build Understanding

Money Power
Materials: Play money
Groups: 3–5 students

A. Johnny emptied his bank. He wanted to trade his pennies for dimes and his dimes for dollars. He knew that

10 pennies make 1 dime.   10 dimes make 1 dollar.

Suppose Johnny had 2 dollars, 9 dimes, and 15 pennies.

a. Use your play money to show Johnny's money. Then trade 10 pennies for 1 dime.

b. Trade 10 dimes for 1 dollar.

  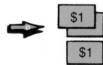 

c. Show the final amount: 3 dollars, 0 dimes, and 5 pennies.

Johnny had 3 dollars, 0 dimes, and 5 pennies.

B. Suppose Maxine has 2 dollars, 0 dimes, and 7 pennies. She needs dimes to play the machine at the video arcade.

a. Use your play money to show Maxine's money.

b. Trade 1 dollar for 10 dimes.

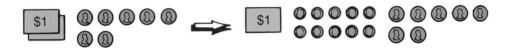

c. Show the final amount: 1 dollar, 10 dimes, and 7 pennies.

Maxine will have 1 dollar, 10 dimes, and 7 pennies.

c. Johnny and Maxine wrote the amount of money each had after the trades in the place-value boxes below.

$	d	p
3	0	5

Johnny

$	d	p
1	10	7

Maxine

■ **Talk About Math** In Example A, explain what will happen if you start trading with the dimes first.

Check Understanding

For another example, see Set A, pages 142–143.

Use your play money to show each problem.
Then record the answer.

1. How many pennies can you get for 1 dime?

2. How many pennies can you get for 2 dimes?

3. How many dimes can you get for 30 pennies?

4. How many dimes can you get for 57 pennies?

Practice

For More Practice, see Set A, pages 144–145.

Use your play money. Trade pennies for dimes and
dimes for dollars. Record how many dollars, dimes,
and pennies you have when you finish.

5.

$	d	p
4	3	12

6.

$	d	p
2	14	5

7.

$	d	p
0	13	4

8.

$	d	p
3	3	17

9.

$	d	p
1	15	11

10.

$	d	p
2	13	10

11.

$	d	p
4	9	12

12.

$	d	p
1	9	10

13.

$	d	p
0	8	23

Use play money for each amount. Make the trade. Now record how many dollars, dimes, and pennies you have.

14. Trade 1 dime for 10 pennies.

$	d	p
3	5	7

15. Trade 1 dime for 10 pennies.

$	d	p
2	8	1

16. Trade 1 dollar for 10 dimes.

$	d	p
4	3	5

17. Trade 1 dime for 10 pennies.

$	d	p
1	4	0

18. Trade 1 dollar for 10 dimes.

$	d	p
5	0	1

19. Trade 1 dollar for 10 dimes.

$	d	p
1	2	6

Problem Solving

Critical Thinking Find the mystery numbers.

20. I am a 3-digit number less than 300. My tens digit is less than my hundreds digit and my ones digit is less than my tens digit. Who am I?

21. I am a number between 600 and 700. My ones digit is 4. My tens digit is the difference between my ones and hundreds digits. Who am I?

Choose a _____ Strategy

Fun with Phones

22. Barry's phone number is 176-8204. Find the sum of the digits.

23. Rosa's phone number has some digits that are different from Barry's but the sum is the same. What could the number be?

PROBLEM SOLVING STRATEGIES

Choose an Operation
Find a Pattern
Use Logical Reasoning

CONSUMER CONNECTION

Exploring Three-Digit Addition

Build Understanding

Birthday Money
Materials: Play money
Groups: 3–5 students

A. Jim and Joanne put their money together to buy a birthday present for their mother. How much did they have altogether?

	$	d	p
Jim's money →	2	8	7
Joanne's money →	1	7	5

a. Use your play money to show each amount. Put the money together.

b. Trade 10 pennies for 1 dime.

c. Trade 10 dimes for 1 dollar.

d. Show the final amount: 4 dollars, 6 dimes, and 2 pennies.

Jim and Joanne had $4.62 in all.

B. What is the total amount in the
place-value box?

$	d	p
2	2	7
+ 1	0	2

a. Use your play money to show
both amounts.

b. Put them together.

c. Trade if you can.   Not enough pennies or dimes to trade.

d. Show the final amount with
play money:
3 dollars, 2 dimes, and 9 pennies.

There is $3.29 in all.

▪ **Talk About Math**   Why is it important
to start with pennies when trading?

Check Understanding

For another example, see Set B, pages 142–143.

Look at the place-value box. Use your play
money to help you answer the questions.

1. Look at these two amounts of money.
How many pennies are there
altogether?

2. How many dimes can be made?
How many dimes are there altogether?

3. How many dollars can be made?

$	d	p
2	4	6
+ 1	5	5

Practice

For More Practice, see Set B, pages 144–145.

Use play money to show each amount of money in the place-value chart. Trade 10 pennies for 1 dime if you can. Then try to trade 10 dimes for 1 dollar. Write how much in all.

4.

$	d	p
4	2	7
+ 1	5	6

5.

$	d	p
2	8	1
+ 2	6	4

6.

$	d	p
3	7	9
+ 3	1	0

7.

$	d	p
2	4	5
+ 1	8	6

8.

$	d	p
3	2	6
+ 2	5	3

9.

$	d	p
0	4	5
+ 1	5	7

10.

$	d	p
3	6	2
+ 1	7	0

11.

$	d	p
3	4	2
+ 4	4	9

12.

$	d	p
2	9	5
+ 3	0	5

Number Sense Make up a money addition problem like the ones in this lesson that makes you

13. trade 10 pennies for a dime.

14. trade 10 dimes for 1 dollar.

15. have no trades.

16. trade both 10 pennies for a dime *and* 10 dimes for a dollar.

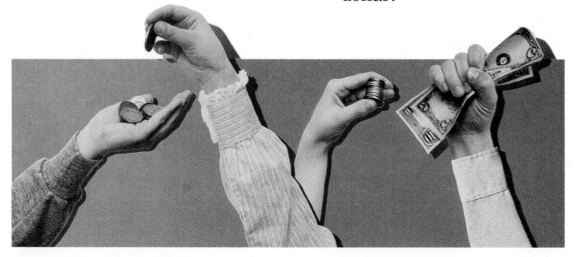

Problem Solving

Jim and Jamelle played this game.

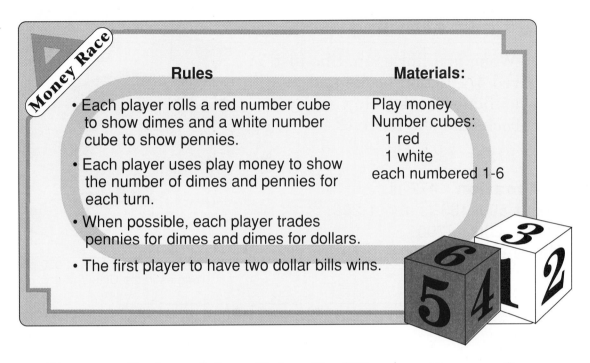

Money Race

Rules

- Each player rolls a red number cube to show dimes and a white number cube to show pennies.

- Each player uses play money to show the number of dimes and pennies for each turn.

- When possible, each player trades pennies for dimes and dimes for dollars.

- The first player to have two dollar bills wins.

Materials:

Play money
Number cubes:
1 red
1 white
each numbered 1-6

17. Here are Jim's and Jamelle's rolls. Who won the game?

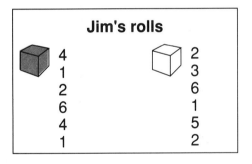

Jim's rolls	
4	2
1	3
2	6
6	1
4	5
1	2

Jamelle's rolls	
3	6
2	3
6	4
1	2
3	6
4	9

18. Play a game of Money Race with a friend. Play until someone has at least 2 dollar bills.

19. Critical Thinking Suppose you roll a 6 and a 2. Would you rather that the red cube show the 6 or the 2? Explain your answer.

TIPS FOR PROBLEM SOLVERS

Think about your own thinking. Pause to ask, "How is this going to help me solve the problem?"

117

Adding Three-Digit Numbers

Build Understanding

A. Mrs. Wong is a librarian. She just received 472 fiction books and 183 nonfiction books. How many new books did she receive?

Find 472 + 183.

Estimation 472 is about 500. 183 is about 200.
500 + 200 = 700
The answer should be about 700.

There are more than 14,000 public libraries in the United States.

Add the ones. ➡	Add the tens. Rename. ➡	Record. ➡	Add the hundreds.

```
  472            472                      1          1
 +183           +183    15 tens =        472        472
 ────           ────    1 hundred       +183       +183
    5              5    and 5 tens      ────       ────
                                          55        655
```

Mrs. Wong received 655 new books.

B. Find 123 + 271.

Add the ones. ➡	Add the tens. ➡	Add the hundreds.

```
  123           123           123
 +271          +271          +271
 ────          ────          ────
    4            94           394
```

■ **Talk About Math** Look at Examples A and B. What extra step did you have to do in Example A? Why was it necessary?

For another example, see Set C, pages 142–143.

Check Understanding

Answer each question to find the missing digits.

1. What number should replace the ▦?

2. What number should replace the ▦?

3. What does the number for ▦ mean?

4. Find 635 + 147.

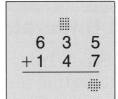

```
      ▦
    6 3 5
  + 1 4 7
      ▦
```

Practice

For More Practice, see Set C, pages 144–145.

Find each sum. **Remember** to estimate
before you find the exact answer.

5. 539 +247	**6.** 285 +453	**7.** 72 +137	**8.** 403 +382	**9.** 367 +150
10. 690 +153	**11.** 821 +176	**12.** 339 +202	**13.** 264 +570	**14.** 651 +285

15. 127 + 453   **16.** 543 + 345   **17.** 681 + 127   **18.** 328 + 259

19. 325 + 219 + 173   **20.** 189 + 127 + 85   **21.** 109 + 190 + 901

Skills **Review**   page 545

What time is it?

1.    **2.**    **3.**    **4.**

Three- and Four-Digit Addition

Build Understanding

Girl Scout Troop 115 spent the fall collecting aluminum cans to be recycled. They placed containers at two places: one in front of the school and one in the supermarket parking lot.

How many cans altogether did they collect in September?

Find 1,459 + 1,043.

Estimation 1,459 is about 1,500. 1,043 is about 1,000. 1,500 + 1,000 = 2,500 The answer should be about 2,500.

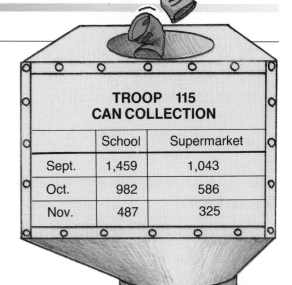

TROOP 115 CAN COLLECTION		
	School	Supermarket
Sept.	1,459	1,043
Oct.	982	586
Nov.	487	325

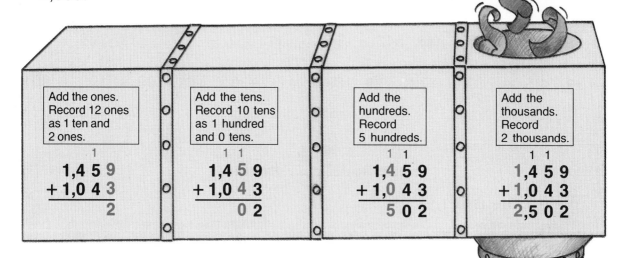

Add the ones. Record 12 ones as 1 ten and 2 ones.	Add the tens. Record 10 tens as 1 hundred and 0 tens.	Add the hundreds. Record 5 hundreds.	Add the thousands. Record 2 thousands.
$\begin{array}{r} 1 \\ 1,459 \\ +1,043 \\ \hline 2 \end{array}$	$\begin{array}{r} 1\ 1 \\ 1,459 \\ +1,043 \\ \hline 0\ 2 \end{array}$	$\begin{array}{r} 1\ 1 \\ 1,459 \\ +1,043 \\ \hline 5\ 0\ 2 \end{array}$	$\begin{array}{r} 1\ 1 \\ 1,459 \\ +1,043 \\ \hline 2,5\ 0\ 2 \end{array}$

There were 2,502 cans collected in September. That is very close to your estimate of 2,500.

■ **Talk About Math** Does the estimate tell you that your answer is correct? Explain.

120

Check Understanding

For another example, see Set D, pages 142–143.

Estimation   Find each answer.

1. Estimate how many cans were collected in October. Then find the exact number. How close was your estimate?

2. Estimate how many cans were collected in November. Then find the exact number. How close was your estimate?

Practice

For More Practice, see Set D, pages 144–145.

Find each sum. **Remember** to estimate first.

3. 4,840 +1,023	**4.** 6,029 +1,416	**5.** 5,520 + 715	**6.** 387 +763	**7.** 398 +249

8. 6,058 + 819	**9.** 5,727 +1,609	**10.** 8,731 + 273	**11.** 9,540 + 482	**12.** 8,694 + 457

13. 8,704 + 918	**14.** 5,360 + 315	**15.** 5,462 + 923	**16.** 2,640 +3,173	**17.** 1,847 +6,259

18. 4,983 + 390   **19.** 3,519 + 23   **20.** 387 + 2,980 + 4,257

Problem Solving

Explore ———— Math

21. Start with 99. Add 11.

22. Make a table to record the number sentence.

23. Add 11 to each sum until you reach 198.

24. Describe the pattern you discover in the sums.

Number Sentences			
99	+ 11	=	110
110	+ 11	=	▨
▨	+ 11	=	▨

Choose a Computation Method

Build Understanding

Dan's Cub Scout troop had a pinewood car derby. Each car was judged on speed and style. The chart shows the scores for some of the best cars.

TROOP 157 DERBY		
Car	Speed	Style
Firebird	627	812
Gazelle	712	790
Rampage	600	700
Eagle	64	78

A. What was Firebird's total score?

Find 627 + 812.

Calculator This can be a hard problem. You might choose to do it with a calculator:

627 + 812 = 1,439

B. Find 600 + 700.

Mental Math This is an easy problem to do with mental math.

Think: 600 + 700 = 1,300

C. Find 64 + 78.

Paper and Pencil This is not a very hard problem, but you might not be able to do it mentally. Use paper and pencil.

$$\begin{array}{r} 1 \\ 64 \\ +\ 78 \\ \hline 142 \end{array}$$

Talk About Math How might you be able to find the answer to Example C using a mental math strategy?

Check Understanding

For another example, see Set E, pages 142–143.

Use paper and pencil, mental math, or a calculator
to find each answer. Tell what method you used.

1.	50	**2.**	359	**3.**	8	**4.**	86	**5.**	903
	+40		+102		+6		+42		+878

Practice

For More Practice, see Set E, pages 144–145.

Use paper and pencil, mental math, or a calculator
to find each answer. Tell what method you used.

6.	603	**7.**	4	**8.**	36	**9.**	47	**10.**	2,743
	+1,457		+2		+20		+12		+9,189

11.	86	**12.**	563	**13.**	67	**14.**	4,787	**15.**	746
	+80		+210		+29		+1,896		+120

16. 8,354 + 2,498   **17.** 600 + 320   **18.** 217 + 328

Problem Solving

Use the chart on page 122 to solve each problem.

19. How much greater was
Eagle's style score than its
speed score?

20. Which car had the greatest
total score?

Critical Thinking Find the
missing numbers. Within each
exercise, the same shape
represents the same missing digit.

21.	40▦	**22.**	45▦	**23.**	45▦	**24.**	7▦3
	+2▦9		+1▦7		+1△2		+19▦
	△64		△12		▦30		△59

Use Data from a Picture

Build Understanding

This map shows some of the trails that the pioneers used in the 1800s.

Part of the path from Boston to Independence was called the Mohawk Trail. How many miles was it from Boston to Independence?

PROBLEM SOLVING GUIDE

Understand
QUESTION
FACTS
KEY IDEA

Plan and Solve
STRATEGY
ANSWER

Look Back
SENSIBLE ANSWER
ALTERNATE APPROACH

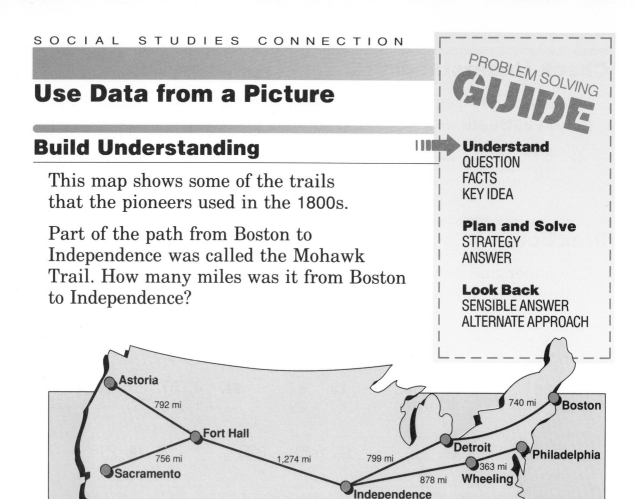

Understand

QUESTION   How far was Independence from Boston?

FACTS   The map shows the information you need. Where do you need to start? Find Boston. Where do you need to go? Find Independence. Can you go directly, or do you need to go through another city? How far is it from Boston to Detroit? How far is it from Detroit to Independence?

KEY IDEA   You are joining the two distances.

Plan and Solve

You should add.

$$\begin{array}{r} 7\,4\,0 \\ +\,7\,9\,9 \\ \hline 1{,}5\,3\,9 \end{array}$$

It was 1,539 miles from Boston to Independence.

Look Back   Did you use the correct map information?

■ **Write About Math**   Is the trip from Boston to Independence longer or shorter than the trip from Philadelphia to Independence? Explain.

Check Understanding

Use the map on page 124 to answer each question.

1. What city must you go through to get from Independence to Astoria?

2. What two smaller trips make the total trip from Independence to Astoria?

3. How long was the Oregon Trail between Independence and Astoria?

Practice

Use the map on page 124 to solve each problem.

4. What city must you go through to get from Independence to Sacramento?

5. What two smaller trips make the total trip from Independence to Sacramento?

6. How many miles is it from Boston to Sacramento?

7. How many miles is it from Philadelphia to Sacramento?

Reading ———— Math

Diagrams and Pictures   Are these statements True or False? Use the map on page 124.

1. The number 792 is the name of a highway.

2. It is 1,274 miles from Independence to Astoria.

3. The number 792 is the number of miles from Astoria to Fort Hall.

4. It is about 800 miles from Independence to Detroit.

Exploring Three-Digit Subtraction

$1.29

Build Understanding

Spending Spree
Materials: Play money
Groups: 3–5 students

How many kinds of house plants can you name?

A. Toni and Chris had $4.62 to spend. They bought a plant that cost $1.29. How much did they have left?

a. Use your play money to show the amount they started with.

	$	d	p
Their money →	4	6	2
Cost of plant →	1	2	9

b. Try to take away 9 pennies. There are not enough pennies. Trade 1 dime for 10 pennies.

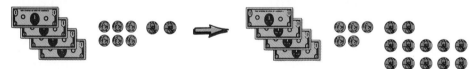

c. Now take away 9 pennies.

d. Take away 2 dimes.

e. Take away 1 dollar.

f. Show the amount left.

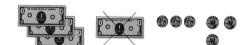

Toni and Chris had $3.33 left.   3 dollars   3 dimes   3 pennies

126

$	d	p
3	3	3
− 1	1	2

B. Suppose you have 3 dollars, 3 dimes, and 3 pennies. Take away 1 dollar, 1 dime, and 2 pennies. How much money is left?

a. Show 3 dollars, 3 dimes, and 3 pennies. Take away 2 pennies.

b. Take away 1 dime. Then take away 1 dollar.

c. Show the amount left.

There is $2.21 left.

■ **Talk About Math**   Why is it important to take away pennies first? What could happen if you start with the dimes?

Check Understanding

For another example, see Set F, pages 142–143.

Suppose you have 6 dollars, 4 dimes, and 2 pennies. Take away 5 dollars, 9 dimes, and 1 penny.

$	d	p
6	4	2
− 5	9	1

1. Look at these two amounts of money. What would be your first step?

2. Do you need to do any trading to solve this problem?

3. If so, what would you have to trade?

4. What would you get in exchange?

Practice

For More Practice, see Set F, pages 144–145.

Use your play money to show how much you have.
Take away the amount you spend. You may have
to trade a dime for 10 pennies. You may have to
trade a dollar for 10 dimes. Write how much you have left.

5.

	$	d	p
Have:	8	9	1
Spend:	5	1	7

6.

	$	d	p
Have:	5	8	5
Spend:	3	7	4

7.

	$	d	p
Have:	4	6	7
Spend:	3	7	5

8.

	$	d	p
Have:	9	9	6
Spend:	5	2	2

9.

	$	d	p
Have:	4	3	0
Spend:	1	4	3

10.

	$	d	p
Have:	3	5	8
Spend:	2	6	6

11.

	$	d	p
Have:	8	3	2
Spend:	2	4	8

12.

	$	d	p
Have:	9	2	0
Spend:	7	4	1

13.

	$	d	p
Have:	6	0	2
Spend:	1	0	3

Number Sense Make up a money subtraction
problem like the ones in this lesson that makes you

14. trade a dime for 10 pennies.   **15.** trade a dollar for 10 dimes.

16. trade both a dollar for   **17.** make no trades.
10 dimes *and* a dime for
10 pennies.

Tell how many dollars, dimes, and pennies
you have if you trade

1. pennies for dimes.

$	d	p
3	6	13

2. 1 dime for 10 pennies.

$	d	p
6	7	8

3. Tell how much you have in all.

$	d	p
1	8	2
3	7	1

4. Tell how much you have left.

$	d	p
4	7	2
1	4	3

Add.

5. 451
    +275

6. 482
    +359

7. 208
    +320

8. 3,086
    +5,027

9. 7,134
    +1,098

Add. Use mental math, paper and pencil, or a calculator
to find each answer. Tell what method you used.

10. 562
     +164

11. 248
     +127

12. 28
     +32

13. 4,274
     +3,899

14. 6,259
     +1,362

15. What is the shortest distance between Woodruff and Slinger?

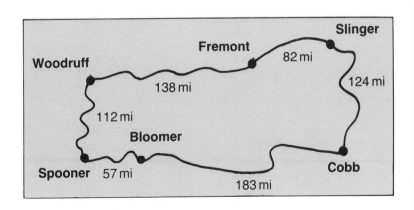

Problem Solving WORKSHOP

Critical Thinking Activity

CLUES

- There are 3 chips in the red box.
- There are 9 chips altogether in the yellow and blue boxes.
- There are 8 chips altogether in the yellow and red boxes.

1. How many chips are in the blue box?

2. How many chips are there altogether?

Hint: Counters may help you.

Math-at-Home Activity

Play this game with someone at home. Put out 21 black-eyed peas or dry beans. Take turns removing 1, 2, or 3 peas. The player who takes away the last pea is the winner.

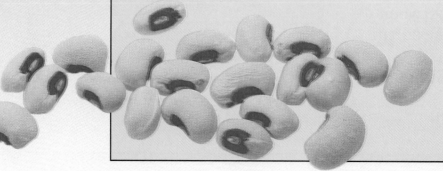

Number-Sense Project

Look back at pages 108-109.

1. Look at the dots on the green dominoes.

    a. Estimate how many dots there are.

    b. Count the dots.

    c. Was your estimate close to the actual number of dots? Explain how you found your estimate.

2. Look at the red dominoes.

    a. Tell how you could estimate the number of dots. Then give the estimate.

    b. Compare your estimate and method with a classmate. Which one has the better method for estimating?

Explore as a Team

1. Follow the pattern to make bigger and bigger squares.

2. How many yellow squares will be in the next biggest square after d? How many red?

3. Talk and write about number patterns you see.

TIPS FOR
WORKING TOGETHER
Work as a group. If you understand, help another group member. Don't work ahead of the others.

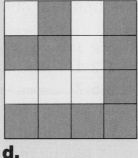

d.

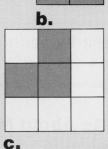

c.

a.

b.

Subtracting Three-Digit Numbers

Build Understanding

Ramón's class is getting ready for a school party. The boys need to make 481 hats. They have already made 124 hats. How many more hats do they have to make?

Find 481 − 124.

Estimation   481 is about 500. 124 is about 100. 500 − 100 = 400 The answer should be about 400.

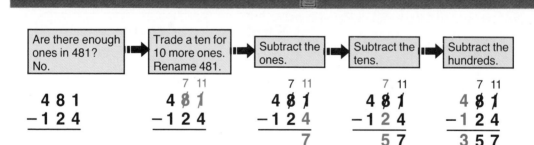

Are there enough ones in 481? No.	Trade a ten for 10 more ones. Rename 481.	Subtract the ones.	Subtract the tens.	Subtract the hundreds.
4 8 1 − 1 2 4	7 11 4 8̸ 1̸ − 1 2 4	7 11 4 8̸ 1̸ − 1 2 4 ——— 7	7 11 4 8̸ 1̸ − 1 2 4 ——— 5 7	7 11 4 8̸ 1̸ − 1 2 4 ——— 3 5 7

The boys have 357 more hats to make. That is close to your estimate of 400.

Check by adding.
$$\begin{array}{r} 4\,8\,1 \\ -\,1\,2\,4 \\ \hline 3\,5\,7 \end{array}$$
← These two should be the same. →
$$\begin{array}{r} 3\,5\,7 \\ +\,1\,2\,4 \\ \hline 4\,8\,1 \end{array}$$

■ **Write About Math**   Write a subtraction problem in which you do not have to rename.

132

Check Understanding

For another example, see Set G, pages 142–143.

Do you need to rename the top number in each exercise? Why? Tell how you would rename each.

1. 463
    −147

2. 406
    −134

3. 243
    − 32

4. 158
    − 39

5. 762
    −481

6. Find the differences for Exercises 1–5.

Practice

For More Practice, see Set G, pages 144–145.

Find each difference. **Remember** to estimate first.

7. 521
    −370

8. 654
    −108

9. 194
    −157

10. 197
    − 16

11. 585
    −469

12. 863
    −735

13. 120
    − 40

14. 654
    −542

15. 984
    −951

16. 876
    −219

17. 473 − 170   **18.** 419 − 336   **19.** 323 − 82   **20.** 4,930 − 1,052

Mixed Practice Use paper and pencil or mental math to find each answer. Tell what method you used.

21. 157
    − 90

22. 246
    +549

23. 984
    −951

24. 128
    + 50

25. 176
    − 68

Problem Solving

Solve each problem.

26. 🖩 **Calculator** What two 3-digit numbers have a sum of 1,325 and a difference of 367?

27. **Use Data** Use the chart on page 122. How many more speed points did Firebird get than Eagle?

Zeros in Subtraction

Build Understanding

The students in Edgar School were part of a Reading Marathon. The graph shows how many books the students in each grade read.

How many more books did the fifth graders read than the fourth graders?

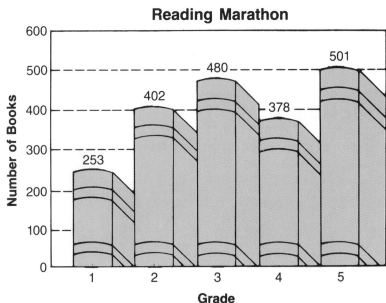

Reading Marathon

Find 501 − 378.

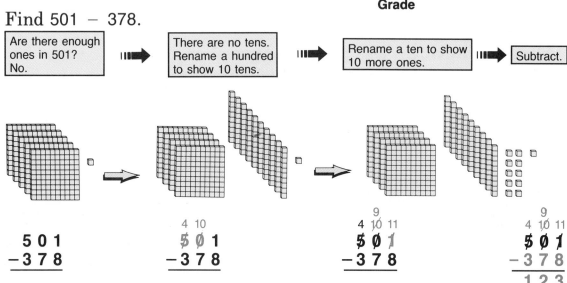

| Are there enough ones in 501? No. | ➡ | There are no tens. Rename a hundred to show 10 tens. | ➡ | Rename a ten to show 10 more ones. | ➡ | Subtract. |

$$
\begin{array}{r} 5\ 0\ 1 \\ -\ 3\ 7\ 8 \\ \hline \end{array}
\qquad
\begin{array}{r} {}^{4\ 10} \\ 5\ \cancel{0}\ 1 \\ -\ 3\ 7\ 8 \\ \hline \end{array}
\qquad
\begin{array}{r} {}^{9} \\ {}^{4\ 10\ 11} \\ 5\ \cancel{0}\ \cancel{1} \\ -\ 3\ 7\ 8 \\ \hline \end{array}
\qquad
\begin{array}{r} {}^{9} \\ {}^{4\ 10\ 11} \\ 5\ \cancel{0}\ \cancel{1} \\ -\ 3\ 7\ 8 \\ \hline 1\ 2\ 3 \end{array}
$$

The fifth graders read 123 more books.

■ **Write About Math** Do you always have to rename when there are zeros in a subtraction problem? Write several problems to explain your answer.

Check Understanding

For another example, see Set H, pages 142–143.

In which of these exercises would you need
10 more ones?
In which would you need 10 more tens?
In which would you need both?

1. 403 −251	**2.** 673 −205	**3.** 730 −156	**4.** 800 −475	**5.** 436 −138

6. Find the differences for Exercises 1–5.

Practice

For More Practice, see Set H, pages 144–145.

Find each difference.

7. 306 − 57	**8.** 580 −137	**9.** 801 −160	**10.** 507 −372	**11.** 860 −503
12. 402 − 36	**13.** 650 −309	**14.** 700 −160	**15.** 900 −708	**16.** 300 −193

Mixed Practice Use paper and pencil or mental math
to find each answer. Then tell which method you used.

17. 100 − 57	**18.** 201 −118	**19.** 902 −209	**20.** 400 −195	**21.** 140 +627
22. 703 −376	**23.** 659 +128	**24.** 303 −128	**25.** 714 +386	**26.** 504 −337
27. 673 + 59	**28.** 815 −269	**29.** 472 +758	**30.** 827 −458	**31.** 980 +124

32. 504 − 87   **33.** 638 + 28   **34.** 624 − 46

Three- and Four-Digit Subtraction

Build Understanding

A. Abraham Lincoln was born on February 12, 1809. He died on April 15, 1865. How old was he then?

Find 1,865 − 1,809.

Are there enough ones in 1,865? No.	➡	Rename a ten to show 10 more ones.	➡	Subtract.

$$
\begin{array}{r}
1{,}8\,6\,5 \\
-\,1{,}8\,0\,9 \\
\hline
\end{array}
\qquad
\begin{array}{r}
{}^{5}\ {}^{15} \\
1{,}8\,\cancel{6}\,\cancel{5} \\
-\,1{,}8\,0\,9 \\
\hline
\end{array}
\qquad
\begin{array}{r}
{}^{5}\ {}^{15} \\
1{,}8\,\cancel{6}\,\cancel{5} \\
-\,1{,}8\,0\,9 \\
\hline
5\,6
\end{array}
$$

President Lincoln was 56 when he died.

B. Find 8,006 − 4,927.

Are there enough ones in 8,006? No.	➡	There are no tens. There are no hundreds. Rename a thousand to show 10 hundreds.	➡	Rename a hundred to show 10 tens.	➡	Rename a ten to show 10 more ones.	➡	Subtract.

$$
\begin{array}{r}
8{,}0\,0\,6 \\
-\,4{,}9\,2\,7 \\
\hline
\end{array}
\quad
\begin{array}{r}
{}^{7}\ {}^{10} \\
\cancel{8}{,}0\,0\,6 \\
-\,4{,}9\,2\,7 \\
\hline
\end{array}
\quad
\begin{array}{r}
{}^{9} \\
{}^{7}\ \cancel{10}\ {}^{10} \\
\cancel{8}{,}\cancel{0}\,0\,6 \\
-\,4{,}9\,2\,7 \\
\hline
\end{array}
\quad
\begin{array}{r}
{}^{9}\ {}^{9} \\
{}^{7}\ \cancel{10}\ \cancel{10}\ {}^{16} \\
\cancel{8}{,}\cancel{0}\,\cancel{0}\,6 \\
-\,4{,}9\,2\,7 \\
\hline
\end{array}
\quad
\begin{array}{r}
{}^{9}\ {}^{9} \\
{}^{7}\ \cancel{10}\ \cancel{10}\ {}^{16} \\
\cancel{8}{,}\cancel{0}\,\cancel{0}\,6 \\
-\,4{,}9\,2\,7 \\
\hline
3{,}0\,7\,9
\end{array}
$$

■ **Talk About Math** Tell why addition works as a check for subtraction.

Check Understanding

For another example, see Set I, pages 142–143.

In which of these exercises would you
need to rename in the thousands place?
Tell why.

1. 5,187
  − 3,156

2. 4,672
  − 1,826

3. 5,000
  − 2,654

4. 6,002
  − 3,005

5. Find the differences for Exercises 1–4.

Practice

For More Practice, see Set I, pages 144–145.

Subtract.

6. 434
  − 326

7. 7,002
  − 3,064

8. 481
  − 293

9. 9,004
  − 7,539

10. 6,757
  − 4,902

11. 8,001
  − 1,197

12. 3,926
  − 2,842

13. 6,003
  − 751

14. 504
  − 420

15. 1,005
  − 811

16. 9,007 − 4,345

17. 3,502 − 1,201

18. 5,342 − 2,091

Problem Solving

Mental Math   Solve each problem.

19. In 1976, the United States
celebrated its 200th birthday.
In what year was it "born"?

20. Ronald Reagan turned 70 in
1981, the same year he
became President. In what
year was he born?

Skills ——— Review   pages 84–85

Find each sum.
1. 72 + 54 + 23
2. 84 + 51 + 92
3. 20 + 34 + 8 + 13

Use Data from a Table

Build Understanding

PROBLEM SOLVING
GUIDE

▶ **Understand**
QUESTION
FACTS
KEY IDEA

Plan and Solve
STRATEGY
ANSWER

Look Back
SENSIBLE ANSWER
ALTERNATE APPROACH

To solve problems, you may need to get information from a table.

Some of the students in Mrs. Shaw's third-grade class made a table to show things about themselves.

Which 9-year-old likes cats best?

Student	Age	Hair Color	Weight	Favorite Animal
Nori	9	Black	52 lb	Dog
Timmy	8	Brown	57 lb	Cat
Anne	9	Brown	61 lb	Dog
Adela	9	Black	58 lb	Cat

▶ **Understand** QUESTION Which 9-year-old likes cats best?

FACTS There are many facts in the table. You do not need to use all of them.

KEY IDEA Pick the facts you need. The first row tells you what information you will find in the chart: each student's name, age, hair color, weight, and favorite animal. You will find the information you want to know in the columns under age and favorite animal.

Plan and Solve Nori, Anne, and Adela are 9 years old. Adela is the only 9-year-old who likes cats.

Look Back Have you answered the question? Is there anything else you need to find out?

■ Talk About Math Could you have started in another column other than the one for Age? Explain how this would change the way you solved this problem.

Check Understanding

Solve the problem by answering Questions 1–4.

Which 9-year-old has brown hair?

1. What two things have to be true about the student you find?

2. Which two columns do you have to look at?

3. Could Nori be the student? Why or why not?

4. Explain why each of the rest of the students either could or could not be the student.

Practice

Use the table on page 138 to solve each problem.

5. Which student is the youngest?

6. Which student weighs the most?

7. Which student weighing less than 60 pounds has brown hair?

8. Which student with black hair likes cats?

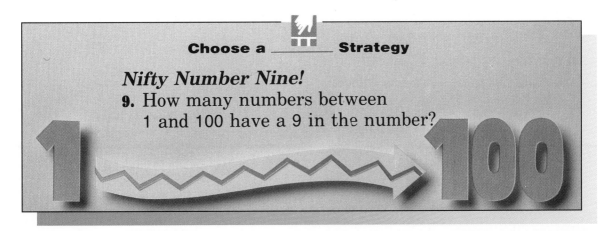

Choose a _____ Strategy

Nifty Number Nine!
9. How many numbers between 1 and 100 have a 9 in the number?

Problem Solving REVIEW

Solve each problem.

Town	Number of homes with Pets
Fairfield	7,373
Hartford	7,410
Tolland	1,091
Middleton	1,228

1. Use the chart to answer which town has the most homes with pets. Which town has the least?

2. John wanted to go to one of two community colleges. Westtown had 5,395 students. Eastville had 2,816. What is the difference in the number of students?

3. Dana has 7 coins in his pocket worth 39¢. What coins are they?

4. I am the smallest number in a family of facts. The other two numbers are 7 and 5. What am I?

5. A grocery coupon saves Mrs. Nova 50¢ on cereal if she buys milk too. Another coupon gives her 30¢ off on two cans of tuna. She can get a third can of cat food free if she buys 2 of them. What is the least number of items that Mrs. Nova will buy if she uses all of these coupons?

6. Find the number. The sum of the hundreds and ones digits is double the tens digit. Their difference is 0. The number is between 300 and 400.

7. **Data File** Use data from pages 248–249. Find the distance in miles between the following cities in California: Los Angeles and San Diego. Santa Barbara and San Diego. Which city is closer to San Diego? How much closer?

8. **Make a Data File** Find sale advertisements for 5 pieces of furniture. Tell the item, the sale price and the regular price.

Explore with a Calculator

Using Estimation Strategies

Estimation and calculators work well together.

Look at the numbers in the box.

Look at 1a.
Find two numbers whose sum is 1,696.

If you choose the first number in the box, 239, the other number needs to be about 1,500 since 1,696 is close to 1,700 and 239 is close to 200.

Are there any numbers in the box close to 1,500? No. So 239 is not one of the numbers. Try another number. Estimate and find the difference. If the estimates look like they might work, prove it by using your calculator.

239	2,696	931
765	**652**	8,188
2,409	1,703	2,003
363	4,025	737

1. Look at the numbers in the box to

a. find two numbers whose sum is 1,696.
__?__ and __?__

b. find two numbers whose sum is 3,146.
__?__ and __?__

c. find three numbers whose sum is 5,344.
__?__ , __?__ , and __?__

d. find three numbers whose sum is 6,402.
__?__ , __?__ , and __?__

e. find four numbers whose sum is 7,424.
__?__ , __?__ , __?__ , and __?__

Reteaching

Set A pages 110–113

You have 2 dollars and 1 dime. You need more dimes for the bus. Trade 1 dollar for 10 dimes.

You have 1 dollar and 11 dimes.

Remember that you can trade dimes for dollars if you have 10 or more dimes.

Record how many dollars, dimes, and pennies you have after the trade.

1. Trade 1 dollar for 10 dimes.

$	d	p
4	3	6

Set B pages 114–117

Find how much money is shown in this chart.

	$	d	p
	3	6	7
+	4	4	8

Add: 7$ 10d 15p

Trade 10 pennies for 1 dime.
7 dollars   11 dimes   5 pennies
Trade 10 dimes for 1 dollar.
   8 dollars   1 dime   5 pennies

Remember to trade pennies for dimes first, if you can. Then trade dimes for dollars if you can. Find how much money is shown in each chart.

1.

	$	d	p
	2	3	6
+	4	5	9

2.

	$	d	p
	3	3	4
+	1	8	7

Set C pages 118–119

Find 374 + 195.

```
        1
 374    374    Record 16 tens as
+195   +195    1 hundred 6 tens
   9    569
```

Remember to estimate before you find the exact answer. Find each sum.

1. 364
      + 255

2. 439
      + 380

Set D pages 120–121

Find 2,084 + 2,547.

```
    1       1 1       1 1
 2,084    2,084     2,084
+2,547   +2,547    +2,547
    1       31      4,631
```

Remember to estimate first. Find each sum.

1. 4,165
      + 1,267

2. 5,246
      + 2,375

Set E   pages 122-123

Use a calculator to add large numbers with renaming.

Use mental math to add when there is no renaming.

Use paper and pencil for other addition problems.

Remember to estimate first.

Use paper and pencil or a calculator. Tell what method you used.

1. 2,006
   + 3,997

2. 87
   + 36

3. 30 + 147

Set F   pages 126-128

How much money is left? To subtract pennies, trade 1 dime.

	$	d	p
Have:	7	8	3
Spend:	4	2	6

$	d	p
7	7	13
4	2	6

3$ 5d 7p

Remember to subtract pennies first.
Write how much is left.

1.
$	d	p
6	7	3
3	2	6

2.
$	d	p
3	4	6
1	1	8

Set G   pages 132-133

Find 691 − 563.

Trade a ten for 10 more ones.

       8 11
     69̸1̸
   − 563
     128

Remember to check by adding. Estimate, then subtract.

1. 637
   − 219

2. 284
   − 146

3. 348 − 140

Set H   pages 134-135

Find 403 − 286.
Rename a hundred to show tens.

 3 10
 40̸3   Rename a ten to
−286   show 10 more ones.

        9
      3 10 13
      40̸3̸
    − 286
      1 1 7

Remember that you may not have to rename when there are zeros. Find each difference.

1. 506
   − 127

2. 202
   − 82

3. 401
   − 103

Set I   pages 136-137

Find 6,007 − 4,135.

          5 10
Rename a   6,0̸07   Rename a
thousand. − 4,135   hundred.

              9
           5 10 10
         6,0̸0̸7
       − 4,135
         1,872

Remember to check by adding. Subtract.

1. 4,006
   − 1,241

2. 5,006
   − 2,457

More Practice

Set A   pages 110–113

Use your play money. Trade pennies for dimes
and dimes for dollars. Record how many dollars,
dimes, and pennies you have when you finish.

1.

$	d	p
3	5	14

2.

$	d	p
4	12	5

3.

$	d	p
2	13	12

Make these sets of money with your play money.
Record how many dollars, dimes, and pennies
you have when you finish trading.

4. Trade 1 dime for
10 pennies.

$	d	p
2	6	8

5. Trade 1 dime for
10 pennies.

$	d	p
4	5	3

6. Trade 1 dollar for
10 dimes.

$	d	p
3	7	2

Set B   pages 114–117

Use play money to show each amount of money in the place-value
chart. Trade whenever you can. Write how much in all.

1.

	$	d	p
	1	4	6
+	4	3	5

2.

	$	d	p
	3	3	8
+	2	7	3

3.

	$	d	p
	2	5	0
+	3	8	8

Set C   pages 118–119

Find each sum. **Remember** to estimate first.

1. 325
  + 117

2. 174
  + 283

3. 605
  + 384

4. 734 + 375

5. 484 + 519

Set D   pages 120–121

Find each sum.

1. 3,641
  + 4,308

2. 5,367
  + 2,027

3. 675
  + 455

4. 5,760 + 465

5. 3,427 + 44

Set E pages 122–123

Use paper and pencil, mental math, or a calculator
to find each answer. Tell what method you used.

1. 1,007 + 898	2. 785 + 336	3. 85 + 14	4. 682 + 317	5. 74 + 98

6. 5,284 + 3,469   **7.** 300 + 150   **8.** 400 + 563

Set F pages 126–128

Use your play money to show how much you
have. Take away the amount you spend.
Write how much you have left.

1.

	$	d	p
Have:	6	7	2
Spend:	2	4	6

2.

	$	d	p
Have:	2	4	9
Spend:	1	5	3

3.

	$	d	p
Have:	4	3	0
Spend:	2	6	2

Set G pages 132–133

Find each difference. **Remember** to estimate first.

1. 483 − 191	2. 274 − 238	3. 536 − 409	4. 785 − 341	5. 340 − 160

Set H pages 134–135

Find each difference.

1. 370 − 236	2. 408 − 49	3. 500 − 240	4. 630 − 106	5. 904 − 362

6. 400 − 230   **7.** 240 − 206   **8.** 300 − 109   **9.** 608 − 421

Set I pages 136–137

Subtract.

1. 6,005 − 2,076	2. 543 − 265	3. 467 − 198	4. 8,435 − 5,713	5. 3,004 − 1,265

6. 5,806 − 3,402   **7.** 7,004 − 4,253   **8.** 9,463 − 4,082

Enrichment

Estimation Strategies

Adam has begun collecting stamps from all over the world.

Estimate how many stamps he has in all.

United States: 336

Japan: 256

Mexico: 147

One easy way is to use only the *front-end* digits:

$$3\ 3\ 6$$
$$1\ 4\ 7$$
$$+2\ 5\ 6$$

$3 + 1 + 2 = 6$
6 hundreds

Adam has more than 600 stamps in his collection.

A more accurate way is to use the front-end digits and *adjust* the estimate by using the tens digits.

$$3\ 3\ 6$$
$$1\ 4\ 7$$
$$+2\ 5\ 6$$

$3 + 1 + 2 = 6$ $3 + 4 + 5 = 12$
6 hundreds   12 tens

The tens make at least one more hundred. So a more accurate estimate would be 700 stamps.

Use front-end estimation to estimate each sum. Adjust the estimate if you can.

1. 517 + 285 + 161   **2.** 410 + 324 + 19   **3.** 383 + 242 + 400

4. 253 + 13 + 745   **5.** 273 + 382 + 29   **6.** 219 + 86 + 548

7. 112 + 508 + 354   **8.** 526 + 411 + 689   **9.** 282 + 860 + 58

10. 36 + 9 + 273   **11.** 94 + 118 + 6   **12.** 7 + 50 + 231

Chapter 4 Review/Test

1. Rename 1 dollar as 10 dimes. Write the new amount.

   2 dollars, 2 dimes, 7 pennies

Tell how many dollars, dimes, and pennies

2. there are in all.   3. are left.

$	d	p
5	4	7
+ 3	6	9

$	d	p
7	2	4
− 5	5	1

Add.

4. 931
   + 54

5. 276
   +481

6. 6,893 + 510

Subtract.

7. 482
   −315

8. 905
   −273

9. 7,261
   −3,521

10. 4,200
    − 374

Use paper and pencil, mental math, or a calculator to find each answer. Tell which method you used.

11. 75
    +20

12. 5
    +3

13. 143
    +869

City-Wide Children's Art Fair
The Most Entries Ever!

Grade	Number of Paintings	Number of Clay Models
2	122	218
3	59	236
4	249	114

Use the data in the picture.

14. Which prize was won by a painting of an animal?

Read this problem. Then answer the questions below.

How many more third-graders made clay models than paintings?

15. What facts from the table would you use to solve this problem?

16. Solve the problem above.

17. ■ **Write About Math**
    Write a subtraction problem in which you need to rename hundreds as tens.

Time, Measurement, and Geometry

Did You Know:
Electric clocks came into use in many homes in the 1920s. Digital clocks became popular in the late 1970s. Some of the earliest clocks were sundials and water clocks. They were made many thousands of years ago.

Number-Sense Project

Estimate
Estimate how many clocks you have in your home. Predict: Do your classmates have more digital clocks or more standard clocks in their homes?

Gather Data
Record the number, type, and location of all the clocks in your home.

Analyze and Report
Be ready to add your results to a class chart. Check to see whether you and your classmates have more digital or more standard clocks in your homes.

149

Telling Time: Nearest 5 Minutes and Minute

Build Understanding

Do you use a clock to help you to wake up? What time do you get up on school days?

A. The first clock shows the time Christina gets up. The short hand is called the **hour hand.** It points to the hour. What time does Christina wake up?

B. The second clock tells the time that Christina begins to eat lunch. What time is that?

Christina begins lunch at eleven thirty. The time can be written as

11:30
30 minutes after 11 o'clock

The long hand is called the **minute hand.** It points to the minutes.

■ **Talk About Math** Explain how skip-counting can help you tell time.

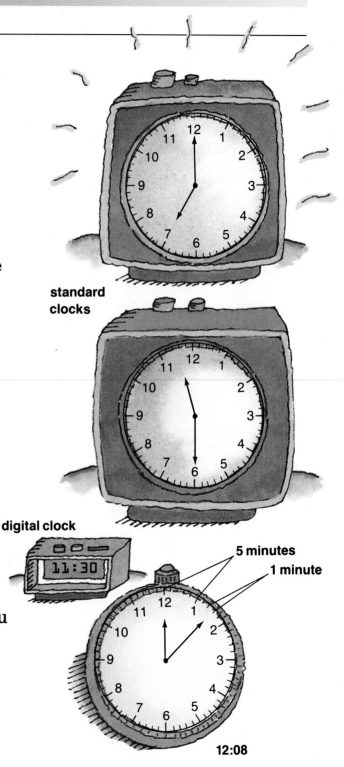

standard clocks

digital clock

5 minutes
1 minute

12:08

150

Check Understanding

For another example, see Set A, pages 178–179.

Write the letter of the clock that shows the time.

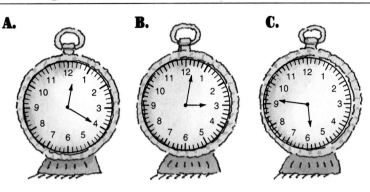

A.   **B.**   **C.**

1. 5:46

2. 12:20

3. 3:02

4. 2 minutes after 3

5. 46 minutes after 5

6. 20 minutes after 12

7. How many minutes are in one hour?

Practice

For More Practice, see Set A, pages 180–181.

Write the letter of the digital clock that shows the same time as each standard clock. **Remember** that the short hand is the hour hand and the long hand is the minute hand.

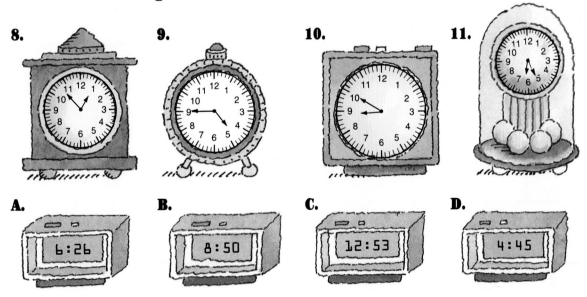

8.   **9.**   **10.**   **11.**

A. 6:26

B. 8:50

C. 12:53

D. 4:45

Write each time in two ways.

12.

13.

14.

15.

Mental Math Use a standard clock to answer the questions.

16. What time does the clock show now?

17. What time will it be in an hour?

18. What time will it be 10 minutes from now?

19. What time will it be 30 minutes from now?

20. How many minutes is 1 hour and 15 minutes?

21. How many hours is 120 minutes?

Problem Solving

22. Diane turned on the television set at two minutes after seven o'clock. Write this time using numerals.

23. The Meng family began eating dinner at twenty minutes after six. Draw a standard clock face showing this time.

24. Roberto read a newspaper in 55 minutes. Flora read it in 1 hour and 10 minutes. How much longer did it take Flora to read the paper?

Visualize the problem in your mind to help you understand it better.

25. Pat began to write a letter at 10:30. She finished it 30 minutes later. What time did she finish the letter?

26. Kei and Lee went out to play at 3:15. Their mother told them to come home in 2 hours. What time should they come back?

Reading ———— Math

Vocabulary   The hands of a clock always move in the same direction. They move *clockwise.*

1. Which faucet is being moved clockwise?

2. What do you think the word *counterclockwise* means?

Reading Calendars: Days, Weeks, Months

Build Understanding

Every September the town of New Harmony holds an International Festival. This calendar shows the events of the festival.

		August				
S	M	T	W	T	F	S
						1
2	3	4	5	6	7	8
9	10	11	12	13	14	15
16	17	18	19	20	21	22
23	24	25	26	27	28	29
30	31					

		October				
S	M	T	W	T	F	S
					1	2	3
4	5	6	7	8	9	10
11	12	13	14	15	16	17
18	19	20	21	22	23	24
25	26	27	28	29	30	31

September

Sunday	Monday	Tuesday	Wednesday	Thursday	Friday	Saturday
		1 Chinese food	2	3	4 Mexican food	5
6	7	8	9	10	11 Italian art	12 Hispanic writing
13	14 Spanish music	15	16 German puppets	17 Russian circus	18	19 African wood carving
20	21 steel drum	22 Caribbean band	23 French opera	24	25	26
27	28 Canadian hockey	29 European soccer	30 English rugby			

A. The 7 days of the week are Sunday, Monday, Tuesday, Wednesday, Thursday, Friday, and Saturday.

B. A week begins on Sunday. It ends on Saturday.

■ **Talk About Math** How many days are there from one Sunday to the next? From one Saturday to the next? Use your answers to explain the phrase "a week from Sunday."

Check Understanding

For another example, see Set B, pages 178–179.

Use the calendar on page 154 to answer the questions.

1. On what day of the week does the Russian circus perform?

2. What happens on the second Saturday of the month?

Practice

For More Practice, see Set B, pages 180–181.

Use the calendar on page 154 to answer the questions.

3. What happens one week after September 16? What day is that?

4. What happens on the second Friday? What date is that?

5. In what week are the most events held? On what dates does that week begin and end?

6. On August 29, Cal bought a ticket for the festival. What day of the week was that?

Problem Solving

Explore ———— Math

Use the calendar on page 154.

7. What date is one week after September 1?

8. Is the date one week after the 1st the same in any month?

9. On what day of the week does October 1 fall?

10. What date is 1 week later than October 1? 2 weeks later? 3 weeks later? 4 weeks later?

11. October 31 is the last date in October. On what day of the week does October end? Use your answer to Exercise 10 to find out.

Customary Lengths: Inches, Feet

Build Understanding

A. Inching Along
Materials: 12-inch ruler
Groups: Partners

a. Spread your fingers as shown in the picture. How far do you think one little finger is from the other little finger? Estimate.

b. Have your partner measure the distance. How close was your estimate?

c. Repeat the activity. Measure your partner's hands.

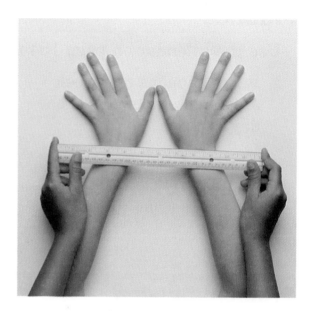

The distance from one little finger to the other is about 12 inches. 12 ***inches*** (in.) is 1 ***foot*** (ft).

B.

This ribbon is about 3 inches long to the nearest inch.

C.

This eraser is about $1\frac{1}{2}$ inches long to the the nearest half inch.

■ **Write About Math** Explain what it means to measure to the nearest inch; the nearest half inch.

Check Understanding

For another example, see Set C, pages 178–179.

Measure to the nearest inch.

1. the width of your bulletin board

2. the length of your shoe

Practice

For More Practice, see Set C, pages 180–181.

Measure to the nearest half inch.

3. the length of your textbook

4. the length of your chair seat

Find the distance between the dot by each animal and the dot by its home. Measure to the nearest half inch.

5. bee   **6.** bird   **7.** fish   **8.** dog

Estimation Estimate each length. Then measure each length to the nearest inch. Use feet and inches when you can.

9. your open math book

10. piece of construction paper

Customary Lengths: Yards, Miles

Build Understanding

The **yard** (yd) and **mile** (mi) are customary units of length. They are used to measure long lengths.

A. Mrs. Awan's stride measures about 1 yard.

1 yard = 3 feet
1 yard = 36 inches

B. Mrs. Awan takes about 1,760 strides to run 1 mile.

1 mile = 1,760 yards
1 mile = 5,280 feet

■ **Talk About Math** Explain what would happen if you tried to use inches to measure a city block.

1 yard

Check Understanding

For another example, see Set D, pages 178–179.

Tell whether you would use yards or miles to measure the following.

1. Length of a football field

2. Length of a bus trip

3. Distance from California to China

4. Distance from one street corner to the next

158

Practice

For More Practice, see Set D, pages 180–181.

Write inches, feet, yards, or miles to tell which you would use to measure the following.

5. Width of a piece of paper

6. Distance from one town to another

7. Depth of a swimming pool

8. Length of a soccer field

9. Length of a classroom

10. Length of a leaf

Copy and complete each sentence.

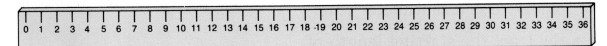

11. There are ▦ inches in 1 yard.

12. There are ▦ inches in 1 foot.

13. One mile is the same as ▦ feet.

14. Two feet is the same as ▦ inches.

15. There are ▦ yards in 6 feet.

16. Use Data What is the length in inches of the note pad on page 94?

Problem Solving

17. Critical Thinking The little finger is also called a pinky. Suppose you told a friend that a desk was 17 pinkies long. Would your friend know exactly how long that is? Why or why not?

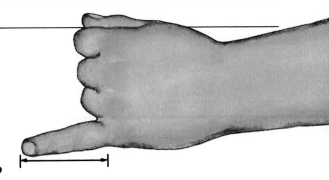

Metric Lengths: Centimeters, Decimeters

Build Understanding

A. Measuring Up
Materials: Centimeter ruler

Does plant food help plants grow taller? Al chose two plants with stems 4 centimeters long. He fed Plant A. He did not feed Plant B. The picture at the right shows how the plants looked a week later.

a. Measure the stem of each plant from the edge of the cup up to the leaves. Use a centimeter ruler.

b. Subtract the starting length of each plant. How much did each plant grow?

B. Scientists use metric measurements. *Centimeters* (cm) and *decimeters* (dm) are metric units of length.

10 centimeters = 1 decimeter

← one centimeter →
← one decimeter →

| 1 | 2 | 3 | 4 | 5 | 6 | 7 | 8 | 9 | 10 | 11 | 12 | 13 | 14 | 15 | 16 | 17 |

■ **Talk About Math** Why should you line up the left edge of the object you are measuring with the zero point on the ruler?

Check Understanding

For another example, see Set E, pages 178–179.

Measure each line segment to the nearest centimeter.

1. _____   2. _____

3. _____

Practice

For More Practice, see Set E, pages 180–181.

Estimation   Without using a ruler, draw a line
segment that you think has the length given.
Then measure the line segment with a ruler.

4. 1 centimeter   **5.** 8 centimeters   **6.** 6 centimeters

7. 12 centimeters   **8.** 2 decimeters   **9.** 2 centimeters

Problem Solving

10. A stem 8 centimeters long
grew 4 centimeters. How
long is it now?

11. How could you measure the
length of a desk with
beans?

Midchapter ———— Checkup

Answer each question.
1. At 1:30, to what number
does the minute hand
point?

2. What is the date a week
after May 9?

Copy and complete each sentence.
3. One foot is the same as
▦ inches.

4. There are ▦ feet in
1 yard.

5. One decimeter is the same as
▦ centimeters.

Real-Life Decision Making

You can go to the movies if you work in the yard at least 60 minutes. The chart shows what needs to be done and how many minutes each job should take.

1. How many minutes should it take to weed the garden and sweep the driveway?

2. Decide which jobs you will do.

Task	Minutes it should take
weed garden	25
rake leaves	20
sweep driveway	15
water lawn	15
pick vegetables	20

Problem Solving WORKSHOP

Number-Sense Project

Look back at pages 148-149.

The water clock was invented about 3,000 years ago. It was a glass jar filled with water. Over time the water trickled out of the jar. The water left in the jar showed how much time had passed since the jar was filled.

1. If a water clock contained 6 quarts of water at 8 o'clock in the morning and 2 quarts of water at 12 noon,

    a. how much water had trickled out of the jar?

    b. how much time had passed?

2. For the water clock in Exercise 1, how much water stood for one hour?

Explore as a Team

1. Cut a piece of string that is the length of your height.

2. Guess how many times your shoe will fit along the length of the string. Check your guess.

TIPS FOR **WORKING TOGETHER**

Tell someone when he or she does or says something that helps you.

Math-at-Home Activity

1. Keep a tally of traffic at or near your home. Make a tally mark for each car, bus, or truck that drives by in 10 minutes.

2. Write some things about your tally.

163

Metric Lengths: Meters, Kilometers

Build Understanding

Meters (m) and *kilometers* (km) are metric units of length. They are used to measure long lengths.

A. The length of $3\frac{1}{2}$ pieces of construction paper is about 1 meter.

1 meter = 100 centimeters
1 meter = 10 decimeters

B. The length of 3,500 pieces of construction paper is about 1 kilometer.

1 kilometer = 1,000 meters

■ **Talk About Math** Suppose you were to measure something in meters and then in centimeters. For which measurement would you use *more* units? For which would you use *fewer* units? Explain.

35,000 trees could be saved each year if people recycled used newspapers and boxes.

Check Understanding

For another example, see Set F, pages 178–179.

Tell whether you would use meters or kilometers to measure the following:

1. Length of a city block

2. Length of a picnic bench

3. Distance between cities

4. Length of your school

Practice

For More Practice, see Set F, pages 180–181.

Tell whether you would use centimeters, meters, or kilometers to measure the following.

5. Length of a diving board

6. Length of a baseball bat

7. Distance across Canada

8. Height of a skyscraper

9. Width of a tennis racket

10. Distance along a highway

Copy and complete each sentence.

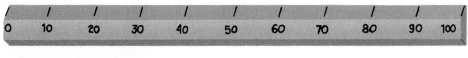

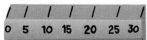

11. One meter is the same as ⬛ centimeters.

12. There are ⬛ meters in 1 kilometer.

Number Sense Copy and complete the sentence.

13. One kilometer is the same as 1,000 meters, so 2 kilometers is the same as ⬛ meters.

Mixed Practice Copy and complete each sentence.

14. There are ⬛ feet in 1 yard.

15. In 1 foot there are ⬛ inches.

16. One mile is the same as ⬛ feet.

17. One meter is the same as ⬛ centimeters.

18. In 1 kilometer, there are ⬛ meters.

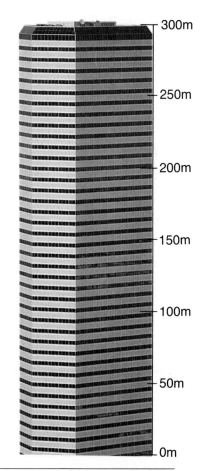

Make a Table

Build Understanding

The class read a story called "Robbery at the Amusement Park." The robber was Sue or Theo or Willa or Fred. Each was at the park on a different day, Wednesday, Thursday, Friday, or Saturday.

The robbery happened on Friday. Was Willa the robber?

PROBLEM SOLVING GUIDE

Understand
QUESTION
FACTS
KEY IDEA

➤ **Plan and Solve**
STRATEGY
ANSWER

Look Back
SENSIBLE ANSWER
ALTERNATE APPROACH

Clue 1: No one's name begins with the same letter as the day he or she was at the park.

Clue 2: Willa spent Thursday and Friday at the beach.

Clue 3: Theo was at the park three days before Willa.

Clue 4: Fred was at the park one day after Theo.

Understand Willa is the robber if she was at the park on Friday.

Plan and Solve STRATEGY Make a table. Use the clues. Mark an X when you know a person was not at the park on that day. Use O to show that a person was at the park.

Red x's: Clue 1
Blue x's: Clue 2

Day	Sue	Theo	Willa	Fred
Wednesday			X	
Thursday		X	X	
Friday			X	X
Saturday	X			

ANSWER Willa was at the park only on Saturday. She could not be the robber.

Look Back Are there any clues which have not been used?

■ **Talk About Math** Suppose you know a person was *not* at the park on Friday. How can this help you decide who the robber was?

Check Understanding

Copy the table on page 166. Fill in more of the table as you answer the questions.

1. Use Clue 3. What day was Theo at the park? Put an O in the table to show when he was there.

2. Put an X in your table for each day when Theo was not at the park.

3. Use Clue 4. When was Fred at the park?

4. For each day, put an O or an X under Fred's name.

Practice

Complete your table to find out who the robber was.

5. How many Xs do you now have in the row for Friday? What do those Xs tell you?

6. Put X or O in every space in your table. Who was at the park on Friday? Who was the robber?

Use the three clues below to answer the question.

7. Brad, Hannah, Celia, and Don each read a book about a different animal. The animals were a horse, a beaver, a deer, and a cat. Which animal did each child read about?

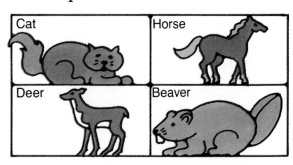

Clue 1: No child's name has the same number of letters as the name of the animal in his or her book.

Clue 2: No child's name begins with the same letter as the name of the animal in his or her book.

Clue 3: Celia's book was not about a deer.

Perimeter

Build Understanding

Jason is a carpenter. He is putting wood trim around a window. To do this, he needs to know the distance around the window.

Perimeter is the distance around a figure. What is the perimeter of this window?

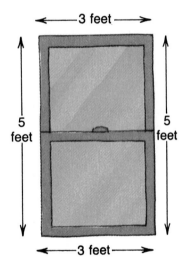

To find the perimeter, add the lengths of the sides.

3 + 5 + 3 + 5 = 16

The perimeter of the window is 16 feet.

■ **Talk About Math** Explain why 16 inches or 16 yards is not a reasonable answer.

Check Understanding

For another example, see Set G, pages 178–179.

Find the perimeter of each window.

1.

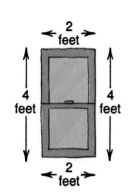

2.

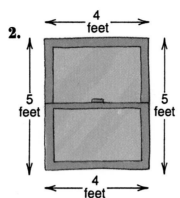

3.

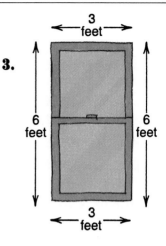

Practice

For More Practice, see Set G, pages 180–181.

Use a ruler to measure the sides of each figure.
Use the units named. Then find the perimeter.

4.

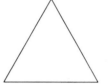

The perimeter is
▦ centimeters

5.

The perimeter is
▦ inches.

6.

The perimeter is
▦ centimeters.

Use paper and pencil or mental math to
find the perimeter of each figure. Tell
which method you used.

7.

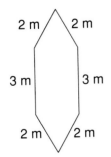

8.

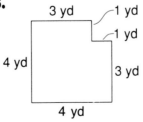

9.

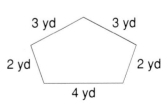

10. 🖩 **Calculator** The sides of a playground
are 262 feet, 311 feet, 195 feet, and 278 feet
long. Find the perimeter.

Counting Squares to Find Area

Build Understanding

A. Covering the Cover
Materials: math books, play pennies, paper clips, inch grid paper, paper rectangles of various sizes, scissors
Groups: 3 to 5 students

a. Cover one math book with play pennies. Do not overlap the pennies. Record how many pennies you used.

b. Repeat *a* using paper clips.

c. Repeat *a* using squares cut from inch grid paper.

You can write the answer to *c* as 80 *square inches.*
This tells you the **area** of the cover.

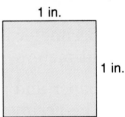

1 in.

1 in.

1 square inch

B. A *square centimeter* is smaller than a square inch. If you covered your math book with squares of this size, would you need more than 80 squares or fewer than 80?

The area of your math book is about 500 square centimeters.

1 cm

1 cm

1 square centimeter

■ **Talk About Math** The answers for parts *a, b,* and *c* of the Activity are different. Explain why.

Check Understanding

Work in groups. Cover each object with
1-inch squares. Tell the area.

1. the front cover of your
   spelling book

2. the paper rectangle your
   teacher gives to your group

Practice

Find the area of each figure in square centimeters.

3.

4.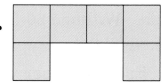

5.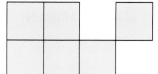

6.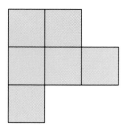

7.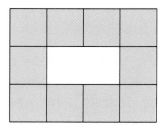

8.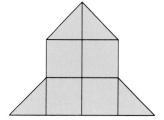

Problem Solving

Explore ———— Math

How could you find the area of your hand?
Try tracing your hand on centimeter grid paper.

9. How many whole boxes are inside your
   tracing?

10. How many partial boxes are inside it? About
    how many whole boxes do the partial boxes make?

11. What is the area of your hand in
    square centimeters?

Deciding When an Estimate Is Enough

Build Understanding

Angela wants 6 streamers for her party. Each streamer will be 12 feet long. Crepe paper comes in rolls of 50 feet or 100 feet. What should Angela buy?

Understand QUESTION Will one 50-foot roll be enough?

FACTS Each streamer will be 12 feet. Rolls of crepe paper are 50 feet or 100 feet.

KEY IDEA Angela does not need to know the exact number of feet. She needs to know only if one roll of 50 feet is enough.

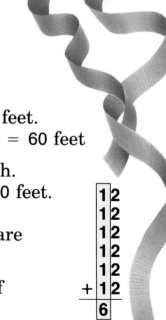

Plan and Solve Angela can estimate.

12 feet is a little more than 10 feet.
10 + 10 + 10 + 10 + 10 + 10 = 60 feet

One roll of 50 feet is not enough. Angela must buy one roll of 100 feet.

Look Back Look at the tens digits. There are 6 tens.

Angela needs at least 60 feet of crepe paper.

$$\begin{array}{r} 1\,2 \\ 1\,2 \\ 1\,2 \\ 1\,2 \\ 1\,2 \\ +\ 1\,2 \\ \hline 6 \end{array}$$

■ **Talk About Math** Why doesn't Angela need to know the exact number of feet the streamers will be?

Problem Solving Guide

Understand
QUESTION
FACTS
KEY IDEA

Plan and Solve
STRATEGY
ANSWER

Look Back
SENSIBLE ANSWER
ALTERNATE APPROACH

Check Understanding

Tell whether you need to find an exact answer or an estimate.

1. You need 5 bows, each 18 inches. Spools of ribbon are 75 inches and 125 inches.

2. Framing is cut to order. You need wood to frame a picture that is 8 inches on each side.

Practice

Tell whether you need to find an exact answer or an estimate. Then tell what Angela should buy for her party.

3. Angela needs string for 4 balloons. Each string is 32 inches. String comes in rolls of 100 or 200 inches.

4. Angela needs fabric for 12 costumes. Each costume uses 3 yards of fabric. Fabric is cut to order.

5. Angela needs ribbon for 5 favors. Each ribbon is 18 inches. Ribbon comes in spools of 100 or 150 inches.

6. Angela needs 6 bows. Each bow is 14 inches. Ribbon comes in spools of 75 or 125 inches.

Choose a ____ Strategy

7. ***Race to the Finish!*** Suppose you are in a race. There are 4 runners ahead of you, 8 runners behind you, and 5 runners who have dropped out of the race. How many runners were in the race at the start?

PROBLEM SOLVING
STRATEGIES

Choose an Operation
Find a Pattern
Use Logical Reasoning
Make a Table

Temperature

Build Understanding

When the temperature outdoors is 30°C, do you need a coat?

The thermometers give the temperature in degrees *Celsius* (°C) and *Fahrenheit* (°F). A thermometer measures temperature.

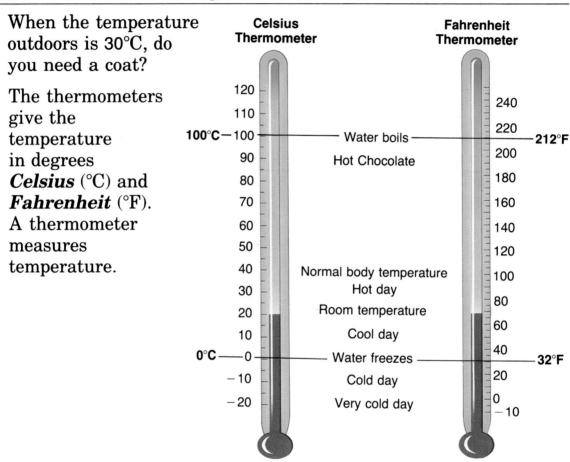

Celsius Thermometer

Fahrenheit Thermometer

100°C — 100 — Water boils — 212°F

Hot Chocolate

Normal body temperature
Hot day
Room temperature
Cool day

0°C — 0 — Water freezes — 32°F

Cold day

Very cold day

You do not need a coat when the temperature is 30°C.

■ **Talk About Math** Are the units on both thermometers the same size? Explain your answer.

Check Understanding

For another example, see Set H, pages 178–179.

1. Is 0°F warmer or colder than 0°C?

2. If −1°F means one degree below zero, what does 5°F mean?

Practice

For More Practice, see Set H, pages 180–181.

Write the temperature in °C or °F.

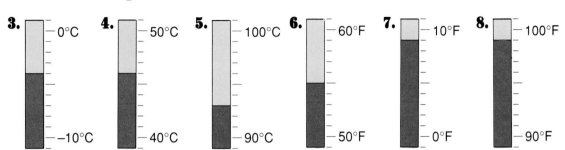

3. 0°C −10°C   **4.** 50°C 40°C   **5.** 100°C 90°C   **6.** 60°F 50°F   **7.** 10°F 0°F   **8.** 100°F 90°F

Estimation Choose the more sensible measure.

9. temperature of a classroom
32°F   69°F

10. a person with a fever
99°C   40°C

11. temperature of hot soup
78°F   179°F

12. blizzard weather
−15°C   15°C

Problem Solving

Ty graphed the temperature at 9:00 every morning.

13. What was the highest temperature?

14. What was the lowest?

15. What was the difference between Monday's and Friday's temperatures?

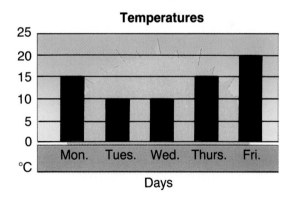

Temperatures

Days

Skills _____ **Review**   pages 118–119, 132–133

Add or subtract.

1. 665 − 231   **2.** 409 + 356   **3.** 873 + 22   **4.** 803 − 157

Solve each problem.

1. Mr. Hill drove 325 miles on Thursday and 378 miles on Friday. How many miles did he drive in all?

2. Sheena weighs 70 pounds. Her mother weighs 118 pounds, and her father weighs 162 pounds. A small boat can hold 330 pounds. Can all three ride in it at the same time?

3. If you need 1 ticket for every 2 adults and 1 ticket for every 3 children, how many tickets do you need for 2 adults and 5 children?

4. Linda is older than Anna. Cathy was born before Anna. Anna is older than Louise. Cathy was born before Linda. Who is the oldest? The youngest?

5. Will $2.00 be enough to buy two 49¢-notepads and a 98¢-pen? Estimate.

6. **Data File** Use data from pages 248-249. The Amazon River is how many miles longer than the Yangtze River in China?

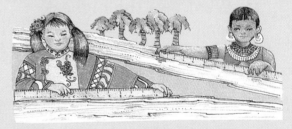

7. **Make a Data File** Look in the newspaper. Record the high and low temperatures in your area for a week. Make a table.

Problem Solving REVIEW

Explore with a Calculator

Figures Don't Lie.

We interviewed some geometric figures. All of them told us some facts about themselves. They even told us their perimeters. Use the facts given and your calculator to find the missing fact about the length of one side of each figure.

1. "I am a rectangle. My perimeter is 18 yards. My width is 4 yards. What is my length?"

2. "I am a rectangle. My length is 14 inches. My perimeter is 48 inches. What is my width?"

3. "I am a 4-sided figure. Each of my sides is a different length. My perimeter is 97 centimeters. Three of my sides measure 18, 24, and 36 centimeters. What is the length of my fourth side?"

4. "I am a triangle. My perimeter is 84 centimeters. Each of my 3 sides is a different length. Two sides have lengths of 21 and 35 centimeters. What is the length of my third side?"

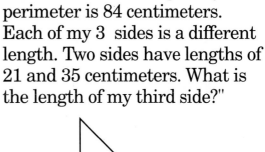

5. "I am a 5-sided figure My perimeter is 128 inches. Four of my sides measure 23, 18, 27, and 29 inches. What is the length of my fifth side?"

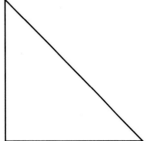

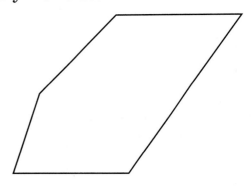

Reteaching

Set A   pages 150–153

Write the time in two ways.

12:35; 35 minutes after 12 o'clock.

Remember that the short hand points to the hour.

Write the time in two ways.

Set B   pages 154–155

What day is October 4?

OCTOBER

Sunday	Monday	Tuesday	Wednesday	Thursday	Friday	Saturday
	1	2	3	4	5	6
7	8	Columbus Day	10	11	12	13
14	15	16	17	18	19	20
21	22	23	United Nations Day	25	26	27
28	29	30	Halloween			

Thursday

Remember that a week begins on Sunday and ends on Saturday. Use the calendar at the left to answer the questions.

1. What day is October 22?

2. What is the date of the third Friday?

Set C   pages 156–157

How long is the pencil to the nearest half inch?

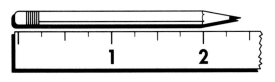

$2\frac{1}{2}$ inches

Remember to line up the end of the ruler with the edge of what you are measuring.

1. Measure the length of your desk to the nearest half inch.

Set D   pages 158–159

The foot and the yard are used to measure lengths that are not as small as a pencil and not as long as the distance between cities.

Remember that 1 mile equals 1,760 yards and also equals 5,280 feet.

1. Would you use inches, feet, yards, or miles to find the length of a car?

Set E   pages 160–161

The width of a large paper clip is 1 centimeter. The length is about 5 centimeters.

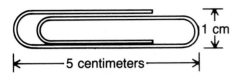

Remember that

10 centimeters = 1 decimeter

1. Without using a ruler, draw a line segment that is 3 centimeters long. Then measure your line segment with a ruler.

Set F   pages 164–165

The width of a door is about 1 meter. The width of 1,000 doors is about 1 kilometer.

1 kilometer = 1,000 meters

Remember that it takes more units to measure something in centimeters than in meters.

1. Tell whether you would use centimeters, meters, or kilometers to measure the length of a city block.

Set G   pages 168–169

Find the perimeter of this desk.

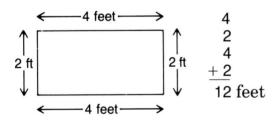

$$\begin{array}{r} 4 \\ 2 \\ 4 \\ +\ 2 \\ \hline 12 \text{ feet} \end{array}$$

Remember that perimeter means the distance around a figure.

1. Find the perimeter of this mirror.

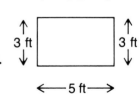

Set H   pages 174–175

What temperature is shown?

Each mark is 1 degree. Start at 30°C and count to 36°C.

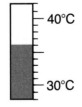

Remember that each unit is bigger on the Celsius scale than on the Fahrenheit scale.

1. Write the temperature shown at the right.

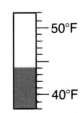

More Practice

Set A pages 150–153

Write each time in two ways.

1.

2.

Mental Math

3. The time is 10:20. What time will it be 30 minutes from now?

4. How many minutes is 1 hour and 35 minutes?

Set B pages 154–155

Use the calendar on page 154 to answer these questions.

1. What happens one week after September 21? What day is that?

2. What happens on the third Wednesday? What date is that?

3. Labor Day is the first Monday in September. What date is that?

4. Al's birthday is one week after the French opera. Name the date.

Set C pages 156–157

Measure to the nearest half inch.

1.

2.

Set D pages 158–159

Write inches, feet, yards, or miles to tell which you would use to measure the following.

1. Length of a hairbrush

2. Height of a refrigerator

3. Distance from earth to the moon

4. Length of a football field

Set E pages 160-161

Estimation Without using a ruler, draw a line
segment that you think has the length given.
Then measure the line segment with a ruler.

1. 4 centimeters   **2.** 7 centimeters   **3.** 9 centimeters

Set F pages 164-165

Tell whether you would use centimeters, meters, or
kilometers to measure the following.

1. Length of a toothbrush   **2.** Length of a river

3. Height of tree   **4.** Width of a street

Number Sense Copy and complete the sentence.

5. One meter is the same as 100 centimeters, so
3 meters is the same as ▦ centimeters.

Set G pages 168-169

Use paper and pencil or mental math to find the
perimeter of each figure.

Tell which method you used.

1. 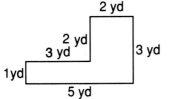   **2.** 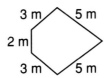   **3.**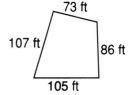

Set H pages 174-175

Write the temperature in °C or
°F.

1. 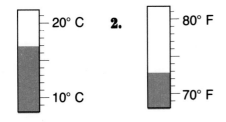 **2.**

Estimation Choose the more
sensible measure.

3. Making ice cubes
50°F   32°F

4. A cup of hot cocoa
80°C   50°C

Enrichment

Area and Perimeter

Are these two rectangles the same size?

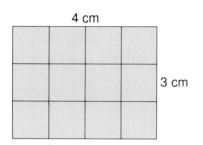

4 cm

3 cm

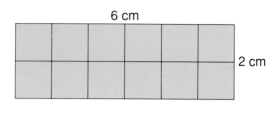

6 cm

2 cm

1. Find the area of each rectangle.

2. Find the perimeter of each rectangle.

3. Is the area of both rectangles the same?

4. Is the perimeter of both rectangles the same?

Use grid paper to make rectangles for each exercise. Then find the area and perimeter of each. Record your findings in a table.

5. 8 across and 2 down

6. 4 across and 4 down

7. 10 across and 2 down

8. 12 across and 1 down

9. 5 across and 4 down

10. 3 across and 2 down

Exercise	Area	Perimeter
5.		
6.		
7.		
8.		
9.		
10.		

11. Which rectangles have the same area?

12. Which rectangles have the same perimeter?

13. Do any rectangles have the same area and perimeter?

Chapter 5 Review/Test

What time is shown on each clock?

1.  **2.**

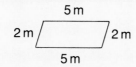

	AUGUST					
S	M	T	W	T	F	S
		1	2	3	4	5
6	7	8	9	10	11	12
13	14	15	16	17	18	19
20	21	22	23	24	25	26
27	28	29	30	31		

3. What is the date of the third Monday in August?

4. Measure the line segment to the nearest inch and centimeter.

_____

Choose the more sensible unit of measure.

5. Length of a truck

mile   foot

6. Length of a pencil

centimeter   kilometer

7. Find the perimeter.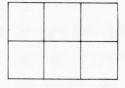

8. Find the area of the figure in square centimeters.

9. Choose the most sensible temperature for snow skiing.

20°F   68°F   90°F

10. John needs string to tie up 6 boxes. For each box he needs 24 inches of string. Should he buy a 100-inch roll of string or a 200-inch roll?

Read this problem. Then make a table to answer the questions below.

Ted, Nan, and Joe are wearing hats. One hat is green, one orange, and one blue. Neither of the boys has a blue hat. Joe wishes he had a green hat. What color is each child's hat?

11. Who has the blue hat?

12. Who has the orange hat?

13. Who has the green hat?

14. ■ **Write About Math**
Explain why you chose the measure you did in Item 5.

Multiplication Concepts

6

LIGHT BULBS

LIGHT BULBS

2 in pack

4 in pack

EGGS

ONE DOZEN

EGGS

ONE DOZEN

Number-Sense Project

Estimate
Estimate how many 2-packs of light bulbs you would need if you replaced every bulb in your house.

Gather Data
Record the number of bulbs you have in your home. How many packages of light bulbs do you need?

Analyze and Report
Make charts with your classmates to compare the number of bulbs you would need with the number of packages you would need.

Joining Groups of Equal Size

Build Understanding

What do you like to do at picnics?

Judy bought some of the supplies for the Waller Company picnic. She got 3 six-packs of juice. How many cans of juice did she get?

Add the number in each pack to find the number in all.

6 + 6 + 6 = 18

■ **Talk About Math**   Tell how you can find how many cans there would be if Judy bought 30 six-packs of juice.

Each American drinks about 5½ gallons of juice in one year.

Check Understanding

For another example, see Set A, pages 212–213.

Choose all the number names that tell how many there are of each. Use the picture on this page to help you.

1. How many forks?

2. How many plates?

3. How many napkins?

4. How many straws?

A. 2 groups of 100
B. 5 + 5 + 5 + 5
C. 4 groups of 5
D. 10 + 10
E. 100 + 100
F. 4 groups of 20
G. 200
H. 2 groups of 10
I. 20 + 20 + 20 + 20

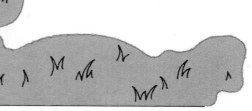

Mental Math In Exercises 5 and 6, tell an easy way to find the answer.

5. 10 + 10 + 10 + 10 + 10 + 10   **6.** 100 + 100 + 100 + 100

Practice

For More Practice, see Set A, pages 214–215.

Tell how many.

7. 8 + 8 + 8 + 8   **8.** 9 + 9 + 9   **9.** 6 + 6 + 6 + 6 + 6

10. 5 + 5 + 5   **11.** 7 + 7 + 7 + 7   **12.** 2 + 2 + 2 + 2 + 2

13. 10 + 10 + 10   **14.** 100 + 100   **15.** 10 + 10 + 10 + 10

Mixed Practice Tell which is greater.

16. 5 + 5 or 2 + 9   **17.** 8 − 4 or 3 + 3

18. 20 + 10 or 34   **19.** 80 or 35 + 35

20. 22 + 22 or 25 + 25   **21.** 50 − 20 or 20 + 20

Problem Solving

Write an addition sentence for Exercises 22–25. Tell how many in all. Use the picture on this page to help you.

22. 4 packages of plates

23. 2 packages of forks

24. 2 packages of napkins

25. 8 packages of cups

187

Meaning of Multiplication: Repeated Addition

Build Understanding

A. All the Same
Materials: Small objects
Groups: 3–5 students

How many toy cars are in the picture?

a. Each of you show 3 objects.

b. Tell how many are in 2 groups of 3.
Write an addition sentence.

You can write a multiplication sentence to show 2 groups of 3.

2 × 3 = 6
2 times 3 equals 6

c. Repeat *step b* with 3, 4, and 5 groups of 3. Write an addition and a multiplication sentence for each set.

Use objects to find the number of cars. Write an addition and a multiplication sentence.

B. You can show multiplication in many ways.

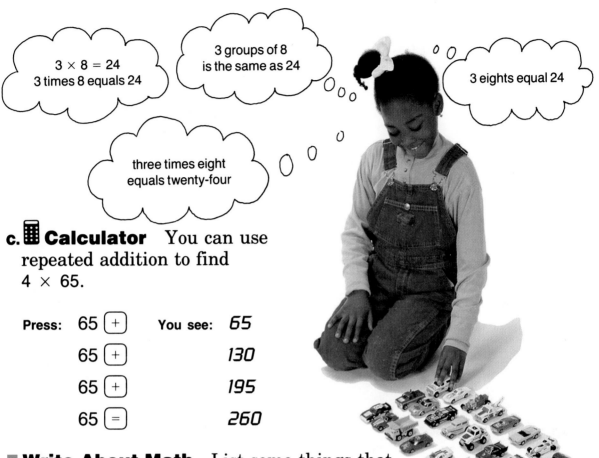

3 × 8 = 24
3 times 8 equals 24

3 groups of 8
is the same as 24

3 eights equal 24

three times eight
equals twenty-four

c. ▓ **Calculator** You can use repeated addition to find 4 × 65.

Press:		You see:	
65	+		*65*
65	+		*130*
65	+		*195*
65	=		*260*

■ **Write About Math** List some things that come in groups. Write multiplication sentences to describe them.

Check Understanding

For another example, see Set B, pages 212–213.

Use the ideas in Example B to help you write 4 sentences to describe each exercise.

1.

2.

3. 4 groups each with 3 toy trucks

4. 6 bags each with 2 toy dinosaurs

Practice

For More Practice, see Set B, pages 214–215.

Write an addition and a multiplication sentence for each exercise. **Remember** to use objects to help you.

5.

6.

7.

8.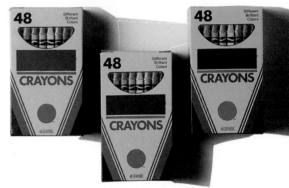

9. 5 shelves each with 5 toy dogs

10. 4 bags each with 3 balls

11. 3 boxes each with 9 stuffed animals

12. 2 bags each with 100 marbles

13. 4 boxes each with 200 building blocks

14. 5 checker games each with 24 checkers

Estimation Use what you know about estimating sums to estimate in multiplication. Estimate each answer.

15. 86 + 86 + 86   **16.** 3 × 32   **17.** 104 + 104

18. 2 × 197   **19.** 22 + 22 + 22 + 22   **20.** 4 × 18

Problem Solving

Solve each problem. Use objects to help you.

21. Jerry saw 3 toy train displays. Each train had 12 cars. How many cars were there in all?

22. Susan bought 4 boxes of tracks for her train set. Each box had 20 pieces of track. How many pieces of track did she buy?

Be flexible. If you get stuck, try another idea.

Write a story problem for each exercise.

23. $4 \times 3 = 12$ 24. $10 \times 6 = 60$ 25. $100 \times 4 = 400$

Use Data Look at the picture on page 186. Write a multiplication sentence to tell how many

26. forks.   27. plates.   28. napkins.   29. straws.

Visual Thinking Tom folded cards in two and punched holes in them. Then he unfolded the cards. How many holes are there in each card?

30.    31.

Skills _____ Review

Use a calculator, paper and pencil, or mental math to find each answer. Tell which method you used.

1. 84
   + 15

2. 523
   + 469

3. 602
   + 176

4. 265
   + 846

5. 493
   + 78

6. 4,215
   + 5,532

7. 6,821
   +   400

8. 1,578
   + 2,322

9. 80
   + 54

10. 3,999
    + 2,003

Exploring Multiplication Using Arrays

Build Understanding

Hurray for Arrays!
Materials: Small objects
Groups: Partners

Bert has some wood carvings. He put them in a display case that has 6 rows with 5 places in each row. How many carvings does he have?

a. Use small objects to show what Bert did. An **array** shows **rows** and **columns**.

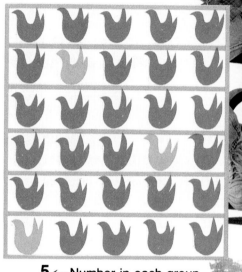

$5 \times 6 = 30$

—Number in each group
—Number of groups

$$\begin{array}{r} 5 \leftarrow \text{Number in each group} \\ \times\ 6 \leftarrow \text{Number of groups} \\ \hline 3\,0 \end{array}$$

Bert has 30 carvings.

b. Make an array to show 4 rows of 8 carvings. Write a multiplication sentence to tell how many carvings there are in all.

What hobbies do your classmates like?

■ **Write About Math** List at least 5 things you see displayed as arrays.

Check Understanding

For another example, see Set C, pages 212–213.

Number Sense   True or False. Each exercise matches the array.

1. $3 \times 6 = 18$ 2. $3 + 3 = 6$

3. $2 \times 9 = 18$ 4. $6 + 6 + 6 = 18$

5. three fives   6. $6 \times 3 = 18$

7. three sixes equal eighteen

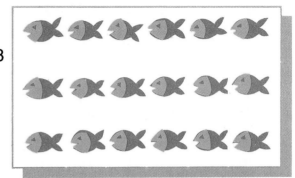

Practice

For More Practice, see Set C, pages 214–215.

Make an array and write a multiplication sentence for each.

8. 2 rows of 4   9. $3 + 3 + 3$ 10. 4 sixes   11. 5 rows of 7

12. $9 + 9 + 9$ 13. 4 fours   14. 3 rows of 5   15. $8 + 8$

16. 5 fives   17. 2 rows of 6   18. $2 + 2 + 2 + 2$ 19. 5 twos

Problem Solving

Solve each problem. **Remember** that making arrays may help you.

20. How many wood blocks are in 4 packages if there are 12 blocks in one package?

21. Bert sold 38 carvings. If he started with 214 carvings, how many did he have left?

Explore ———— Math

22. Make as many arrays of 16 objects as you can. Write a multiplication sentence for each array.

23. What shapes are arrays for multiplication sentences?

Multiplication with Fives

Build Understanding

How many happy face stickers do you see?

You can look at them in two different ways.

Turn your book so that the column on the left becomes the row across the bottom. Now you see an ear, two eyes, and a nose. There are 5 columns of 4 stickers.

When your book is not turned, you see two eyes, a nose, and a mouth. There are 4 columns of 5 stickers.

You can multiply when all the groups are the same size.

$5 \times 4 = 20$ **$4 \times 5 = 20$**

Think of 5 groups of 4.   Think of 4 groups of 5.

There are 20 stickers in all.

■ **Write About Math**   Why do we count by 5? What are some things we count by 5?

Check Understanding

For another example, see Set D, pages 212–213.

1. For each fact, draw an array and write the answer.

2	3	4	5	6	7	8	9
$\times 5$	$\times 5$	$\times 5$	$\times 5$	$\times 5$	$\times 5$	$\times 5$	$\times 5$

Write two multiplication sentences for each array.

2.  **3.**  **4.**

Practice

For More Practice, see Set D, pages 214–215.

Find each answer.

5. 4 ×5	**6.** 3 ×5	**7.** 5 ×2	**8.** 8 ×5	**9.** 6 ×5	**10.** 7 ×5

11. 5 ×4	**12.** 5 ×5	**13.** 2 ×5	**14.** 5 ×9	**15.** 5 ×6	**16.** 5 ×7

17. 5 × 5   **18.** 5 × 3   **19.** 5 × 9   **20.** 8 × 5   **21.** 4 × 5

Mixed Practice   Use paper and pencil or mental math to find each answer. Tell which method you used.

22. 46 + 29   **23.** 191 − 82   **24.** 5 × 6   **25.** 489 − 291

26. 9,836 − 400   **27.** 9 × 5   **28.** 3,076 + 925   **29.** 7 × 5

Problem Solving

Explore _____ Math

30. In the answers to Exercise 1, what pattern do you see?

Use the pattern to tell the ones digits in these answers.

31. 5 × 12   **32.** 5 × 17   **33.** 5 × 34   **34.** 5 × 103

Twos: Doubling

Build Understanding

Have you ever been to a baseball doubleheader? A doubleheader is 2 games.

In one doubleheader, the Cubs played 9 innings in each game. How many innings did they play in all?

There are 2 equal groups of 9. You can multiply.

2 × 9 = 18

The Cubs played 18 innings.

Mets	0	0	1	0	0	2	0	0	1
Cubs	0	0	0	1	1	0	0	0	0

Mets	0	0	0	3	0	0	1	0	0
Cubs	0	0	0	1	1	1	0	0	2

■ **Talk About Math** What are some other things that come in doubles or pairs?

Check Understanding

For another example, see Set E, pages 212–213.

1. Could the number 8 come out of the Doubling Machine?

2. Could the number 11 come out of the Doubling Machine?

3. What number comes out of the Doubling Machine when 5 goes in?

4. If 20 comes out of the Doubling Machine, what number went in?

DOUBLING MACHINE

IN	OUT
2	4
3	6
5	▦
20	40
50	100

5. Which of the numbers from 1 to 20 could come out of the Doubling Machine?

6. **Number Sense** What happens when you put 0 in the Doubling Machine?

7. For each fact, draw an array and write the answer.

$$\begin{array}{cccccccc} 2 & 3 & 4 & 5 & 6 & 7 & 8 & 9 \\ \times 2 & \times 2 & \times 2 & \times 2 & \times 2 & \times 2 & \times 2 & \times 2 \end{array}$$

Practice

For More Practice, see Set E, pages 214–215.

Find each answer.

8.	9.	10.	11.	12.	13.
$\begin{array}{r} 5 \\ \times 2 \end{array}$	$\begin{array}{r} 3 \\ \times 2 \end{array}$	$\begin{array}{r} 2 \\ \times 8 \end{array}$	$\begin{array}{r} 9 \\ \times 2 \end{array}$	$\begin{array}{r} 2 \\ \times 4 \end{array}$	$\begin{array}{r} 2 \\ \times 7 \end{array}$

14.	15.	16.	17.	18.	19.
$\begin{array}{r} 2 \\ \times 2 \end{array}$	$\begin{array}{r} 2 \\ \times 3 \end{array}$	$\begin{array}{r} 2 \\ \times 9 \end{array}$	$\begin{array}{r} 8 \\ \times 2 \end{array}$	$\begin{array}{r} 2 \\ \times 6 \end{array}$	$\begin{array}{r} 4 \\ \times 2 \end{array}$

20. 2×6 21. 5×2 22. 8×2 23. 2×7 24. 2×2

Find the missing number.

25. $2 \times \blacksquare = 14$ 26. $2 \times \blacksquare = 10$ 27. $\blacksquare \times 2 = 8$

28. **Number Sense** Look at the answers to Exercise 7. What pattern do you see?

Midchapter _____ **Checkup**

For each exercise, draw an array and write an addition and a multiplication sentence.

1. 2 groups of 6   2. 3 groups of 9   3. 4 groups of 10

4.	5.	6.	7.	8.
$\begin{array}{r} 5 \\ \times 8 \end{array}$	$\begin{array}{r} 6 \\ \times 5 \end{array}$	$\begin{array}{r} 3 \\ \times 2 \end{array}$	$\begin{array}{r} 9 \\ \times 5 \end{array}$	$\begin{array}{r} 2 \\ \times 7 \end{array}$

Problem Solving WORKSHOP

Explore as a Team

1. Use grid paper to cut out rectangles. *Rule:* Each rectangle must have at least two rows.

2. Can you make rectangles with these numbers of squares?

8 15 11 20 12
7 10 16 30 9

3. Write number sentences for the rectangles you were able to make.

Number-Sense Project

Look back at pages 184-185. Light bulbs come in 2-packs and 4-packs. Suppose you bought 3 of each size package. Then you used 1 light bulb from each package.

1. How many bulbs are left in each package now?

2. How could you use addition to find out how many bulbs are left?

3. How can you use addition and multiplication to find out how many bulbs are left?

Real-Life Decision Making

Your family has many huge baskets full of nuts. You need to put the nuts in bags. Your mother wants about 40 nuts in each bag.

1. You can usually pick up 5 nuts in one handful. How can you use your handfuls to fill each bag with about 40 nuts?

2. What other ways are there to fill the bags with about 40 nuts without counting each nut?

Explore With a Computer

Use the *Number Sense Workshop Project* for this activity.

1. Suppose you are planning a seating arrangement. You have 4 rows and 8 chairs in each row. Make an array to show the chairs in the pattern.

2. In what other pattern can you arrange the same number of chairs to have equal numbers of chairs in each row? Try your plan on the computer.

Draw a Picture

Build Understanding

For Me and For You

There is 1 on the table
And 6 on the floor,
3 on each chair,
Of which there are 4;

5 under the blanket
With 9 more on top.
I know I counted 7
Behind the dust mop.

And in each drawer
of the chest having 2,
There were 8 of them hiding
From me and from you.

Christine Rakow

PROBLEM SOLVING GUIDE

Understand
QUESTION
FACTS
KEY IDEA

Plan and Solve
STRATEGY
ANSWER

Look Back
SENSIBLE ANSWER
ALTERNATE APPROACH

How many things are mentioned in the *first stanza* of the poem?

Understand   Things are on the table, the floor, and on 4 chairs.

Plan and Solve   STRATEGY   Draw a picture of a table, the floor, and 4 chairs. Draw the number of things on each.

Count how many things in all.

ANSWER   There are 19 things in the first stanza.

Look Back   You could use multiplication to find the number of things on the chairs. Then add that answer to the number of things on the floor and table.

■ **Talk About Math**   What do you think the things are? How many things would there be if there were 5 chairs?

Check Understanding

To solve the problem, answer Questions 1-3.
Draw a picture to help you.

How many things are in the chest of drawers?

1. How many drawers are in the chest?

2. How many things are in each drawer?

3. How many things are in the chest of drawers?

4. How many things would there be if there were 5 drawers in the chest?

Practice

Solve each problem. Draw a picture to help you.

5. How many things are mentioned in the second stanza?

6. How many things are mentioned in the entire poem?

7. If they shared them evenly, how many things would each person get?

8. If the things are pennies, how many nickels would they be worth?

Choose a _____ Strategy

Too Many Cycles

9. There are 7 children. Each child has either a bicycle or a tricycle. In all, there are 17 wheels. How many bicycles and how many tricycles are there?

PROBLEM SOLVING STRATEGIES

Choose an Operation
Find a Pattern
Use Logical Reasoning
Make a Table
Draw a Picture

Threes: Adding to a Known Fact

Build Understanding

If 8 carrot sticks are put in each lunch, how many are needed for 3 lunches?

You know that 2 × 8 will tell you how many carrot sticks are needed for 2 lunches. For 3 lunches, add another set of 8 sticks.

A balanced diet includes 4 servings of fruits and vegetables each day.

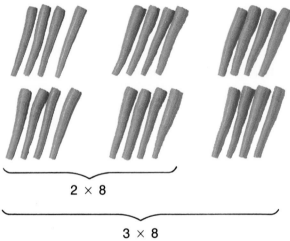
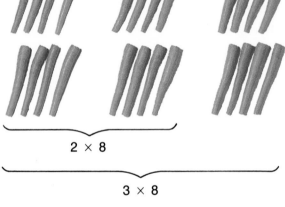

2 × 8

3 × 8

3 × 8 = 24

You need 24 carrot sticks for 3 lunches.

■ **Write About Math** Explain how 8 lunches with 3 carrot sticks is related to the example.

Check Understanding

For another example, see Set F, pages 212–213.

1. Draw an array for each fact. Find each answer.

2	3	4	5	6	7	8	9
×3	×3	×3	×3	×3	×3	×3	×3

Number Sense How much more is

2. 3 × 9 than 2 × 9?   **3.** 3 × 9 than 3 × 8?   **4.** 4 × 3 than 4 × 2?

Practice

For More Practice, see Set F, pages 214–215.

Find each answer.

5. 6 ×3	**6.** 8 ×3	**7.** 3 ×2	**8.** 9 ×3	**9.** 3 ×5	**10.** 3 ×3

11. 3 × 5   **12.** 3 × 7   **13.** 6 × 3   **14.** 8 × 3   **15.** 3 × 9

16. 3 × 2   **17.** 3 × 4   **18.** 7 × 3   **19.** 3 × 3   **20.** 9 × 3

Calculator If 3 × 5 = 15, how much is

21. 3 × 50?   **22.** 3 × 500?   **23.** 3 × 5,000?

Problem Solving

Number Sense Solve each problem.

24. Is 2 × 14 more or less than 3 × 14?

25. How much more is 3 × 100 than 2 × 100?

Reading ——— Math

Vocabulary
1. What do *trio, triplet, tricycle, triangle,* and *triple* mean?

2. What do these words have in common?

3. What is the meaning of *tricolor?*

4. Name something that is tricolor.

Fours: Doubling a Known Fact

Build Understanding

How many shapes are there in all?

You can double a twos fact to help you multiply by 4.

There are 2 groups of 6 squares. $2 \times 6 = 12$

There are 2 groups of 6 circles. $2 \times 6 = 12$

So 4 groups of 6 shapes is the same as 2×6 plus 2×6.

$$4 \times 6 = 24$$

Factors ↑ ↑   ↑ Product

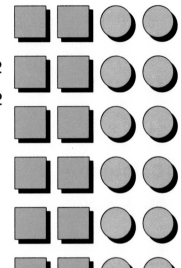

■ **Write About Math**   What fact could you double to find 4×8?

Check Understanding

For another example, see Set G, pages 212–213.

1. For each fact, draw an array and write the answer.

2	3	4	5	6	7	8	9
×4	×4	×4	×4	×4	×4	×4	×4

What fact could you double to find the products?

2. ☆ ☆ ☆ ☆ ☆ ☆ ☆
☆ ☆ ☆ ☆ ☆ ☆ ☆
☆ ☆ ☆ ☆ ☆ ☆ ☆
☆ ☆ ☆ ☆ ☆ ☆ ☆

3. △△△△△△△△
△△△△△△△△
▢▢▢▢▢▢▢▢
▢▢▢▢▢▢▢▢

Practice

For More Practice, see Set G, pages 214–215.

Find each product.

4. 6 ×4	5. 4 ×3	6. 4 ×8	7. 5 ×4	8. 2 ×4	9. 4 ×4

10. 5 × 4   **11.** 7 × 4   **12.** 4 × 3   **13.** 8 × 4   **14.** 2 × 4

15. 9 × 4   **16.** 4 × 7   **17.** 6 × 4   **18.** 4 × 9   **19.** 4 × 4

Find the missing factor.

20. 4 × ▦ = 8   **21.** 4 × ▦ = 16   **22.** ▦ × 4 = 28

Mental Math   Find each answer.

23. 18 − 9   **24.** 10 + 10   **25.** 4 × 7   **26.** 7 − 2   **27.** 3 × 5

28. 4 + 6   **29.** 8 − 5   **30.** 2 × 8   **31.** 7 + 8   **32.** 3 × 9

Problem Solving

Solve each problem.

33. A room has 7 tables. At each table there are 4 chairs. How many chairs are there in all?

34. There are 9 calculators. If 4 are being used, how many are not being used?

Explore ———— Math

You know that 4 × 6 is the same as 2 × 6 plus 2 × 6.
Write each exercise by doubling a twos fact.
35. Exercise 8   **36.** Exercise 9   **37.** Exercise 12

38. Why can you say that 2 × 2 × 6 is the same as 4 × 6?

Too Much Information

Build Understanding

How many nature trails are in
the River City Park System?

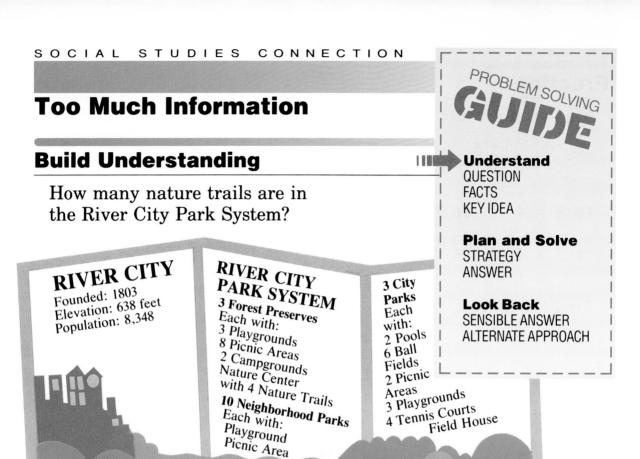

RIVER CITY
Founded: 1803
Elevation: 638 feet
Population: 8,348

**RIVER CITY
PARK SYSTEM**
3 Forest Preserves
Each with:
3 Playgrounds
8 Picnic Areas
2 Campgrounds
Nature Center
with 4 Nature Trails
10 Neighborhood Parks
Each with:
Playground
Picnic Area

**3 City
Parks**
Each
with:
2 Pools
6 Ball
Fields
2 Picnic
Areas
3 Playgrounds
4 Tennis Courts
Field House

PROBLEM SOLVING
GUIDE

Understand
QUESTION
FACTS
KEY IDEA

Plan and Solve
STRATEGY
ANSWER

Look Back
SENSIBLE ANSWER
ALTERNATE APPROACH

Understand   QUESTION   How many nature trails are there?

FACTS   You don't need to use all the
information given. Look for nature trails under
each type of park. There are 4 trails in each of
3 forest preserves.

KEY IDEA   Since the same number of trails are
in each preserve, you can multiply.

**Plan
and Solve** $3 \times 4 = 12$

River City has 12 nature trails.

Look Back   Make sure you have used all the information
you need.

■ **Write About Math** Draw a picture to show all the different areas one city park has.

Check Understanding

Solve the problem by answering Questions 1–4.

How many playgrounds are in the park system?

1. How many playgrounds are in each forest preserve? How many are in all the forest preserves?

2. How many playgrounds are in each neighborhood park? How many are in all the neighborhood parks?

3. How many playgrounds are in each city park? How many are in all the city parks?

4. How many playgrounds are in the entire River City park system?

Practice

Use the chart on page 206 to solve each problem.

5. How many different types of parks are in the park system?

6. How many ball fields are in the park system?

7. River City had 317 settlers when it was founded. How many more people live in River City now?

8. Are there more nature centers or more field houses in the park system? How many more?

 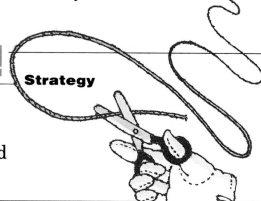

Choose a Strategy

No Strings Attached!
9. To cut a string into 8 pieces, how many cuts would you need to make?

Zero and One in Multiplication

Build Understanding

A. At the pet shop, Charlie put out 5 empty fish bowls. How many fish are there in all?

5 groups of 0

$0 + 0 + 0 + 0 + 0 = 0$

$5 \times 0 = 0$

There are 0 fish.

B. Charlie put 1 fish in each bowl. How many fish are there in all?

5 groups of 1

$1 + 1 + 1 + 1 + 1 = 5$

$5 \times 1 = 5$

There are 5 fish.

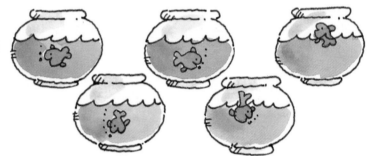

■ **Talk About Math** Charlie put a second fish in each bowl. Draw a picture to show how many fish in all. Write an addition and multiplication sentence for the picture.

Check Understanding

For another example, see Set H, pages 212–213.

1. **Number Sense** Copy the multiplication sentence at the right. Replace the ☿ with a number between 0 and 15.

$$☿ \times 0 = ▦$$

2. Find the product.

3. Try it three more times with different numbers.

4. What can you say about multiplying any number by 0?

5. Repeat Exercises 1–3 with this number sentence.

$$\text{❄} \times 1 = \text{❑}$$

6. What can you say about multiplying any number by 1?

Practice

For More Practice, see Set H, pages 214–215.

Find each product.

7. $\begin{array}{r} 0 \\ \times 5 \\ \hline \end{array}$	**8.** $\begin{array}{r} 0 \\ \times 1 \\ \hline \end{array}$	**9.** $\begin{array}{r} 1 \\ \times 7 \\ \hline \end{array}$	**10.** $\begin{array}{r} 5 \\ \times 0 \\ \hline \end{array}$	**11.** $\begin{array}{r} 1 \\ \times 3 \\ \hline \end{array}$	**12.** $\begin{array}{r} 2 \\ \times 0 \\ \hline \end{array}$
13. $\begin{array}{r} 6 \\ \times 0 \\ \hline \end{array}$	**14.** $\begin{array}{r} 0 \\ \times 0 \\ \hline \end{array}$	**15.** $\begin{array}{r} 1 \\ \times 8 \\ \hline \end{array}$	**16.** $\begin{array}{r} 6 \\ \times 1 \\ \hline \end{array}$	**17.** $\begin{array}{r} 8 \\ \times 0 \\ \hline \end{array}$	**18.** $\begin{array}{r} 1 \\ \times 5 \\ \hline \end{array}$

19. 0×7 **20.** 9×1 **21.** 9×0 **22.** 1×7 **23.** 1×1

24. 2×1 **25.** 79×1 **26.** 1×45 **27.** 0×82 **28.** 36×0

Problem Solving

Write a multiplication sentence for each problem. Then solve it.

Shari had 3 bowls with 5 fish in each bowl.

29. Shari sold 1 bowl of fish. How many fish are left?

30. Shari sold another bowl of fish. How many fish are left?

31. Shari sold the last bowl of fish. How many fish are left?

32. **Use Data** Tell the number of playgrounds in the neighborhood parks in River City. Use the data found on page 206.

Solve each problem.

1. As the holiday shop opened for business, 7 customers arrived. In the next 30 minutes, 2 more customers came in, 5 went out, 4 came in, 3 went out, 6 came in, 1 came in, and 5 went out. How many customers are in the store now?

2. What number am I? I am more than 2 fives and less than 4 threes.

3. In the next game, Nella scored 10,000 points more than her previous high. Is that enough to pass Steve's high score?

Flight Patrol high scores	
Jose G.	114,000
Steve P.	105,000
Nella A.	96,000

4. How many different shapes are there having an area of 3 square units and a perimeter of 8 units? Sketch them.

5. Eight groups of 5 tourists fit on a trolley ride at an amusement park. How many people will fit into 2 trolleys?

6. It is 10:45. The next show starts at 11:20. It takes 25 minutes to get to the theater. Tania will be ready in 5 minutes. Will she get to the theater in time?

7. **Data File** Use data from pages 248-249. What time should Marta catch the bus at the Highland stop in order to arrive in Chicago at 7:51 A.M.?

8. **Make a Data File** Record the prices of 5 different brands of cold cereal. Use the same size of box for all brands. Order the prices from least to greatest.

Problem Solving REVIEW

Explore with a Calculator

These are 4 hands in a game of "Math Matchup." The
object of the game is to get matching sets of 3 cards.
The first player to get 2 matching sets wins.

Find the cards that match.

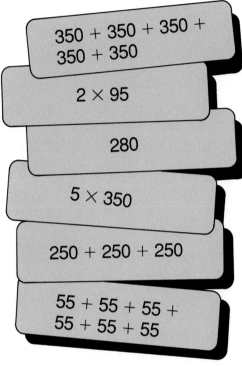

350 + 350 + 350 + 350 + 350

2 × 95

280

5 × 350

250 + 250 + 250

55 + 55 + 55 + 55 + 55 + 55

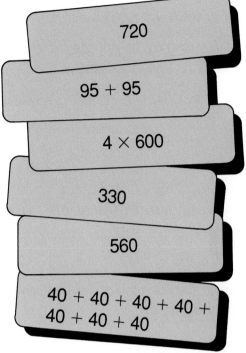

720

95 + 95

4 × 600

330

560

40 + 40 + 40 + 40 + 40 + 40 + 40

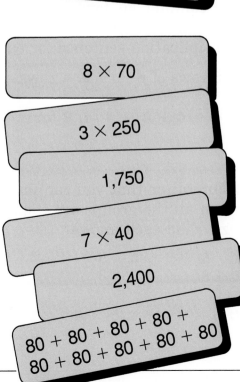

8 × 70

3 × 250

1,750

7 × 40

2,400

80 + 80 + 80 + 80 + 80 + 80 + 80 + 80 + 80 + 80

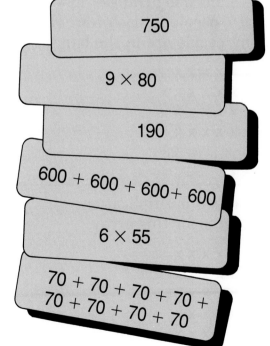

750

9 × 80

190

600 + 600 + 600 + 600

6 × 55

70 + 70 + 70 + 70 + 70 + 70 + 70 + 70

Reteaching

Set A   pages 186–187

Each table at the picnic has room for 8 people. How many people can sit at 5 tables?

Add the number of people at each table to find the number in all.

8 + 8 + 8 + 8 + 8 = 40

Remember that counting by twos is the same as adding twos, counting by threes is the same as adding threes, and so on.
Tell how many.

1. 3 + 3 + 3 + 3 + 3   **2.** 4 + 4 + 4

Set B   pages 188–191

There are 3 cartons of eggs. Each carton has 12 eggs. Write an addition and a multiplication sentence to show this.

12 + 12 + 12 = 36   3 × 12 = 36

Remember that multiplication is repeated addition.

Write an addition and a multiplication sentence for each.

1. 6 cases each with 8 cans

2. 7 boxes each with 4 bulbs

3. 4 shelves each with 10 books

Set C   pages 192–193

The band was arranged in 4 rows with 7 people in each row. How many people are in the band?

x x x x x x x
x x x x x x x
x x x x x x x
x x x x x x x
4 × 7 = 28

Remember that rows go across and columns go down.
Make an array and write a multiplication sentence for each.

1. 5 rows of 6   **2.** 4 rows of 9

3. 4 + 4 + 4 + 4   **4.** 8 fours

Set D   pages 194–195

Write two multiplication sentences for this array.

x x x x x x
x x x x x x
x x x x x x
x x x x x x
x x x x x x
5 × 6 = 30   6 × 5 = 30

Remember that you can multiply when all the groups are the same size. Find each answer.

1.   5
     ×8

2.   5
     ×3

3.   9
     ×5

4. 5 × 4   **5.** 5 × 2   **6.** 7 × 5

Set E   pages 196–197

Children's tickets cost $8. Adult tickets cost *double* that amount. How much do adults pay?

$$2 \times 8 = 16$$

An adult ticket costs $16.

Remember that doubling a number means multiplying by 2. Find each answer.

1. 2	**2.** 6	**3.** 7	**4.** 2
$\times 5$	$\times 2$	$\times 2$	$\times 9$

Set F   pages 202–203

If you eat 3 meals a day, how many meals do you eat in 7 days?

xxx xxx xxx xxx xxx xxx xxx

There are 7 groups of 3.

$$7 \times 3 = 21$$

You eat 21 meals in 7 days.

Remember that multiplying a number by 3 means adding the same number 3 times. Find each answer.

1. 3	**2.** 7	**3.** 3	**4.** 3
$\times 4$	$\times 3$	$\times 2$	$\times 8$

Set G   pages 204–205

How many shapes are there in all?

△ △ △ △ △   △ △ △ △ △
△ △ △ △ △   △ △ △ △ △

4 groups of 5 shapes is the same as 2 × 5 plus 2 × 5.
  $$4 \times 5 = 20.$$

Remember that the numbers you multiply are called factors. The answer is called the product.

Find each product.

1. 4	**2.** 4	**3.** 9	**4.** 8
$\times 6$	$\times 7$	$\times 4$	$\times 4$

Set H   pages 208–209

Children can go to the concert free. Adult tickets cost $1. How much does it cost for 4 children?

$$0 + 0 + 0 + 0 = 0 \qquad 4 \times 0 = 0$$

The cost is 0.

How much does it cost for 4 adults?

$$1 + 1 + 1 + 1 = 4 \qquad 4 \times 1 = 4$$

It costs $4 for 4 adults.

Remember that if a factor is 0, the product is 0. If a factor is 1, the product is the other factor. Find each product.

1. 1	**2.** 7	**3.** 0
$\times 0$	$\times 1$	$\times 2$

4. 3×1 **5.** 0×6 **6.** 1×5

213

More Practice

Set A pages 186–187

Tell how many.

1. 4 + 4 + 4 + 4   **2.** 5 + 5 + 5 + 5 + 5   **3.** 7 + 7 + 7 + 7 + 7

4. 10 + 10   **5.** 9 + 9 + 9 + 9   **6.** 100 + 100 + 100

Mixed Practice Tell which is greater.

7. 9 − 3 or 4 + 4   **8.** 7 + 4 or 6 + 6   **9.** 60 or 25 + 25

Set B pages 188–191

Write an addition and a multiplication
sentence for each exercise.

1.

2.
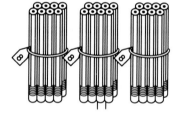

3. 6 bags each with 4 balls   **4.** 5 shelves each with 5 toy cars

5. 4 boxes each with 8 baseball
bats

6. 3 bags each with 200 marbles

Estimation Use what you know about
estimating sums to estimate in
multiplication. Estimate each answer.

7. 47 + 47 + 47   **8.** 4 × 19   **9.** 96 + 96 + 96

10. 95 × 3   **11.** 209 + 209   **12.** 5 × 11

Set C pages 192–193

Make an array and write a
multiplication sentence for each.

1. 4 rows of 9   **2.** 5 + 5 + 5   **3.** 4 sevens   **4.** 5 rows of 6

5. 8 + 8 + 8   **6.** 4 rows of 2   **7.** 6 fours   **8.** 7 + 7

Set D   pages 194–195

Find each answer.

1. 7   **2.** 5   **3.** 8   **4.** 3 × 5   **5.** 6 × 5
  ×5   ×9   ×5

Mixed Practice   Use paper and pencil or mental math
to find each answer. Tell which method you used.

6. 7,386 − 300   **7.** 5 × 5   8. 2,083 + 918   **9.** 8 × 5

Set E   pages 196–197

Find each answer.

1. 2   **2.** 8   **3.** 4   **4.** 7 × 2   **5.** 2 × 5
  ×9   ×2   ×2

Set F   pages 202–203

Find each answer.

1. 1   **2.** 3   **3.** 3   **4.** 4 × 3   **5.** 5 × 3
  ×3   ×2   ×3

6. Number Sense   What pattern do you see in the answers to
  Exercises 1–5?

Set G   pages 204–205

Find each product.

1. 4   **2.** 7   **3.** 8   **4.** 4 × 2   **5.** 4 × 6
  ×5   ×4   ×4

Mental Math   Find each answer mentally.

6. 16 − 8   **7.** 9 + 9   **8.** 3 × 7   **9.** 8 − 2   **10.** 5 × 2

11. 3 + 7   **12.** 9 − 4   **13.** 2 × 9   **14.** 6 + 5   **15.** 8 × 3

Set H   pages 208–209

Find each product.

1. 3   **2.** 4   **3.** 4   **4.** 2 × 1   **5.** 8 × 0
  ×0   ×1   ×0

215

Enrichment

Primes and Composites

Only one rectangle can be made with a **prime** number of blocks.

2 is a prime number.   5 is a prime number.

More than one rectangle can be made with a **composite** number of blocks.

4 is a composite number.   12 is a composite number.

 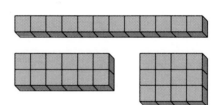

Make as many rectangles as you can for each number. Then copy and complete the chart.

Number	Can you make more than 1 rectangle?	How many rectangles?	Prime or Composite?
1	1 is a special number.		Neither
2	**1.**	**2.**	**3.**
3	**4.**	**5.**	**6.**
9	**7.**	**8.**	**9.**
10	**10.**	**11.**	**12.**
11	**13.**	**14.**	**15.**
15	**16.**	**17.**	**18.**
17	**19.**	**20.**	**21.**
18	**22.**	**23.**	**24.**

Chapter 6 Review/Test

1. Write an addition sentence for this picture.

Write an addition and a multiplication sentence for each picture.

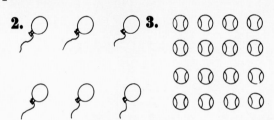

Write each product.

4. $\begin{array}{r} 3 \\ \times 5 \\ \hline \end{array}$	**5.** $\begin{array}{r} 5 \\ \times 2 \\ \hline \end{array}$	**6.** $\begin{array}{r} 2 \\ \times 6 \\ \hline \end{array}$
7. $\begin{array}{r} 7 \\ \times 2 \\ \hline \end{array}$	**8.** $\begin{array}{r} 4 \\ \times 3 \\ \hline \end{array}$	**9.** $\begin{array}{r} 3 \\ \times 7 \\ \hline \end{array}$
10. $\begin{array}{r} 5 \\ \times 4 \\ \hline \end{array}$	**11.** $\begin{array}{r} 4 \\ \times 7 \\ \hline \end{array}$	**12.** $\begin{array}{r} 8 \\ \times 1 \\ \hline \end{array}$
13. $\begin{array}{r} 1 \\ \times 9 \\ \hline \end{array}$	**14.** $\begin{array}{r} 5 \\ \times 0 \\ \hline \end{array}$	**15.** $\begin{array}{r} 0 \\ \times 2 \\ \hline \end{array}$

16. Which picture can help you find the product for 3 times 4?

a. ★ ★ ★ ★
★ ★ ★ ★

b. ★ ★ ★
★ ★ ★

c. ★ ★ ★
★ ★ ★
★ ★ ★

d. ★ ★ ★ ★
★ ★ ★ ★
★ ★ ★ ★

17. Ramon's aquarium has 2 starfish and 6 guppies. Each starfish has 5 arms. How many arms are there in all?

Read this problem. Then answer the question below.

An ice-cream truck has 4 wheels. If 3 trucks and 4 dogs pass by Jan's house, how many wheels are there in all?

18. Which information is *not* needed to solve the problem?
a. 4 wheels
b. 3 trucks
c. 4 dogs

19. ■ **Write About Math** For the picture you chose in Exercise 16, write a sentence telling how many groups there are and the number in each group.

Multiplication Facts

7

Did You Know:
It is estimated that twins occur once in every 89 births, triplets once in every 7,900 births, quadruplets once in every 705,000 births, and quintuplets once in every 85 million births.

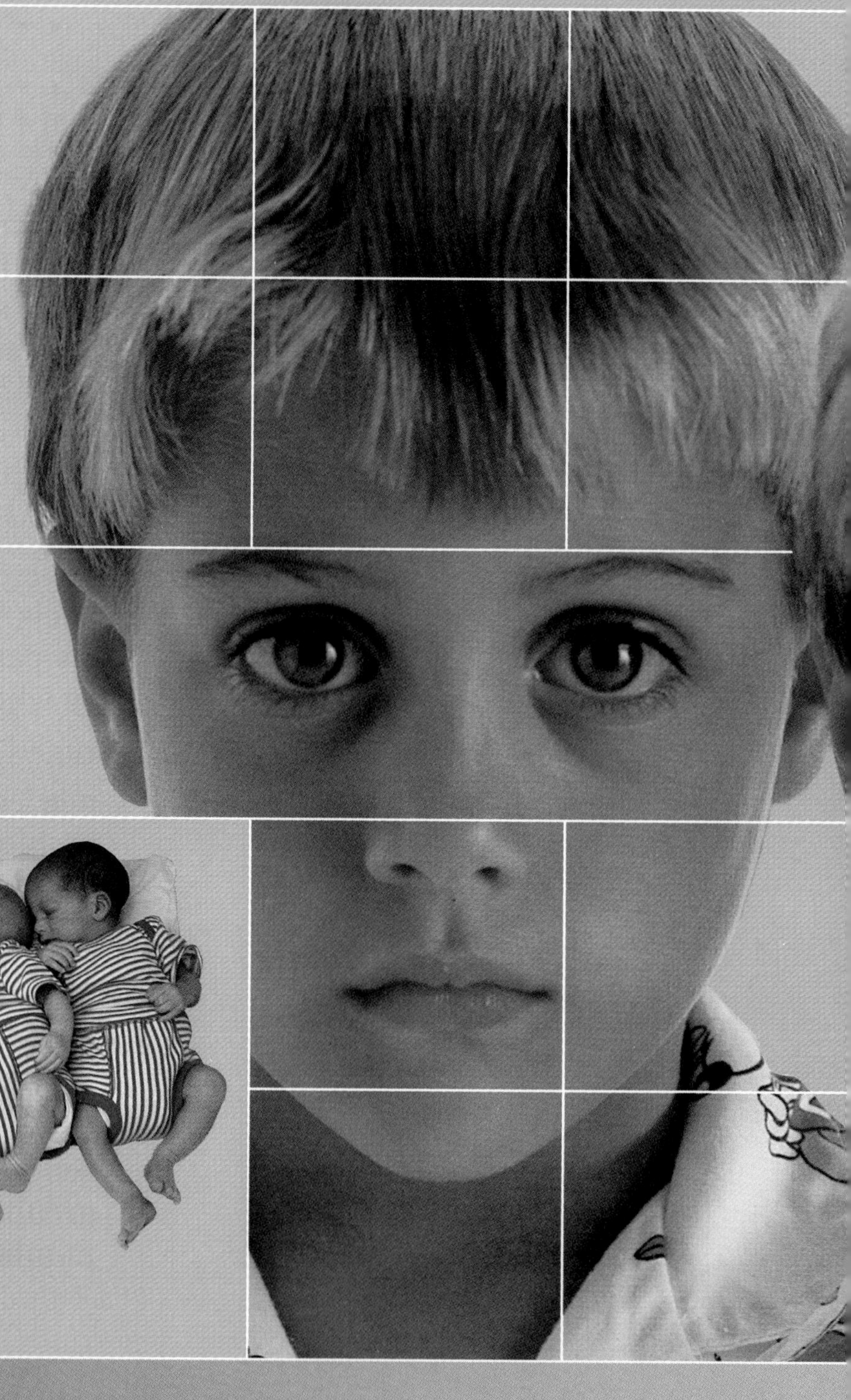

218

Number-Sense Project

Estimate
Predict how many students in your class have a parent or grandparent who was born as part of a set of twins, quadruplets, or quintuplets.

Gather Data
Find out whether any of your parents or grandparents were part of a set of twins, quadruplets, or quintuplets. Ask an older person in your family, such as a parent or grandparent.

Analyze and Report
Write a summary of the information you collected. Share your findings with other classmates.

Using Order to Multiply with 6 Through 9

Build Understanding

A.

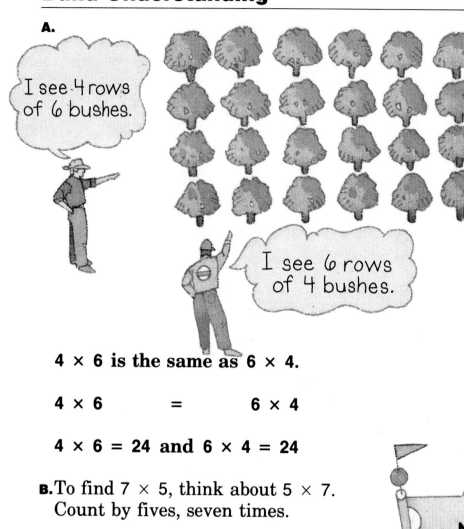

I see 4 rows of 6 bushes.

There are 24 bushes in all.

I see 6 rows of 4 bushes.

4 × 6 is the same as 6 × 4.

4 × 6   =   6 × 4

4 × 6 = 24 and 6 × 4 = 24

B. To find 7 × 5, think about 5 × 7. Count by fives, seven times.

5,   10,   15,   20,   25,   30,   35
 1   2   3   4   5   6   7

5 × 7 = 35 and 7 × 5 = 35

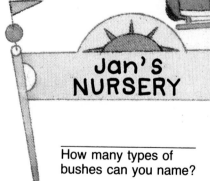

Jan's NURSERY

How many types of bushes can you name?

■ **Talk About Math** You can reverse the order of the numbers when you multiply. Can you do that when you add? When you subtract? Use examples to help explain.

220

Check Understanding

For another example, see Set A, pages 242–243.

Write two ways to find each product.

1. 8×2 **2.** 9×3 **3.** 7×4 **4.** 6×5 **5.** 5×8

6. Number Sense Use repeated addition to find 12×3. Is it easier to add twelve 3s or three 12s?

Practice

For More Practice, see Set A, pages 244–245.

Find each product. Use the order property to help you.

7.
$$\begin{array}{r} 8 \\ \times 4 \\ \hline \end{array}$$
8.
$$\begin{array}{r} 9 \\ \times 3 \\ \hline \end{array}$$
9.
$$\begin{array}{r} 6 \\ \times 5 \\ \hline \end{array}$$
10.
$$\begin{array}{r} 2 \\ \times 8 \\ \hline \end{array}$$
11.
$$\begin{array}{r} 5 \\ \times 7 \\ \hline \end{array}$$
12.
$$\begin{array}{r} 9 \\ \times 2 \\ \hline \end{array}$$

13. 3×6 **14.** 4×7 **15.** 7×3 **16.** 8×5 **17.** 5×9

18. 7×2 **19.** 9×4 **20.** 4×6 **21.** 3×8 **22.** 14×3

Mental Math Find each answer.

23. $15 - 6$ **24.** 5×8 **25.** $9 + 7$ **26.** 4×5 **27.** $16 - 9$

28. $7 + 7$ **29.** 3×9 **30.** $14 - 6$ **31.** 4×4 **32.** $7 + 8$

Problem Solving

Solve each problem.

33. The workers planted 3 rows of 6 daisies. How many daisies did they plant?

34. They planted 9 oak and 4 maple trees. How many trees did they plant?

35. There is a square foot of land for every bedding plant. How many square feet is the area for 5 rows of 8 plants?

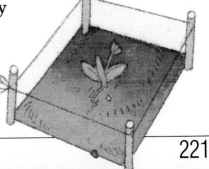

Multiplication with 6 Through 9 on the Number Line

Build Understanding

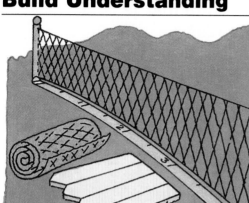

Custom-Designed Fences

Fence Type	Section Lengths
light iron	8 feet
redwood slat	7 feet
stockade	9 feet
heavy iron	6 feet
split rail	10 feet
picket	5 feet

How long is a fence with 5 sections of light iron?

$$5 \times 8 = 40$$

— number of feet

— number of sections

A fence with 5 sections of light iron is 40 feet long.

■ **Talk About Math** A section of stockade fence is 6 feet high and 9 feet long. Which of the two measures should you use to find how much fencing you need to go around your yard?

Check Understanding

For another example, see Set B, pages 242–243.

1. What is the length of 3 sections of redwood slat fencing?

2. Some *multiples* of 6 are 6, 12, 18, 24, and 30. Give 3 more multiples of 6.

Practice

For More Practice, see Set B, pages 244–245.

Find each product. **Remember** to use a number line if you need it.

3. 4 ×8	**4.** 7 ×3	**5.** 2 ×6	**6.** 8 ×3	**7.** 3 ×9	**8.** 6 ×5
9. 5 ×8	**10.** 9 ×2	**11.** 6 ×3	**12.** 9 ×4	**13.** 7 ×5	**14.** 8 ×2

15. 4 × 7   **16.** 6 × 4   **17.** 9 × 5   **18.** 7 × 2   **19.** 3 × 9

Problem Solving

Use the chart on page 222 to solve each problem.

20. How long is a fence with 9 sections of picket boards?

21. How long is a fence with 4 sections of redwood slats?

22. One section of each type of fence is displayed along a wall. How long is the display?

23. The perimeter of a yard is 72 feet. Leaving a 6-foot opening, how much fencing will be needed?

24. How many section lengths of split rail fencing do you need to go around a yard with a perimeter of 80 feet?

25. **Critical Thinking** Would you need more sections of light iron or heavy iron fencing for a fence of 60 feet? Explain.

Skills _____ Review   pages 132–133

Use a calculator, paper and pencil, or mental math to find each answer. Tell which method you used.

1. 745 − 133   **2.** 62 − 42   **3.** 704 − 128   **4.** 5,642 − 1,764

5. 4,200 − 382   **6.** 15 − 9   **7.** 794 − 500   **8.** 682 − 349

Choose an Operation

Build Understanding

The Frisbee Club sold Frisbees for $1.00.
The amounts collected by the members
on Tuesday are shown on the Frisbees
below. How much did the boys in the
club collect?

PROBLEM SOLVING
GUIDE

Understand
QUESTION
FACTS
KEY IDEA

IIII➤ **Plan and Solve**
STRATEGY
ANSWER

Look Back
SENSIBLE ANSWER
ALTERNATE APPROACH

Understand There are 3 boys. Each collected $8.

IIII➤ **Plan and Solve** STRATEGY Choose an operation. Since each boy
collected the same amount of money, you can use
multiplication to find the answer.

3 × 8 = 24

ANSWER The boys collected $24 dollars.

Look Back Since multiplication is repeated addition, you could
use addition to find the answer. 8 + 8 + 8 = 24

■ **Write About Math** Use the information in the
picture to write a problem that could be solved by
using subtraction.

Check Understanding

Use the picture on page 224. Tell whether you *add*, *subtract*, or *multiply*. Then find each answer.

1. How much did Kimi and Dina collect?

2. How much more did Maria collect than José?

3. Estimation   Tell how you could estimate the total amount collected on Tuesday.

Practice

	Ben	Dina	Kimi	Hank	Jose	Maria	**Total**
Monday	$0	$3	$9	$2	$10	$1	▦
Tuesday	$8	$8	$9	$8	$8	$10	$51
Wednesday	$3	$5	$9	$0	$15	$6	$38
Total	$11	$16	▦	$10	$33	$17	▦

Use the chart to solve each problem. Tell whether you *add, subtract,* or *multiply*. Then find each answer.

4. How much did Kimi collect in all?

5. How much was collected on Monday?

6. How much more did José collect on Wednesday than on Tuesday?

7. How much more was collected on Tuesday than on Monday?

Choose a _____ Strategy

What's the Difference?
8. Find two digits with a sum of 9, a product of 8, and a difference of 7.

Square Products

Build Understanding

Shapely Numbers
Materials: Objects of same size, 10 × 10 grid paper
Groups: 3–5 students

A. Have you ever made designs using colored disks?

Billy was using disks to make different designs. Some designs formed squares. He noticed a pattern.

There are some numbers that are called *square products.* Can you tell why?

a. Look at the arrays Billy made. Write a multiplication fact for each.

b. Make arrays to show 6 × 6, 7 × 7, 8 × 8, and 9 × 9. What are the products?

c. What shape is formed by each of the arrays?

d. Make arrays to show 6 × 5, 7 × 4, and 3 × 8. What are the products?

e. What shape is formed by these new arrays?

B. Using 36 objects, make as many different arrays as you can. Write the multiplication fact for each.

■ **Talk About Math** In Example B, which factors make squares? Which make rectangles?

Check Understanding

For another example, see Set C, pages 242–243.

1. List the square products for the factors 0 through 9.

2. Number Sense You know that $4 \times 8 = 32$. How can you use this to help you find 8×8?

Practice

For More Practice, see Set C, pages 244–245.

Find each product.

3.	**4.**	**5.**	**6.**	**7.**	**8.**
4	8	3	7	6	9
$\times 4$	$\times 8$	$\times 3$	$\times 7$	$\times 6$	$\times 9$

9. 2×2 **10.** 0×0 **11.** 5×5 **12.** 1×1 **13.** 10×10

14. 8×8 **15.** 3×3 **16.** 9×9 **17.** 6×6 **18.** 7×7

Problem Solving

Make or draw arrays to help you solve this problem.

19. Critical Thinking Write the next two numbers in this pattern.   2   4   8   16   32   ▦   ▦

Midchapter ———— Checkup

Find each product.

1. 4×8 **2.** 9×9 **3.** 9×5 **4.** 6×6 **5.** 3×8

6. 4×9 **7.** 5×6 **8.** 3×7 **9.** 7×7 **10.** 8×8

Tell whether you *add, subtract,* or *multiply.*

11. There are 25, 13, and 37 cards in boxes. How many cards are there in all?

12. Kiri tiled a floor. She used 8 tiles in each of 8 rows. How many tiles did she use?

Visual-Thinking Activity

Which photo did Natalia take?

a.

b.

c.

Problem Solving WORKSHOP

1. Use grid paper to draw a secret rectangle. Make each side between 2 and 9 squares long.

2. Cover a part of your rectangle with another piece of paper, hiding parts of two sides of your rectangle.

3. Take turns showing the uncovered part of your rectangles to the rest of your team. Then they can try to figure out how many squares are in the whole rectangle.

Explore as a Team

TIPS FOR **WORKING TOGETHER**
When you are unsure, ask someone in your group for help or say you don't understand.

Explore with a Computer

For this activity use the *Geometry Workshop Project.*

1. Use the **Measure** menu to find the perimeter and area of the rectangle.

2. Use the **Stretch** option to make a different rectangle. Estimate the change in the perimeter and area. Then use the **Measure** menu to check your estimates.

3. Try to stretch the rectangle to make the number of units for the perimeter and the area the same.

Number-Sense Project

Mr. Wong gives each child in his class 8 sheets of colored paper. Does he need more for the Ruiz twins or for the McMahon triplets?

Using Tens to Multiply with 9

Build Understanding

Suki is giving each of her 9 friends paper and 7 stamps. How many stamps will she need to buy?

Since she plans to give each friend the same number of stamps, she could multiply.

Suki knows that 10 × 7 is 70.
So 9 × 7 is 7 less than 70.

70 − 7 = 63

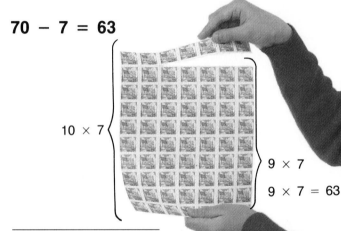

10 × 7

9 × 7

9 × 7 = 63

The Post Office sells over 30 billion stamps a year.

She will need to buy 63 stamps.

■ **Talk About Math** Tell how you can use tens to find 9 × 9.

Check Understanding

For another example, see Set D pages 242–243.

Mental Math Find each product.

1. How much less than 10 × 8 is 9 × 8? Find 9 × 8.

2. Complete: 6 × 10 = 60, so 6 × 9 = 60 − ▒. Find 6 × 9.

Practice

For More Practice, see Set D pages 244–245.

Find each product.

3. 9 $\times 2$	**4.** 7 $\times 9$	**5.** 9 $\times 6$	**6.** 9 $\times 9$	**7.** 5 $\times 9$	**8.** 9 $\times 8$

9. 3×9 **10.** 9×1 **11.** 7×9 **12.** 0×9 **13.** 9×9

14. 5×9 **15.** 9×8 **16.** 6×9 **17.** 9×2 **18.** 9×4

Mental Math   Find each answer.

19. $17 - 9$ **20.** 5×5 **21.** $9 + 6$ **22.** $4 + 8$ **23.** $11 - 3$

24. 4×7 **25.** 7×2 **26.** $12 - 6$ **27.** 3×9 **28.** $8 + 5$

Problem Solving

Draw a picture to help you solve each problem.

29. Stamps usually come in a 10×10 sheet. How many stamps are in one sheet?

30. Marti has a 4×9 array of stamps and a 6×9 array. How many stamps does she have in all?

Visualize the problem in your mind to help you understand it better.

Explore _____ Math

31. Add the digits of each product. What do you notice?
$9 \times 5 = 45$ $9 \times 8 = 72$ $9 \times 4 = 36$

32. Are the results in Exercise 31 true for all the multiplication facts of 9? How is this information helpful?

The Last Three Facts:
6×7, 6×8, 7×8

Build Understanding

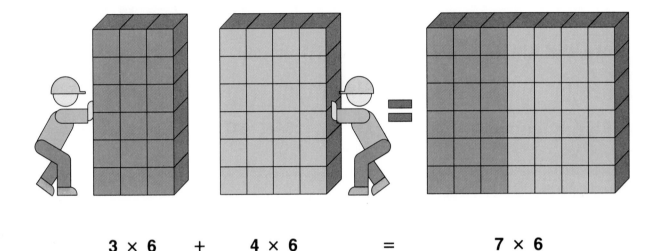

3×6	$+$	4×6	$=$	7×6
18	$+$	24	$=$	42

3 groups of 6 plus 4 groups of 6 is the same as 7 groups of 6.

$$7 \times 6 = 42$$

■ **Write About Math** Draw arrays to show two smaller facts that you could use to find 7×8.

Check Understanding

For another example, see Set E, pages 242–243.

Number Sense Answer each question.

1. Which is greater, 4×6 or 5×6? How much greater? Explain your thinking.

2. Which is less, 7×5 or 8×5? How much less? Explain your thinking.

3. Explain how to use 3×8 to find the answer to 6×8.

4. What fact could you find using 5×9 plus 4×9?

Practice

For More Practice, see Set E, pages 244–245.

Copy and complete each table.

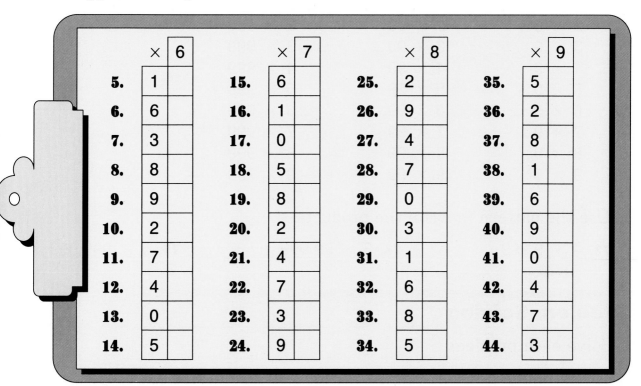

×	6		×	7		×	8		×	9
5. 1		**15.** 6		**25.** 2		**35.** 5	
6. 6		**16.** 1		**26.** 9		**36.** 2	
7. 3		**17.** 0		**27.** 4		**37.** 8	
8. 8		**18.** 5		**28.** 7		**38.** 1	
9. 9		**19.** 8		**29.** 0		**39.** 6	
10. 2		**20.** 2		**30.** 3		**40.** 9	
11. 7		**21.** 4		**31.** 1		**41.** 0	
12. 4		**22.** 7		**32.** 6		**42.** 4	
13. 0		**23.** 3		**33.** 8		**43.** 7	
14. 5		**24.** 9		**34.** 5		**44.** 3	

Complete each number sentence.

45. $6 \times \text{▦} = 42$ **46.** $\text{▦} \times 9 = 63$ **47.** $\text{▦} \times 8 = 48$

▮ Mixed Practice Use a calculator, paper and pencil, or mental math to find each answer. Tell which method you used.

48. 521
− 70

49. 48
−31

50. 7
×9

51. 231
+ 4,160

52. 9
×3

53. 6,007
− 985

54. 4
×4

55. 936
−846

56. 458
+ 31

57. 8
×6

58. 8×8

59. $975 - 620$

60. $16 - 7$

61. 6×7

62. 1×629

63. $27 - 17$

64. $86 + 5$

65. 0×248

66. $5 + 38$

67. 8×3

68. 36×1

69. $256 + 90$

▦ Calculator   Use your calculator to find each product. Then try to find the patterns in the products.

70. 1 × 9
  2 × 9
  3 × 9
  4 × 9
  5 × 9
  6 × 9
  7 × 9
  8 × 9
  9 × 9

71. 1 × 99
  2 × 99
  3 × 99
  4 × 99
  5 × 99
  6 × 99
  7 × 99
  8 × 99
  9 × 99

72. 1 × 999
  2 × 999
  3 × 999
  4 × 999
  5 × 999
  6 × 999
  7 × 999
  8 × 999
  9 × 999

Use the pattern to write the products.

73. 4 × 9,999

74. 3 × 99,999

75. 5 × 999,999

Problem Solving

Solve each problem.

76. While at camp, Arthur is reading a 360-page book. He has read 88 pages of the book. How many pages does he have left to read?

77. In a craft session, Carla made a button doll. She used 3 cards of buttons. Each card had 8 buttons. How many buttons did Carla use?

78. The chart shows the number of Calories in the breakfast foods served at camp. Jane had milk, cereal, and juice. How many Calories were in Jane's breakfast?

Food	Calories
milk	90
juice	85
toast	95
cereal	195
egg	125

79. Timmy, Mike, Yoshi, and Will are going to summer camp for 2 weeks. Each boy will bring 5 shirts to camp. How many shirts will the 4 friends bring to camp in all?

234

Use Data Use the chart on page 222 to solve this problem.

80. Carey bought 9 sections of redwood slat fencing and a 9-foot gate to put around his yard. What is the perimeter of the yard?

Choose a _____ Strategy

Bead Necklaces These necklaces are shaped like triangles. Answer the questions below to find how many beads will be on each side of the sixth necklace and how many beads there will be in the sixth necklace.

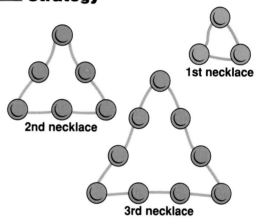

1st necklace

2nd necklace

3rd necklace

81. How many beads are on each side of the first necklace? the second necklace? the third necklace?

82. How many beads are in the first necklace? the second necklace? the third necklace?

83. Copy and complete the table to show your answers.

Necklace	1st	2nd	3rd
Number of beads on each side	2		
Total number of beads	3		

PROBLEM SOLVING
STRATEGIES

Choose an Operation
Find a Pattern
Use Logical Reasoning
Make a Table
Draw a Picture

84. How many beads are on each side of the sixth necklace? How many beads are in the sixth necklace?

Find a Pattern

Build Understanding

Lester found a pattern in the products for multiplication facts for 4. What pattern might he have found?

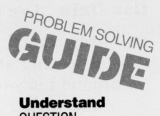
PROBLEM SOLVING GUIDE

Understand
QUESTION
FACTS
KEY IDEA

➤ **Plan and Solve**
STRATEGY
ANSWER

Look Back
SENSIBLE ANSWER
ALTERNATE APPROACH

Understand To help find the pattern, you could write the multiplication facts for 4.

1	2	3	4	5	6	7	8	9
×4	×4	×4	×4	×4	×4	×4	×4	×4
4	8	12	16	20	24	28	32	36

➤ **Plan and Solve** STRATEGY You need to use at least three of the products before you can see if there is a pattern. Look at the products.

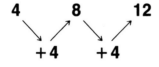

4   8   12   To get the second product, add 4.

+4   +4   To get the third product, add 4.

ANSWER The pattern is to add 4. Each number in the products for the multiplication facts for 4 is four more than the number before it.

Look Back Check to see if the pattern continues. Add 4 to each number. Do your answers match the products for the facts of 4?

■ **Talk About Math** In what other ways could you find patterns?

Check Understanding

Look at the ones digit for the products of the following pairs of facts for 4. What do you notice?

1. 1 × 4 and 6 × 4   **2.** 2 × 4 and 7 × 4   **3.** 3 × 4 and 8 × 4

4. Look at the ones digit for the product of 5 × 4. What should the ones digit for the product of 10 × 4 be?

5. What is the pattern made by the ones digits in the facts of 4?

Practice

Do Problems 6–8 to find patterns in the multiplication facts for 3, 6, and 8. (Do not use 0 as a factor.)

6. Write the multiplication facts for 3, 6, and 8 in order.

7. For each set of facts, add the digits in each product until you get a one-digit sum.

8. For each set of facts, find the pattern in the sums.

9. Find the pattern made by the sum of the digits in each product of the facts for 9.

Explore _____ Math

Find a pattern in these numbers.

What is the difference between
10. 1 and 4?   **11.** 4 and 9?   **12.** 9 and 16?   **13.** 16 and 25?

14. What is the pattern?

Using Multiplication

Build Understanding

Block Tower
Materials: Blocks
Groups: 3–5 students

Pepe and Irma used blocks to build a tower. Can you tell how many blocks they used?

a. Make the tower. Each layer has 2 rows with 4 blocks in each row. Make 5 layers.

b. Find how many blocks are in the whole tower.

You can use multiplication because the number of blocks in each row is the same. Also, the number of blocks in each layer is the same.

Find $2 \times 4 \times 5$.

First, find the number of blocks in one layer. $\qquad 2 \times 4 = 8$

Then multiply this answer by the number of layers. $\quad 5 \times 8 = 40$

There are 40 blocks in the whole tower.

■ **Talk About Math** You know that you can multiply numbers in any order. What would be the best order in which to multiply $2 \times 9 \times 5$? What is the product?

Check Understanding

For another example, see Set F, pages 242–243.

Use blocks or multiplication to find how many in all.

1. Each layer has 2 rows with 3 blocks in each row. Make 7 layers.

2. Each layer has 5 rows with 2 blocks in each row. Make 3 layers.

Practice

For More Practice, see Set F, pages 244–245.

Tell how many layers, how many rows in each layer, and how many in each row. Then find the product.

3.

▦ × ▦ × ▦ = ▦

4.

▦ × ▦ × ▦ = ▦

5.

▦ × ▦ × ▦ = ▦

6.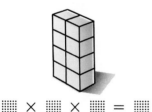

▦ × ▦ × ▦ = ▦

7.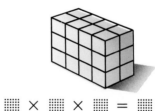

▦ × ▦ × ▦ = ▦

8.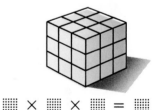

▦ × ▦ × ▦ = ▦

Use blocks or multiplication to find each product.

9. 5 × 3 × 2   **10.** 4 × 0 × 5   **11.** 9 × 2 × 1   **12.** 5 × 4 × 2

Reading ——— Math

Vocabulary Use this number sentence to answer each problem.   4 × 2 × 7 = 56

1. Tell the product.   **2.** Tell each factor.

3. Complete this sentence: ▦ is a multiple of ▦, ▦, and ▦.

Problem Solving REVIEW

Solve each problem.

1. A number is greater than 350 and less than 400. Its tens digit is 4 times its ones digit. What is the number?

2. Steve bought 2 tapes. They were labeled B and C. Use the chart to find out how much he spent.

Tape	Price
A	$5
B	$6
C	$7
D	$8

3. Would you use inches or feet to measure the width of the window in your bedroom for a window shade?

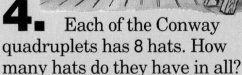

4. Each of the Conway quadruplets has 8 hats. How many hats do they have in all?

5. Would it take more postcards or math books to cover the area of your classroom floor? Why?

6. Write the next 3 numbers in the pattern. Describe the pattern as a multiplication pattern and as an addition pattern. 6, 12, 18, 24, . . .

7. **Data File** Use data from pages 248-249. Jane wants to make a double-size recipe of baked rice pudding. How much of each ingredient should she use?

8. **Make a Data File** Use this year's calendar to find out how many Mondays there are between July 15th and December 15th. Check a calendar for another year. Is the number always the same? Explain.

Cracking the Code

If Mauricio can crack the code,
he can find a treasure. The code is
hidden in the patterns found in each
exercise. Help him crack the code.

1. Complete.

a.   1 $\boxed{\times}$ 9 $\boxed{+}$ 2 $\boxed{=}$ **d.**   1234 $\boxed{\times}$ 9 $\boxed{+}$ 5 $\boxed{=}$

b.   12 $\boxed{\times}$ 9 $\boxed{+}$ 3 $\boxed{=}$ **e.**   12345 $\boxed{\times}$ 9 $\boxed{+}$ 6 $\boxed{=}$

c.   123 $\boxed{\times}$ 9 $\boxed{+}$ 4 $\boxed{=}$

Do you see a pattern? Use the pattern to complete the following.

f.   123456 $\boxed{\times}$ 9 $\boxed{+}$ 7 $\boxed{=}$ **g.**   1234567 $\boxed{\times}$ 9 $\boxed{+}$ 8 $\boxed{=}$

What is the next exercise in the pattern? What is the answer?

2. Complete.

a.   1 $\boxed{\times}$ 9 $\boxed{-}$ 1 $\boxed{=}$ **d.**   4321 $\boxed{\times}$ 9 $\boxed{-}$ 1 $\boxed{=}$

b.   21 $\boxed{\times}$ 9 $\boxed{-}$ 1 $\boxed{=}$ **e.**   54321 $\boxed{\times}$ 9 $\boxed{-}$ 1 $\boxed{=}$

c.   321 $\boxed{\times}$ 9 $\boxed{-}$ 1 $\boxed{=}$

Do you see a pattern? Use the pattern to complete the following.

f.   654321 $\boxed{\times}$ 9 $\boxed{-}$ 1 $\boxed{=}$ **g.**   7654321 $\boxed{\times}$ 9 $\boxed{-}$ 1 $\boxed{=}$

What is the next exercise in the pattern? What is the answer?

3. Name the two digits which repeat in each answer. Add them.
This is the secret number that cracks the code. What is it?

241

Reteaching

Set A pages 220–221

To find 8 × 4, think about 4 × 8. Count by fours, eight times.

4, 8, 12, 16, 20, 24, 28, 32
1 2 3   4   5   6   7   8

4 × 8 = 32 and 8 × 4 = 32

Remember that you can reverse the order of the numbers when you multiply.

1. 5
  ×8

2. 9
  ×3

3. 7
  ×6

Set B pages 222–223

One section of fence is 7 feet long. How long is a fence with 4 sections? Use a number line.

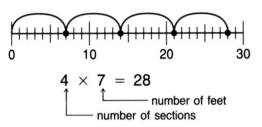

4 × 7 = 28
↑   ↑
| |———— number of feet
|———— number of sections

Remember to use the number line if you need help to find a product. Find each product.

1. 5
  ×7

2. 9
  ×3

3. 6
  ×4

4. 3
  ×8

5. 5
  ×6

6. 9
  ×5

Set C pages 226–227

You can make a square array to show 4 × 4. So 4 × 4 is a square product.

○ ○ ○ ○
○ ○ ○ ○
○ ○ ○ ○
○ ○ ○ ○

Fact: 4 × 4 = 16

Remember that any number multiplied by itself is a square product.

1. 5
  ×5

2. 8
  ×8

3. 9
  ×9

Set D pages 230–231

This array shows how to use tens to find 9 × 6.

10 × 6 = 60

X X X X X X X X X X
X X X X X X X X X X
X X X X X X X X X X
X X X X X X X X X X
X X X X X X X X X X
X X X X X X X X X X

9 × 6 = 54

Remember that 9 × 9 is 9 less than 10 × 9 and that 9 × 8 is 8 less than 10 × 8. Find each product.

1. 9
  ×3

2. 9
  ×5

3. 9
  ×7

4. 4 × 9   **5.** 9 × 6   **6.** 9 × 0

Set E pages 232–235

Draw arrays to show two number facts that you can use to find 6×8.

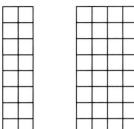

$$2 \times 8 + 4 \times 8 = 6 \times 8$$
$$16 + 32 = 48$$
So $6 \times 8 = 48$.

Remember that you can also use the doubling method to find 6×8. You would use $(3 \times 8) + (3 \times 8)$. Copy and complete each table.

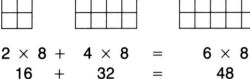

	×	7
1.	4	▦
2.	8	▦
3.	6	▦
4.	0	▦
5.	3	▦

	×	8
6.	5	▦
7.	7	▦
8.	3	▦
9.	9	▦
10.	4	▦

Set F pages 238–239

These blocks show that
$$4 \times 2 \times 3 = 24.$$

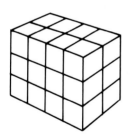

Number of blocks in one layer:
$$4 \times 2 = 8$$

Multiply this answer by the number of layers.
$$3 \times 8 = 24$$

Remember that you can change the order of the numbers to make the multiplication easier.

Tell how many layers, how many rows in each layer, and how many in each row. Then find the product.

1. 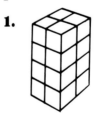 **2.**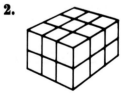

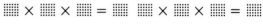

▦ × ▦ × ▦ = ▦ ▦ × ▦ × ▦ = ▦

3. 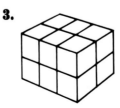 **4.**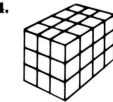

▦ × ▦ × ▦ = ▦ ▦ × ▦ × ▦ = ▦

More Practice
Set A   pages 220–221

Find each product. Use the order property to help you.

1. 7
  $\times 5$

2. 3
  $\times 8$

3. 6
  $\times 7$

4. 9
  $\times 5$

5. 8
  $\times 9$

6. 8
  $\times 6$

7. 2×9

8. 5×6

9. 7×4

10. 6×3

11. 9×4

Mental Math   Find each answer.

12. $14 - 8$

13. $7 + 5$

14. 8×3

15. $15 - 9$

16. $9 + 9$

17. $4 + 8$

18. 5×5

19. 8×3

20. 9×3

21. $17 - 8$

Set B   page 222–223

1. 4
  $\times 6$

2. 8
  $\times 5$

3. 4
  $\times 9$

4. 7
  $\times 2$

5. 6
  $\times 5$

6. 9
  $\times 5$

7. 6×3

8. 7×4

9. 8×3

10. 3×9

11. 5×7

Set C   pages 226–227

Find each product.

1. 6
  $\times 6$

2. 3
  $\times 3$

3. 1
  $\times 1$

4. 5
  $\times 5$

5. 2
  $\times 2$

6. 9
  $\times 9$

7. 8×8

8. 4×4

9. 7×7

10. 9×9

11. 6×6

Set D   pages 230–231

Find each product.

1. 9
  $\times 4$

2. 3
  $\times 9$

3. 9
  $\times 1$

4. 9
  $\times 2$

5. 8
  $\times 9$

6. 6
  $\times 9$

7. 9×7

8. 0×9

9. 9×3

10. 9×9

11. 9×5

Mental Math   Find each answer.

12. $13 + 8$

13. $14 - 8$

14. 8×8

15. $15 - 9$

16. 3×7

17. 4×6

18. 5×3

19. $6 + 9$

20. 8×5

21. $12 - 5$

Set E pages 232-235

Copy and complete each table.

	×	6
1.	5	
2.	2	
3.	7	
4.	9	
5.	8	

	×	7
6.	9	
7.	0	
8.	5	
9.	8	
10.	7	

	×	8
11.	2	
12.	6	
13.	3	
14.	8	
15.	9	

	×	9
16.	3	
17.	8	
18.	1	
19.	7	
20.	6	

Mixed Practice Use a calculator, paper and pencil, or mental math to find each answer. Tell which method you used.

21. 346 − 81

22. 483 + 5,316

23. 68 − 34

24. 7 × 6

25. 37 + 23

26. 610 − 395

27. 9 × 9

28. 17 − 9

29. 76 + 6

Set F pages 238-239

Tell how many layers, how many rows in each layer, and how many in each row.

1.

▦ × ▦ × ▦ = ▦

2.

▦ × ▦ × ▦ = ▦

3.

▦ × ▦ × ▦ = ▦

4.

▦ × ▦ × ▦ = ▦

5.

▦ × ▦ × ▦ = ▦

6.
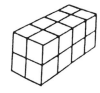

▦ × ▦ × ▦ = ▦

Use blocks or multiplication to find each product.

7. 6 × 2 × 2

8. 8 × 3 × 1

9. 9 × 3 × 0

10. 2 × 9 × 5

Enrichment

Multiplying with Greater Numbers

You can use multiplication facts and what you know about place value to multiply greater numbers.

Here is how Pete found 7×14.

He thought of 14 as $10 + 4$.

Then he multiplied 7×10 and 7×4.

He added the products to find 7×14.

$$7 \times 14 = 98$$

$$\left.\begin{array}{l} 7 \times 10 = 70 \\ 7 \times\ \ 4 = \underline{28} \end{array}\right\} \text{Add}$$

$$98$$

Find each product.

1. 8×12 **2.** 6×18 **3.** 5×16 **4.** 4×19 **5.** 7×13

6. 9×14 **7.** 3×17 **8.** 8×15 **9.** 7×16 **10.** 6×12

Copy and complete the multiplication table.

	×	0	1	2	3	4	5	6	7	8	9	10	11	12
11.	0													
12.	1													
13.	2													
14.	3													
15.	4													
16.	5													
17.	6													
18.	7													
19.	8													
20.	9													
21.	10													
22.	11													
23.	12													

Chapter 7 Review/Test

1. A section of fence is 6 feet long.

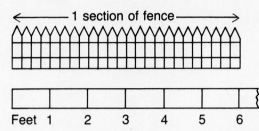

Which product shows the length of 4 sections of the fence?

a. 4×7 **b.** 6×4 **c.** 4×8

Find each product.

2. $\begin{array}{r} 6 \\ \times 3 \\ \hline \end{array}$ **3.** $\begin{array}{r} 6 \\ \times 6 \\ \hline \end{array}$ **4.** $\begin{array}{r} 8 \\ \times 6 \\ \hline \end{array}$

5. $\begin{array}{r} 7 \\ \times 5 \\ \hline \end{array}$ **6.** $\begin{array}{r} 9 \\ \times 7 \\ \hline \end{array}$ **7.** $\begin{array}{r} 8 \\ \times 8 \\ \hline \end{array}$

8. $\begin{array}{r} 6 \\ \times 7 \\ \hline \end{array}$ **9.** $\begin{array}{r} 7 \\ \times 8 \\ \hline \end{array}$ **10.** $\begin{array}{r} 9 \\ \times 9 \\ \hline \end{array}$

11. $\begin{array}{r} 6 \\ \times 9 \\ \hline \end{array}$ **12.** $\begin{array}{r} 8 \\ \times 9 \\ \hline \end{array}$ **13.** $\begin{array}{r} 9 \\ \times 2 \\ \hline \end{array}$

14. Write the multiplication facts for 8 in order, starting with 0×8. What pattern is made by the ones digits?

15. How many layers? How many rows? How many in each row? How many in all?

$\blacksquare \times \blacksquare \times \blacksquare = \blacksquare$

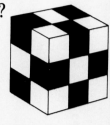

Tell whether you would add, subtract, or multiply to solve each problem.

16. A laundromat has 3 rows of driers. There are 5 driers in each row. How many driers are there in all?

17. Carlos has 3 model airplanes, 2 model spaceships, 4 model helicopters, and 1 model space station. How many models does he have in all?

18. All of the neighborhood children are having a bicycle parade. If there are 8 rows and 5 children in each row, how many are riding in all?

19. Solve Problem 18.

20. ■ **Write About Math**
Write an addition sentence and show an array for Exercise 3.

247

Data File

1. Mileage Guide
Read across the row and down the column to find the distance in miles between two cities.

2. Chart
The chart shows the seven longest rivers in the world.

3. Bus Schedule
This bus takes passengers to the train station.

4. Recipe Card
This is a recipe for rice pudding.

5. Recipe Card
This is a recipe for making bread modeling dough.

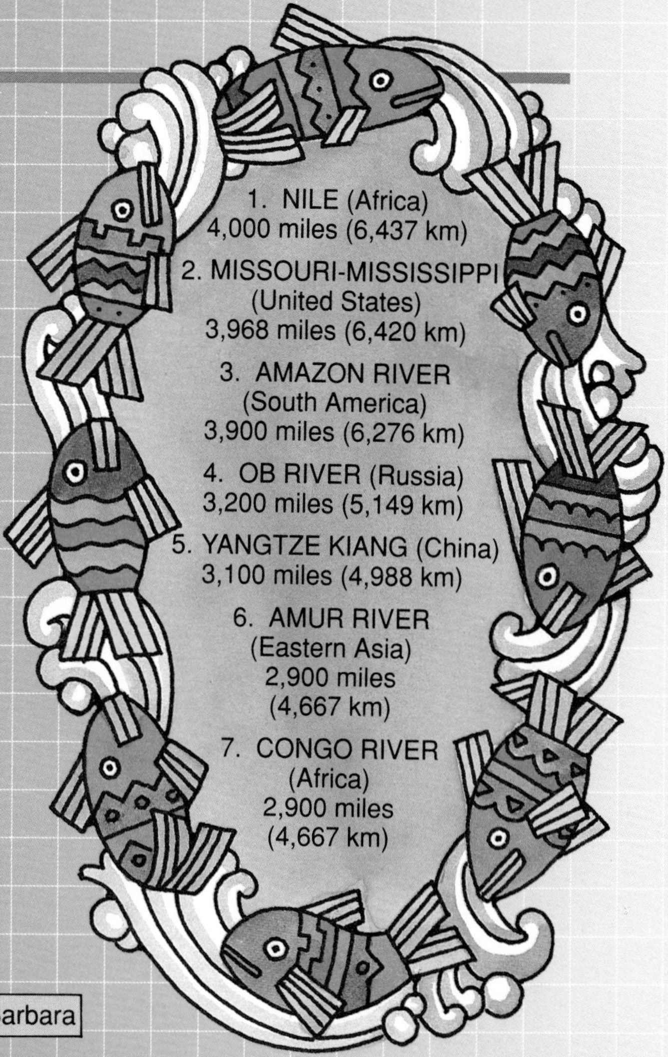

1. NILE (Africa)
4,000 miles (6,437 km)

2. MISSOURI-MISSISSIPPI (United States)
3,968 miles (6,420 km)

3. AMAZON RIVER (South America)
3,900 miles (6,276 km)

4. OB RIVER (Russia)
3,200 miles (5,149 km)

5. YANGTZE KIANG (China)
3,100 miles (4,988 km)

6. AMUR RIVER (Eastern Asia)
2,900 miles (4,667 km)

7. CONGO RIVER (Africa)
2,900 miles (4,667 km)

2. River Chart

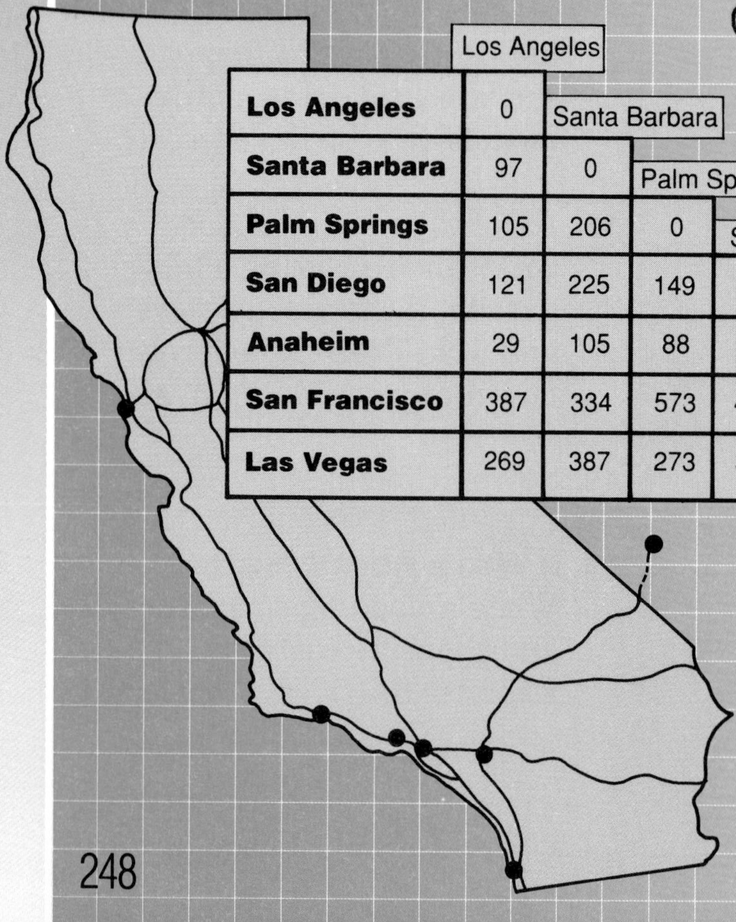

	Los Angeles	Santa Barbara	Palm Springs	San Diego	Anaheim	San Francisco	Las Vegas
Los Angeles	0						
Santa Barbara	97	0					
Palm Springs	105	206	0				
San Diego	121	225	149	0			
Anaheim	29	105	88	90	0		
San Francisco	387	334	573	497	403	0	
Las Vegas	269	387	273	330	295	676	0

1. Mileage Guide

ROUTE 602							Trains to		
WEEK DAY MORNING							**Chicago**		
1	2	3	4	5	6	7			
ABBEYWOOD	GLEN/LAKE	HIGHLAND	SALEM	SCHAUMBERG	WISE	ROSELLE STATION	TRAIN LEAVES ROSELLE	TRAIN ARRIVES CHICAGO	
5:32 A.M.	5:37 A.M.	5:48 A.M.	5:49 A.M.	5:54 A.M.	6:01 A.M.	6:12 A.M.	6:17 A.M.	7:02 A.M.
6:20 A.M.	6:25 A.M.	6:33 A.M.	6:37 A.M.	6:42 A.M.	6:49 A.M.	7:00 A.M.	7:10 A.M.	7:51 A.M.
6:50 A.M.	6:55 A.M.	7:03 A.M.	7:07 A.M.	7:12 A.M.	7:19 A.M.	7:30 A.M.	7:38 A.M.	8:18 A.M.

3. Bus Schedule

5. Recipe Card

Recipe

BREAD MODELING DOUGH

You Will Need:

2 slices day old white bread

2 tablespoons white household glue

2 drops glycerine

4 drops white vinegar

food coloring or poster paint

How To Make:
Remove crust and break bread into
small pieces in a bowl. Add glue,
glycerine, and vinegar. Mix with your
hands until it isn't sticky. Divide dough
and add a few drops of the desired color
to each portion. Mix until blended.

How to Use:
Use hand lotion on your hands to keep
dough from sticking. Make small objects
such as jewelry or flowers. Allow to dry
1 to 2 days. Paint with a mixture of
1 tablespoon white glue and 1 tablespoon
of water. Allow to dry, then apply one or
two more coats. Bake at 225 degrees, for
4 minutes.

4. Recipe Card

BAKED RICE PUDDING

4 eggs   **1 cup sugar**   **1 quart milk**

1 teaspoon cinnamon   **2 cups cooked rice**

2 tablespoons butter

1. Preheat oven to 250 degrees F. butter 9 x 13 inch baking dish.

2. Break eggs into bowl and beat lightly with beater or fork.

3. Measure and add sugar, salt and cinnamon. Beat again.

4. Add milk and rice. Mix together.

5. Pour slowly into baking dish. Dot with butter.

6. Place in oven and bake about $1\frac{1}{2}$ hours. (Use pot holders.)

MAKES 8 SERVINGS

249

Give the letter for the correct answer.

1. Which number sentence is true?

   A 199 > 202   **C** 225 < 178
   B 211 > 189   **D** 194 < 149

2. Estimate the sum. First round both numbers to the nearest ten.

   67 + 11

   A 70   **B** 90   **C** 80   **D** 60

3. Add.

      38
   + 17

   A 45   **B** 41   **C** 55   **D** 51

4. Add.

    473
   + 56

   A 439   **B** 519   **C** 429   **D** 529

5. Add.

   5,914
   + 265

   A 5,179   **B** 5,779   **C** 6,179   **D** 6,279

6. Estimate the difference. First round both numbers to the nearest ten.

   48 − 36

   A 10   **B** 20   **C** 30   **D** 0

7. Subtract.

    682
   − 38

   A 654   **B** 644   **C** 554   **D** 656

8. Subtract.

    963
   − 272

   A 791   **B** 711   **C** 611   **D** 691

9. Subtract.

   4,208
   − 1,343

   A 2,965   **B** 2,165   **C** 2,865   **D** 3,965

10. Which number sentence should be used to solve the problem?

Mark had 26 pennies. He spent 17 of them. How many pennies did he have left?

   A 26 + 19 = ▦
   B 17 − 15 = ▦
   C 17 + 15 = ▦
   D 26 − 17 = ▦

11. What time is shown on this clock?

   A 9:30   **B** 6:45   **C** 6:15   **D** 7:45

12. Choose the most sensible unit of measure.

Length of a ladder

A Centimeters **C** Kilometers
B Meters **D** Square meters

13. Multiply.

6
×5

A 11
B 30
C 35
D 25

14. Multiply.

7
×9

A 63
B 56
C 64
D 16

15. Multiply.

8
×6

A 64
B 48
C 56
D 42

16. Multiply.

7
×7

A 81
B 35
C 49
D 45

Solve Problems 17–19.

17. Marta wrote 2 letters. Each was 6 pages long. How many pages did she write in all?

A 10 **B** 16 **C** 6 **D** 12

18. There are 8 chairs around a table. Each chair has 4 legs. How many legs are there in all?

A 32 **B** 24 **C** 12 **D** 36

19. Beth, Carl, Joy, and Rick have backpacks. One is blue, one red, one green, and one orange. Neither Joy nor Carl has the green backpack. Rick's backpack is blue. Joy's backpack is not orange. Who has the orange backpack?

A Beth **B** Carl **C** Joy **D** Rick

Read the problem below. Then answer the question.

A computer instruction book has 5 parts. Each part has 88 pages. How many pages in all are there?

20. Which number sentence would you choose to solve the problem?

A 88 + 5 = ▦
B 88 − 5 = ▦
C 88 × 5 = ▦
D 88 + 88 = ▦

Geometry and Measurement

Did You Know: Food companies usually put the "net weight" on their packages. The "net weight" is the weight of just the contents without the container.

Ketchup

NET WT. 14 OZ. – 397 GRAMS

Bread

ENRICHED BREAD

NET WT. 12 OZ.

Number-Sense Project

Estimate
Estimate the total weight in ounces of each item. Remember that some containers weigh more than others.

Gather Data
Look at containers of different types of food. Find the net weight of each when full. Then estimate the total weight with the container.

Analyze and Report
Make a poster with drawings or cut outs of different items. List the net weight under each item.

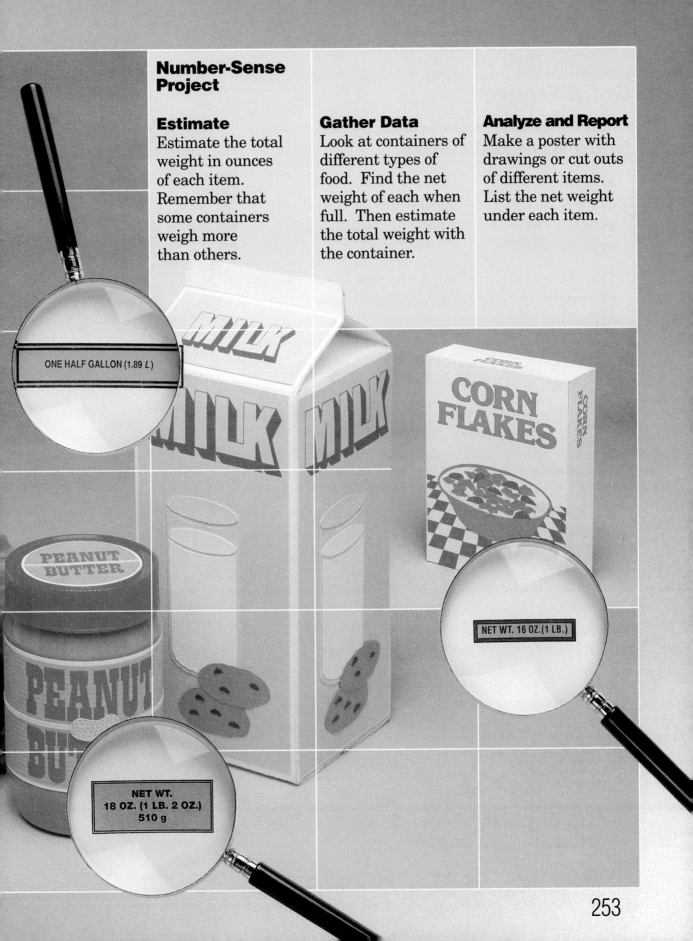

ONE HALF GALLON (1.89 *L*)

NET WT. 16 OZ.(1 LB.)

NET WT.
18 OZ. (1 LB. 2 OZ.)
510 g

Solid Figures

Build Understanding

A. Shape Up!
Materials: Old magazines and newspapers,
scissors, glue, large piece of paper
Groups: Partners

The pictures show solid shapes. They show
cylinders, cubes, spheres, and rectangular
prisms.

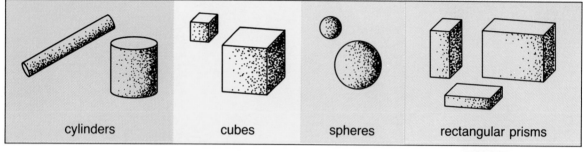

| cylinders | cubes | spheres | rectangular prisms |

a. Look through old magazines and
newspapers. Cut out three or four pictures
of objects that match each solid shape.

b. Fold a large piece of paper in half. Then
fold the paper in half again. Unfold the
paper. Write the names of the solid
shapes in the 4 sections as shown.

c. Glue each magazine picture in
the proper section.

d. Which of the 4 shapes was the
hardest to find?

e. Which shape was easiest to find?

f. Why do you think there is more of
one shape than another?

B. How many *surfaces,* or sides, does a rectangular prism have?

A rectangular prism has 6 surfaces. Each surface is called a *face.*

When two surfaces meet, they form an *edge.* How many edges does the rectangular prism have?

When three edges meet, they form a *corner.* How many corners does the rectangular prism have?

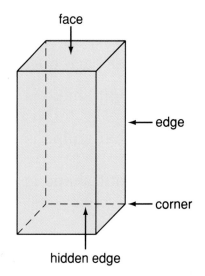

■ **Talk About Math** Which solid shapes have curved or rounded surfaces? Which have only flat surfaces? Which have both flat and curved surfaces?

Check Understanding

Name the shape of each object. Write *cylinder, cube, sphere,* or *rectangular prism.*

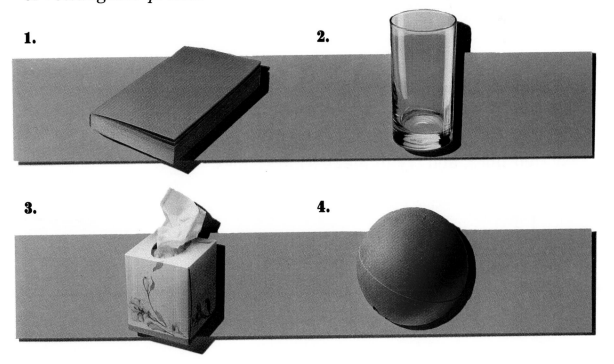

1.

2.

3.

4.

Practice

Answer each question.

5. What shape is a baseball?

6. What shape is a brick?

7. What shape is a soup can?

8. What shape is a nickel?

9. What shape is a box of crayons?

10. What shape is a child's block?

11. What shape has only two edges?

12. What shape has only one surface?

Do the pictures show two different views of the same object? Explain your answers.

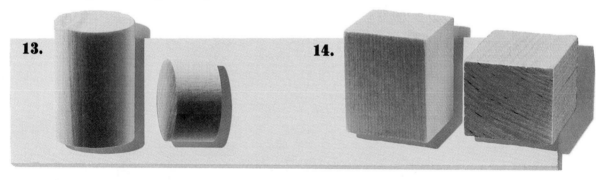

13.

14.

Problem Solving

Cut out figures like those below. Fold along the dotted lines, and try to make solid shapes.

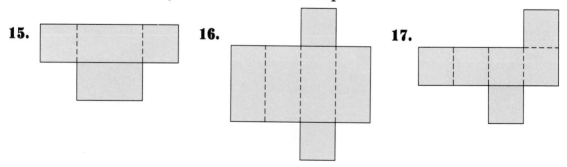

15.

16.

17.

18.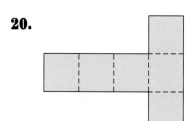

19.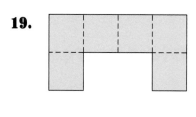

20.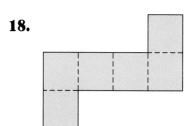

21.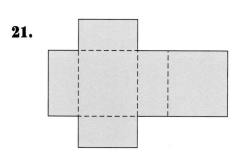

22. Which figures can be folded into solid shapes?

23. Which figures cannot be folded into solid shapes?

Choose a Strategy

City Needs New Tower

24. Four solid shapes are needed to build the new city tower. A cylinder, a rectangular prism, a sphere, and a cube are needed.

Use all four clues below to draw a picture of the new tower.

a. The cylinder will not touch the ground.

b. The rectangular prism is not between the cube and the sphere.

c. The cube is under the cylinder and above the rectangular prism.

d. The sphere is above the cylinder.

PROBLEM SOLVING STRATEGIES

Choose an Operation
Find a Pattern
Use Logical Reasoning
Make a Table
Draw a Picture

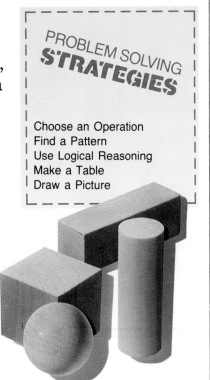

Geometric Figures

Build Understanding

A. Lori used sponges and ink to make designs on wrapping paper.

a. What are the solid shapes of the sponges above?

Lori dipped one face of each sponge into ink and pressed it onto her paper. Each made a *geometric figure.*

The faces of solid shapes form geometric figures. Seven geometric figures are shown at the right.

b. Name the solid shape that has a face which makes
   • a circle.
   • a square.
   • a rectangle.

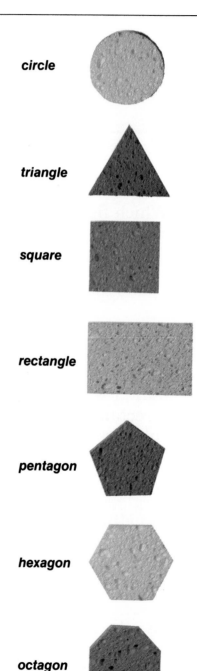

circle

triangle

square

rectangle

pentagon

hexagon

octagon

A decagon has 10 sides.

258

B. Geometric figures have *curves* or *line segments* as *sides.* Two sides meet at a *corner* of a figure.

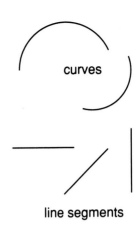

curves

a. Which geometric figure has no corners?

b. On grid paper, draw the geometric figures pictured on page 258. Do not draw the circle.

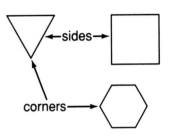

line segments

c. Count the number of sides each figure has. Then count the number of corners.

■ **Talk About Math** What do you notice about the number of sides and the number of corners a geometric figure has?

←sides→

corners→

Check Understanding

For another example, see Set A, pages 288–289.

Use the picture of the flag to answer Exercises 1 and 2.

1. What figure is each stripe on the flag?

2. What other geometric figures do you see on the flag?

3. What is the difference between squares and other rectangles?

4. Which has more sides, a pentagon or an octagon?

5. Name something in your classroom that has the shape of a circle.

Practice

For More Practice, see Set A, pages 290–291.

Give the name of each geometric figure. Then give the number of sides and corners each figure has.

6.

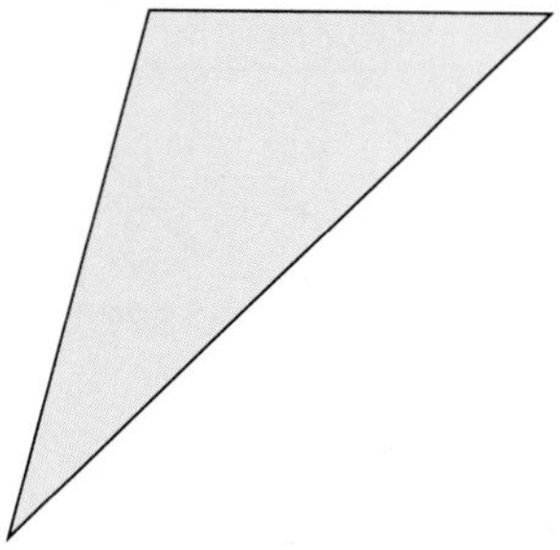

7.

8.

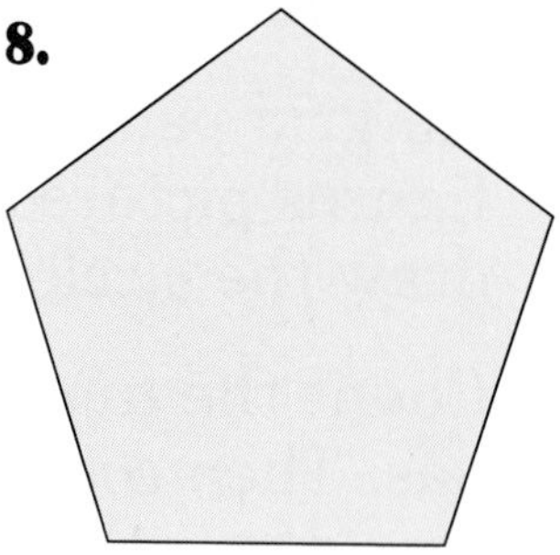

9.

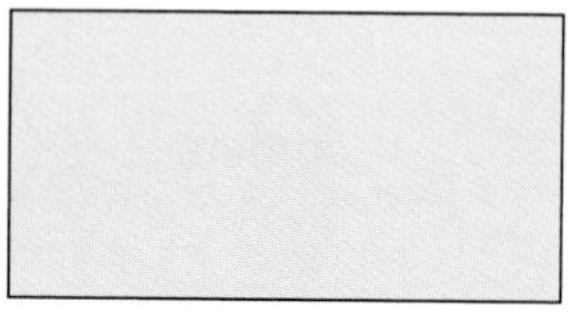

10.

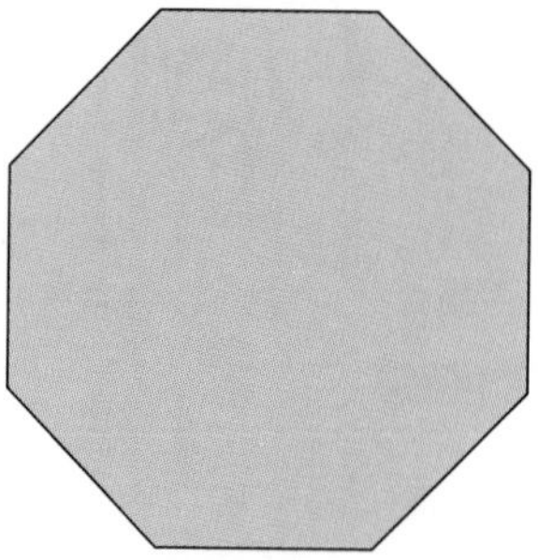

11.

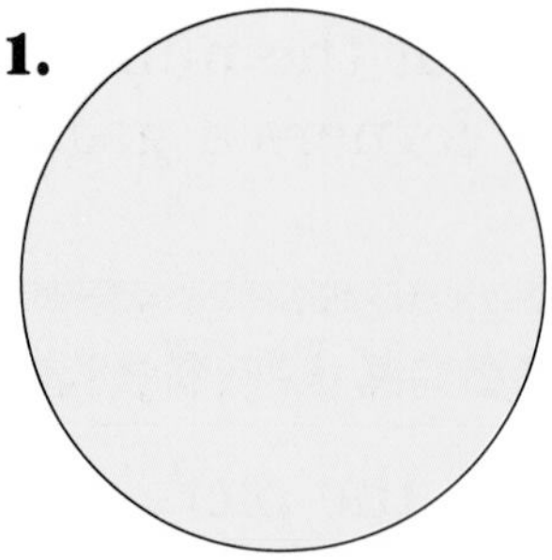

12.

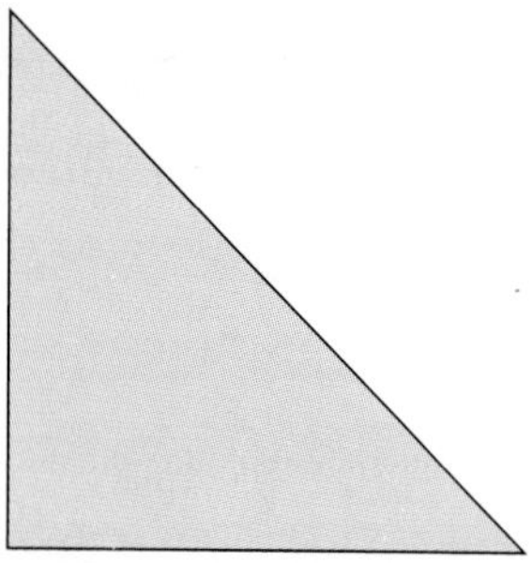

13.

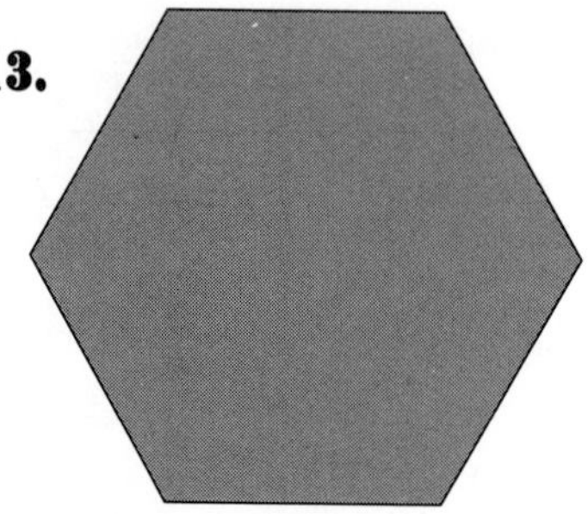

14.

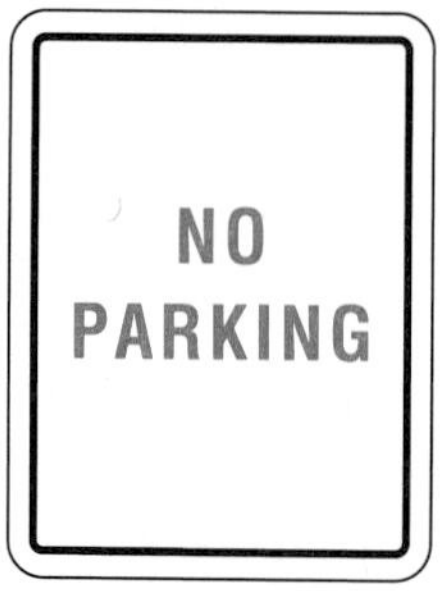
NO
PARKING

15.

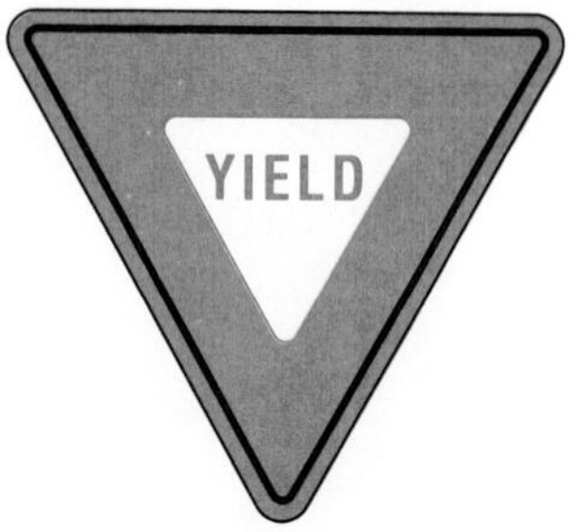
YIELD

16.

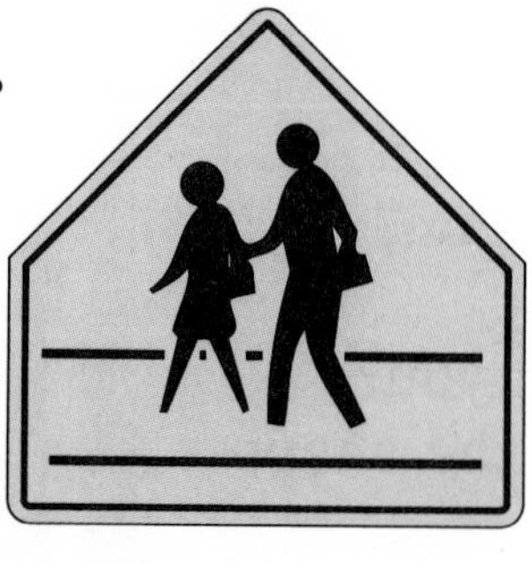

17.

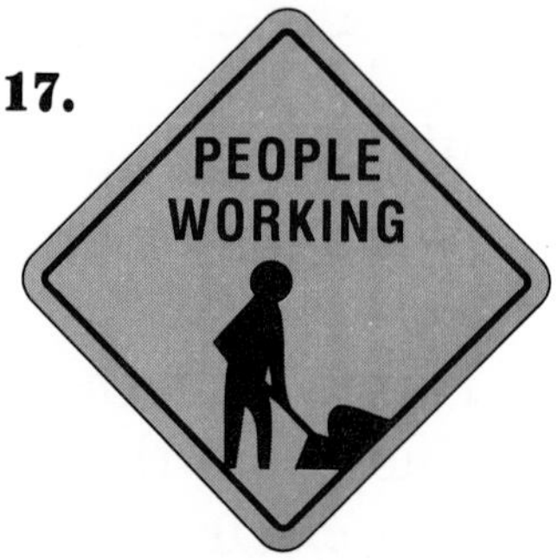
PEOPLE
WORKING

Problem Solving

Trace each figure on grid paper. Cut each one out. Put two or more figures together in different ways to answer Problems 18–23.

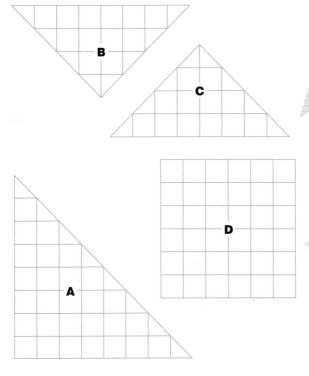

18. What is the largest triangle you can make?

19. What is the largest square you can make?

20. What is the largest rectangle, not square, you can make?

21. What different geometric figures can you make with Figures B and C?

22. What other geometric figures can you make using four figures? Show your work by drawing the new figures on grid paper.

23. Write the number of sides and corners of each shape you made in Problem 22.

24. **Use Data** What geometric figures can you see in the clock faces in Exercises 8–11 on page 151?

Angles

Build Understanding

A. Two sides of a geometric figure that meet at a corner form an **angle.** The pictures below show angle R, angle S, and angle T.

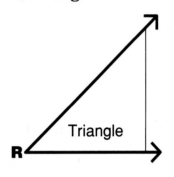

Triangle

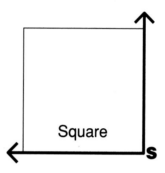

Square

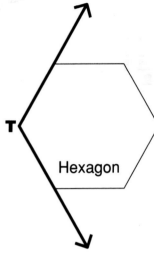

Hexagon

Each corner of a figure forms an angle. How many angles are in a triangle? How many angles are there in a square? in a hexagon?

B. Look at the pictures at the right. The edges of solid shapes form angles at the corners too.

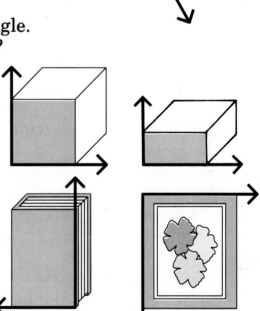

C. Angles that form square corners are called **right angles.** The pictures at the right show right angles.

■ **Write About Math** Write the names of several objects in your classroom that have angles. Tell which sides or edges form the angles.

Check Understanding

For another example, see Set B, pages 288–289.

Does each picture show an angle?
Write *yes* or *no*.

1.    **2.**    **3.**    **4.**

5. Which pictures in Exercises 1–4 show one or more right angles?

Practice

For More Practice, see Set B, pages 290–291.

How many angles are in each figure? Are they right angles? Write *yes* or *no*.

6.    **7.**   **8.**    **9.**

10.   **11.**   **12.**   **13.**

Problem Solving

14. Visual Thinking Name a time when the hands of a clock form a right angle.

15. Draw a figure with 7 angles and 7 corners.

16. Mental Math Tell the perimeter of the figure at the right.

5m 5m 5m

Symmetry

Build Understanding

A butterfly can fold its wings so that the two parts match.

A. Match Making

Materials: Paper, markers, scissors

a. Fold a piece of paper in half. Draw curves to look like a butterfly wing. Begin and end your drawing at the fold. Your paper might look like the one at the right.

b. With the paper still folded, cut along the curves and unfold. Have you made a butterfly with two matching wings?

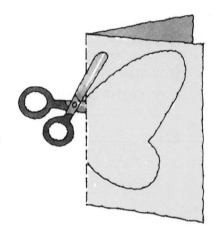

B. A figure is *symmetric* if you can fold it and make the two parts match. The fold line is the *line of symmetry.*

Make another symmetric figure by folding and cutting.

line of symmetry

not a line of symmetry

c. Some figures, such as the one at the right, do not have a line of symmetry. Draw a figure that has no line of symmetry.

■ **Talk About Math** How can you tell that the figure in Example C does not have a line of symmetry?

Check Understanding

For another example, see Set C, pages 288–289.

Which line, the red one or the blue one, shows the line of symmetry? If there is no line of symmetry, write *none*.

1.

2.

3.

Practice

For More Practice, see Set C, pages 290–291.

Does each figure look symmetric? Write *yes* or *no*.

4.

5.

6.

7.

8.

9.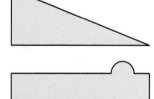

Problem Solving

Explore ———— Math

10. Use folding and cutting to make a figure having 4 lines of symmetry.

11. Try folding and cutting differently. Can you make 8 lines of symmetry?

Congruence

Build Understanding

A. Angelo's job in the pillow factory is to inspect the pillow pieces. The top and bottom pieces must be exactly the same size and shape.

Figures that have the same size and shape are ***congruent.***

  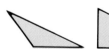

Congruent   Not congruent

B. Angelo keeps pairs of congruent pieces and throws away pairs that are not congruent.

Look at the pairs of pieces in *a*, *b*, and *c*. What will Angelo do with each pair?

Angelo will keep the two pieces in pair *a*. The pieces are the same size and shape. They are congruent.

Angelo will throw away the pieces in pair *b*. They are not congruent because they are not the same size and shape.

Angelo will keep the pair of pieces in *c*. They are congruent.

a.

b.

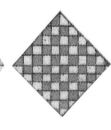 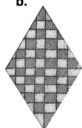

c.

■ **Write About Math** Describe how you can tell that the pieces in *c* are congruent. Describe two ways you can tell that figures are not congruent.

Check Understanding

For another example, see Set D, pages 288–289.

Are the figures congruent? Write *yes* or *no*. Explain.

1.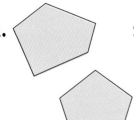

2.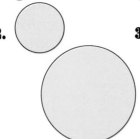

3.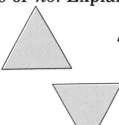

4.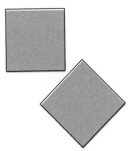

Practice

For More Practice, see Set D, pages 290–291.

Match the congruent figures. Write the letter
for each number.

5.   a. 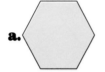   6.   d.

7.   b.   8.   e.

9.   c.   10.   f.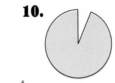

✓ Midchapter _____ Checkup

1. What shape is a cereal box?   2. What shape is a straw?

3. How many corners does a hexagon have?   4. Name a figure that has a right angle.

5. Which figures at the right are symmetric?   a.   b.   c.

6. Which figures at the right are congruent?   a.   b.   c.

Explore as a Team

1. Use squares to see how many shapes you can make with 5 squares. They can be called *pentominoes*. *Rule:* Squares must share at least one full side with another square.

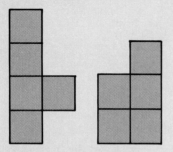

These are pentominoes.

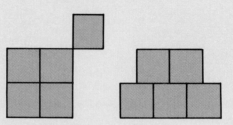

These are not pentominoes.

If one pentomino can fit exactly on another, they are the same.

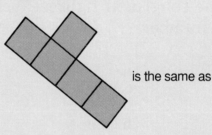

is the same as

2. Record the pentominoes your group made on grid paper.

3. Guess which pentominoes can be folded into an open box. Check your guess by cutting and folding.

Visual Thinking Activity

The pattern can be folded into the cube shown. Which color is on the bottom?

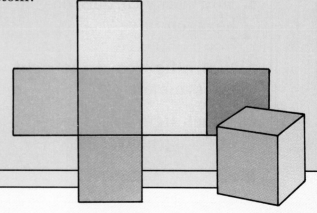

TIPS FOR
WORKING TOGETHER

Help keep your group
on task.

Problem Solving WORKSHOP

Number-Sense Project

Look back at pages 252-253.

1. Estimate the net weight of each of the following.

Item	Total Weight	Net Weight
a. Box of cereal	20 oz.	
b. Loaf of bread	25 oz.	
c. Glass jar of strawberry jam	16 oz.	
d. Box of instant gelatin	8 oz.	

2. In writing, tell how total weight is different from net weight.

Explore with a Computer

Use the *Geometry Workshop Project* for this activity. At the computer, you will make lines of symmetry with the figures.

1. Slide, flip, and turn one of the figures. Then move the two figures so the sides that touch make a line of symmetry.

2. How many different ways can you do this?

Use Data from a Graph

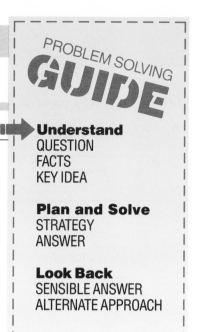

Build Understanding

The graph tells about the favorite books of Mrs. Gordon's students. Compare Adventure Books and Fairy Tales. How many more students chose Adventure Books?

Understand   QUESTION   How many more students chose Adventure Books than Fairy Tales?

We LOVE to Read!

Frog and Toad Books	📖📖📖 📖
Little House Books	📖📖
Fairy Tales	📖📖📖 📖📖📖
Mystery Books	📖📖📖 📖
Adventure Books	📖📖📖 📖📖📖 📖📖📖

Each 📖 equals one vote

FACTS   The right column of the graph tells how many students chose a certain type of book as their favorite. 6 students chose Fairy Tales. 9 children chose Adventure Books.

KEY IDEA   The graph shows number information that you can use to compare students' favorite kinds of books.

Plan and Solve   Subtract to find how many more.

9 − 6 = 3

3 more students chose Adventure Books as their favorite.

Look Back   Did you look in the correct rows to find the numbers?

■ **Talk About Math**   Explain how you can find the number of children in the class if each child had one vote shown on the graph.

Check Understanding

1. How many children liked Mystery Books best?

2. What kind of book was the most popular?

3. Did more students like Frog and Toad Books or Fairy Tales?

4. How many more students chose Fairy Tales than Mystery Books?

Practice

The graph at the right shows how many books some children read for a library contest.

How Many Books Read?

Shauna					
John				
Lisa		
Karl							
Pam		

Each ▯ equals one book.

5. Who read the most books?

6. How many more books did Shauna read than John?

7. Who read 4 more books than John?

8. Which two people read the same number of books?

9. Which children read more books than Lisa?

Choose a ___ Strategy

Missing Shapes   Copy these puzzles.
10. Some shapes are missing from the puzzles. What shapes can you put in the empty squares to show a pattern?

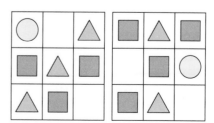

Counting Cubes to Find Volume

Build Understanding

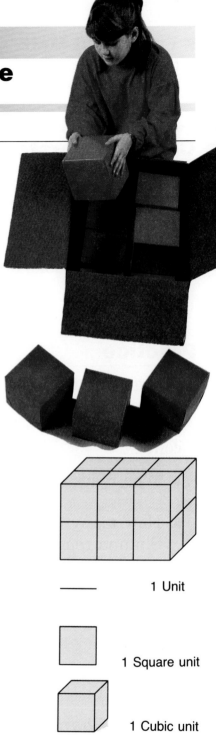

A. Fill It Up!
Materials: Cubes, chalkboard erasers or crayon boxes, empty boxes of various sizes
Groups: 3 to 5 students

a. Fill a box with chalkboard erasers or small crayon boxes. Record how many erasers or small boxes you use.

b. Repeat Part *a* using cubes.

B. The box in the picture holds 2 layers of cubes. Each layer has 6 cubes. The box holds 12 cubes. It holds 12 cubic units.

The number of cubic units something holds is its *volume.* You can say the box has a volume of 12 cubic units.

■ **Talk About Math** The answers for Part *a* and Part *b* are different. Explain why. Which way measures volume in cubic units?

——— 1 Unit

1 Square unit

1 Cubic unit

Check Understanding

1. Box A holds 16 bricks. Box B holds 12 bricks. Which box has the greater volume?

2. If a box holds exactly 5 rows of 4 cubes, what is the volume of the box in cubic units?

Practice

Find the volume of each solid shape in cubic units.
Remember to watch out for hidden cubes.

3.

4.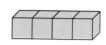

5.

6.

7.

8.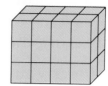

9.

10.

11.

Problem Solving

12. Use cubes to build stacks. The first layer has 4 cubes. How many cubes are in a 2-layer stack? a 3-layer stack? a 7-layer stack?

1 layer   2 layers   3 layers

Use cubes to build shapes like those on the right. What is the volume of each?

13.

14.

15.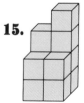

Customary Units of Capacity

Build Understanding

Jorge is a baker. To make a cake, he measures liquids. Customary units for measuring liquids are the *cup* (c), the *pint* (pt), the *quart* (qt), and the *gallon* (gal).

Customary units for liquids tell how much liquid a container will hold.

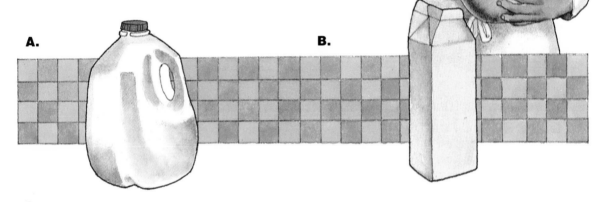

A.

A gallon is 4 quarts.
1 gal = 4 qt

B.

A quart is 2 pints.
1 qt = 2 pt

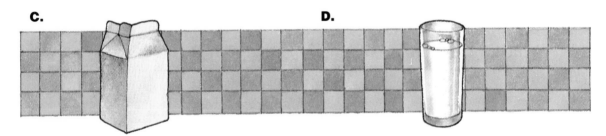

C.

A pint is 2 cups.
1 pt = 2 c

D.

A drinking glass can hold about 1 cup.

■ **Write About Math** Tell how you could find the number of cups in a gallon.

Check Understanding

For another example, see Set E, pages 288–289.

Choose the unit of measure you would use
to find how much the container holds.

1. Cereal bowl
 cup   quart

2. Bathtub
 quart   gallon

3. Watering can
 cup   gallon

Choose the more sensible liquid measure
for the container.

4. Sand pail
 2 qt   2 gal

5. Auto fuel tank
 15 pt   15 gal

6. Flower vase
 2 c   2 gal

Practice

For More Practice, see Set E, pages 290–291.

Estimation   Choose the more sensible
customary measure for each.

7. Drinking glass
 quart   cup

8. Jug of cider
 cup   gallon

9. Cat's water bowl
 cup   quart

10. Wading pool
 25 pt   25 gal

11. Juice pitcher
 2 pt   2 gal

12. Baby bottle
 1 c   1 qt

Write *cups, pints, quarts,* or *gallons* to tell which
you would use to measure how much each holds.

13. Can of soup

14. Washing machine

15. Thermos bottle

Problem Solving

Solve the problem.

16. Jorge needs 6 gallons of milk to
make a day's supply of bread.
He has 3 one-gallon containers,
8 one-quart containers, and
8 one-pint containers of milk. Does
he need to buy more milk? Explain.

TIPS FOR PROBLEM SOLVERS

**Share your thinking
with others.** Explaining
your ideas helps you think
better.

Metric Units of Capacity

Build Understanding

Metric units used for measuring liquids are
the *milliliter* (mL) and the *liter* (L).

A. This small spoon holds
about 5 milliliters.

B. This bottle holds
about 1 liter.
A liter is
1,000 milliliters.
1 L = 1,000 mL

■ **Talk About Math**   Which is more, 750 mL
or 750 L? Explain why.

Check Understanding

For another example, see Set F, pages 288–289.

Choose the unit of measure you would use
to find how much the container holds.

1. Bucket

milliliter   liter

2. Water cup in bird cage

milliliter   liter

Choose the more sensible liquid measure
for the container.

3. Flower vase

1 mL   1 L

4. Paper cup

200 mL   200 L

5. Tea kettle

2 mL   2 L

6. Number Sense   Write these liquid measurements
in order from least to greatest.

50 L   5 mL   5 L   50 mL

Practice

For More Practice, see Set F, pages 290–291.

Estimation   Choose the more sensible metric measure for each.

7. Wading pool

   100 mL   100 L

8. Kitchen sink

   20 mL   20 L

9. Thermos jug

   3 mL   3 L

10. Liquid soap bottle

   80 mL   80 L

11. Fish tank

   15 mL   15 L

12. Medicine dropper

   1 mL   1 L

Write *liter* or *milliliter* to tell which you would use to measure how much each holds.

13. Bathtub

14. Juice glass

15. Water tower

16. Oil barrel

17. Bottle cap

18. Doll's bottle

Reading ——— Math

Vocabulary   In each sentence, one word has some missing letters. Copy each of these words and write one letter in each to complete the word. Use the Glossary at the back of the book if you need help with spelling.

1. The __?__ __?__ r __?__ m e t __?__ r of a figure is the distance around the figure.

2. The number of square units that cover a figure is the __?__ r __?__ a.

3. The number of cubic units that a shape can hold is its __?__ o __?__ u __?__ e.

Customary Units of Weight

Build Understanding

Mrs. Kennedy is ordering cheese at the deli counter of a grocery store. She tells the clerk how much she needs, and the clerk weighs the cheese. The customary units for measuring weight are the **ounce** (oz) and the **pound** (lb).

A. This slice of cheese for a sandwich weighs about 1 ounce.

B. This loaf of bread weighs about 1 pound. A pound is 16 ounces. 1 lb = 16 oz

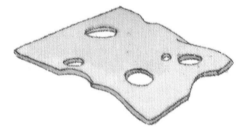

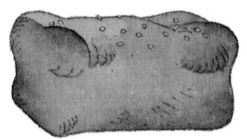

■ **Talk About Math** Which is more, 15 ounces or 15 pounds? Explain why.

Check Understanding

For another example, see Set G, pages 288–289.

Should each amount of food pictured be weighed in *ounces* or *pounds*? Write your answer.

1.

2.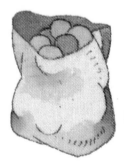

3.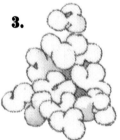

4.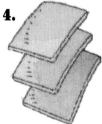

Practice

For More Practice, see Set G, pages 290–291.

Estimation Choose the more sensible customary measure for each.

5. Pair of socks

6 oz   6 lb

6. Football player

200 oz   200 lb

7. Baby's teddy bear

8 oz   8 lb

8. Large dog

70 oz   70 lb

9. Newborn baby

9 oz   9 lb

10. Bag of potatoes

5 oz   5 lb

Write *ounces* or *pounds* to tell which you would use to measure how much each weighs.

11. 10 dimes

12. Bookcase

13. 5 dictionaries

14. Pencil

15. 4 nails

16. Bar of soap

Mixed Practice Use the chart at the right to tell which customary measures a store uses to sell each product.

17. Largest container of milk

18. Whole turkey

19. Sliced ham for sandwiches

20. Small drinks of lemonade

Customary Measures	
Capacity	Weight
Cup Pint Quart Gallon	Ounce Pound

Problem Solving

Solve each problem.

21. Frances bought 9 ounces of peanuts and 6 ounces of walnuts. How can you tell if she has enough to make a pound?

22. ▦ **Calculator** Mary wants 2 pounds of sliced turkey. The scale reads 17 ounces. How many more ounces does she need?

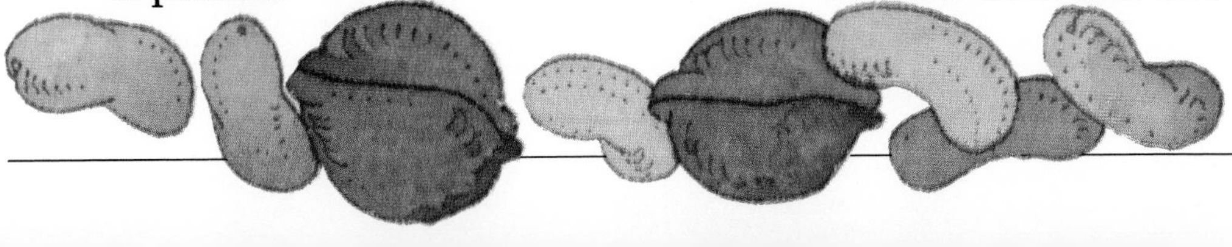

Metric Units of Mass

Build Understanding

Metric units used for measuring mass are the **gram** (g) and the **kilogram** (kg).

A. A dollar bill has a mass of about 1 gram.

B. A baseball bat has a mass of about 1 kilogram. A kilogram is 1,000 grams.

1 kg = 1,000 g

■ **Talk About Math** About how many five-dollar bills would it take for your money to weigh 1 kilogram? Explain why.

Check Understanding

For another example, see Set H, pages 288–289.

Should the object in the picture be measured in grams or kilograms?

1.

2.

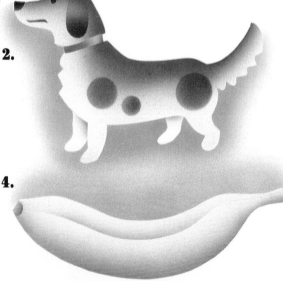

3.

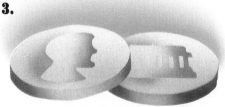

4.

Practice

For More Practice, see Set H, pages 290–291.

Estimation Choose the more sensible metric measure for each.

5. Ballpoint pen

2 g   2 kg

6. Piano

400 g   400 kg

7. Typewriter

15 g   15 kg

Write *grams* or *kilograms* to tell which you
would use to measure how much each weighs.

8. Slice of bread

9. Letter

10. Watermelon

11. School bus

12. Bicycle

13. Spoon

14. Toothpicks

15. Car tire

16. 10 grapes

Problem Solving

Number Sense Solve each problem.

17. Would 2,000 dollar bills weigh more or
less than 1 kilogram?

18. The label on a can of soup shows
251 grams. How many cans could
make 1 kilogram? Tell how you found
your answer.

Skills _____ Review

pages 168–169

For Exercises 1–3, tell whether you would use mental math
or paper and pencil. Then find each perimeter.

1.

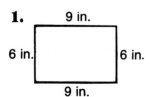

9 in.

6 in.   6 in.

9 in.

2.

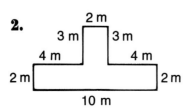

2 m

3 m   3 m

4 m   4 m

2 m   2 m

10 m

3.

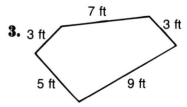

7 ft

3 ft   3 ft

5 ft   9 ft

281

Too Little Information

Build Understanding

PROBLEM SOLVING
GUIDE

Katie is making salad for a holiday picnic. She needs to make enough for 16 servings. How many apples should she buy?

Understand
QUESTION
FACTS
KEY IDEA

Plan and Solve
STRATEGY
ANSWER

Look Back
SENSIBLE ANSWER
ALTERNATE APPROACH

Understand

QUESTION How many apples should she buy?

FACTS The recipe tells you how many cups of diced apples Katie needs for 8 servings.

KEY IDEA If you know the amount for 8 servings, you need to double it for 16 servings.

Plan and Solve

Multiply everything in the recipe by 2 to double it.

ANSWER You need 8 cups of diced apples for 16 servings, but you still cannot tell how many apples to buy. The problem does not give you enough information to find out.

Look Back

The missing information is the number of cups of diced apples you get from one apple.

PICNIC APPLE SALAD

4 cups of diced apples

2 cups of plain yogurt

1 teaspoon of lemon juice

1 tablespoon of honey

Mix everything together.

Chill

Makes 8 servings

■ **Talk About Math** What happens if you don't have enough information to solve a problem?

Check Understanding

Use the recipe for Oh Jay Drink to answer the following questions.

1. Is there enough information to make this recipe?

2. What information do you need?

3. Why are units of measure important?

Practice

Tell how you solve each problem. If there is missing information, tell where you could find it.

4. Emily wants to make tuna salad. She needs 18 ounces of tuna for her recipe. How many cans should she buy?

5. Tyrone wants to take 16 packages of fruit juice to the picnic. How many 3-packs of juice should he buy?

6. Tanya asked the deli clerk for 3 pounds of potato salad. The clerk gave her four 8-ounce containers and one 16-ounce container. Did Tanya get the right amount?

7. Mr. Gomez plans to serve baked ham at a family party. The recipe says to bake 1 pound of ham for each diner. If he buys one ham, will there be enough for him and 15 guests?

Estimating Weights and Volumes

Build Understanding

A. About how many cubes do you think it will take to fill the carton?

  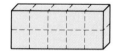

It takes 10 cubes to fill the carton.
The volume is 10 cubic units.

B. The carrot weighs about 4 ounces. How many carrots do you think it will take to make one pound?

Remember that 16 oz = 1 lb.

4 oz + 4 oz + 4 oz + 4 oz = 16 oz = 1 lb

It will take about 4 carrots to make a pound.

Talk About Math Explain what is the same and what is different about estimating volume and estimating weight.

What are some other kinds of root vegetables?

284

Check Understanding

1. Which is the correct volume for the box, 4 cubic units or 12 cubic units?

2. The banana weighs 8 ounces. About how many bananas will it take to make a pound?

Practice

Is the correct volume shown for each picture?
Write *yes* or *no*.

3.

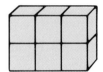

less than 5 cubic units

4.

more than 6 cubic units

5.

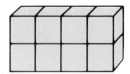

exactly 8 cubic units

6.

less than 8 cubic units

Tell how many of each object would make about 1 pound.

7. 1-ounce cracker

8. 2-ounce hotdog

9. 8-ounce bunch of grapes

10. 5-ounce tomato

Solve each problem.

1. Jason built a tower in the shape of a rectangular prism. It was 3 layers high with 4 cubes in the bottom layer. How many cubes did the tower have?

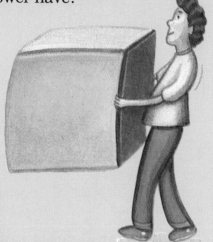

2. Which solid shape has 6 congruent faces?

3. Tell which letters of the alphabet are made with only line segments. Then tell which ones are symmetric.

4. How many cups are in 2 pints?

5. Luke traced the bottoms of several cans. Were the figures he drew congruent? Why or why not?

6. **Data File** Use data from pages 402-403. How many more grams of fat are in cream cheese than in the same amount of mozzarella cheese?

7. **Make a Data File** Find 4 items that come in at least 3 different sizes. Make a chart telling the items and the 3 sizes for each.

Problem Solving REVIEW

Explore with a Calculator

Multiple Measurements

1. To find the amount of trim needed to go around a bulletin board, Carlene measured each side in inches. This is the key sequence she used.

34 ⊞ 28 ⊞ 34 ⊞ 28 ⊟

Troy used this key sequence.

34 ⊞ 28 ⊠ 2 ⊟

a. What answers did they get?

b. Why does Troy's sequence work?

2. Write 2 key sequences that will help solve each problem.

a. What is the perimeter of this calendar?

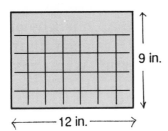

9 in.

←——— 12 in. ———→

b. What is the area of this floor?

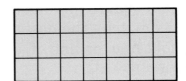

c. What is the volume of this display box of *Crazy Cubes?*

d. Betina was giving Thomas a crazy cube for his birthday. How much ribbon did she need to go around the present?

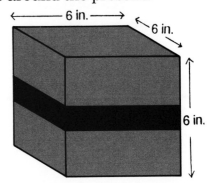

←——— 6 in. ———→ ↖ 6 in.

6 in.

Reteaching

Set A
pages 258–261

This stop sign is an octagon.

It has 8 corners and 8 sides.

Remember that geometric figures have curves or line segments as sides. Give the number of sides and corners.

1.  **2.**

Set B
pages 262–263

When two sides of a figure meet, they form an angle.

This hexagon has six angles, because it has six corners.

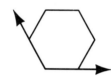

Remember that right angles form square corners. How many angles are there in each figure? Are they right angles?

1.   **2.**

Set C
pages 264–265

You can fold a square and make the two parts match. The dashed line is the fold line, or line of symmetry.

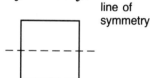

line of symmetry   no line of symmetry

Remember that some figures have more than one line of symmetry. Does each figure look symmetric? Write yes or no.

1.  **2.**

Set D
pages 266–267

Congruent figures have the same size and shape.

The triangles are congruent.

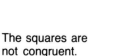

The squares are not congruent.

Remember that figures are congruent if you can place one on the other and they match.

Tell which is congruent to the figure at the right.

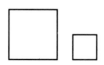

a. 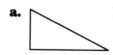 **b.**

288

Set E pages 274-275

John knows these facts:

A glass of water is about 1 cup.
Two cups make 1 pint.
Two pints make 1 quart.
Four quarts make 1 gallon.

He knew that the water in a fish tank is measured in gallons.

Remember that customary units for liquids tell how much liquid a container will hold.

Choose the more sensible customary measure for each.

1. Gas tank
  pint gallon

2. Flower vase
  pint gallon

Set F pages 276-277

Amy knows these facts:

5 milliliters is about 1 teaspoon.
1 liter is 1,000 milliliters.

Knowing this, she knew that the water in the fish bowl is measured in liters.

Remember that milliliters are used when very small amounts of liquid are involved.

Write liter or milliliter to tell which you would use to measure how much each holds.

1.   **2.**

Set G pages 278-279

José knows these facts:

A thin slice of bread weighs about 1 ounce.
A loaf of bread weighs about 1 pound.

José's dog could weigh 15 pounds, but not 15 ounces.

Remember that ounces are used to measure "dry" items and fluid ounces are used to measure liquid items.

Write ounces or pounds to tell which you would use to measure

1. a couch.   **2.** an eraser.

Set H pages 280-281

Loo knows these facts:

A dollar bill has a mass of 1 gram.
A baseball bat has a mass of 1 kilogram.

She knew that the mass of an insect was measured in grams.

Remember that grams are used when very small amounts of mass are involved.

Write grams or kilograms to tell which you would use to measure

1. a medicine pill.   **2.** a truck.

More Practice

Set A   pages 258-261

Give the name of each shape. Then give the
number of sides and corners each shape has.

1.   2.   3.

Set B   pages 262-263

How many angles are there in each figure?
Are they right angles? Write yes or no.

1.   2.   3.   4.

Set C   pages 264-265

Does each figure look symmetric? Write *yes*
or *no*.

1.   2.   3.   4.

Set D   pages 266-267

Match the congruent figures. Write the letter
for each number.

1.   a.   4.   d.

2.   b.   5.   e.

3.   c.   6.   f.

Set E   pages 274–275

Estimation   Choose the more sensible
customary measure for each.

1.

2 c   2 gal

2.

1 c   1 qt

3.

1 qt   1 gal

Set F   pages 276–277

Estimation   Choose the more sensible
metric measure for each.

1.

10 mL   10 L

2.

4 mL   4 L

3.

250 L   250 mL

Set G   pages 279–279

Estimation   Choose the more sensible
customary measure for each.

1.

5 oz   5 lb

2.
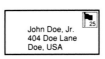

1 oz   1 lb

3.

10 oz   10 lb

Set H   pages 280–281

Estimation   Choose the more sensible
metric unit for each.

1.

2 g   2 kg

2.

100 g   100 kg

3.

40 g   40 kg

Enrichment

Angles of Geometric Figures

Two line segments that meet form an angle. The sides of many geometric figures are line segments. When two sides meet at a corner, they form an angle. How many angles does a triangle have?

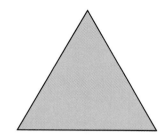

There are three angles, one at each corner of the triangle. Angle 1 is formed by sides CA and BA. The sides meet at corner A. This angle is named angle CAB or angle BAC. Is angle CAB the same as angle BAC? Every angle has two names made of three letters. The middle letter tells the corner where the angle is.

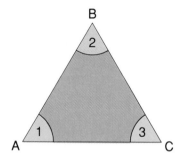

1. Write two names for angle 2.

2. What are two names for angle 3?

3. How many angles are in this square?

4. Name the angles. Give two names for each angle.

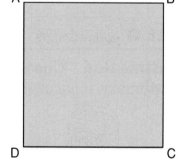

5. How many angles can you find in this rectangle? Write two names for each angle.

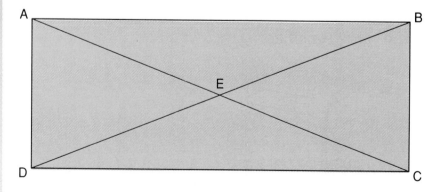

Chapter 8 Review/Test

Give the name for each shape. Use *sphere, cube, square,* or *hexagon.*

1.

2.

3. Is this angle a right angle?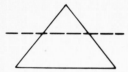

4. Is the broken line a line of symmetry?

5. Which two figures are congruent?

   a.   b.   c.

6. Find the volume in cubic units.

Choose the more sensible measure for each.

7. Can of tomato soup
   cup   quart

8. Perfume bottle
   milliliter   liter

9. Weight of a giraffe
   ounce   pound

10. Mass of a ruler
    gram   kilogram

11. Mass of a chair
    gram   kilogram

12. Write how many 4-ounce peaches would make about 1 *pound.*

Winners of Weekly Spell-off	
Erin	X X X
Jacob	X X
André	X X X X
Elena	X X X
X = 1 spell-off won	

13. Which problem can be solved with data from the graph?

    a. How many words did Erin spell correctly?
    b. How many more times did André win than Jacob?
    c. How many children did not win a spell-off?

14. Solve the problem you chose in Exercise 13.

15. ■ **Write About Math**
    Explain your reason for your answer to Exercise 4.

293

Division Concepts

9

Did You Know: In 1977, Peter Dowdeswell set a record for eating pancakes by eating 62 buttered pancakes with syrup in just under 7 minutes.

294

Number-Sense Project

Estimate
How many in your family would like to have some of these pancakes?

Gather Data
In your family, if these 18 pancakes were divided equally, how many would each person get?

Analyze and Report
Compare your results with other students.

295

Sharing

Build Understanding

ACTIVITY

Deal Out the Daisies
Materials: Small objects
Groups: 3–5 students

A. Suppose you work at your aunt's flower shop. She hands you 15 flowers and 5 vases. You must put the same number of flowers in each vase. How many should go in each vase?

a. Use 15 small objects.

b. Show a place on your desk for each group.

c. Start by putting 1 object in each group.

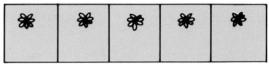

d. Do you have enough to put 1 more in each group? Try.

e. Keep going until you do not have enough objects to put 1 in each group.

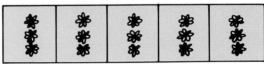

When you put the same number of objects into groups this way, you are ***sharing*** the objects equally among the groups.

You would put 3 flowers in each vase.

B. On another day you have 5 baskets to fill.

   a. If you have 10 flowers, how many go in each basket?

   b. If you have 20 flowers, how many go in each basket?

   c. If you have 25 flowers, how many go in each basket?

c. You have 24 tulips. Your aunt wants you to put the same amount into each vase.

   a. If you have 3 vases, how many flowers go in each vase?

   b. If you have 6 vases, how many go in each vase?

   c. If you have 8 vases, how many go in each vase?

■ **Talk About Math** In Example C, when you have more than 8 vases, will you put more or fewer flowers in each vase? How can you tell?

Check Understanding

For another example, see Set A, pages 322–323.

Look at the box at the right.
Then answer the questions.

1. If you had 12 flower seeds, what would you do first to find how many seeds there would be in each group?

2. What would you do next?

3. How many would be in each group?

4. If there were 20 seeds in all, how many would be in each group?

VIOLETS

12 seeds in all
4 groups
▦ seeds in each group

Practice

For More Practice, see Set A, pages 324–325.

For each exercise use small objects or draw pictures to find each answer.

5. 16 in all
4 equal groups
How many in
each group?

6. 9 in all
3 equal groups
How many in
each group?

7. 12 in all
3 equal groups
How many in
each group?

8. 10 in all
2 equal groups
How many in
each group?

9. 25 in all
5 equal groups
How many in
each group?

10. 18 in all
2 equal groups
How many in
each group?

11. 14 in all
7 equal groups
How many in
each group?

12. 24 in all
2 equal groups
How many in
each group?

13. 12 in all
4 equal groups
How many in
each group?

Problem Solving

Choose a _____ Strategy

14. A flower arrangement has 36 flowers. The same number of flowers are on each side of a candle. How many flowers are on each side?

PROBLEM SOLVING
STRATEGIES

Choose an Operation
Find a Pattern
Use Logical Reasoning
Make a Table
Draw a Picture

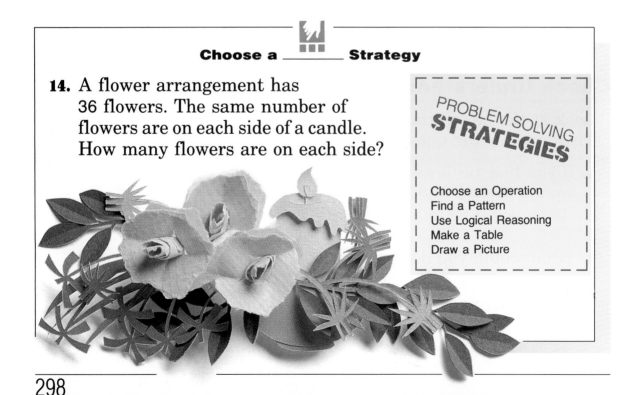

Tell the shape of each object in Exercises 1–8.
Use the pictures to help you.

sphere

cube

cylinder

rectangular prism

circle

square

triangle

rectangle

1. baseball

2. envelope

3. can of peas

4. shoe box

5. sail on boat

6. stick of butter

7. ring

8. photo 3 inches high and 3 inches wide

Tell whether you would use grams or kilograms
to measure the weight of each object.

9. TV set   **10.** comb   **11.** piece of paper

Tell whether you would use milliliters
or liters to measure how much each holds.

12. Juice glass   **13.** Bathtub

14. Soup bowl

299

Grouping

Build Understanding

Gerbil Family Photos
Materials: Small objects
Groups: 3–5 students

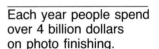

A. Your class has been raising gerbils as a science project. Last week Geraldine and Billy Gerbil had babies. The teacher picked you to take pictures of them. Now you have 20 photos to put in the class album. If you want 4 photos on each page, how many pages will you use?

a. Count out 20 small objects. You will make a group for each page.

b. Start by making 1 group of 4.

c. Are there enough to make another group of 4? Try.

Each year people spend over 4 billion dollars on photo finishing.

d. Keep going until you do not have enough objects to make another group of 4. When you put objects together this way, you are ***grouping*** the objects.

You would use 5 pages in the album.

B. You have more album pages to fill. Put 4 photos on each page.

a. If you have 12 field trip photos, how many pages will you fill?

b. If you have 24 class play photos, how many pages will you fill?

c. If you have 28 school picnic photos, how many pages will you fill?

In Example B, the total number of photos changes but the number of photos on a page stays the same. What can you say about the number of pages?

C. You took 24 photos of your science project for your album.

a. How many pages will you fill if you put 3 photos on a page?

b. How many pages will you fill if you put 6 photos on a page?

c. How many pages will you fill if you put 8 photos on a page?

■ **Talk About Math** In Example C, the total number of photos stays the same but the number of photos on a page changes. What can you say about the number of pages?

Check Understanding

For another example, see Set B, pages 322–323.

Use the numbers to write a story problem about gerbils. Find the answer.

1. 27 in all, 3 in each group   **2.** 15 in all, 3 in each group

Number Sense Suppose you have 20 objects. You want to make equal groups with no objects left over. Can you have equal groups of

3. 7 objects?   **4.** 6 objects?

5. 5 objects?   **6.** 4 objects?

7. 3 objects?   **8.** 2 objects?

Practice

For More Practice, see Set B, pages 324–325.

Use small objects or draw pictures to find each answer.

9. 12 in all
4 in each group
How many
groups?

10. 18 in all
3 in each group
How many
groups?

11. 30 in all
5 in each group
How many
groups?

12. 8 in all
4 in each group
How many
groups?

13. 15 in all
3 in each group
How many
groups?

14. 12 in all
2 in each group
How many
groups?

15. 10 in all
2 in each group
How many
groups?

16. 16 in all
4 in each group
How many
groups?

17. 24 in all
6 in each group
How many
groups?

Problem Solving

Solve each problem.

TIPS FOR PROBLEM SOLVERS

Don't give up. Some problems take longer than others.

18. The class had 9 goldfish. They put 3 fish in each bowl. How many bowls did they use?

19. Mr. Hughes has 63 science books for his third graders. If he orders 49 more books, how many will he have?

20. For his project, Steve planted 3 rows of seeds. Each row had 25 seeds. How many seeds did he plant?

Explore ———— Math

Calculator   You want to put 28 objects into groups of 7 each. You can use repeated subtraction to find the number of groups.

Press:	You see:	Make a ✔ each time you subtract.
28 − 7 =	*21*	✔
− 7 =	*14*	✔
− 7 =	*7*	✔
− 7 =	*0*	✔

Count how many 7s you subtracted from 28. There are 4 groups of 7 in 28.

Do repeated subtraction on your calculator to find the number of groups.

21. 16 in all, 2 in each group

22. 21 in all, 3 in each group

23. 10 in all, 5 in each group

24. 24 in all, 6 in each group

Meaning of Division

Build Understanding

A. During story hour, 6 children will read 12 pages orally. How many pages will each child read if each reads an equal number of pages?

Say: 12 pages divided equally among 6 children is 2 pages for each child.

12 divided by 6 is 2.

Write: **12 ÷ 6 = 2**

B. 18 books in all. 9 books on each shelf. How many shelves?

Say: 18 books divided by putting 9 on each shelf is 2 shelves.

18 divided by 9 is 2.

Write: **18 ÷ 9 = 2**

■ **Talk About Math**   Look at Examples A and B. Which shows sharing? Which shows grouping?

Check Understanding

For another example, see Set C, pages 322–323.

Number Sense   Answer each question.

1. What does the term *divide* mean?

2. If 12 ÷ ☐ = △, what is 12 ÷ △?

Use the picture to help answer each question.

3. How many books are on the table?

4. How many groups of 2 books could you make?
Complete: 12 ÷ 2 = ▦

5. If you make 6 equal groups, how many would be in each group?
Complete: 12 ÷ 6 = ▦

Practice

For More Practice, see Set C, pages 324–325.

Write the division sentence for each exercise.
Draw pictures to help you.

6. 28 in all
4 in each group
▦ groups
28 ÷ 4 = ▦

7. 21 in all
3 groups
▦ in each group
21 ÷ 3 = ▦

8. 16 in all
2 in each group
▦ groups
16 ÷ 2 = ▦

9.

▦ in all
3 bowls
▦ ÷ 3 = △

10.

▦ in all
3 boxes
▦ ÷ 3 = △

11.

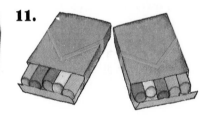

▦ in all
5 in each box
▦ ÷ 5 = △

12.

▦ in all
△ bowls
▦ ÷ △ = ◇

13.

▦ in all
△ in each stack
▦ ÷ △ = ◇

14.

▦ in all
△ groups
▦ ÷ △ = ◇

Dividing by Two and Three

Build Understanding

The P. E. teacher says biking is a healthy exercise. Her bike club has 18 bikers. If there are 3 bikers on a team, how many teams are there?

You can use repeated subtraction to help you find the number of groups. How many times can 3 be subtracted from 18? 6 times.

$$18 - 3 = 15$$
$$15 - 3 = 12$$
$$12 - 3 = 9$$
$$9 - 3 = 6$$
$$6 - 3 = 3$$
$$3 - 3 = 0$$

$18 \div 3 = 6$

There are 6 teams.

■ Talk About Math

How many teams would there be if there were 9 bikers on a team?

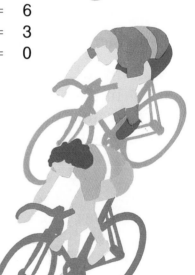

Where have you ridden a bicycle?

Check Understanding

For another example, see Set D, pages 322–323.

For Exercises 1–4, tell how you can use counting by 2s or 3s to help find the answer. Then write each answer.

1. $16 \div 2$ **2.** $9 \div 3$ **3.** $10 \div 2$ **4.** $6 \div 3$

5. Use repeated subtraction to find $24 \div 3$.

Practice

For More Practice, see Set D, pages 324–325.

Write each answer. **Remember** to draw pictures to help you.

6. 18 ÷ 2   **7.** 15 ÷ 3   **8.** 6 ÷ 2   **9.** 9 ÷ 3

10. 14 ÷ 2   **11.** 4 ÷ 2   **12.** 21 ÷ 3   **13.** 6 ÷ 3

14. 27 ÷ 3   **15.** 18 ÷ 3   **16.** 16 ÷ 2   **17.** 8 ÷ 2

18. 24 ÷ 3   **19.** 12 ÷ 3   **20.** 10 ÷ 2   **21.** 12 ÷ 2

Problem Solving

Solve each problem.

22. Critical Thinking In the example on page 306, how could you use addition or multiplication to find the answer?

23. Your school volleyball club has 14 players. The coach wants to make 2 equal teams. How many children will be on each team?

24. There are 12 members on the skating team. 4 of them started skating this year. How many started before this year?

25. The hiking club has 7 teams with 3 members in each team. How many members are there in all?

26. Estimation Carl has 23 decorations for the soccer team party. He wants to put them in 3 rooms. If he divided them as evenly as possible, about how many will be in each room?

Dividing by Four

Build Understanding

A. Julie wants to make 20 candles. She has 4 different candle molds. She will make an equal number of each. How many should she make in each mold?

You can use multiplication facts to help find the number of each kind.

Think: 4 times what number is 20?

$4 \times \boxed{} = 20$
$4 \times 5 = 20$

20 ÷ 4 = 5

Julie can make 5 candles using each mold.

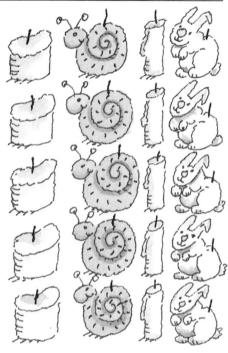

B. You can write division another way.

$$20 \div 4 = 5 \qquad 4\overline{)20}$$

Quotient — 5
Divisor
Dividend

■ **Talk About Math** In the division fact, 20 is called the dividend. What is 20 called in the multiplication fact? What are 4 and 5 called in the multiplication fact?

Check Understanding

For another example, see Set E, pages 322–323.

Number Sense Copy each sentence and write number words to complete. Then draw a picture to match the sentence.

1. ? paint brushes divided into groups of 4 are ? groups.

2. ? jars of paint divided into 4 sets are ? jars in each set.

Copy each exercise. Then write each quotient.

3. 8 ÷ 4   **4.** 12 ÷ 4   **5.** 16 ÷ 4   **6.** 20 ÷ 4

7. 4)‾24‾   **8.** 4)‾28‾   **9.** 4)‾32‾   **10.** 4)‾36‾

11. On your paper, circle each quotient in Exercises 3–6. Put a box around each divisor in Exercises 7–10.

12. Find the words *quotient, dividend,* and *divisor* in the Glossary. Write the meaning for each in your journal.

Practice

For More Practice, see Set E, pages 324–325.

Find each quotient. **Remember** to use multiplication facts to help you.

13. 20 ÷ 4   **14.** 16 ÷ 4   **15.** 12 ÷ 4   **16.** 8 ÷ 4

17. 28 ÷ 4   **18.** 24 ÷ 4   **19.** 32 ÷ 4   **20.** 12 ÷ 4

21. 4)‾32‾   **22.** 4)‾16‾   **23.** 4)‾20‾   **24.** 4)‾36‾

Mental Math   Find each answer.

25. 42 + 7   **26.** 12 ÷ 2   **27.** 3 × 4   **28.** 16 − 4   **29.** 12 ÷ 3

30. 25 − 14   **31.** 9 ÷ 3   **32.** 18 + 6   **33.** 5 × 7   **34.** 20 − 8

Midchapter _____ Checkup

Write each answer.

1. 14 in all
7 equal groups
How many in each group?

2. 24 in all
3 in each group
How many groups?

Find each quotient.

3. 24 ÷ 4   **4.** 15 ÷ 3   **5.** 6 ÷ 2   **6.** 18 ÷ 2   **7.** 27 ÷ 3

Number-Sense Project

Food	How many would like some?	Would each get an equal amount?	How many would I get?
15 pancakes	5	no	6
12 apples	4	no	1
8 slices of pizza	5	no	2
10 biscuits	5	no	3
15 strawberries	3	yes	5

Look back at pages 294-295.
Allan thought about how different foods would be divided in his family. He recorded the information above.

Would Allan get more or less of these items if they were divided equally in his family of five?

1. Pancakes **2.** Biscuits

3. Apples **4.** Strawberries

Critical Thinking Activity

Copy the two loops. Write the numbers in the correct loop or loops.

4 12 18 10 9 16 2 14 6 8 15

Two is a factor of   Three is a factor of

8   6   15

Real-Life Decision Making

You need to buy some new pencils. Two stores near your home are having a sale. How many pencils would you buy? Where would you buy them? Why? How much would they cost?

SALE
2 PENCILS FOR 18¢

15¢ each

15¢ each

All PENCILS SALE 5¢ off

Math-at-Home Activity

Write the numbers 2, 2, 3, 3, 4, 4, 5, 5, 6, 7, 8, and 9 on individual pieces of paper and put them in a bag. Each member of your family should draw out 3 numbers. (Put in extra 2s, 3s, 4s, and 5s if you need them so everyone can have 3 numbers.)

You must look for items around your home that come in multiples of the numbers you have drawn. When everyone has found their items, make a list. Which multiple was easiest to find items for? Which was the hardest?

Try and Check

Build Understanding

Brian's father weighs 100 pounds more than Brian. Together they weigh 240 pounds. How much does Brian weigh?

PROBLEM SOLVING
GUIDE

Understand
QUESTION
FACTS
KEY IDEA

Plan and Solve
STRATEGY
ANSWER

Look Back
SENSIBLE ANSWER
ALTERNATE APPROACH

Understand Brian's father weighs 100 pounds more than Brian. The sum of their weights is 240 pounds.

Plan and Solve STRATEGY Guess Brian's weight. Add 100 pounds to find his father's weight. Check to see if those weights total 240 pounds.

If Brian weighs 60 pounds, then Brian's father weighs 60 + 100 or 160 pounds. Their total weight is 60 + 160 or 220 pounds. That is too small.

Try other weights. Make a table to help you.

	Brian	Father	Total	
Try 60 pounds.	60	160	220	too small
Try 80 pounds.	80	180	260	too large
Try 70 pounds.	70	170	240	correct

ANSWER Brian weighs 70 pounds.

Look Back Is the computation correct? Does Brian's father weigh 100 pounds more than Brian? Do the two weights total 240 pounds?

312

■ **Talk About Math** Can you think of another way to figure out Brian's weight?

Check Understanding

Solve the problem by answering Questions 1–5.

Ann and Amy are twins. Bob and Bill are twins. The girls are 2 years older than the boys. The sum of all four ages is 40. How old are they?

1. If Ann and Amy are 9 years old, how old are Bob and Bill?

2. If Ann and Amy are 9 years old, what is the sum of all four ages?

3. Are Ann and Amy older or younger than 9 years old?

4. What number could you try next for the age of Ann and Amy?

5. Try different numbers for the ages of Ann and Amy. Find the ages of Bob and Bill. Do this until you find four ages which total 40.

Practice

Solve each problem. Use *Try and Check* to find the answers.

6. There are 100 math and science books on a shelf. There are 20 more math books than science books. How many of each kind are there?

7. There are 16 cans of either corn or peas in the cupboard. There are 3 times as many cans of corn as there are peas. How many cans of each are there?

8. John and his sister Cindy have 50 tapes. Cindy has 10 more tapes than John. How many tapes does each child have?

9. Noreen has 2 dozen eggs. She has 4 fewer white eggs than brown eggs. How many eggs of each color are there?

Dividing by Five

Build Understanding

A. You can get a nickel for 5 pennies. How many groups of 5 pennies can be made from 35 pennies?

35 ÷ 5 = 7   5 × 7 = 35

You can get 7 nickels for 35 pennies.

B. If you divide the 35 pennies equally among 5 people, how many pennies would each person get?

35 ÷ 5 = 7

Each person would get 7 pennies.

Remember:
You can write division in two ways.

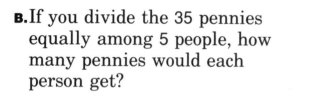

$$35 \div 5 = 7 \qquad 5\overline{)35}$$

Quotient — Divisor — Dividend

■ **Talk About Math** Explain how you can use multiplication to check division.

Check Understanding

For another example, see Set F, pages 322–323.

Match each picture to a division sentence.

1.

2.

3.

a. 25 ÷ 5 = 5

b. 20 ÷ 5 = 4

c. 15 ÷ 5 = 3

For each multiplication fact, write a division exercise with 5 as the divisor.

4. $2 \times 5 = 10$ **5.** $6 \times 5 = 30$ **6.** $9 \times 5 = 45$ **7.** $7 \times 5 = 35$

Practice

For More Practice, see Set F, pages 324–325.

Write each quotient.

8. $30 \div 5$ **9.** $45 \div 5$ **10.** $10 \div 5$ **11.** $20 \div 5$

12. $35 \div 5$ **13.** $40 \div 5$ **14.** $15 \div 5$ **15.** $25 \div 5$

16. $5 \overline{)30}$ **17.** $5 \overline{)40}$ **18.** $5 \overline{)35}$ **19.** $5 \overline{)45}$

Mixed Practice   Use mental math or paper and pencil to find each answer. Tell which method you used.

20. 6×5 **21.** $24 \div 4$ **22.** $18 + 209$ **23.** $20 \div 5$ **24.** $37 - 29$

25. $30 \div 5$ **26.** $16 \div 2$ **27.** $153 - 94$ **28.** $27 \div 3$ **29.** 4×9

Problem Solving

Solve each problem.

30. Deanne has 40 cents. All of the coins are nickels. How many nickels does she have?

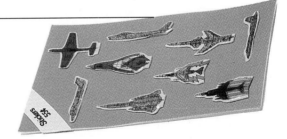

31. Su Lin has 7 nickels in his pocket. How much money is that?

32. Sasha has 9 nickels. He wants stickers that cost 55 cents. Does he have enough money?

33. Kelly has 15 cents in nickels in one hand and 6 nickels in her other hand. How many nickels does she have in all?

34. **Use Data**   Write division facts for the arrays in Exercises 2–4 on page 195.

Write a Number Sentence

Build Understanding

T. J. is buying tapes at a store in the mall. Each package has 3 tapes. How many packages should T. J. buy to have 15 tapes in all?

Understand   You know how many in all. You know how many in each group. You need to find how many groups.

IIIII▶ **Plan and Solve**   STRATEGY   You can use a number sentence to show how the parts of a problem are related.

Write the numbers and math signs for the words.

▦ packages	of 3 tapes each	is 15 tapes.
↓	↓	↓
▦	× 3	= 15

To find the missing number, think of the division fact.

$15 ÷ 3 = ▦$ $15 ÷ 3 = 5$

ANSWER   T. J. needs to buy 5 packages of tapes.

Look Back   Read the question again. Does the answer make sense?

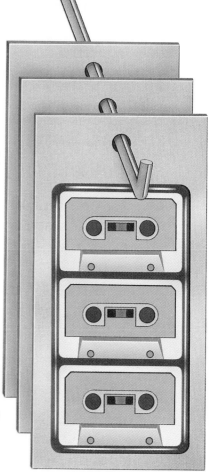

■ **Write About Math**   Explain how you could use objects to solve T. J.'s problem.

Check Understanding

Solve the problem by answering Questions 1–4.

Angie has to buy muffin pans. Each muffin pan will hold 6 muffins. How many muffin pans should Angie buy to bake 24 muffins?

1. What are you asked to find?

2. What facts are you given?

3. Which number sentence can help solve this problem?
   a. 24 − 6 = ▦
   b. ▦ + 6 = 24
   c. ▦ × 6 = 24

4. Write the answer to the problem in a complete sentence.

Practice

Write a number sentence for each problem. Then solve the problems.

5. The mall has parking space for 1,280 cars in the north lot and 975 cars in the east lot. How many parking spaces are there in the two lots?

6. Brienne's Card Shop ordered 560 greeting cards in May. They ordered 435 cards in June. How many more cards did they order in May?

7. Cari wants to buy 12 pairs of socks. The socks are sold 3 pairs to a package. How many packages should Cari buy?

8. At the book store, a display shelf holds 8 books. There are 4 display shelves. How many books can be displayed?

Choose a _____ Strategy

9. There are 5 children and 2 adults in each van. There are 40 children in all. How many vans are there? What is the total number of adults?

Families of Facts

Build Understanding

A. You can write 2 multiplication sentences about the poster.

$2 \times 3 = 6$
$3 \times 2 = 6$

You also can write 2 division sentences about the poster.

$6 \div 2 = 3$
$6 \div 3 = 2$

These four sentences are a *family of facts.*

B. This family of facts has only 2 number sentences.

$4 \times 4 = 16$
$16 \div 4 = 4$

■ **Talk About Math**   What can you say about the numbers that make up a family of facts?

Check Understanding

For another example, see Set G, pages 322–323.

1. Write two number sentences to complete this family of facts.

$2 \times 5 = 10$ $10 \div 5 = 2$

2. Choose a multiplication fact. Draw a picture for it. Write the family of facts for it.

318

Practice

For More Practice, see Set G, pages 324–325.

Write the number sentences to complete
each family of facts. Write each answer.

3. $4 \times 5 =$ **4.** $3 \times 4 =$ **5.** $4 \times 2 =$ **6.** $5 \times 5 =$

$20 \div 4 =$ $12 \div 4 =$ $2 \times 4 =$

Write the family of facts using the given numbers.

7. 3, 5, 15   **8.** 2, 2, 4   **9.** 2, 5, 10   **10.** 4, 4, 16

Problem Solving

Solve each problem.

11. Choose one family of facts from Exercises 3–5. Write a word problem for each fact.

12. Use Data Will the families of facts for Exercises 3–18 on page 227 have 2 or 4 sentences? Why?

13. Critical Thinking Write 4 facts for the picture. You may use addition, subtraction, multiplication, and division.

Reading ———— Math

Vocabulary Match the number sentences to the problems.

1. Carl buys 6 packs with 4 toys each. How many are there in all?

2. Carl separates 28 baseball cards into 4 equal piles. How many are in each pile?

3. Carl has 28 cans and gives 4 away. How many does he have left?

a. $28 - 4 =$

b. $28 \div 4 =$

c. $6 \times 4 =$

d. $6 - 4 =$

Solve each problem.

1. How many apples did Chet pick?

Number of Apples Picked				
ROSA	🍎	🍎	🍎	
JOE	🍎	🍎		
DANIELLE	🍎			
CHET	🍎	🍎	🍎	🍎

Each 🍎 stands for 2 apples.

2. How many more apples did Rosa pick than Joe?

3. Father bought 3 packages of ground beef. Each package weighed between 2 and 3 pounds Could he have 7 pounds? Could he have 10 pounds? Explain.

4. Delia has 17 pairs of socks in 4 colors. There are 3 pairs more of blue than pink socks. She has 5 pairs of white socks and 1 pair of red. How many pairs of blue socks does Delia have?

5. Marta and Chuck each bought 18 books. Marta's bookcase has 3 shelves. Chuck's bookcase has 2 shelves. Who has more books on a shelf if the books are shared equally on the shelves? How many more?

6. **Data File** Use data from pages 402-403. Bonita can toast 4 slices of bread at one time. How many sets of toast will she make if she uses the entire loaf?

7. **Make a Data File** Find the number of players on 5 different team sports. Make a table to show your findings.

Problem Solving REVIEW

Explore with a Calculator

Pick 'Em Game

1. Play "Pick 'Em." Complete each number sentence by "picking" one number and one sign from each tree. Once you have picked a number and a sign, it cannot be used again. You should have used them all when you are finished.

a. ■ □ 4 = 36

b. 7 □ ■ = 12

c. 24 □ 6 = ■

d. 37 □ ■ = 46

e. ■ □ 7 = 21

f. 47 □ ■ = 41

g. 64 □ ■ = 8

h. 2 □ 2 = ■

Reteaching
Set A   pages 296–298

There are 3 students in each art class group. Your group was given 27 crayons to share equally. How many will each student receive?

This picture shows that each student will receive 9 crayons.

Remember that you are sharing when you find how many objects are in each group.

For each exercise, use small objects or draw pictures to find each answer.

1. 16 in all
  8 equal groups
  How many in each group?

2. 12 in all
  4 equal groups
  How many in each group?

Set B   pages 300–303

Tony has 30 stamps to put in his stamp book. Each page will hold 6 stamps. How many pages will the stamps fill?

xx	xx	xx	xx	xx
xx	xx	xx	xx	xx
xx	xx	xx	xx	xx

The stamps will fill 5 pages.

Remember that the number of pages will be less if you put more stamps on each page.

Use small objects or draw pictures to find each answer.

1. 9 in all
  3 in each group
  ⬚ groups?

2. 21 in all
  7 in each group
  ⬚ groups?

Set C   pages 304–305

There are 4 students in each science class group. Amy's group has to collect 24 leaves for a science project. How many leaves will each student have to collect?

Say: 24 leaves divided equally
    among 4 students is 6
    leaves for each student.
    24 divided by 4 is 6.

Write: 24 ÷ 4 = 6

Remember that to divide means to share objects equally or to group objects equally.

Write the division sentence for each exercise. Draw pictures to help you.

1. 27 in all
  9 in each group
  ⬚ groups

2. 24 in all
  3 groups
  ⬚ in each group

Set D   pages 306–307

The hiking club has 12 members. Each team has 2 people. How many teams are in the club?

Count the number of times you can subtract 2 from 12.

$$12 - 2 = 10$$
$$10 - 2 = 8$$
$$8 - 2 = 6$$
$$6 - 2 = 4$$
$$4 - 2 = 2$$
$$2 - 2 = 0$$

$12 \div 2 = 6$ There are 6 teams.

Remember that you can use counting by 2s to divide by 2, and counting by 3s to divide by 3.

Write each answer.

1. $10 \div 2$ **2.** $12 \div 3$

3. $16 \div 2$ **4.** $15 \div 3$

5. $14 \div 2$ **6.** $21 \div 3$

Set E   pages 308–309

You can use multiplication facts to find $24 \div 4$.

Think: 4 times what number is 24?

$$4 \times \blacksquare = 24$$
$$4 \times 6 = 24$$
$$24 \div 4 = 6$$

Remember that the quotient is the answer to a division problem.

Find each quotient.

1. $28 \div 4$ **2.** $16 \div 4$

3. $4\overline{)12}$ **4.** $4\overline{)28}$

Set F   pages 314–315

Each row in the plane has 5 seats. How many rows will 35 people fill? Find $35 \div 5$.

Think: $5 \times \blacksquare = 35$
         $5 \times 7 = 35$
         $35 \div 5 = 7$ It will take 7 rows.

Remember that you can write a division problem by using $\div$ or $\overline{)}$. Write each quotient.

1. $20 \div 5$ **2.** $30 \div 5$ **3.** $5\overline{)25}$

Set G   pages 318–319

You can write a family of facts about this picture.

□ □ □
□ □ □
□ □ □
□ □ □

$$3 \times 4 = 12$$
$$4 \times 3 = 12$$
$$12 \div 3 = 4$$
$$12 \div 4 = 3$$

Remember that a family of facts for some numbers has only two number sentences.

Write the number sentences to complete each family of facts.

1. $4 \times 6 = 24$ **2.** $3 \times 5 = 15$
    $24 \div 6 = 4$

More Practice

Set A pages 296–298

For each exercise use small objects or draw
pictures to find each answer.

1. 18 in all
   3 equal groups
   How many in
   each group?

2. 15 in all
   3 equal groups
   How many in
   each group?

3. 12 in all
   2 equal groups
   How many in
   each group?

4. 10 in all
   5 equal groups
   How many in
   each group?

5. 21 in all
   7 equal groups
   How many in
   each group?

6. 18 in all
   6 equal groups
   How many in
   each group?

Set B pages 300–303

Use small objects or draw pictures to find
each answer.

1. 10 in all
   5 in each group
   How many groups?

2. 12 in all
   3 in each group
   How many groups?

3. 18 in all
   6 in each group
   How many groups?

4. 24 in all
   8 in each group
   How many groups?

5. 16 in all
   2 in each group
   How many groups?

6. 30 in all
   6 in each group
   How many groups?

Set C pages 304–305

Write the division sentence for each exercise.
Draw pictures to help you.

1. 24 in all
   4 groups
   ▦ in each group
   $24 \div 4 = $ ▦

2. 15 in all
   3 in each group
   ▦ groups
   $15 \div 3 = $ ▦

3. 25 in all
   5 in each group
   ▦ groups
   $25 \div 5 = $ ▦

4. 9 in all
   3 groups
   ▦ in each group
   $9 \div 3 = $ ▦

5. 20 in all
   5 in each group
   ▦ groups
   $20 \div 5 = $ ▦

6. 16 in all
   4 groups
   ▦ in each group
   $16 \div 4 = $ ▦

Set D pages 306–307

Write each answer.

1. $10 \div 2$ **2.** $24 \div 3$ **3.** $9 \div 3$ **4.** $14 \div 2$ **5.** $18 \div 3$

6. $8 \div 2$ **7.** $18 \div 2$ **8.** $21 \div 3$ **9.** $27 \div 3$ **10.** $24 \div 2$

Set E pages 308–309

Find each quotient.

1. $28 \div 4$ **2.** $16 \div 4$ **3.** $32 \div 8$ **4.** $12 \div 4$ **5.** $36 \div 4$

6. $4\overline{)12}$ **7.** $4\overline{)8}$ **8.** $4\overline{)20}$ **9.** $4\overline{)32}$ **10.** $4\overline{)24}$

Mental Math   Find each answer.

11. $31 + 8$ **12.** 3×5 **13.** $15 - 3$ **14.** $18 \div 2$ **15.** $19 + 7$

16. 5×8 **17.** $26 - 15$ **18.** $15 \div 3$ **19.** 4×7 **20.** $30 - 9$

Set F pages 314–315

Write each quotient.

1. $40 \div 5$ **2.** $35 \div 5$ **3.** $45 \div 5$ **4.** $30 \div 5$

5. $5\overline{)20}$ **6.** $5\overline{)25}$ **7.** $5\overline{)10}$ **8.** $5\overline{)15}$

Mixed Practice   Use mental math or paper and pencil
to find each answer. Tell which method you used.

9. 4×6 **10.** $40 \div 5$ **11.** $16 + 107$ **12.** $48 - 19$

13. $24 \div 3$ **14.** $15 \div 3$ **15.** $136 - 87$ **16.** 7×4

Set G pages 318–319

Copy the number sentences and write each answer.
Write the number sentences to complete each family of facts.

1. $3 \times 6 = $ ▦   **2.** $4 \times 9 = $ ▦   **3.** $5 \times 2 = $ ▦   **4.** $3 \times 3 = $ ▦
    $18 \div 3 = $ ▦ $36 \div 4 = $ ▦ $2 \times 5 = $ ▦

Write the family of facts using the given numbers.

5. 2, 4, 8   **6.** 5, 5, 25   **7.** 4, 5, 20   **8.** 4, 6, 24

Enrichment

Using Place Value to Divide

You can use place value to help you divide large numbers.

Find 26 ÷ 2.

You can break the greater number into its expanded form.

26 = 20 + 6

Divide 20 by 2. Divide 6 by 2.

You can count by 2 to find how many twos are in 20.

2, 4, 6, 8, 10, 12, 14, 16, 18, 20

There are 10 twos in 20.

You can use division to find how many twos are in 6. There are 3 twos in 6.

Add the number of twos in 20 and the number of twos in 6.

10 + 3 = 13

26 ÷ 2 = 13

If there are 10 twos in 20, how many will be in

1. 40?   **2.** 60?   **3.** 80?

If there are 10 threes in 30, how many will be in

4. 60?   **5.** 90?

Find each quotient.

6. 68 ÷ 2   **7.** 46 ÷ 2   **8.** 84 ÷ 2   **9.** 22 ÷ 2

10. 39 ÷ 3   **11.** 63 ÷ 3   **12.** 36 ÷ 3   **13.** 93 ÷ 3

Chapter 9 Review/Test

The art class has 9 tables with 1 cup on each table.

1. If you have 27 markers, how many go in each cup?

2. If you have 18 markers, how many go in each cup?

The art class has 30 students.

3. If the students work in groups of 6, how many groups will there be?

4. If the students work in groups of 10, how many groups will there be?

5. Complete.

▦ in all

4 cups

▦ ÷ 4 = ▦

Write each quotient.

6. $14 \div 2$ **7.** $9 \div 3$

8. $16 \div 4$ **9.** $45 \div 5$

10. $2\overline{)12}$ **11.** $3\overline{)27}$

12. $4\overline{)32}$ **13.** $5\overline{)25}$

Complete each number sentence. Then write three more sentences to make a family of facts.

14. $3 \times 8 =$ ▦   **15.** $5 \times 9 =$ ▦

16. $4 \times 7 =$ ▦   **17.** $2 \times 6 =$ ▦

18. The school library has 500 books. There are 10 more books in the fiction section than in the nonfiction section. How many books of each kind are there?

Read this problem. Then answer the questions below.

Chin needs 25 invitations for his party. Each package has 5 invitations. How many packages should he buy?

19. What does the underlined statement mean?

  a. Chin must find a package with 25 invitations.

  b. Chin must buy more than one package.

  c. Chin can only invite 5 people.

20. Solve the problem above.

21. ■ **Write About Math** How can you use multiplication to help find a quotient?

Division Facts

10

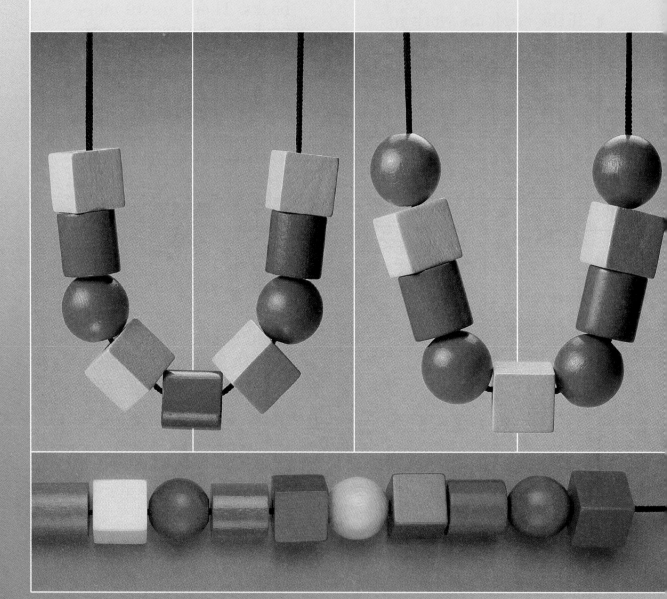

Number-Sense Project

Estimate
Predict which necklace design will be the most popular.

Gather Data
Ask 3 people who are not in your class which necklace they like the best. Tally the results.

Analyze and Report
Share your results with other students. Was your prediction of the most popular necklace correct?

Did You Know: People like different shapes and different colors. The most popular color in the U.S. is blue.

Dividing by Six

Build Understanding

Arrays on Display
Materials: Small objects
Groups: 3–5 students

A. Amy is a window dresser. She wants to display 18 figurines. She wants to put the same number of figurines in each row. If she puts 6 in each row, how many rows will she make?

a. Count out 18 objects.

b. Make a row with 6 objects.

c. Make as many more rows of 6 as you can.

d. How many rows could you make?

18 ÷ 6 = 3

Amy will make 3 rows with 6 figurines in each row.

B. Make an array with 24 objects. Put 6 in each row. How many rows are there?

■ **Talk About Math** What multiplication facts could you write for the arrays you made?

Check Understanding

For another example, see Set A, pages 352–353.

Make or draw an array for each fact. Write
the related multiplication fact for each.

1. 36 ÷ 6   **2.** 30 ÷ 6   **3.** 12 ÷ 6   **4.** 42 ÷ 6   **5.** 54 ÷ 6

Practice

For More Practice, see Set A, pages 354–355.

Write each quotient. **Remember** to make or draw arrays to help
you.

6. 12 ÷ 6   **7.** 24 ÷ 6   **8.** 54 ÷ 6   **9.** 48 ÷ 6

10. 42 ÷ 6   **11.** 30 ÷ 6   **12.** 18 ÷ 6   **13.** 36 ÷ 6

14. $6\overline{)30}$ **15.** $6\overline{)42}$ **16.** $6\overline{)36}$ **17.** $6\overline{)18}$

Mixed Practice   Find each answer.

18. 42 ÷ 6   **19.** 30 ÷ 6   **20.** 24 ÷ 4   **21.** 43 − 29

22. 25 ÷ 5   **23.** 8 × 5   **24.** 90 − 13   **25.** 18 ÷ 2

26. 9 × 8   **27.** 54 ÷ 6   **28.** 28 + 64   **29.** 28 ÷ 4

Problem Solving

Solve each problem.

30. Millie displayed 6 of
27 outfits in one window.
How many outfits are
left to display?

31. If 6 mannequins fill
1 window, how many are
needed to fill 5 windows?

32. Suppose David must move
48 mannequins. If 6 fit in
the elevator with him, how
many trips will he have to
make?

33. Critical Thinking
Suppose you begin with 72.
Predict how many times
you would need to subtract
6 to reach 0. Check your
prediction.

Dividing by Seven

Build Understanding

Bobby has 56 new models to put on 7 shelves at the hobby shop. If he wants the same number on each shelf, how many models will go on each?

You can use multiplication to help you with division.

$7 \times$  $= 56$

$7 \times 8 = 56$ So $56 \div 7 = 8$.

He can place 8 models on each shelf.

■ **Talk About Math**   Explain how you can use multiplication to check division. Then tell how you might use division to check multiplication.

Check Understanding

For another example, see Set B, pages 352–353.

Write two division sentences for each picture.

1.

2.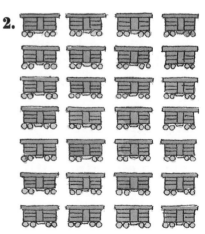

Use each multiplication sentence to write
two division sentences.

3. 5 × 7 = 35   **4.** 9 × 7 = 63   **5.** 3 × 7 = 21

Practice

For More Practice, see Set B, pages 354–355.

Write each quotient.

6. 21 ÷ 7   **7.** 42 ÷ 7   **8.** 63 ÷ 7   **9.** 56 ÷ 7

10. 49 ÷ 7   **11.** 14 ÷ 7   **12.** 28 ÷ 7   **13.** 35 ÷ 7

14. 7)‾63‾   **15.** 7)‾28‾   **16.** 7)‾49‾   **17.** 7)‾56‾

Mental Math   Find each answer.

18. 46 + 53   **19.** 24 ÷ 6   **20.** 41 − 11

21. 32 ÷ 4   **22.** 8 × 7   **23.** 38 − 21

24. 27 ÷ 3   **25.** 15 + 16   **26.** 49 ÷ 7

27. 9 × 4   **28.** 5 × 6   **29.** 56 ÷ 7

Problem Solving

Solve each problem.

30. Crystal bought 14 packs of
red yarn, 7 packs of green
yarn, and 7 packs of yellow
yarn. How many packs of
yarn did she buy?

31. Andy bought 28 wooden
houses for his train display.
If he puts 7 houses on each
block, how many blocks can
he set up?

32. The Brownie troop had
85 pieces of balsa wood.
They bought some more and
now they have 117 pieces.
How many pieces did they
buy?

33. Fallon and his friends have
9 radio-controlled cars. If
each car needs 8 AA
batteries, how many
batteries will they need in
all?

Dividing by Eight

Build Understanding

Nicole is helping her science teacher set up 40 microscopes. She will place 8 microscopes on each table. How many tables will Nicole be able to fill?

40 ÷ 8 = 5   since 5 × 8 = 40

■ **Talk About Math**   Explain how you could draw an array to show that 40 ÷ 8 = 5.

What kinds of things can you look at under a microscope?

Check Understanding

For another example, see Set C, pages 352–353.

Write two division sentences for each picture.

1.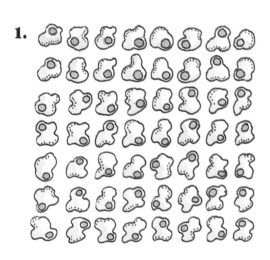

2.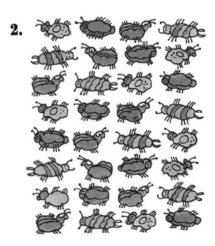

Write a multiplication sentence that would help you find each quotient; then write each quotient.

3. 64 ÷ 8   **4.** 72 ÷ 8   **5.** 16 ÷ 8   **6.** 48 ÷ 8

Practice

For More Practice, see Set C, pages 354–355.

Write each quotient.

7. 40 ÷ 8   **8.** 72 ÷ 8   **9.** 16 ÷ 8   **10.** 48 ÷ 8

11. 24 ÷ 8   **12.** 56 ÷ 8   **13.** 32 ÷ 8   **14.** 64 ÷ 8

15. 8)‾32   **16.** 8)‾56   **17.** 8)‾16   **18.** 8)‾64

Mixed Practice Use mental math or paper and pencil to do each exercise. Tell which method you used.

19. 24 ÷ 8   **20.** 410 − 26   **21.** 56 ÷ 8   **22.** 99 + 37

23. 7 × 7   **24.** 189 + 72   **25.** 24 ÷ 3   **26.** 66 − 57

27. 56 ÷ 7   **28.** 40 ÷ 5   **29.** 28 + 32   **30.** 6 × 4

Problem Solving

Number Sense Find each quotient. Then write the next two facts of the pattern.

31. 16 ÷ 8, 24 ÷ 8, 32 ÷ 8, __?__, __?__

32. 72 ÷ 8, 64 ÷ 8, 56 ÷ 8, __?__, __?__

TIPS FOR PROBLEM SOLVERS

Take risks. Try your hunches. They often work.

Skills _____ Review   pages 274–275

Choose the more sensible measure for each container.

1. Soup bowl   **2.** Teakettle   **3.** Kitchen sink

    1 cup   1 quart   2 quarts   2 gallons   20 cups   20 gallons

4. Baby bottle   **5.** Juice pitcher   **6.** Wading pool

    1 cup   1 quart   2 pints   2 gallons   25 pints   25 gallons

Dividing by Nine

Build Understanding

Stickers	Price
Hearts	6¢ each
Stars	7¢ each
Ducks	8¢ each
Bears	9¢ each

Stephanie wants to buy some bear stickers. How many bear stickers can she buy for 54 cents?

$$54 \div 9 = 6 \quad \text{since } 6 \times 9 = 54$$

Stephanie can buy 6 bear stickers.

■ **Write About Math**   Draw two arrays to show that $54 \div 9 = 6$ and $54 \div 6 = 9$.

Check Understanding

For another example, see Set D, pages 352–353.

Write two division sentences for each picture.

1.

2.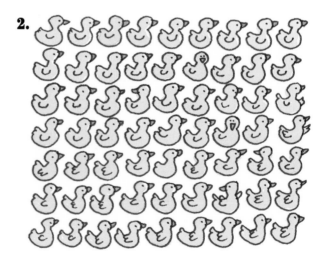

Write a multiplication sentence that would help you find each quotient; then write each quotient.

3. $81 \div 9$ **4.** $54 \div 9$ **5.** $18 \div 9$ **6.** $72 \div 9$

Practice

For More Practice, see Set D, pages 354–355.

Write each quotient.

7. 45 ÷ 9   **8.** 54 ÷ 9   **9.** 81 ÷ 9   **10.** 27 ÷ 9

11. 72 ÷ 9   **12.** 18 ÷ 9   **13.** 36 ÷ 9   **14.** 63 ÷ 9

15. 9)$\overline{54}$ **16.** 9)$\overline{27}$ **17.** 9)$\overline{72}$ **18.** 9)$\overline{36}$

Mixed Practice Use mental math, paper and pencil, or a calculator to find each answer. Tell which method you used.

19. 35 ÷ 5   **20.** 100 − 26   **21.** 81 ÷ 9   **22.** 25 + 13

23. 7 × 7   **24.** 2,118 − 243   **25.** 8 × 4   **26.** 28 ÷ 4

27. 54 ÷ 6   **28.** 42 ÷ 7   **29.** 9 × 4   **30.** 3,045 + 933

Problem Solving

Use the chart on page 336 to solve Problems 31–33.

31. How many heart stickers could you buy for 48 cents?

32. Dante bought 5 bear and 7 star stickers. How much did he spend?

33. David spent 54 cents to buy some heart and some duck stickers. How many of each did he buy?

34.  **Calculator** If 63 ÷ 9 = 7, what is 6,300 ÷ 9? 6,300 ÷ 90? 6,300 ÷ 900?

35. Estimation Carrie needed 52 stickers. One package has 6 stickers. She thought: Since 6 × 8 = 48 and 6 × 9 = 54, I should get 9 packages. Use Carrie's process to find how many packages of 8 stickers you would buy to get at least 47 stickers.

Families of Facts

Build Understanding

A. There are two multiplication sentences that describe this picture.

3 × 7 = 21

7 × 3 = 21

There are also two division sentences that describe this picture.

21 ÷ 3 = 7

21 ÷ 7 = 3

These four sentences form a family of facts.

B. This family of facts has only two number sentences.

6 × 6 = 36

36 ÷ 6 = 6

■ **Talk About Math** How does knowing fact families help you in math?

Check Understanding

For another example, see Set E, pages 352–353.

1. Write a family of facts for this picture.

2. Complete this family of facts.

$5 \times 8 = 40 \quad 40 \div 8 = 5$

3. Write a family of facts that has only two number sentences.

Practice

For More Practice, see Set E, pages 354–355.

Write the family of facts for each picture.

4.

5.

6.

Copy. Then write each answer. Write number sentences to complete each family of facts.

7. $6 \times 9 = $ ▦

$54 \div 9 = $ ▦

8. $7 \times 5 = $ ▦

$35 \div 7 = $ ▦

9. $8 \times 8 = $ ▦

10. $9 \times 4 = $ ▦

$36 \div 9 = $ ▦

11. $4 \times 7 = $ ▦

12. $7 \times 7 = $ ▦

13. $8 \times 9 = $ ▦

14. $6 \times 3 = $ ▦

Midchapter _____ Checkup

For each exercise, draw an array and write the family of facts.

1. $18 \div 9$ **2.** $64 \div 8$ **3.** 14×7

Find each quotient.

4. $72 \div 9$ **5.** $64 \div 8$ **6.** $49 \div 7$ **7.** $36 \div 6$

8. $9\overline{)81}$ **9.** $7\overline{)63}$ **10.** $8\overline{)48}$ **11.** $6\overline{)42}$

Number-Sense Project

Look back at pages 328-329.

1. How many of this necklace can Delia make if she has these beads on hand?

2. Delia also likes the third necklace in the picture on pages 328-329. How many of these necklaces can she make with the beads she has?

Type of Bead	Number on Hand
cube	40
cylinder	24
sphere	18

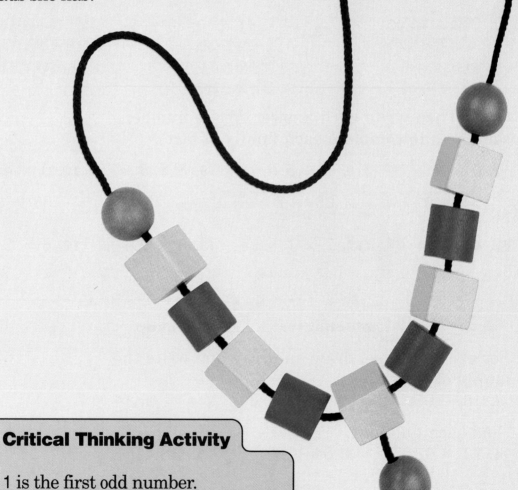

Critical Thinking Activity

1 is the first odd number.
3 is the second odd number.
What is the tenth odd number?

Problem Solving WORKSHOP

The teacher asks you to find enough helpers to carry 30 math books from the book room to your classroom. You and your helpers need to carefully bring all 30 books in one trip. How many helpers do you need?

Explore as a Team

1. Without counting past 10, estimate how many squares are shaded.

2. Write about the method your group used to solve the problem.

TIPS FOR WORKING TOGETHER
Be a good tutor. Make up similar problems or easier ones to help someone understand.

Choose an Operation

Build Understanding

The students in Mrs. Hillary's class collected insects for a science project. Stanley caught 36 crickets. He put 4 crickets in each jar. How many jars did he use?

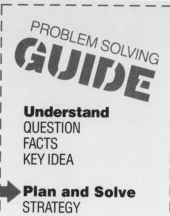

PROBLEM SOLVING GUIDE

Understand
QUESTION
FACTS
KEY IDEA

Plan and Solve
STRATEGY
ANSWER

Look Back
SENSIBLE ANSWER
ALTERNATE APPROACH

Understand Stanley separated 36 into equal groups with 4 in each group.

Plan and Solve STRATEGY Choose an operation. Since you are separating into equal groups, you can use division to find the number of groups.

36 ÷ 4 = 9

ANSWER Stanley used 9 jars.

Look Back You can check division by using multiplication.
$9 \times 4 = 36$

■ **Talk About Math** How many jars would Stanley have used if he had put 6 crickets in each jar?

Check Understanding

Solve this problem by answering Questions 1–5.

Matt caught 15 grasshoppers. He used 8 of them for his project and let the rest go. How many grasshoppers did he let go?

1. What are you asked to find?

2. List the facts you need.

3. Should you add, subtract, multiply, or divide to solve this problem?

4. How did you decide which operation you should use?

5. How many grasshoppers did Matt let go?

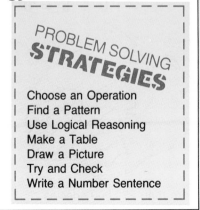

Practice

Tell whether you should *add, subtract, multiply,* or *divide.* Then find each answer.

6. Teresita arranged her insects in a box. She made 7 rows with 7 in each row. How many insects did Teresita have in all?

7. The class caught 8 moths. They caught 6 more butterflies than moths. How many butterflies did they catch?

8. Jamie caught 7 June bugs, 8 dragonflies, and 4 fireflies. How many insects did he catch in all?

9. Of the 14 butterflies caught, 9 were monarchs. The rest were swallowtails. How many were swallowtails?

10. If 4 butterfly nets were shared equally by 24 students, how many students used each net?

Choose a _____ Strategy

What a Difference!
11. Think of 2 one-digit numbers. Their difference is double their quotient. What are the numbers?

PROBLEM SOLVING STRATEGIES

Choose an Operation
Find a Pattern
Use Logical Reasoning
Make a Table
Draw a Picture
Try and Check
Write a Number Sentence

Zero and One in Division

Build Understanding

A. Tasha has 5 zinnia plants in a flat. How many groups of 5 does she have?

$$5 \div 5 = 1$$

B. Tasha put 1 plant in each of 5 different pots. How many groups of 1 did she make?

$$5 \div 1 = 5$$

C. The flat has no plants in it now. How many groups of 5 are there?

D. Tasha bought 5 more plants. How many groups of 0 are there?

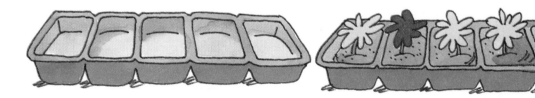

$$0 \div 5 = 0$$

$$5 \div 0 = \text{?}$$

We would not use any of the plants if we made groups of 0. So this question doesn't make sense.

■ **Talk About Math** What is the family of facts for Example A?

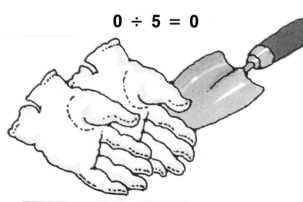

More than 250,000 species of flowering plants exist.

Check Understanding

For another example, see Set F, pages 352–353.

Write each quotient.

1. 4 ÷ 4   **2.** 8 ÷ 1   **3.** 0 ÷ 2   **4.** 9 ÷ 9   **5.** 7 ÷ 1

6. What is the quotient when any number is divided by itself?

7. What is the quotient when any number is divided by 1?

8. What is the quotient when 0 is divided by any nonzero number?

Practice

For More Practice, see Set F, pages 354–355.

Write each quotient.

9. 9 ÷ 1   **10.** 0 ÷ 3   **11.** 7 ÷ 7   **12.** 6 ÷ 1   **13.** 8 ÷ 8

14. 0 ÷ 5   **15.** 4 ÷ 1   **16.** 3 ÷ 3   **17.** 0 ÷ 6   **18.** 2 ÷ 2

19. 0 ÷ 4   **20.** 2 ÷ 1   **21.** 0 ÷ 7   **22.** 1 ÷ 1   **23.** 0 ÷ 8

24. 0 ÷ 1   **25.** 8 ÷ 1   **26.** 35 ÷ 35   **27.** 67 ÷ 1   **28.** 0 ÷ 93

Problem Solving

Critical Thinking Write a multiplication/division family of facts in which

29. all of the numbers in the number sentences are the same.

30. one of the factors is 1.

31. Use Data Draw an array and write the family of facts for one of Exercises 7–24 on page 209.

Remainders

Build Understanding

Button Up Your Socks
Materials: 27 small objects
Groups: 2–3 students

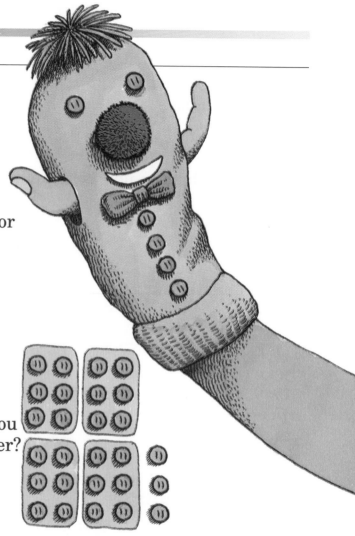

A. Have you ever made
a puppet out of a sock?

Teddy makes hand puppets. For
each one he uses 6 buttons—
4 for the puppet's shirt and
2 for the eyes. If Teddy has
27 buttons, how many hand
puppets can he make?

a. Use 27 small objects.

b. Make groups of 6.

c. How many groups of 6 did you
make? Are there any left over?

27 divided by 6 is 4 with a
remainder of 3.

B. Divide 14 into 4 equal groups.

a. Show 14 objects.

b. Divide them equally into 4 groups.

c. Tell how many are in each group.
Tell how many are left over.

What is 14 divided by 4?
What is the remainder?

■ **Talk About Math** How could you write
the answers for the problems in the examples?

Check Understanding

For another example, see Set G, pages 352–353.

Use small objects to help you with each exercise.

1. Show 20 in all.
Make groups of 3.
How many groups?
What is the remainder?

2. Show 18 in all.
Make 4 equal groups.
How many in each group?
What is the remainder?

3. 8 ÷ 3   **4.** 9 ÷ 4   **5.** 7 ÷ 2   **6.** 10 ÷ 6   **7.** 15 ÷ 9

Practice

For More Practice, see Set G, pages 354–355.

Use small objects to help you with each exercise.
Remember to tell the remainder.

8. 17 ÷ 3   **9.** 11 ÷ 2   **10.** 14 ÷ 4   **11.** 15 ÷ 8   **12.** 13 ÷ 6

13. 19 ÷ 4   **14.** 16 ÷ 5   **15.** 14 ÷ 6   **16.** 10 ÷ 7   **17.** 20 ÷ 5

18. 21 ÷ 5   **19.** 22 ÷ 5   **20.** 23 ÷ 5   **21.** 24 ÷ 5   **22.** 25 ÷ 5

Problem Solving

Explore ———— Math

23. If you make 7 groups, what
is the greatest number
that could be left over?

24. If you make groups of
3 objects, could 3 objects
be left over?

25. Compare the remainder with the divisor
in each of Exercises 8-22. Which is always
greater, the divisor or the remainder?

Interpret the Remainder

PROBLEM SOLVING

GUIDE

Understand
QUESTION
FACTS
KEY IDEA

▸ **Plan and Solve**
STRATEGY
ANSWER

Look Back
SENSIBLE ANSWER
ALTERNATE APPROACH

Build Understanding

A class of 28 students is going to the history museum. A car can carry 5 students. How many cars are needed for the trip?

Understand   They need enough cars to carry all 28 students, even if it means one car will have some empty seats.

▸ **Plan and Solve**   STRATEGY   Draw 28 Xs. Circle groups of 5.

ANSWER   There are 5 groups of 5 with 3 left over.

Five cars could carry only 25 students. So 6 cars are needed for the 28 students.

Look Back   SENSIBLE ANSWER $6 \times 5 = 30$. So 6 cars will be enough to carry 28 students.

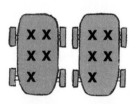

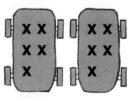

■ **Talk About Math**   If 2 of the 28 students were absent, would they still need 6 cars? Why?

Check Understanding

Solve this problem by answering Questions 1–4.

Daniel has 55 cents. He wants to spend it on stickers in the gift shop. If each sticker costs 7 cents, how many could he buy?

1. What do you need to divide?

2. How many Xs should you draw? How many Xs will you put in each group?

3. How many groups did you make? How many Xs were left over?

4. How many stickers can Daniel buy? Will he have money left? How much?

Practice

Draw a picture to help you solve each problem.

5. The class has 15 pictures of the trip to put on 4 poster boards. They put the same number of pictures on each board. How many pictures were not used?

6. Mr. Chang says his class will go to the history museum in vans. There are 24 students. Each van holds 9 students. How many vans will they need?

7. There are 50 people going into the museum lunch room. Only 6 people can sit at each table. How many tables are needed to seat the people?

8. The gift shop sells lava rocks. Each bag holds 3 rocks. How many bags can Nicky fill if she has 19 rocks?

Reading ———— Math

Main Idea Tell which phrase best describes the remainder in Problem 7.

a. The number of people who will sit at a table that is not full

b. The number of people who do not get to eat

c. The number of tables that are needed

Solve each problem.

1. What am I? I am used on cars to make them shine. All symmetric are the 3 letters of mine.

2. Mrs. Killany has 3 kittens. Each kitten eats 3 meals a day. A box of soft kitten food has 8 meal-sized packets. Does Mrs. Killany need more than 1 box a day?

3. Mr. Lewis started making a wooden puzzle by cutting an 8-inch by 9-inch board into 1-inch squares. How many puzzle pieces were there?

4. Jessica took 24 photos with one roll of film and 36 photos with another. How many photos did she take?

5. **Data File** Use data from pages 402–403. To make each decoration, Victor needs 6 stars, 8 pine branches, and 7 snowflakes. How many decorations can he make if he has one bag of each?

6. **Make a Data File** Look at the information on the labels of 5 types of food. List the number of grams of carbohydrates, fat, and protein there is in one serving.

Explore with a Calculator

Palindromes

The Palindrome gnome made a game.
Said forward or backward the same
Are numbers and letters you name.

1. Find the palindrome the gnome
made for each number.

Reverse the digits of the number.
Add them. Repeat until the sum reads
the same backwards as forwards.

```
   37     reverse the digits
 + 73     add
  110     reverse the digits
 + 011    add
  121     This is a palindrome. It reads the same
          forward and backward.
```

Find a palindrome for each.

a. 457   **b.** 96   **c.** 148

d. 84   **e.** 199   **f.** 6,509

2. Words can be palindromes too.
Write 3 more palindrome words.

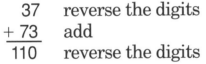

MOM DAD

Reteaching

Set A   pages 330–331

If you have 12 objects, you can make an array that has 6 objects in each row.

x x x x x x
x x x x x x

You can make 2 rows with 6 objects in each row.

$$12 \div 6 = 2$$

Remember that the quotient is the answer to a division problem.

Write each quotient.

1. $18 \div 6$ **2.** $36 \div 6$

3. $6\overline{)24}$ **4.** $6\overline{)54}$

Set B   pages 332–333

Allen has collected 42 model cars. He wants to display them on 7 shelves. If he places the same number of cars on each shelf, how many cars will he place on each?

You can use multiplication to help you with division.

$$7 \times \text{▦} = 42$$
$$7 \times 6 = 42$$
So $\quad 42 \div 7 = 6$

He can place 6 cars on each shelf.

Remember that if the product of the quotient and the divisor is the dividend, the quotient is correct.

Write each quotient.

1. $49 \div 7$ **2.** $14 \div 7$

3. $7 \div 7$ **4.** $28 \div 7$

5. $7\overline{)42}$ **6.** $7\overline{)21}$

7. $7\overline{)14}$ **8.** $7\overline{)35}$

Set C   pages 334–335

This array shows two division sentences.

x x x x x x x x
x x x x x x x x
x x x x x x x x
x x x x x x x x
x x x x x x x x
x x x x x x x x

$48 \div 6 = 8 \qquad 48 \div 8 = 6$

Remember that you can use multiplication to help you find a quotient. Write each quotient.

1. $56 \div 8$ **2.** $16 \div 8$

3. $24 \div 8$ **4.** $64 \div 8$

5. $8\overline{)32}$ **6.** $8\overline{)48}$

7. $8\overline{)24}$ **8.** $8\overline{)40}$

Set D pages 336–337

These arrays show divisions.

$36 \div 4 = 9$ $36 \div 9 = 4$

```
x x x x x x x x x        x x x x x x x x x
x x x x x x x x x        x x x x x x x x x
x x x x x x x x x        x x x x x x x x x
x x x x x x x x x        x x x x x x x x x
```

Remember that the dividend is the number being separated into groups. Write each quotient.

1. $27 \div 9$ **2.** $45 \div 9$ **3.** $54 \div 9$

4. $9\overline{)81}$ **5.** $9\overline{)63}$ **6.** $9\overline{)45}$

Set E pages 338–339

This family of facts describes this array.

```
x x x x x x    4 × 6 = 24
x x x x x x    6 × 4 = 24
x x x x x x    24 ÷ 6 = 4
x x x x x x    24 ÷ 4 = 6
```

Remember that you can use one multiplication or division fact to help you write a family of facts.

Write the family of facts for this picture.

```
x x x x x x x x x
x x x x x x x x x
```

Set F pages 344–345

This array shows that $4 \div 4 = 1$.

```
x x x x
```

Knowing this division fact, you can write a family of facts.

$4 \div 1 = 4$
$4 \times 1 = 4$
$1 \times 4 = 4$

Remember that dividing a number by 0 makes no sense.

Write each quotient.

1. $9 \div 9$ **2.** $8 \div 1$

3. $6 \div 1$ **4.** $0 \div 5$

5. $86 \div 86$ **6.** $92 \div 1$

Set G pages 346–347

Divide 13 into groups of 4.

```
x x x    x x x    x x x    x
```

You can divide 13 into 3 groups of 4 with 1 left over. So $13 \div 4$ is 3 with a remainder of 1.

Remember that the remainder should be less than the divisor.

Use small objects to help you answer each exercise.

1. $9 \div 2$ **2.** $14 \div 3$

3. $17 \div 5$ **4.** $16 \div 4$

5. $22 \div 4$ **6.** $13 \div 5$

More Practice

Write each quotient.

1. $18 \div 6$ 2. $12 \div 6$ 3. $36 \div 6$ 4. $42 \div 6$

5. $6\overline{)12}$ 6. $6\overline{)48}$ 7. $6\overline{)54}$ 8. $6\overline{)24}$

Mixed Practice   Find each answer.

9. 7×5 10. $36 \div 4$ 11. $36 - 27$ 12. $42 \div 6$

13. $57 + 38$ 14. 8×7 15. $45 \div 5$ 16. $24 \div 4$

17. $21 \div 3$ 18. $70 - 39$ 19. $24 \div 6$ 20. $16 \div 2$

Write each quotient.

1. $14 \div 7$ 2. $35 \div 7$ 3. $49 \div 7$ 4. $56 \div 7$

5. $7\overline{)42}$ 6. $7\overline{)28}$ 7. $7\overline{)21}$ 8. $7\overline{)35}$

Mental Math   Find each answer.

9. 8×4 10. $17 + 26$ 11. $46 - 13$ 12. $24 \div 3$

13. $36 \div 4$ 14. $42 \div 6$ 15. $42 \div 7$ 16. 9×6

Write each quotient.

1. $16 \div 8$ 2. $64 \div 8$ 3. $24 \div 8$ 4. $72 \div 8$

5. $8\overline{)24}$ 6. $8\overline{)40}$ 7. $8\overline{)32}$ 8. $8\overline{)48}$

Mixed Practice   Use mental math or paper and pencil to do each exercise. Tell which method you used.

9. $27 \div 3$ 10. $620 - 48$ 11. $87 + 29$ 12. 6×7

13. $17 + 33$ 14. $84 - 37$ 15. $35 \div 5$ 16. 8×8

17. $42 \div 6$ 18. 8×4 19. 7×4 20. $23 + 39$

Independent Study MORE PRACTICE

Set D pages 336–337

Write each quotient.

1. 27 ÷ 9   **2.** 72 ÷ 9   **3.** 36 ÷ 9   **4.** 63 ÷ 9

5. 9)‾45   **6.** 9)‾18   **7.** 9)‾63   **8.** 9)‾81

Mixed Practice Use mental math, paper and pencil, or a calculator to find each answer. Tell which method you used.

9. 45 ÷ 5   **10.** 90 − 36   **11.** 6 × 6   **12.** 4,088 + 811

Set E pages 338–339

Write the family of facts for each picture.

1. X X X X X X
    X X X X X X
    X X X X X X

2. X X X X X X X
    X X X X X X X
    X X X X X X X
    X X X X X X X

3. X X X X X X X X X
    X X X X X X X X X

Copy and complete each sentence. Write number sentences to complete each family of facts.

4. 7 × 8 = ▦
    56 ÷ 8 = ▦

5. 9 × 3 = ▦
    27 ÷ 9 = ▦

6. 8 × 4 = ▦
    32 ÷ 8 = ▦

7. 9 × 9 = ▦

8. 3 × 8 = ▦   **9.** 6 × 9 = ▦   **10.** 7 × 3 = ▦   **11.** 6 × 7 = ▦

Set F pages 344–345

Write each quotient.

1. 4 ÷ 4   **2.** 8 ÷ 1   **3.** 0 ÷ 5   **4.** 1 ÷ 1

5. 0 ÷ 182   **6.** 47 ÷ 47   **7.** 103 ÷ 1   **8.** 94 ÷ 94

Set G pages 346–347

Use small objects to help you answer each exercise.

1. 7 ÷ 2   **2.** 11 ÷ 3   **3.** 14 ÷ 5   **4.** 21 ÷ 3

5. 23 ÷ 4   **6.** 17 ÷ 8   **7.** 21 ÷ 6   **8.** 12 ÷ 7

Enrichment

Missing Factors and More

When you divide, you are looking for a *missing factor.*

40 ÷ 8 = ▦ is the same as **8 ×** ▦ **= 40.**

Complete each number sentence.

1. 6 × ▦ = 54   **2.** 35 ÷ ▦ = 5

3. ▦ × 7 = 42   **4.** 24 ÷ ▦ = 8

5. 4 × ▦ = 16   **6.** 9 × ▦ = 63

7. 8 × ▦ = 72   **8.** ▦ × 2 = 14

9. 27 ÷ ▦ = 3   **10.** ▦ ÷ 5 = 6

Divide. Then decide if you should replace the ▦ with >, <, or = .

11. 48 ÷ 8 ▦ 56 ÷ 7   **12.** 72 ÷ 8 ▦ 27 ÷ 3

13. 18 ÷ 3 ▦ 14 ÷ 2   **14.** 42 ÷ 6 ▦ 81 ÷ 9

15. 30 ÷ 5 ▦ 36 ÷ 6   **16.** 18 ÷ 2 ▦ 36 ÷ 9

Which of the numbers 1 to 9 will make each sentence true? Each exercise may have more than one answer.

17. 54 ÷ 6 < 3 × ▦   **18.** 4 × ▦ > 40 ÷ 5

19. 3 × ▦ > 36 ÷ 9   **20.** 24 ÷ ▦ < 35 ÷ 7

21. 6 × 6 > 8 × ▦   **22.** 16 ÷ 4 < 2 × ▦

Chapter 10 Review/Test

Write each quotient.

1. $48 \div 6$ **2.** $3 \div 1$

3. $36 \div 9$ **4.** $40 \div 8$

5. $0 \div 2$ **6.** $42 \div 7$

7. $6\overline{)24}$ **8.** $7\overline{)63}$

9. $8\overline{)56}$ **10.** $9\overline{)54}$

Copy and write each answer. Circle the fact that does not belong to the family of facts.

11. $24 \div 3$ **12.** $16 \div 8$
 3×8 4×4
 $24 \div 4$ $16 \div 4$
 8×3
 $24 \div 8$

Divide. Write each quotient and remainder.

13. $17 \div 8$ **14.** $32 \div 6$

15. $61 \div 7$ **16.** $85 \div 9$

Tell whether you would add, subtract, multiply, or divide to solve each problem.

17. Of the 32 cans on the shelf, 8 are soup cans. How many are not soup cans?

18. If each car can carry 5 children, how many cars are needed for 15 children?

19. Susie's cat book has 42 pages. Her horse book is 15 pages longer. How many pages does the horse book have?

20. Solve Problem 18.

Pablo has 36 photographs. He will put 8 on each page of his album.

21. Choose the most sensible answer for the number of pages Pablo needs for his pictures.

   a. 4 pages   **c.** 28 pages
   b. 44 pages   **d.** 5 pages

22. If all the album pages are empty at first, how many pictures will Pablo put on the last page he uses?

23. ■ **Write About Math** In Exercise 12, tell why the fact you chose does not belong to that family.

Fractions and Decimals

11

Did You Know: Apatosaurus (Brontosaurus) was 70 feet long and weighed over 60,000 pounds. It lived in what is now Colorado, Oklahoma, Utah, and Wyoming.

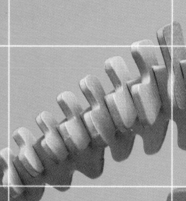

Number-Sense Project

Estimate
Predict which dinosaur is the best known.

Gather Data
Show 4 people pictures of 4 dinosaurs and have them try to name each one. Record which ones they could name.

Analyze and Report
Was your prediction correct? Compare your results with other students. Did everyone come up with the same answer?

USA
25 *Pteranodon*

Fractions: Part of a Whole

Build Understanding

A. Fraction Cut-ups
Materials: Unlined paper, red crayon, tracing paper, scissors

Lee is helping to make 4 clown costumes for the school play. How can he cut a piece of cloth into 4 equal parts? Equal parts are all the same size. You can use a piece of paper to show how to make 4 equal parts.

a. Fold a piece of paper in two. Then fold it again.

b. Open the paper. Cut along each fold. Are the parts equal?

 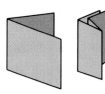

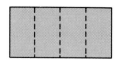

B. How many equal parts of the whole does each picture show?

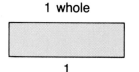
1 whole
1

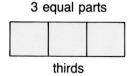
2 equal parts
halves

3 equal parts
thirds

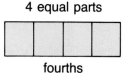
4 equal parts
fourths

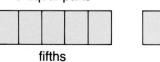
5 equal parts
fifths

6 equal parts
sixths

8 equal parts
eighths

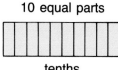
10 equal parts
tenths

c. This figure is divided into sixths.

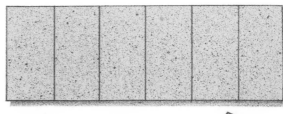

a. Trace the figure and cut it out. Then cut it apart along the lines.

b. Pick up one part. This part is one sixth of the whole figure. *Fractions* name equal parts of a whole, so one sixth is a fraction.

You write one sixth as $\frac{1}{6}$.

numerator ⟶ **1** ⟵ number of parts set aside
denominator ⟶ **6** ⟵ number of equal parts in all

c. Pick up the parts of the figure to show two sixths, three sixths, four sixths, and five sixths.

■ **Talk About Math**   Is each part of this circle one third of the whole circle? Explain.

Check Understanding

For another example, see Set A, pages 396–397.

Write the fractions.

1.

2. Two thirds

3.

Number Sense   Answer each question.

4. In Exercises 1–3, what is the denominator of each fraction?

5. What does the denominator of a fraction stand for?

6. In Exercises 1–3, what is the numerator of each fraction?

7. What does the numerator of a fraction stand for?

Copy and complete the table.

8.	Equal parts	2	3	4	5	6	7	8	9	10	12
	Name	Halves									

Which fraction names the shaded part?

9.

$\frac{1}{3}$ $\frac{1}{2}$ $\frac{1}{4}$

10.

$\frac{2}{4}$ $\frac{1}{3}$ $\frac{2}{3}$

11.

$\frac{1}{3}$ $\frac{2}{2}$ $\frac{1}{1}$

12.

$\frac{1}{2}$ $\frac{1}{3}$ $\frac{4}{6}$

13.

$\frac{4}{6}$ $\frac{2}{6}$ $\frac{4}{4}$

14.

$\frac{4}{10}$ $\frac{3}{5}$ $\frac{1}{2}$

Which picture is shaded to show the fraction?

15. Two thirds

a.

b.

16. Three eighths

a.

b.

17. Six tenths

a.

b.

18. One half

a.

b.

Write a fraction to name the shaded part.
Write the fraction as a number and with words.

19.

20.

21.

Problem Solving

Solve each problem.

22. Kim, Chaz, and Rob cut a ribbon into 3 equal parts. Each took 1 part. What part of the whole ribbon did each get?

23. Mikey cut a piece of cloth into 6 equal pieces. How can he cut the cloth again to get 12 equal pieces?

Explore _____ Math

24. Show $\frac{3}{4}$ of this figure.

a. Trace the figure. Cut out your tracing.

b. Fold the tracing in two. Can you fold it in two again to make 4 equal parts? Try it.

c. Open the paper. Are there 4 equal parts? If not, try folding again until you get 4 equal parts.

d. Color 3 of the equal parts. How many equal parts in all? What fraction of the tracing is colored?

Fractions: Part of a Set

Build Understanding

How many students in your class would like to be in a singing group? You can use a fraction to name that part of the whole class.

A. There are 7 out of 15 students in Maria's class who want to be part of a singing group. This fraction shows what part of the class wants to be in the group.

$$\frac{\text{number of singers} \longrightarrow}{\text{number of students in all} \longrightarrow} \quad \frac{7}{15}$$

The fraction $\frac{7}{15}$ shows what part of the class wants to be in a singing group.

B. Three of the singers are also guitar players. Maria used a fraction to show what part of the singers are also guitar players.

$$\frac{\text{number of guitar players} \longrightarrow}{\text{number of singers} \longrightarrow} \quad \frac{3}{7}$$

The fraction $\frac{3}{7}$ shows what part of the singers are also guitar players.

■ **Talk About Math** If a group is divided into fourths, must each fourth be exactly like the other fourths? Why or why not?

What are some of your favorite songs?

Check Understanding

For another example, see Set B, pages 396–397.

1. What fraction would you use for the whole class?

2. What fraction of the whole class did not want to sing?

3. What fraction of the singers did not play guitar?

4. The guitar players make up what fraction of the class?

Practice

For More Practice, see Set B, pages 398–399.

What fraction stands for the blue part of each group?

Write the letter. **a.** $\frac{1}{6}$ **b.** $\frac{5}{8}$ **c.** $\frac{3}{4}$ **d.** $\frac{4}{6}$ **e.** $\frac{3}{5}$ **f.** $\frac{1}{2}$ **g.** $\frac{1}{3}$

5.

6.

7.

8.

9.

10.

Problem Solving

What fraction of the song books have

11. blue covers?

12. the word *singing* in the titles?

13. the word *songs* in the titles?

14. covers that are not blue?

Equal Fractions

Build Understanding

The Jackson twins are making cards. They use a sheet of construction paper to make each card.

Jackie folded her pink paper in half. Julie folded her paper in fourths. Then the twins opened their papers.

Jackie saw that one half of her paper was the same as two fourths of Julie's paper.

The fractions $\frac{1}{2}$ and $\frac{2}{4}$ are equal.

■ **Talk About Math** Suppose a friend of the twins folded the paper in sixths. Do you think $\frac{3}{6}$ is the same as $\frac{1}{2}$ and $\frac{2}{4}$? Why or why not?

Check Understanding

For another example, see Set C, pages 396–397.

Julie wants to make yellow cutouts, all the same size, to paste on the green card. She begins by folding a sheet of yellow construction paper.

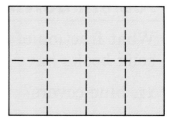

1. How many equal parts are there?

2. How many of these parts make up one half of the sheet?

3. How many of these parts make up one fourth of the sheet?

How many eighths are there in

4. one half?　　　**5.** one fourth?　　　**6.** one whole?

Practice

For More Practice, see Set C, pages 398–399.

Complete each number sentence to show equal fractions.

7.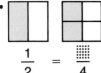

$$\frac{1}{2} = \frac{\text{▨}}{4}$$

8.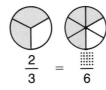

$$\frac{2}{3} = \frac{\text{▨}}{6}$$

9.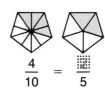

$$\frac{4}{10} = \frac{\text{▨}}{5}$$

10.

$$\frac{6}{8} = \frac{\text{▨}}{\text{▨}}$$

11.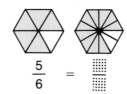

$$\frac{5}{6} = \frac{\text{▨}}{\text{▨}}$$

12.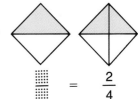

$$\frac{\text{▨}}{\text{▨}} = \frac{2}{4}$$

13.

$$\frac{\text{▨}}{\text{▨}} = \frac{\text{▨}}{\text{▨}}$$

14.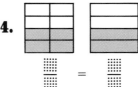

$$\frac{\text{▨}}{\text{▨}} = \frac{\text{▨}}{\text{▨}}$$

15.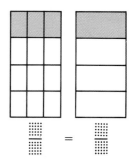

$$\frac{\text{▨}}{\text{▨}} = \frac{\text{▨}}{\text{▨}}$$

16. Number Sense Name two equal fractions and tell how you know they are equal.

Skills ——— Review

pages 118–133, 232–233, 336–337

Use a calculator, paper and pencil, or mental math to find each answer. Tell which method you used.

1. 48 ÷ 8   **2.** 982 − 495   **3.** 9)‾63   **4.** 874 + 619   **5.** 7 × 6

6. 8 × 7   **7.** 265 + 79   **8.** 72 ÷ 9   **9.** 300 − 257   **10.** 8)‾24

Finding Fractional Parts

Build Understanding

Keegan has 18 rabbits for his magic act. If $\frac{1}{3}$ of the rabbits are brown, how many rabbits are brown?

A. Think of dividing the whole set of rabbits into 3 equal groups. How many rabbits will be in each group?

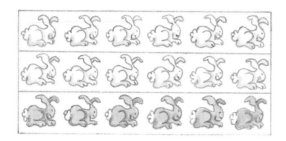

There are six brown rabbits.

B. Suppose Keegan puts bow ties on $\frac{1}{2}$ of the rabbits. How many rabbits wear bow ties?

To find $\frac{1}{2}$ of a number, you can divide the number by 2. Find $\frac{1}{2}$ of 18.

■ Mental Math

Think: $18 \div 2 = 9$
So $\frac{1}{2}$ of $18 = 9$.

There are 9 rabbits wearing bow ties.

■ **Talk About Math** What division fact could you use to answer the question in Example A? Do you prefer to divide a set into equal groups or use division to find the answer? Why?

Check Understanding

For another example, see Set D, pages 396–397.

Answer the questions about the problem. **Remember** to use small objects if you need help.

If $\frac{1}{2}$ of the hats have red bands, how many hats have red bands?

1. How many hats are there?

2. How many groups will you make?

3. How many hats will be in each group?

4. What number will you find $\frac{1}{2}$ of?

5. Which division fact can help you solve the problem?

6. How many hats have red bands?

Practice

For More Practice, see Set D, pages 398–399.

Find each number.

7. $\frac{1}{6}$ of 12

8. $\frac{1}{3}$ of 9

9. $\frac{1}{4}$ of 16

10. $\frac{1}{5}$ of 10

11. $\frac{1}{8}$ of 32

12. $\frac{1}{5}$ of 5

13. $\frac{1}{4}$ of 24

14. $\frac{1}{6}$ of 48

15. $\frac{1}{9}$ of 36

16. $\frac{1}{5}$ of 25

17. $\frac{1}{2}$ of 14

18. $\frac{1}{3}$ of 33

19. **Calculator** Use your calculator to find $\frac{1}{16}$ of 288.

Problem Solving

Solve each problem.

20. A magician has 6 magic wands. Three of the wands are broken. What fraction are broken?

21. Draw 12 top hats. Color $\frac{1}{3}$ of the hats red. Color $\frac{1}{2}$ of the hats black.

369

Try and Check

Build Understanding

Sarah saw 7 clowns in the circus. Each clown was on a bicycle or tricycle. Sarah counted 16 wheels in all. How many clowns were on bicycles?

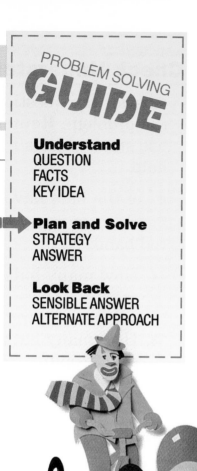

Understand Sarah needs to know how many clowns rode bicycles. She knows each clown was on a bicycle or tricycle. Sarah also knows that there were 16 wheels. The sum of the bicycle wheels and the tricycle wheels must equal 16.

IIII➡ **Plan and Solve**

STRATEGY Sarah can make a guess and then check to see if she is correct.

Number of Bicycles	Number of Tricycles	Bicycle Wheels	Tricycle Wheels	Total Wheels
4	3	8	9	17
6	1	12	3	15
5	2	10	6	16

too many wheels

too few wheels

correct

Look Back Is Sarah's computation correct? Is the number of bicycles and tricycles equal to 7? Is the number of wheels equal to 16?

■ **Write About Math** How could you draw a picture to help find the answer?

Check Understanding

Solve this problem by answering Questions 1–4.

The 7 clowns had 27 pompoms on their clown suits. Some suits had 5 pompoms, and some suits had 3 pompoms. How many suits had 5 pompoms each?

1. What is the total number of pompoms on the clown suits?

2. How many pompoms could be on one clown suit?

3. If only one clown had 5 pompoms, how many pompoms would there be in all?

4. Try different numbers until you get 27 pompoms on 7 suits. How many clowns had 5 pompoms?

Practice

Solve each problem.

5. The circus charges $2 for each child under 12 and $5 for each child over 12. Sarah gave the cashier $18 for 6 children. How many were under 12? How many were over 12?

6. In a parade, there are dogs in clown shoes and people in clown shoes. In all, there are 24 shoes. One half of the clowns are people. How many are dogs?

7. In another act, each clown juggles 3 balls or 6 balls. In all, the clowns juggle 27 balls. One half of the clowns juggle 3 balls. How many clowns are juggling 6 balls?

8. In one act, the clowns wear red or blue. Twice as many clowns wear blue as red. If 33 clowns are in the act, how many are wearing blue? How many are wearing red?

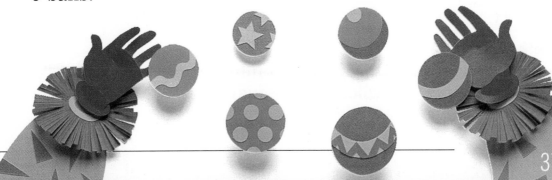

371

Comparing Fractions

Build Understanding

A. Kelly is making salad dressing. His recipe calls for $\frac{1}{2}$ cup of yogurt and $\frac{1}{3}$ cup of oil. Does he need more yogurt or oil?

You can see that $\frac{1}{2}$ cup is more than $\frac{1}{3}$ cup.

So $\frac{1}{2}$ is greater than $\frac{1}{3}$.

$$\frac{1}{2} > \frac{1}{3}$$

You can see that $\frac{1}{3}$ cup is less than $\frac{1}{2}$ cup.

$$\frac{1}{3} < \frac{1}{2}$$

B. Which is greater, $\frac{1}{3}$ cup or $\frac{2}{3}$ cup?

You can see that $\frac{2}{3}$ cup is more than $\frac{1}{3}$ cup.

So $\frac{2}{3}$ is greater than $\frac{1}{3}$.

$$\frac{2}{3} > \frac{1}{3}$$

Also, $\frac{1}{3}$ cup is less than $\frac{2}{3}$ cup.

So $\frac{1}{3}$ is less than $\frac{2}{3}$.

$$\frac{1}{3} < \frac{2}{3}$$

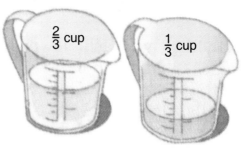

What types of foods do you like to cook?

■ **Talk About Math** Suppose there are two pizzas of equal size. One is divided into 6 equal parts. The other is divided into 7 equal parts. Which pizza has larger pieces? Explain.

Check Understanding

Use < or > to complete each number sentence.

1.

$$\frac{1}{4} \text{ ⬚ } \frac{3}{4}$$

2.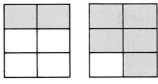

$$\frac{2}{6} \text{ ⬚ } \frac{5}{6}$$

3.

$$\frac{9}{10} \text{ ⬚ } \frac{7}{10}$$

4. In Example A the two fractions have the same numerator but different denominators. Explain how to tell which is larger.

5. In Example B the two fractions have the same denominator but different numerators. Explain how to tell which is larger.

Practice

Write each number sentence using <, >, or =.

6.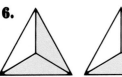

$$\frac{2}{3} \text{ ⬚ } \frac{1}{3}$$

7.

$$\frac{4}{7} \text{ ⬚ } \frac{2}{7}$$

8.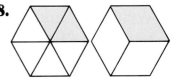

$$\frac{2}{6} \text{ ⬚ } \frac{1}{3}$$

9. $\frac{5}{12} \text{ ⬚ } \frac{7}{12}$

10. $\frac{3}{5} \text{ ⬚ } \frac{2}{5}$

11. $\frac{1}{5} \text{ ⬚ } \frac{1}{4}$

12. $\frac{1}{4} \text{ ⬚ } \frac{2}{3}$

Problem Solving

Write a fraction for each of the following problems.

13. Four of the 6 cooking club members are from Ms. Barr's class.

14. Two of the six cooking club members are from Mr. Lane's class.

15. Use > or < to compare the fractions.

Ordering Fractions

Build Understanding

A. In Oakdale, many children walk to school. Stella walks $\frac{1}{3}$ mile. CJ walks $\frac{1}{2}$ mile. Lou walks $\frac{1}{4}$ mile. Who has the longest walk? Who has the shortest?

The fraction bars on page 375 can help you find the answers.

You can see that $\frac{1}{3} < \frac{1}{2}$. The fraction bars show that $\frac{1}{4} < \frac{1}{2}$ and $\frac{1}{4} < \frac{1}{3}$. From least to greatest the order of the fractions is $\frac{1}{4}, \frac{1}{3}, \frac{1}{2}$.

CJ's $\frac{1}{2}$-mile walk is the longest. Lou's $\frac{1}{4}$-mile walk is the shortest.

B. Write $\frac{1}{3}$, $\frac{4}{6}$, and $\frac{2}{8}$ in order from greatest to least. Use the fraction bars.

Find the bar for thirds. $\frac{1}{3}$ is one section. Draw a line on your paper to show how long this is. Find the bar for sixths. $\frac{4}{6}$ is four sections. Draw a line to show how long this is. Find the bar for eighths. $\frac{2}{8}$ is two sections. Draw a line to show how long this is. From greatest to least the order of the fractions is

$\frac{4}{6}, \frac{1}{3}, \frac{2}{8}$.

■ **Talk About Math** Explain how comparing fractions is related to ordering fractions.

$\frac{1}{2}$		$\frac{1}{2}$	

$\frac{1}{3}$		$\frac{1}{3}$		$\frac{1}{3}$	

$\frac{1}{4}$	$\frac{1}{4}$	$\frac{1}{4}$	$\frac{1}{4}$

$\frac{1}{5}$	$\frac{1}{5}$	$\frac{1}{5}$	$\frac{1}{5}$	$\frac{1}{5}$

$\frac{1}{6}$	$\frac{1}{6}$	$\frac{1}{6}$	$\frac{1}{6}$	$\frac{1}{6}$	$\frac{1}{6}$

$\frac{1}{8}$	$\frac{1}{8}$	$\frac{1}{8}$	$\frac{1}{8}$	$\frac{1}{8}$	$\frac{1}{8}$	$\frac{1}{8}$	$\frac{1}{8}$

$\frac{1}{10}$	$\frac{1}{10}$	$\frac{1}{10}$	$\frac{1}{10}$	$\frac{1}{10}$	$\frac{1}{10}$	$\frac{1}{10}$	$\frac{1}{10}$	$\frac{1}{10}$	$\frac{1}{10}$

Check Understanding

For another example, see Set E, pages 396–397.

Read the problem. Then use the fraction bars to answer the questions below and solve the problem.

From least to greatest, what is the order of these fractions? $\frac{7}{8}, \frac{3}{4}, \frac{5}{6}$

1. Which two fraction bars will you look at first?

2. What will those bars tell you?

3. Which two fraction bars will you look at next?

4. What will those bars tell you?

5. Which two fraction bars will you look at last?

6. Write the fractions in order from least to greatest.

Practice

For More Practice, see Set E, pages 398–399.

Write the fractions in order from least to greatest.
Remember to use the fraction bars to help.

7. $\frac{1}{4}, \frac{1}{6}, \frac{5}{6}$ **8.** $\frac{2}{3}, \frac{2}{5}, \frac{1}{3}$ **9.** $\frac{5}{8}, \frac{5}{6}, \frac{4}{5}$

10. $\frac{2}{5}, \frac{2}{3}, \frac{3}{8}$ **11.** $\frac{4}{10}, \frac{4}{5}, \frac{8}{8}$ **12.** $\frac{2}{5}, \frac{5}{8}, \frac{3}{5}, \frac{1}{2}$

Use the fraction bars to find a fraction
between the two that are given.

13. $\frac{1}{5}$ and $\frac{1}{3}$ **14.** $\frac{3}{5}$ and $\frac{2}{3}$ **15.** $\frac{3}{10}$ and $\frac{2}{5}$

Problem Solving

Explore ———— Math

Mary used fraction bars to make a number line. What are
the missing numbers?

For 3 feet, the unit is feet.
You can think of a fraction
as a unit.

For 3 fourths, the unit is
fourths.

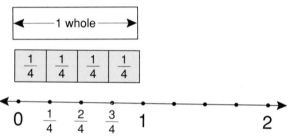

16. Look at Mary's number
line and count by fourths.
How many units are there
from 0 to 1 fourth? 0 to
2 fourths? 0 to 3 fourths? 0 to 1?

17. Keep counting by fourths.
The next number is 1 and
1 fourth. You write this as
$1\frac{1}{4}$. How would you write
1 and 2 fourths?

18. Copy Mary's number line.
Fill in the numbers
between 1 and 2. What
number did you write for
1 and 3 fourths?

19. A number made up of a
whole number and a
fraction is a **mixed
number.** What are the
mixed numbers on your
number line?

Write a fraction that names the shaded part.

1. 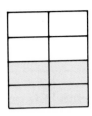   **2.**   **3.**   **4.**

Use the fractions $\frac{4}{8}$, $\frac{1}{4}$, $\frac{1}{2}$, $\frac{2}{6}$, and $\frac{1}{3}$ for Exercises 5–8.

5. Write a number sentence using > to compare two fractions.

6. Write a number sentence using < to compare two fractions.

7. Write a number sentence to show equal fractions.

8. Write three fractions in order from least to greatest.

9. Write a fraction to show how many apples are red.

10. Find $\frac{1}{3}$ of the apples.

11. What division fact can help you find $\frac{1}{8}$ of 32?

12. Find $\frac{1}{6}$ of 30.

Solve each problem.

13. The pet shop has parakeets and kittens. In all, the parakeets and kittens have 24 feet. One half of the pets are parakeets. How many of each pet are there?

14. A game board has 33 squares. Each square is green or yellow. The number of green squares is double the number of yellow squares. How many squares of each color are there?

Problem-Solving Workshop

Number-Sense Project

Look back at pages 358-359.
One class collected this information

AGE	Number surveyed	Dinosaurs Correctly Named			
		Tyrannosaurus	Apatosaurus (Brontosaurus)	Pterandon	Stegosaurus
Preteen	30	20	15	6	10
Teenage	24	18	6	4	12
Adult	40	10	5	2	4

1. How many preteens were asked to identify the dinosaurs?

2. What fraction of the preteens could correctly name Apatosaurus?

3. If 100 preteens, instead of 30, were asked to identify Apatosaurus, how many do you think would be able to do it?

If your clock strikes 13, what time is it?

ANSWER: Time to get a new clock.

Explore with a Computer

Use the *Fractions Workshop Project* for this activity.

Aunt Sophia cut a pumpkin pie into 6 equal pieces and a blueberry pie into 12 equal pieces to serve at a party. After the party some of each pie was not eaten.

1. At the computer, shade the first unit to show that 2 pieces of pumpkin pie were left. Write the amount as a fraction.

2. Shade the second unit to show that 4 pieces of blueberry pie were left. Write the amount as a fraction.

3. Compare the two pies. Which pie has more left over?

Real-Life Decision Making

Answer these questions. Explain your thinking.

1. You are very hungry. Would you rather have $\frac{1}{4}$ or $\frac{1}{8}$ of a small pizza?

2. Your feet are very tired. Would you rather walk $\frac{1}{3}$ mile or $\frac{1}{4}$ mile to get home?

3. Would you rather wait in line for a movie $\frac{1}{2}$ hour or $\frac{1}{4}$ hour?

Critical-Thinking Activity

• Bonnie lives on the top floor.

• Carole lives below Donna.

• Ann lives above Donna.

Who lives on the second floor?

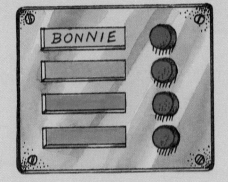

379

Tenths

Build Understanding

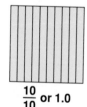

Cover It Up!

Materials: Large decimal models (one whole, tenth sticks)

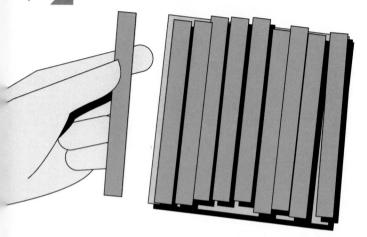

A. a. Cover one whole with tenth sticks.

b. How many tenth sticks cover one whole?

c. What part of one whole is 1 tenth stick?

You can write the fraction $\frac{1}{10}$ as the *decimal* 0.1. You read both $\frac{1}{10}$ and 0.1 as "one *tenth*."

B. a. Put down 1 whole model and 3 tenth sticks.

b. What are the fraction and the decimal for these models?

You read $1\frac{3}{10}$ and 1.3 as "one and three tenths."

c. What number does this model show?

$\frac{10}{10}$ or 1.0

■ **Talk About Math** How are decimals and fractions alike?

380

Check Understanding

Use small decimal models for Exercises 1–5.

1. On a model for one whole, write the whole number and the fraction that names the model.

2. On a tenths model, write the decimal and the fraction that tell what part of the whole one section is.

3. Shade in 4 sections on a tenths model. Write the fraction and the decimal for the shaded sections.

4. Write the decimal and the fraction for the sections that are not shaded in the model for Exercise 3.

5. Shade 3 whole models and 3 sections of another. Write the decimal and fraction.

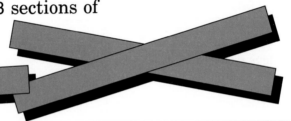

Practice

Show the fraction with a decimal model. Write the decimal.

6. $\frac{4}{10}$ **7.** one tenth   **8.** $\frac{6}{10}$ **9.** two tenths   **10.** $\frac{10}{10}$

Write the decimal and the fraction for the shaded parts.

11.   **12.** 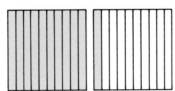   **13.**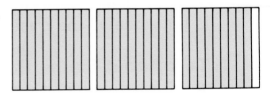

Write the decimal.

14. three tenths   **15.** $\frac{5}{10}$ **16.** seven tenths   **17.** $\frac{9}{10}$

18. 🖩 **Calculator** Find a decimal for $\frac{8}{10}$. **Press:** 8 ÷ 10 = Write the decimal.

Decimal Place Value

Build Understanding

How do you read the digits on a digital thermometer?

Lee took his temperature with a thermometer. His body temperature was normal.

The digits in the place-value box show how many degrees Fahrenheit Lee's temperature was.

Tens	Ones	Tenths
9	**8**	**6**
tens digit	ones digit	tenths digit
9 tens	8 ones	6 tenths
90	8	$\frac{6}{10}$

98.6 ← standard form

The decimal point separates ones from tenths.

Lee's temperature was 98.6°F. You read 98.6 as "ninety-eight and six tenths."

A decimal can also be written as a fraction. The decimal 98.6 is the same as the fraction $98\frac{6}{10}$.

■ **Talk About Math** How is place value with decimals like place value with whole numbers?

Check Understanding

For another example, see Set F, pages 396–397.

Write each number as a decimal and as a fraction.

1.

Ones	Tenths
3	2

2.

Ones	Tenths
1	6

3.

Ones	Tenths
0	3

4. Lee wrote the number fourteen in a place-value box. Did he write it correctly? If not, show how it should be written.

Tens	Ones	Tenths
0	1	4

5. Lee wrote the number one and seven tenths in a place-value box. Write the number correctly if you think Lee is wrong.

Tens	Ones	Tenths
1	7	0

Practice

For More Practice, see Set F, pages 398–399.

Copy each exercise. Underline the tenths digit.

6. 28.1   **7.** 13.9   **8.** 96.8   **9.** 72.7   **10.** 65.8

Tell what place the 4 is in for each exercise.

11. 47.5   **12.** 4.5   **13.** 87.4   **14.** 14.8   **15.** 36.4

16. Write the decimals in Exercises 6–10 in words.

Reading ——— Math

Vocabulary Copy and complete the sentences. Use the words below to fill in the blanks. Use each word only once.

tenths   decimal point   numerator   denominator   fraction bar

In the number 20.5 the digit 5 is in the __1.__ place. In a fraction the __2.__ is the top number and the __3.__ is the bottom number. The __4.__ in 8.7 separates the ones and the tenths.

Hundredths

Build Understanding

Count the Squares
Materials: Large decimal models (one whole, tenth sticks, hundredth squares), 10 × 10 grid paper

A. a. Cover a tenth stick with hundredth squares. How many hundredth squares cover 1 tenth stick?

b. Cover one whole with tenth sticks. Since 10 hundredth squares cover 1 stick, you can count by 10s to find the total number of hundredth squares in 1 whole model. How many hundredth squares are there?

c. What part of one whole is one hundredth square?

You can write $\frac{1}{100}$ as 0.01.

Ones	Tenths	Hundredths
0	0	1

You read both $\frac{1}{100}$ and 0.01 as "one **hundredth**."

B. a. Put down 1 whole model, 3 tenth sticks, and 6 hundredth squares.

b. What number do these models show? You read $1\frac{36}{100}$ and 1.36 as "one and thirty-six hundredths."

Ones	Tenths	Hundredths
1	3	6

c. What number does this place-value box show?

Ones	Tenths	Hundredths
1	**0**	**0**

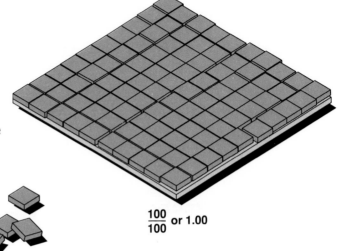

$\frac{100}{100}$ or 1.00

■ **Talk About Math** Tell what the 0 in 3.07 means. Is 3.07 the same as 3.7? Explain.

Check Understanding

Write the fraction and the decimal.

1.   **2.**

Use decimal models to show the numbers.

3. 0.03   **4.** $1\frac{45}{100}$ **5.** two and sixteen hundredths

Number Sense Write the fraction and the decimal for each model.

6.   **7.**

8. Tell whether each pair of models in Exercises 6 and 7 names the same number or different numbers.

Practice

Use decimal models. Write the decimals.

9. $\frac{9}{100}$ **10.** $\frac{66}{100}$ **11.** $1\frac{84}{100}$ **12.** two and three hundredths

Tell whether each pair names the same number.

13. $\frac{50}{100}$, $\frac{5}{10}$ **14.** $8\frac{2}{100}$, 8.02   **15.** $9\frac{47}{100}$, 94.7   **16.** $\frac{37}{100}$, 3.7

Mixed Practice   Answer each question.

17. In 62.5, what digit is in the tenths place?

18. In 3.27, in what place is the 7?

19. In 2.05, in what place is the 0?

20. In 8.97, what digit is in the tenths place?

21. Write the decimal for $\frac{7}{10}$.

22. Write the decimal for $4\frac{63}{100}$.

23. What fraction does the model show?

24. What decimal does the model show?

25. Write a decimal that has 6 in the tenths place.

26. Write a decimal that has 6 in the hundredths place.

27. What fraction does the model show?

28. Write the decimal shown by the models.

Problem Solving

Solve each problem.

29. Of the 100 students at the amusement park, 56 rode on the roller coaster. Write a decimal for the part of the group that did not ride.

30. Twenty-nine of the students were third graders. Write a decimal for the part of the group made up of third graders.

31. Critical Thinking You can write 25¢ as $0.25. How can you write these amounts?

39¢   56¢   4¢

32. Use a sheet of 10 × 10 grid paper. Color each square to make a design. Use five to eight different colors in the design. Then write a decimal for each color to show what part of the grid paper has that color.

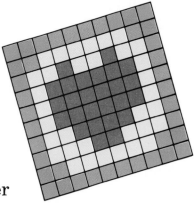

Choose a 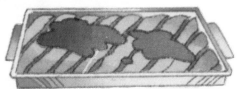 **Strategy**

Lasagna Puzzle

33. A lasagna is in the shape of a rectangle. You want to cut it into 8 equal pieces. What is the least number of cuts you can make? What is the greatest number of cuts you can make?

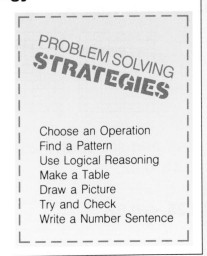

PROBLEM SOLVING
STRATEGIES

Choose an Operation
Find a Pattern
Use Logical Reasoning
Make a Table
Draw a Picture
Try and Check
Write a Number Sentence

Comparing Decimals

Build Understanding

A. Mrs. Lopez has 10 dogs in puppy training class. Out of the 10 puppies, 0.4 are collies and 0.6 are not collies. Are more of the puppies collies or are more not collies?

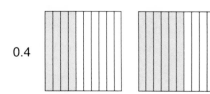

You can see that 0.6 is greater than 0.4.

0.6 > 0.4

More dogs are not collies.

B. Which is less, 0.62 or 0.25?

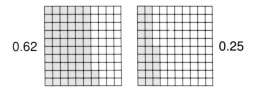

You can see that 0.25 is less than 0.62.

0.25 < 0.62

So 0.25 is less than 0.62.

How many breeds of dogs can you name?

■ **Talk About Math** How is comparing decimals like comparing whole numbers?

Check Understanding

For another example, see Set G, pages 396–397.

Write each number sentence using < or >.

1.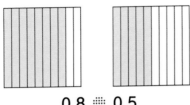

0.8 ⬚ 0.5

2.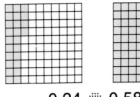

0.24 ⬚ 0.58

Write two number sentences using < and > for each pair of numbers.

3. 0.37, 0.86

4. 1.05, 1.5

Practice

For More Practice, see Set G, pages 398–399.

Write each number sentence using < or >.

5. 1.3 ⬚ 1.4

6. 1.38 ⬚ 1.43

7. 0.8 ⬚ 0.71

8. 2.09 ⬚ 2.1

Write two number sentences using < and > for each pair of numbers.

9. 0.3, 0.5

10. 0.86, 0.37

11. 2.34, 3.65

12. 1.15, 1.51

Problem Solving

Answer each question. Out of 20 dogs in a class,

13. 8 learned to sit on Monday. How many dogs did not learn to sit?

14. there are 14 females. How many are males?

Number Sense Answer each riddle.

15. I am a decimal in hundredths. I am less than 0.4. I am greater than 0.35. The sum of my digits is 10. Who am I?

16. I am a decimal in tenths. I am greater than 0.38. I am less than 0.44. Who am I?

Use Alternate Strategies

Build Understanding

PROBLEM SOLVING GUIDE

Understand
QUESTION
FACTS
KEY IDEA

▶ **Plan and Solve**
STRATEGY
ANSWER

Look Back
SENSIBLE ANSWER
ALTERNATE APPROACH

Kim cut a tamale pie into 10 pieces. Her family ate 0.3 of the pie. Her guests ate 0.5 of the pieces. What part of the pie is left?

Understand You need to find what part of the pie was not eaten. There were 10 pieces in all, and 0.3 and 0.5 were eaten. Think of 0.3 and 0.5 as $\frac{3}{10}$ and $\frac{5}{10}$.

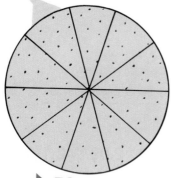

The sum of 3, 5, and the pieces left must equal 10 because $\frac{10}{10}$ equals one whole.

▶ **Plan and Solve**

STRATEGY Draw a picture by shading a decimal model.

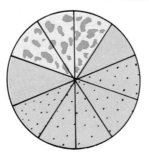

ANSWER The part left is 0.2, or 2 pieces of pie.

STRATEGY Try adding different numbers to 3 and 5. Then check the answer.

$3 + 5 + 4 = 12$ too much
$3 + 5 + 1 = 9$ too small
$3 + 5 + 2 = 10$ correct

ANSWER Two pieces are left. Two pieces are $\frac{2}{10}$, or 0.2 of the pie.

Look Back Which strategy do you like better? Explain.

■ **Talk About Math** Can you think of 0.3 and 0.5 as whole numbers in this problem? Explain.

Check Understanding

1. What part of the pie is 1 piece? Write the decimal.

2. How do you know how many pieces of pie 0.3 and 0.5 are?

3. If 0.2 and 0.4 were eaten, what part would be left?

4. Write a number sentence for Exercise 3 using pieces of pie.

Practice

Write two strategies you could use to solve each problem. Use both ways to find the answer.

5. How many slices of pizza will be on the next tray?

6. Kim cut French bread into 10 equal pieces. She used half the pieces for lunch. She used 0.2 of the pieces for dinner. What part of the bread is left?

7. On one side of the table, Bob is sitting in the middle. Willa is to the left of Greg and to the right of Bob. Rea is to the left of Yuri. In what order are they sitting?

8. Kim has 100 paper plates. She put 0.7 of them at Table A, 0.26 at Table B, and the rest at Table C. How many plates are at each table?

TIPS FOR PROBLEM SOLVERS

Share your thinking with others. Explaining your ideas helps you think better.

391

Using Decimals

Build Understanding

A. Kate has 2 one-dollar bills, 3 dimes, and 9 pennies. How much money does Kate have?

Ones	Tenths	Hundredths
2	3	9

2 dollars	3 dimes	9 pennies
200 cents	30 cents	9 cents
$\frac{200}{100}$	$\frac{30}{100}$	$\frac{9}{100}$

Kate has $2.39.

B. Decimals can be used in many ways. Write each decimal and think about how it is used.

1.09

Decimals can be used to count.

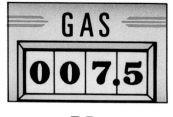

7.5

Decimals can be used to measure.

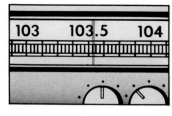

103.5

Decimals can be used to tell order.

C. Estimation You can estimate using decimals. About how long is the stick to the nearest centimeter?

When a centimeter is separated into ten equal parts, you can measure in tenths of a centimeter.

The stick is 4.3 centimeters long. You can see that 4.3 centimeters is closer to 4 centimeters than to 5 centimeters.

The stick is about 4 centimeters long.

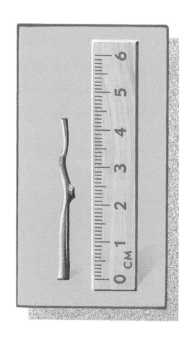

■ **Talk About Math** Where else are decimals used?

Check Understanding

For another example, see Set H, pages 396–397.

Write a decimal and a fraction to answer each question. What part of a dollar is

1. 1 cent? **2.** 1 nickel? **3.** 1 dime? **4.** 1 quarter?

Practice

For More Practice, see Set H, pages 398–399.

Write what the meter will show when the car travels another tenth of a mile.

5.

6.

7. Estimation About how long is the sausage, to the nearest centimeter?

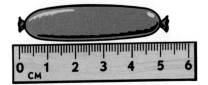

Problem Solving

Calculator You can use your calculator to write $\frac{1}{4}$ as a decimal. Use your calculator to divide 1 by 4.

Press: 1 ÷ 4 =

The display shows *0.25*.

Use your calculator to write each fraction as a decimal.

8. $\frac{1}{5}$ **9.** $\frac{2}{8}$ **10.** $\frac{9}{12}$ **11.** $\frac{12}{16}$ **12.** $\frac{8}{50}$

13. $10\frac{1}{4}$ pounds **14.** $14\frac{1}{2}$ inches **15.** $5\frac{2}{5}$ miles

16. Use Data Use your calculator to help you find the decimals for the fractions in Exercises 19–21 on page 363.

393

Problem-Solving Review

Solve each problem.

1. Jordan peeled an orange and pulled apart the sections. There were 9 sections. If the sections were exactly equal, what fraction would each section represent?

2. A box of Yummy Dog Treats had 27 biscuits in it. Carla has 3 dogs. How many treats will each dog get if they are shared equally?

3. A survey was given to 100 students. Fifty-seven students answered it. Write a decimal to show what part of the students answered the survey.

4. In the fall, Davis planted 24 daffodil bulbs. In the spring, $\frac{1}{8}$ of them did not produce flowers. How many bulbs did make flowers?

5. There were 24 children in a class. On a winter field day, the class equally shared 4 toboggans. How many were in each toboggan?

6. **Data File** Use data from pages 402-403. Find the number of loaves of bread Jonathan will get if he buys $\frac{1}{4}$ of the wheat loaves and $\frac{1}{2}$ of the raisin loaves.

7. **Make a Data File** Use a cookbook. Make a list of 10 ingredients using fractions such as $\frac{1}{2}, \frac{1}{3}, \frac{1}{4}, \frac{1}{8}, \frac{2}{3}$, and $\frac{3}{4}$. Write each fraction, label, and ingredient.

Numerator ÷ Denominator = Decimal

1. One way to compare fractions is to change them to decimals and compare the decimals.

Are $\frac{3}{4}$ and $\frac{15}{20}$ equal fractions ?

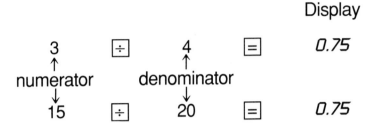

Display

3 ÷ 4 = 0.75

numerator   denominator

15 ÷ 20 = 0.75

The displays are the same, so the fractions are equal.

2. Here are 10 fractions. Change each to a decimal.

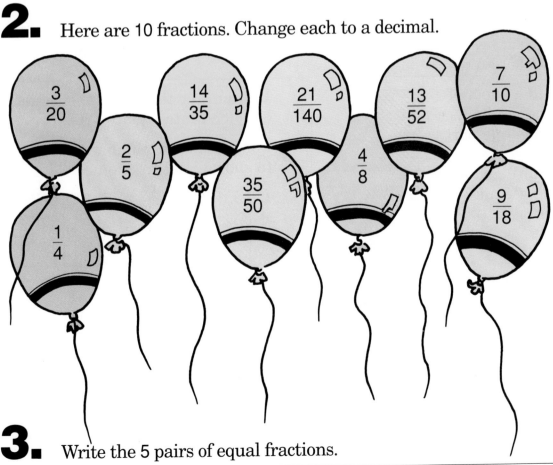

3. Write the 5 pairs of equal fractions.

Reteaching

Set A pages 360-363

Fractions name equal parts of a whole. This figure is divided into 4 equal parts. So each part is one fourth of the whole figure.

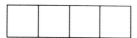

You write one fourth as $\frac{1}{4}$.

Remember that the denominator tells you the number of equal parts. Which fraction names the shaded part?

1.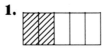

$\frac{2}{5}$ $\frac{3}{5}$ $\frac{1}{2}$

2.

$\frac{1}{4}$ $\frac{1}{3}$ $\frac{3}{4}$

Set B pages 364-365

There are 16 students in the school band. Five of the students play the trumpet. This can be shown as a fraction.

$$\frac{\text{number of trumpet players}}{\text{number of students in all}} = \frac{5}{16}$$

Remember that fractions name parts of a set of objects.

What fraction stands for the blue part of this group?

a. $\frac{2}{5}$ **b.** $\frac{3}{5}$

Set C pages 366-367

Fold a sheet of paper in half. Shade one part.

Fold the paper into 4 equal parts.

So $\frac{1}{2}$ and $\frac{2}{4}$ are equal.

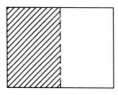

Remember that the paper must be folded into equal parts.

Complete each number sentence to show equal fractions.

1.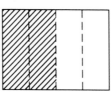

$\frac{2}{3} = \frac{\quad}{6}$

2.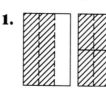

$\frac{\quad}{\quad} = \frac{\quad}{8}$

Set D pages 368-369

Find $\frac{1}{5}$ of 30.

To find $\frac{1}{5}$ of a number you can divide the number by 5. Think:
$30 \div 5 = 6$ So $\frac{1}{5}$ of 30 is 6.

Remember that the denominator of the fraction is the divisor. Answer each question.

1. Find $\frac{1}{6}$ of 30.   **2.** Find $\frac{1}{8}$ of 24.

Set E pages 374–377

Use the fraction bars on page 375 to help you write these fractions in order from greatest to least.

$\frac{1}{3}, \frac{2}{5}, \frac{3}{8}$

The order is: $\frac{2}{5}, \frac{3}{8}, \frac{1}{3}$

Remember that the inequality symbol always points to the smaller number.

Write the fractions in order from least to greatest.

1. $\frac{1}{4}, \frac{1}{5}, \frac{1}{8}$ **2.** $\frac{2}{5}, \frac{2}{6}, \frac{2}{3}$ **3.** $\frac{1}{3}, \frac{5}{8}, \frac{2}{4}$

Set F pages 382–383

Randy ran the distance in 45.6 seconds.

Tens	Ones	Tenths
4	5	6

Read 45.6 as "forty-five and six tenths."

Remember that you read the decimal point as "and."

Tell what place the 3 is in for each exercise.

1. 36.9   **2.** 80.3

3. 73.1   **4.** 46.3

Set G pages 388–389

Compare 0.53 and 0.35.

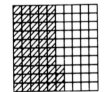 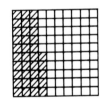

You can see that 0.53 is greater than 0.35.   0.53 > 0.35

Remember that > means "greater than" and < means "less than."

Write each number sentence using < or >.

1. 2.4 ▦ 2.5   **2.** 1.26 ▦ 1.3

3. 0.7 ▦ 0.6   **4.** 0.62 ▦ 0.53

Set H pages 392–393

Decimals are used in many ways. This scale at the supermarket shows two ways.

2.6 lb	$6.35
weight	money

Remember that the decimal point separates ones from tenths.

Write what the meter reading will show when the car travels another tenth of a mile.

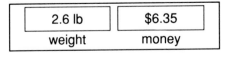

More Practice

Set A   pages 360–363

Which fraction names the shaded part?

1.

$\frac{2}{5}$ $\frac{4}{5}$ $\frac{3}{4}$

2.

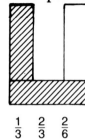

$\frac{1}{3}$ $\frac{2}{3}$ $\frac{2}{6}$

3.

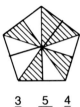

$\frac{3}{5}$ $\frac{5}{10}$ $\frac{4}{5}$

Which picture is shaded to show the fraction?

4. Four fifths

a. 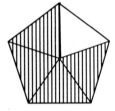   **b.**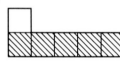

5. Four sixths

a. 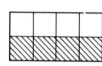   **b.**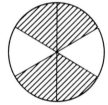

Set B   pages 364–365

What fraction stands for the blue part of each group?

1.

$\frac{1}{3}$ $\frac{4}{6}$ $\frac{4}{5}$

2.

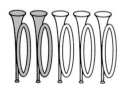

$\frac{1}{5}$ $\frac{2}{5}$ $\frac{3}{5}$

3.

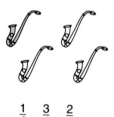

$\frac{1}{4}$ $\frac{3}{4}$ $\frac{2}{4}$

Set C   pages 366–367

Complete each number sentence to show equal fractions.

1.

$\frac{2}{3} = \frac{}{6}$

2.

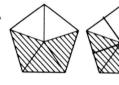

$\frac{3}{5} = \frac{}{10}$

3.

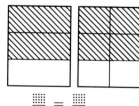

$\frac{}{} = \frac{}{}$

Set D pages 368–369

Find each number.

1. $\frac{1}{3}$ of 12   2. $\frac{1}{8}$ of 24   3. $\frac{1}{3}$ of 27   4. $\frac{1}{7}$ of 35

5. $\frac{1}{4}$ of 28   6. $\frac{1}{6}$ of 30   7. $\frac{1}{4}$ of 32   8. $\frac{1}{8}$ of 64

Set E pages 374–377

Use the fraction bars on page 375 to help you write the fractions in order from least to greatest.

1. $\frac{2}{6}, \frac{2}{3}, \frac{2}{10}$ 2. $\frac{1}{3}, \frac{2}{8}, \frac{2}{4}$ 3. $\frac{3}{8}, \frac{3}{4}, \frac{4}{6}$ 4. $\frac{6}{10}, \frac{6}{8}, \frac{5}{6}$

Set F pages 382–383

Copy each exercise. Underline the tens digit.

1. 36.5   2. 81.9   3. 27.3   4. 59.7   5. 91.8

Tell what place the 5 is in for each exercise.

6. 35.9   7. 56.4   8. 68.5   9. 57.3   10. 91.5

11. Write the decimals in Exercises 1–5 in words.

Set G pages 388–389

Write each number sentence using $<$ or $>$.

1. 1.8 ▦ 1.7   2. 1.83 ▦ 1.96   3. 0.6 ▦ 0.52   4. 3.02 ▦ 3.2

Write two number sentences using $<$ and $>$ for each pair of numbers.

5. 0.6, 0.7   6. 0.72, 0.27   7. 3.48, 3.52   8. 2.1, 2.01

Set H pages 392–393

Write what the meter reading will show when the car travels another tenth of a mile.

1. | | | | | 7 | 6 | 2 | 2. | | | | | 5 | 8 | 8 |

Enrichment

Number Sense with Fractions

Here is a number line showing fractions between the whole numbers 0 and 1. Fractions between any two whole numbers are exactly the same as these.

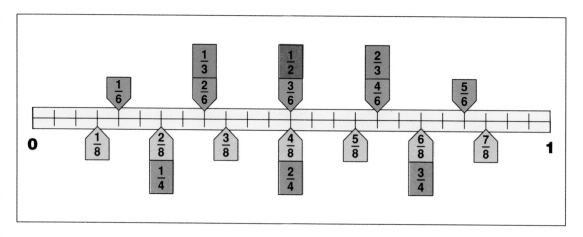

Use the number line. Tell whether the fraction is closer to 0 or to 1.

1. $\frac{4}{6}$ **2.** $\frac{3}{4}$ **3.** $\frac{1}{6}$ **4.** $\frac{5}{8}$ **5.** $\frac{7}{8}$

6. Between which two whole numbers does $9\frac{1}{8}$ lie?

7. To which number is $9\frac{1}{8}$ closer, 9 or 10?

8. To which number is $5\frac{2}{3}$ closer, 5 or 6?

9. To which number is $1\frac{5}{6}$ closer, 1 or 2?

10. To which number is $10\frac{1}{4}$ closer, 10 or 11?

For each exercise, tell what whole number is closest.

11. $7\frac{4}{6}$ **12.** $26\frac{5}{6}$ **13.** $99\frac{1}{3}$ **14.** $47\frac{2}{8}$ **15.** $1\frac{1}{4}$

16. $3\frac{2}{3}$ **17.** $11\frac{7}{8}$ **18.** $9\frac{1}{4}$ **19.** $23\frac{6}{8}$ **20.** $321\frac{1}{8}$

Chapter 11 Review/Test

1. What fraction names the shaded part?

2. What fraction of the balls are yellow?

3. Complete the number sentence to show equal fractions.

$\frac{3}{4}$ =

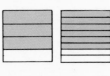

4. Find $\frac{1}{2}$ of 10.

Replace each ⬜ with < or >.

5. 0.7 ⬜ 0.4   **6.** 0.27 ⬜ 0.3

7. $\frac{3}{6}$ ⬜ $\frac{1}{6}$

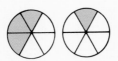

8. Write $\frac{3}{5}$, $\frac{7}{10}$, $\frac{1}{10}$ in order from least to greatest.

Write each decimal.

9. 5 tenths   **10.** 8 tenths

11. thirty-seven hundredths

For each decimal, tell what place the 6 is in.

12. 26.5   **13.** 11.6   **14.** 67.4

15. What decimal part of a dollar is 1 dime?

Read this problem. Then answer the questions below.

Five friends had a race. Ann finished behind Roy and ahead of Lew. <u>Pam finished ahead of Roy</u>, but Pam did not win the race. Tim raced in his new sneakers. What was the order of finish?

16. What does the underlined statement mean?

   a. Pam was behind Roy at the end of the race.

   b. Roy came in last in the race.

   c. Pam got to the finish line before Roy.

17. Solve the problem above.

18. ■ **Write About Math**
Describe a second strategy you could use to solve the problem above.

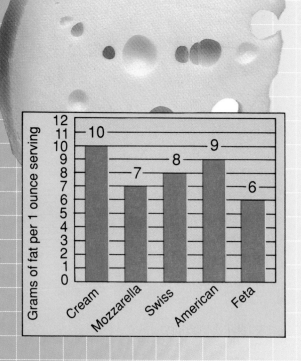
DATA FILE

1. Fats in Cheese

1. Bar Graph
The graph shows grams of fat in different kinds of cheese.

2. Picture Graph
This shows the number of loaves of bread baked daily.

3. Product Label
The label tells the weight and the number of slices in the loaf of bread.

4. Product Labels
These materials are for making crafts.

5. List
This is Ian's weekly shopping list.

Sunshine Bakery
Daily Production Report (Bread)

Wheat	🍞🍞🍞🍞🍞🍞🍞🍞
Rye	🍞🍞🍞🍞
White	🍞🍞
Raisin	🍞🍞🍞🍞🍞
Pumpernickel	🍞🍞🍞🍞

Each 🍞 is 1 loaf of bread

2. Bread Baking

3. Bread Loaf

Bread

Romel's
Wheat Bread
Sandwich Loaf
16 ounces 24 slices

35 COUNT
Red Berry Clusters

48 COUNT
Pine Branches

36 COUNT
Gold Stars

42 COUNT
Snowflakes

4. **Craft Materials**

5. **Shopping List**

6 cans chicken Soup
12 apples
    Peanut Butter
3 rolls paper towels
15 potatoes
2 loaves bread

Give the letter for the correct answer.

1. Add.

134	**A** 156
51	**B** 346
+261	**C** 456
	D 446

2. Subtract.

	A 768
	B 762
886	**C** 758
−128	**D** 752

3. What time is shown?

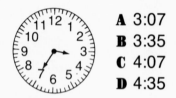

A 3:07
B 3:35
C 4:07
D 4:35

4. What is the length of this line segment to the nearest centimeter?

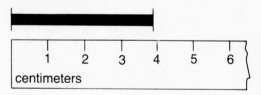

A 4 cm   **C** 6 cm
B 5 cm   **D** 3 cm

5. Find the perimeter.

```
        10 ft
4 ft  [        ]  4 ft
        10 ft
```

A 14 feet   **C** 40 feet
B 6 feet   **D** 28 feet

6. Tell whether you *add, subtract,* or *multiply.* Then find the answer.

Marge made 2 leather bracelets each week for 3 weeks. How many bracelets did Marge make in all?

A Add or multiply; 6
B Subtract; 1
C Add; 5
D Multiply; 9

7. Multiply.

	A 13
	B 1
6	**C** 36
×7	**D** 42

8. Multiply.

	A 15
	B 56
7	**C** 1
×8	**D** 64

9. Which is a right angle?

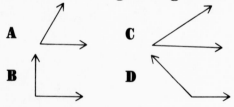

10. Which of the following should be measured in milliliters?

A a raindrop
B the water in a bathtub
C the water in a lake
D the fuel in a car's tank

11. Try and check to solve the problem.

John and his sister Sarah have 35 tapes. Sarah has 15 more tapes than John. How many tapes does each child have?

A Sarah has 10. John has 25.
B Sarah has 30. John has 15.
C Sarah has 25. John has 10.
D Sarah has 15. John has 20.

12. Divide.

$$4\overline{)36}$$

A 12
B 6
C 8
D 9

13. Divide.

$36 \div 9$

A 27
B 4
C 45
D 8

14. Divide.

$5 \div 5$

A 2
B 1
C 10
D 0

15. Divide.

$33 \div 6$

A 6 Remainder 2
B 27 Remainder 1
C 5 Remainder 3
D 14 Remainder 5

16. Solve the problem.

Lance collected 48 rocks. He divided them into 6 equal piles. How many rocks did he put in each pile?

A 288   **B** 8   **C** 42   **D** 54

17. What fraction names the shaded part?

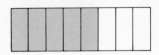

A $\frac{3}{5}$ **C** $\frac{5}{7}$
B $\frac{3}{8}$ **D** $\frac{5}{8}$

18. Which decimal means the same as $\frac{57}{100}$?

A 57.0   **C** 0.57
B 5.7   **D** 0.0057

19. Which number sentence is true?

A 1.5 < 1.05
B 0.5 < 0.3
C 2.09 > 2.1
D 0.75 > 0.37

Read the problem below. Then answer the question.

Ruth did 63 extra math problems in 7 days. She did the same number of problems each day. How many problems did she do each day?

20. Which number sentence would you use to solve the problem?

A 63 + 7 = ▦   **C** 63 × 7 = ▦
B 63 − 7 = ▦   **D** 63 ÷ 7 = ▦

Time and Money

12

Did You Know: When our country was first being settled, coins were scarce. To make more coins, dollars were cut into 8 bits. Two bits equaled 25¢, four bits equaled 50¢, six bits equaled 75¢, and eight bits equaled $1.

Number-Sense Project

Estimate
Predict the year that will appear most often on pennies people have.

Gather Data
Tally the year of each penny you have at home (up to 100). Tally those in banks, in purses, etc. Do not tally pennies in coin collections.

Analyze and Report
Find the total number of pennies for each year. Compare your results with other students.

Minutes Before the Hour

Build Understanding

A. Before and After
Materials: Clock with movable hands, worksheet with clock faces

What did you do at
10 minutes before 9:00 today?

a. Show 8:00 on your clock.

b. Show 8:15. You say:
"15 minutes *after* 8."

c. Show 8:30. You say:
"30 minutes *after* 8."

d. Show 8:50. You say:
"50 minutes *after* 8."

e. Start at the number 12 on your clock. Count by fives as you move backward to the minute hand. You also say: "10 minutes *before* 9" for 8:50.

At 30 minutes after the hour, you can begin counting minutes before the next hour.

B. 3:35
or
35 minutes after 3:00
or
25 minutes before 4:00

c. Estimation What could you do in
1 minute? in 5 minutes? in 10 minutes?

408

■ **Write About Math** Write about what might be happening at the time shown in Example B.

Check Understanding

For another example, see Set A, pages 432–433.

Copy and complete each time.

1.

▦ minutes after ▦

▦ : ▦

2.

▦ minutes after ▦

▦ minutes before ▦

▦ : ▦

3. Why are there three ways to tell the time shown on the clock in Exercise 2 and only two ways to tell the time shown on the clock in Exercise 1?

Practice

For More Practice, see Set A, pages 434–435.

Write each time as minutes before the hour.

4.

5.

6.

7.

Estimation Answer the questions.

8. How many times can you write your name in 1 minute?

9. How long does it take you to get dressed in the morning?

Show each time on your clock. On your
worksheet, draw the hands on a clock.

10. 10 minutes before 6

11. 15 minutes after 2

12. 6 minutes after 9

13. 23 minutes before 12

Write the letter for the most reasonable time.

14. wake up for school

a. 10 minutes before 3:00

15. leave school

b. 15 minutes before 12:00

16. eat lunch

c. 20 minutes before 7:00

Problem Solving

Write the time as minutes before the hour.
Use your clock to help you.

17. It was 25 minutes before 2:00
when Aki began looking for
his money to buy a snack. It
took Aki 5 minutes to find
his money. What time was it
when Aki found his money?

18. Suki's mother was supposed
to pick her up at 2:30. Her
mother was 10 minutes late.
What time was it when
Suki's mother picked her
up?

Use Data Write the time as minutes before the hour. Use the bus schedule on page 414.

19. The bus arrived at Orange Street 15 minutes late. What time did the bus arrive at Orange Street?

20. The bus left school at 3:30 instead of 3:00. What time did it arrive at Apple Street?

Reading ———— Math

Vocabulary Copy and complete the paragraph using the words below to fill in the blanks. Each word may be used more than once.

before   **after**

Suppose you look at your watch and see that the time is 6:40. The time is forty minutes __?__ six. You could also say the time is twenty minutes __?__ seven. In thirty minutes, the time will be ten minutes __?__ seven. Thirty-five minutes after that, the time will be fifteen minutes __?__ eight or forty-five minutes __?__ seven.

Calendar: Year

Build Understanding

JANUARY						
S	M	T	W	Th	F	S
		1	2	3	4	
5	6	7	8	9	10	11
12	13	14	15	16	17	18
19	20	21	22	23	24	25
26	27	28	29	30	31	

FEBRUARY						
S	M	T	W	Th	F	S
						1
2	3	4	5	6	7	8
9	10	11	12	13	14	15
16	17	18	19	20	21	22
23	24	25	26	27	28	

MARCH						
S	M	T	W	Th	F	S
						1
2	3	4	5	6	7	8
9	10	11	12	13	14	15
16	17	18	19	20	21	22
23/30	24/31	25	26	27	28	29

APRIL						
S	M	T	W	Th	F	S
		1	2	3	4	5
6	7	8	9	10	11	12
13	14	15	16	17	18	19
20	21	22	23	24	25	26
27	28	29	30			

MAY						
S	M	T	W	Th	F	S
				1	2	3
4	5	6	7	8	9	10
11	12	13	14	15	16	17
18	19	20	21	22	23	24
25	26	27	28	29	30	31

JUNE						
S	M	T	W	Th	F	S
1	2	3	4	5	6	7
8	9	10	11	12	13	14
15	16	17	18	19	20	21
22	23	24	25	26	27	28
29	30					

JULY						
S	M	T	W	Th	F	S
		1	2	3	4	5
6	7	8	9	10	11	12
13	14	15	16	17	18	19
20	21	22	23	24	25	26
27	28	29	30	31		

AUGUST						
S	M	T	W	Th	F	S
					1	2
3	4	5	6	7	8	9
10	11	12	13	14	15	16
17	18	19	20	21	22	23
24/31	25	26	27	28	29	30

SEPTEMBER						
S	M	T	W	Th	F	S
	1	2	3	4	5	6
7	8	9	10	11	12	13
14	15	16	17	18	19	20
21	22	23	24	25	26	27
28	29	30				

OCTOBER						
S	M	T	W	Th	F	S
			1	2	3	4
5	6	7	8	9	10	11
12	13	14	15	16	17	18
19	20	21	22	23	24	25
26	27	28	29	30	31	

NOVEMBER						
S	M	T	W	Th	F	S
						1
2	3	4	5	6	7	8
9	10	11	12	13	14	15
16	17	18	19	20	21	22
23/30	24	25	26	27	28	29

DECEMBER						
S	M	T	W	Th	F	S
	1	2	3	4	5	6
7	8	9	10	11	12	13
14	15	16	17	18	19	20
21	22	23	24	25	26	27
28	29	30	31			

A. We celebrate Independence Day on the Fourth of July. What day of the week is that on the calendar? What day of the week is your birthday?

B. January has 31 days. How many days does April have?

C. When writing and speaking, we often add the endings "st," "nd," "rd," and "th" to dates. For example, May 16 can be written and said "May sixteenth." How would you write and say August 24?

■ **Talk About Math** Does your birthday fall on the same day of the week each year? Talk about how the calendar changes each year.

412

Check Understanding

For another example, see Set B, pages 432–433.

Write the letter of the correct answer. Use the calendar on page 412 to help you.

1. What day of the week is June 16?

   a. Monday   **b.** Wednesday

2. What is the date of the last Sunday in July?

   a. July 26   **b.** July 27

3. Which month has exactly 30 days?

   a. June   **b.** July

4. How many months have more than 30 days?

   a. 6   **b.** 7

Practice

For More Practice, see Set B, pages 434–435.

Use the calendar on page 412. Write the day of the week.

5. New Year's Day, January 1

6. Flag Day, June 14

7. Labor Day, September 1

8. Columbus Day, October 12

Write the date.

9. Mother's Day, second Sunday in May

10. Thanksgiving Day, fourth Thursday in November

Problem Solving

Use the calendar on page 412 to solve each problem.

11. How many weeks are there in a year?

12. **Calculator** How would you use your calculator to find the number of days in a year? How many days are in a year?

13. In a leap year, there are 29 days in February. Is this a leap-year calendar?

14. How many days are in a leap year?

413

Multiple-Step Problems

Build Understanding

Ann rides the 3:00 bus from school to Lemon Drive. It then takes Ann 15 minutes to walk home from Lemon Drive. What time does Ann get home?

 **Understand**   QUESTION What time does Ann get home?

FACTS The schedule shows that the bus stops at Lemon Drive at 3:25. Then Ann walks for 15 minutes.

KEY IDEA You want to find out what time it is 15 minutes after 3:25.

Plan and Solve   Count by fives to add 15 minutes to 3:25. Ann gets home at 3:40, or 20 minutes before 4:00.

Look Back   Check again that the bus arrives at 3:25. Add 25 and 15 to find how many minutes after 3:00 Ann arrives home.

Bus Schedule Sunflower School	
Leave School:	3:00
Arrive	Time
Apple Street	3:10
Peach Lane	3:15
Lemon Drive	3:25
Cherry Avenue	3:30
Orange Street	3:35
Raisin Lane	3:55
Banana Square	4:00

■ **Talk About Math** Suppose Ann stopped twice on her walk home. What else would you need to know to solve the problem?

Check Understanding

Shirley rides the bus from school to Peach Lane. She walks from Peach Lane to her house in 10 minutes.

Use the schedule on page 414 to answer each question.

School → Peach Lane → Home

1. How long does it take Shirley to ride from school to Peach Lane?

2. How long does it take Shirley to get home from school?

Practice

Answer each question.

3. Paco rides from school to Orange Street. Then he walks 10 minutes to his home. When does he get home?

4. Paco also walks 5 minutes from his classroom to the school bus. How long does it take him to get home?

5. You can ride the bus from Peach Lane to Raisin Lane or from Apple Street to Orange Street. Which ride takes more time? How much more time?

6. Luis gets home at 3:30. Julie gets off the bus at Banana Square and walks home in 12 minutes. How much longer does it take Julie to get home than Luis?

Choose a ⌨ Strategy

Fun at Camp Waterfall Chris goes to Camp Waterfall. She jogs from 8:15 until 8:30. She swims from 8:45 until 9:20.

7. How much time does Chris spend swimming? How much time does she spend jogging?

8. What is the difference between these two times?

Identifying Coins and Bills

Build Understanding

What are the values of different coins and bills?

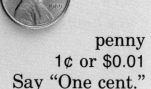

penny
1¢ or $0.01
Say "One cent."

nickel
5¢ or $0.05
Say "Five cents."

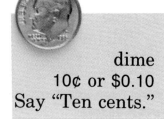

dime
10¢ or $0.10
Say "Ten cents."

quarter
25¢ or $0.25
Say "Twenty-five cents."

half dollar
50¢ or $0.50
Say "Fifty cents."

dollar
100¢ or $1.00
Say "One dollar."

five dollars
500¢ or $5.00
Say "Five dollars."

ten dollars
1,000¢ or $10.00
Say "Ten dollars."

■ **Write About Math** How would you write one dollar, one dime, and one penny together, using a dollar sign and a decimal point?

Check Understanding

For another example, see Set C, pages 432–433.

Tell how many of each it takes to make one dollar.

1. penny   **2.** dime   **3.** nickel   **4.** quarter   **5.** half dollar

Practice

For More Practice, see Set C, pages 434–435.

Write two letters to name each coin or bill.
Use each letter only once.

6. 　　**7.** 　　**8.** 　　**9.**

10. 　　**11.** 　　**12.** 　　**13.**

a. 25¢　　　　**e.** 5¢　　　　　**i.** 25 cents　　**m.** 10¢
b. 1¢　　　　**f.** half dollar　**j.** 5 cents　　**n.** five dollars
c. $10.00　　**g.** $1.00　　　**k.** $5.00　　　**o.** $0.10
d. fifty cents　**h.** ten dollars　**l.** one dollar　**p.** $0.01

Problem Solving

Write the name of the coin or bill.

14. I am the coin worth the least.

15. I am the coin worth the most.

16. I am worth more than 10 cents but less than 50 cents.

17. I am made out of paper and am worth four quarters.

Midchapter **Checkup**

1. What coin is the same as $0.05?

2. How many months are in one year?

3. Write 6:45 in words using minutes before the hour.

4. Al reads 1 hour in the morning and 1 hour at night. How many hours does he read in 5 days?

Problem Solving WORKSHOP

Number-Sense Project

Look back at pages 406-407.

Candice found these pennies at home.

Year	Number of Pennies
1990	15
1989	3
1988	2
1987	4
1986	1
1985	
1984	2
1983	9
1982	4
1981	6
1980	
1979	4

1. In what year do you think Candice collected this information?

2. What was the oldest penny Candice found?

3. Candice recorded the dates of 50 pennies. If she had recorded 100 pennies, how many do you think she would have found dated 1990? 1988? 1979?

Math-at-Home Activity

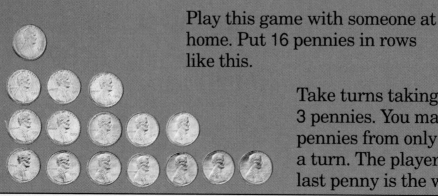

Play this game with someone at home. Put 16 pennies in rows like this.

Take turns taking away 1, 2, or 3 pennies. You may take the pennies from only one row during a turn. The player who takes the last penny is the winner.

Real-Life Decision Making

You are at the carnival. You have 20 minutes to use your last 3 ride tickets.

1. Besides the number of minutes each ride takes, what are some other things to consider that will use up time?

2. Decide if you can take 3 rides and which they will be.

Carnival Rides	
Ride	**Minutes**
Ferris Wheel	5
Merry-Go-Round	4
Roller Coaster	7
Tilt and Spin	7
Roll and Splash	8

Critical Thinking Activity

Clues

a. Danielle has 38¢

b. She has at least one penny, nickel, and dime.

c. She has more pennies than dimes.

d. She has the same number of nickels as pennies.

e. She has 8 coins. How many coins of each type does Danielle have?

Hint: Real or play coins can help you.

Counting Money

Build Understanding

Working for Peanuts
Materials: Play money
Groups: Partners

Peanuts For Sale

Joanne helps the Pep Club sell peanuts at school games. How much money does she have right now?

a. Joanne has two one-dollar bills, one half dollar, three quarters, four dimes, three nickels, and six pennies. Show this with play money.

b. Count the bills first. Then count the coins. Look for combinations that equal one dollar.

These coins equal one dollar.

Each American eats about $6\frac{1}{3}$ pounds of peanuts in one year.

Joanne has $3.86. She has three dollars and eighty-six cents.

■ **Write About Math** What is the least number of coins and bills you could have and still have $3.86?

420

Check Understanding

For another example, see Set D, pages 432–433.

Write the amount of money shown.

1.

2.

Practice

For More Practice, see Set D, pages 434–435.

Use play money to complete Exercises 3–12.
For Exercises 3–6, write each amount in words.

3. $5.62   **4.** $3.73   **5.** $7.82   **6.** $2.36

For Exercises 7–11, write the amount of money.
Remember to use a $ and . in your answers.

7. 1 quarter, 1 dime   **8.** 2 dimes, 3 pennies   **9.** 6 dimes, 4 pennies, 1 nickel

10. 1 half dollar, 1 penny, 1 dime, 1 quarter, 1 nickel, 2 dollars

11. 3 dollars, 2 quarters, 3 nickels, 2 dimes, 1 penny

Problem Solving

Solve the problem.

12. Critical Thinking Suppose you have 8 quarters, 5 dimes, 5 nickels, and 5 pennies. Explain why $2.81 is not a reasonable total for the value of all the coins.

Adding and Subtracting Money

Build Understanding

A. Cameron had $5.38. Then he got $7.50 for his birthday. How much does he have now?

Think:

$5.38	538	Line up the
+ 7.50	+750	decimal points. Place $
$12.88	1288	and . in your answer.

Cameron has $12.88.

"COMPACT DISC SALE"

$9.97

B. Cameron wants a compact disc that is on sale for $9.97. How much money will Cameron have left from his $12.88 if he buys the disc?

Paper and Pencil

$12.88	Line up the decimal points.
− 9.97	Place $ and . in your answer.
$ 2.91	

Calculator

Press: **12.88** − **9.97** =

Display: *2.91*

Cameron has $2.91 left.

Write About Math How is adding and subtracting money different from adding and subtracting whole numbers?

Check Understanding

For another example, see Set E, pages 432–433.

Write the letter for the correct answer.

1. $7.06
   +4.98

2. $6.42
   −3.68

3. $10.19
   + 2.21

   a. $12.40
   b. $12.04
   c. $2.74

4. **Calculator** On a calculator, add $0.25 and $0.25. Explain why there is no 0 after the 5.

Practice

For More Practice, see Set E, pages 434–435.

Add or subtract. **Remember** to line up the decimal points and place $ and . in your answers.

5. $1.19
   +0.79

6. $3.72
   +5.25

7. $3.00
   −2.98

8. $7.88
   +9.45

9. $7.20
   −4.50

10. $9.35
   −3.28

11. $10.05
   + 3.99

12. $40.76
   −30.50

13. $82.34
   − 9.99

14. $26.73
   +66.78

Mixed Practice

Choose mental math, paper and pencil, or calculator to solve each problem. Tell which method you used.

15. $36.11 − $23.09   **16.** 7 × 8   **17.** 49 ÷ 7   **18.** $53.51 + $3.51

Problem Solving

Solve each problem.

19. Carlisle sold two compact discs, one for $9.75 and one for $9.50. How much money did he receive?

20. Sarah wants to buy a compact disc that costs $14.98. She has $12.39. How much more money does she need?

TIPS FOR PROBLEM SOLVERS

Compare problems to help you relate new problems to ones you've solved before.

Skills ———— Review   pages 385, 388–389

Copy each sentence and complete with >, <, or = .
1. 0.23 ⬚ 0.30   **2.** 0.8 ⬚ 0.18   **3.** 0.5 ⬚ 0.50   **4.** 5.76 ⬚ 5.09

Making Change

Build Understanding

A. Quick Change Artist
Materials: Play money
Groups: Work with a partner or small group. Take turns being the clerk and customers.

How much change does the clerk give a customer who pays 2 one-dollar bills for a set of jacks that costs $1.68?

a. Is there any one coin that you can add to $1.68 and get $2.00?

b. What coins could the clerk add to $1.68 to make the total end in 0 or 5?

c. What coins could the clerk then add to $1.70 to make $2.00?

d. Show the correct change using the fewest coins possible.

$6.83

$2.15

$1.68

$2.76

$7.45

$1.23

B. You can also subtract to find out how much change to give a customer.

The customer receives 32 cents.

$$\begin{array}{r} \$2.00 \\ -1.68 \\ \hline \$0.32 \end{array}$$

■ **Talk About Math** Which way of making change do you like better? Why?

Check Understanding

For another example, see Set F, pages 432–433.

Mental Math Choose the letter for the correct amount of change.

1. You gave the clerk $5.00 for a game that costs $3.50.

   a. $1.00   **b.** $1.25   **c.** $1.50

2. You gave the clerk $3.00 for markers that cost $2.25.

   a. $0.50   **b.** $0.75   **c.** $0.85

3. **Number Sense** Why would you give the clerk $24.02 for groceries that cost $23.52? Use play money to find your change.

Practice

For More Practice, see Set F, pages 434–435.

Use the prices on page 424 to answer each question.

4. What is the change from $3.00 for each of these?

   a. ball   **b.** yo-yo   **c.** top

5. What is the change from $10.00 for each of these?

   a. flag   **b.** ball   **c.** hat

What are the fewest coins that will make:

6. $0.25?   7. $0.52?   8. $0.88?

Problem Solving

Explore _____ Math

Penny put a half dollar in the change machine and got back 6 coins.

9. In what way(s) could the machine have given Penny 6 coins for a half dollar?

10. What coins could Penny get if her change had been 5 coins? 7 coins?

Work Backward

Build Understanding

Hank exercised this morning. He lifted weights for 30 minutes. Then he jogged for 20 minutes. Hank finished exercising at 7:30. What time did he begin exercising?

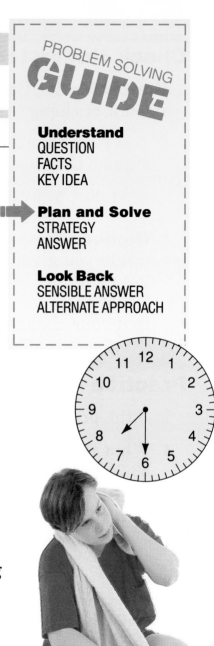

Understand   You want to know when Hank began exercising. You know he finished at 7:30 and spent 20 minutes and 30 minutes exercising.

Plan and Solve   STRATEGY   You can work backward, step by step, to find when Hank began each activity.

What is 20 minutes before 7:30? What is 30 minutes before that?

ANSWER   Hank began jogging 20 minutes before 7:30, so he began jogging at 7:10. He began lifting weights 30 minutes before that, so he began exercising at 6:40.

Look Back   Add 30 minutes and 20 minutes to 6:40 to check that your answer is sensible.

■ **Write About Math**   Explain how you could use a clock to make sure your answer is correct.

Check Understanding

Hank had soup, a sandwich, and dessert for lunch. Hank spent $3.25.

1. What was the cost of the lunch without soup?

2. What was the cost without a sandwich and soup?

3. What was the cost of the dessert?

Practice

Choose mental math, paper and pencil, or calculator to solve each problem.

4. Lisa is 5 years older than Jon. The gym teacher is 22 years older than Lisa. The teacher is 44 years old. How old is Jon?

5. Two weeks ago Lisa spent $15. This week she spent $4. She has $18 left. How much money did she have at first?

6. Jon had 12 peppers. He had 2 more red peppers than green ones. How many green peppers did he have?

7. Jon did some sit-ups. Then he did 16 leg-lifts and 10 bicycles. In all, he did 51 exercises. How many sit-ups did Jon do?

Choose a ⸺ Strategy

Snazzy Sneakers Solve the problem.

8. Karen spent $41.00 for 2 pairs of sneakers. One pair cost $3.00 more than the other. How much did each pair cost?

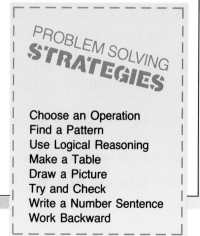

PROBLEM SOLVING
STRATEGIES

Choose an Operation
Find a Pattern
Use Logical Reasoning
Make a Table
Draw a Picture
Try and Check
Write a Number Sentence
Work Backward

Estimation and Money

Build Understanding

Nick has $6. He wants to buy cereal for $2.33, bananas for $1.86, and milk for $1.20. Does Nick have enough money for all three items?

A. You can estimate amounts to the nearest dollar.

Is cereal closer to $2 or $3?	cereal	$2
Are bananas closer to $1 or $2?	bananas	$2
Is milk closer to $1 or $2?	milk	$1
		$5

Nick has $6. He has enough money.

B. Sometimes it is better to estimate a higher amount.

Estimate $1.19 + $1.32 + $2.36 as you did in Example A.

Is your estimate higher or lower than the actual total? Suppose you have $4.00. Does this estimate tell you whether $4.00 is enough?

To get a better answer, estimate to the next higher ten cents.

$0.19 + $0.32 + $0.36 is about
$0.20 + $0.40 + $0.40 = $1.00.

$5.00 is a better estimate of the total than $4.00.

What types of stores are in your neighborhood?

■ **Talk About Math** How is estimating useful when you are shopping?

Check Understanding

For another example, see Set G, pages 432–433.

Use the register tape to answer the questions.

1. Would you estimate $4 or $5 for meat?

2. Would you estimate $1 or $2 for soup?

3. Is $3 a good estimate for milk? Why or why not?

4. **Number Sense** If you wanted to make sure you had enough money, would you estimate $3 or $4 for the last item on the tape? Why?

5. What is the estimated total of the groceries?

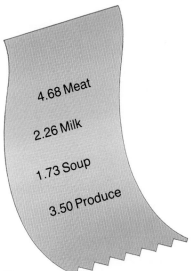

4.68 Meat

2.26 Milk

1.73 Soup

3.50 Produce

Practice

For More Practice, see Set G, pages 434–435.

Estimate to the nearest dollar.
Then use a calculator to find the actual sum.

6. $1.43 + $0.81 + $3.22

7. $6.88 + $4.39 + $0.93

8. $5.22 + $1.44 + $1.91

9. $1.36 + $4.47 + $2.29

10. $31.19 + $12.75 + $19.43

11. $5.62 + $2.16 + $9.99

12. $15.61 + $4.37 + $20.78 + $2.11

Problem Solving

Solve each problem.

13. Cal wants to buy items for $5.67, $3.18, $9.82, and $2.45. He has $21. Estimate the total. Do you think Cal has enough money?

14. **Critical Thinking** Why is it unwise to think you have enough money if your estimated total is the same as the money you have?

Solve each problem.

1. A recipe for bread said to bake for 45 to 55 minutes. If Mrs. Camp put the bread in the oven at 10:35 A.M. when is the earliest the bread should be done? Give the time.

2. Draw a square. Draw diagonal lines to connect the opposite corners. Shade one part. Tell what fraction of the square it is.

3. In Emily's photo album, 6 photos fit on a page. She has 54 photos. How many pages will they fill?

4. Two teams were working on a set of challenge math problems. The Saturn team had finished $\frac{5}{8}$ of the set. The Jupiter team had $\frac{7}{8}$ of the set finished. Which team had finished more problems?

5. A new kind of athletic shoe lets you blow air into it to cushion your feet. If the new shoes cost $150 a pair, how many pairs of $30 sneakers could you buy for the same price?

6. **Data File** Use data from pages 532-533. Jim has $4.50 to spend on dinner. He wants a beverage. What can he order from the menu and still have enough money to pay the bill?

7. **Make a Data File** Make a list of the cost of admission to 5 different types of entertainment.

Problem Solving REVIEW

Explore with a Calculator

Money Sense

1. One pencil costs $0.25. To find the cost of 2 pencils, add.

Paper and pencil   Calculator

$0.25   0.25 + = 0.25 = 0.5   You will need to write a $ sign
+0.25   and a 0 in the hundredths place
 0.50

Write the following displays as money.

a. *0.1*   **b.** *0.07*   **c.** *1.6*

d. *0.3*   **e.** *2.9*   **f.** *23.4*

g. *37.7*   **h.** *10.1*

Solve each problem.

2. If you spent exactly $1.34, what did you buy?

3. If you bought the deluxe crayon set and received $6.25 in change, how much did you give the clerk?

4. If you bought 3 items and spent exactly $1.99, what items did you buy?

5. What is the greatest number of ball-point pens you could buy with $3.00?

6. If you bought 2 items and received $9.00 in change from a $20 bill, what two items did you buy?

SAM'S SCHOOL SUPPLIES

ART BALL POINT PENS ... 59¢

DELUXE CRAYON SET ... $3.75

PENCILS - ½ DOZ ... 35¢

BACK PACK - EACH ... $9.95

FELT TIP PEN - EACH ... 85¢

NOTE BOOK - EACH ... $1.05

TABLETS - 2 FOR ... 49¢

Reteaching

Set A   pages 408–411

Amy got home from band practice at

　　15 minutes before 5.
Show this time on your clock.

At 30 minutes after the hour you can begin counting minutes before the next hour.

15 minutes before 5 is the same as 45 minutes after 4.

Remember that you count backwards starting at 12 on your clock to find the number of minutes before the hour.

Write each time as minutes before the hour.

1.    **2.**

Set B   pages 412–413

The Winkler family vacation began on the fourth Monday of August. Use the calendar on page 412 to write this date.

The fourth Monday is August 25.

When writing and speaking, the endings "st," "nd," "rd," and "th" are often added to the end of dates. You can write and say August 25 as
　　"August twenty-fifth."

Remember that the months of the year do not have the same number of days.

Use the calendar on page 412 to write the date.

1. Father's Day, third Sunday in June

2. Memorial Day, fifth Friday in May

Set C   pages 416–417

There is usually more than one way of using coins to show amounts of money.

Here are three ways to show 57¢.

　1 half-dollar, 1 nickel, 2 pennies
　2 quarters, 1 nickel, 2 pennies
　5 dimes, 1 nickel, 2 pennies

Remember that the penny is the coin that is worth the least.

Give two ways of using coins to show each amount.

1. $0.30　　**2.** 55¢
3. 78¢　　**4.** $0.90

Set D pages 420–421

You have the coins. How much money is this?

3 quarters   4 nickels
3 dimes   6 pennies

3 quarters + 2 dimes + 1 nickel = $1.

This leaves you with 1 dime, 3 nickels, and 6 pennies, or $0.31. You have a total of $1.31.

Remember to look for combinations of coins that equal one dollar when you count coins.

Write the amount of money. Remember to use $ and . in your answers.

1. 3 quarters, 1 nickel, 2 pennies

2. 1 quarter, 4 dimes, 1 nickel

Set E pages 422–423

Ellen spent $25.90 and $9.78. How much did she spend?

$25.90   Line up the decimal points.
+ 9.78   Place $ and . in your answer.
$35.68   Amount spent

Remember to line up the decimal points when you add or subtract. Add or subtract.

1. $8.03   **2.** $73.46
    + 1.98   − 9.87

Set F pages 424–425

Tony bought a hat for $7.56. He gave the clerk $8.00. How much change did he receive?

$8.00   Line up the decimal points.
− 7.56   Place $ and . in your answer.
$0.44

The clerk used the fewest coins possible: 1 quarter, 1 dime, 1 nickel, 4 pennies.

Remember to place $ and . in your answers when you add or subtract money.

What are the fewest coins possible that will make each amount?

1. $0.27   **2.** $0.75

3. $0.16   **4.** $0.90

Set G pages 428–429

Estimate $1.13 + $9.72 + $4.85 by rounding to the nearest dollar.

$1.13 ⟶ $ 1.00
 9.72 ⟶ 10.00
 4.85 ⟶   5.00
       $16.00

Remember that estimating will help you decide if you have enough money.

Estimate the sum by rounding to the nearest dollar.

1. $3.55 + $0.92 + $6.25

More Practice

Set A   pages 408–411

Write each time as minutes before the hour.

1.   **2.**   **3.**   **4.**

Estimation   Answer each question.

5. How long does it take you to travel to school?

6. How long did it take you to do Exercises 1–4 above?

Show each time on your clock. On your worksheet, draw the hands on a clock.

7. 20 minutes before 8

8. 20 minutes after 8

9. 12 minutes after 11

10. 21 minutes before 2

Set B   pages 412–413

Use the calendar on page 412. Write the day of the week.

1. Election Day, November 4

2. Halloween, October 31

3. Memorial Day, May 30

4. Groundhog Day, February 2

Write the date.

5. Abraham Lincoln's Birthday, second Wednesday in February

6. Washington's Birthday, third Monday in February

7. Armed Forces Day, third Saturday in May

8. Martin Luther King, Jr., Day, third Monday in January

Set C   pages 416–417

Give two ways of using coins to show each amount.

1. $0.10   **2.** $0.22   **3.** $0.67   **4.** 75¢   **5.** $0.79

6. $0.18   **7.** 28¢   **8.** $0.35   **9.** $0.60   **10.** $0.99

Set D pages 420–421

Use play money to complete Exercises 1–9.
For Exercises 1–4, write each amount in words.

1. $4.83   **2.** $9.17   **3.** $8.64   **4.** $6.98

For Exercises 5–9, write the amount of money.

5. 1 quarter, 1 nickel   **6.** 4 dimes, 3 nickels   **7.** 2 quarters, 3 pennies

8. 4 dollars, 3 quarters, 2 dimes, 4 nickels, 7 pennies

Set E pages 422–423

Add or subtract.

1. $2.81 $+ 0.38$	**2.** $8.44 $+ 5.67$	**3.** $6.00 $- 3.88$	**4.** $7.01 $+ 3.89$	**5.** $27.88 $+ 39.73$

Mixed Practice Choose mental math,
paper and pencil, or a calculator to solve each
problem. Tell which method you used.

6. $49.36 − $11.04   **7.** 9 × 7   **8.** 54 ÷ 6   **9.** 10 × 9

Set F pages 424–425

Use the prices on page 424 to answer each exercise.

1. What is the change from
$2.00 for each of these?
a. top   **b.** jacks

2. What is the change from $8.00
for each of these?
a. hat   **b.** flag

What are the fewest possible coins that will
make each amount?

3. $0.21   **4.** $0.60   **5.** $0.49   **6.** $0.76

Set G pages 428–429

Estimate each amount by rounding to the
nearest dollar, and find the estimated sum.
Then use a calculator to find the actual sum.

1. $4.09 + $7.81 + $3.20   **2.** $5.91 + $8.42 + $9.64

3. $8.48 + $12.24 + $17.61 + $20.52

Enrichment

Patterns in the Calendar

Look at the red rectangle on the top calendar.

1. What is the sum of the numbers in the dotted ring?

2. What is the sum of the numbers in the solid ring?

3. What do you notice about the two sums?

4. Copy the calendar. Then draw a rectangle around four other numbers. Are the diagonal sums equal?

5. Does any rectangle have both sums equal to the number of days in a week?

Look at the rectangle drawn on the bottom calendar.

6. What is the sum of the numbers in the rectangle?

7. Add the middle number 3 times.

8. What do you notice about this sum and the sum of the numbers in the rectangle?

MAY

S	M	Tu	W	Th	F	S
		1	2	3	4	5
6	7	8	9	10	11	12
13	14	15	16	17	18	19
20	21	22	23	24	25	26
27	28	29	30	31		

JUNE

S	M	Tu	W	Th	F	S
					1	2
3	4	5	6	7	8	9
10	11	12	13	14	15	16
17	18	19	20	21	22	23
24	25	26	27	28	29	30

9. Copy the calendar. Then draw a rectangle around five numbers in a row. Find the sum of the numbers. Add the middle number 5 times. Compare the sums.

Chapter 12 Review/Test

Write each time as minutes before the hour.

1.   **2.**

MAY							JUNE						
S	M	T	W	Th	F	S	S	M	T	W	Th	F	S
					1	2	3	1	2	3	4	5	6	7
4	5	6	7	8	9	10	8	9	10	11	12	13	14
11	12	13	14	15	16	17	15	16	17	18	19	20	21
18	19	20	21	22	23	24	22	23	24	25	26	27	28
25	26	27	28	29	30	31	29	30					

3. Which day of the week is May 25?

4. What is the date of the second Wednesday in June?

Write the name of the coin or bill for each amount.

5. 100 pennies   **6.** 25 cents

Write the amount of money. Use a $ and . in your answers.

7. 3 dimes, 6 pennies

8. 1 dime, 1 half-dollar, 2 nickels

Add or subtract.

9. $35.72
    −   8.49

10. $6.11
    + 0.59

Write the change from $5.00 for a

11. $3.80 ball.   **12.** 49¢ drink.

13. Which is the better estimate for $2.95 + $0.78?

  a. $4.00   **b.** $3.00

14. Janet is 5 years older than Bob. Bob is 2 years older than Pablo. If Janet is 18 years old, how old is Pablo?

Read this problem. Then answer the questions below.

Tim and Roy walked from the park to Roy's home in 25 minutes. Then Tim walked to his home in 20 minutes. If they left the park at 1:30, what time did Tim get home?

15. Which could be the *first step* in solving this problem?

  a. 25 − 20 = 5 minutes
  b. 25 + 20 = 45 minutes
  c. The time 25 minutes before 1:30 is 1:05.

16. Solve the problem above.

17. ■ **Write About Math** What is the least number of coins and bills you could use to make $4.89?

Multiplication Computation

13

Did You Know: The California Giant Sequoias shown at left are among the world's oldest and largest living things. Some are thousands of years old and 200 feet tall.

Number-Sense Project

Estimate
Predict how people would answer the question: "If you were going to be a tree, what kind of tree would you be?"

Gather Data
Ask people of different ages this question.

Analyze and Report
Look to see if a person's age made a difference in the tree they picked. Compare your results with other students.

Exploring Multiplication

Build Understanding

Stamp of Approval
Materials: Place-value materials
Groups: 3–5 students

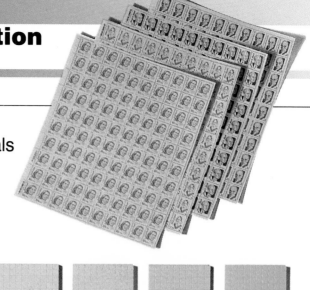

A. A sheet of regular stamps has 100 stamps. How many stamps are in 4 sheets?

Use place-value materials to show 4 hundreds.

There are 400 stamps in all.

B. Special stamps come 50 in a sheet. How many stamps are in 3 sheets?

a. Use ten-sticks to show 50.

b. Now make 3 groups of 50.

3×5 tens $= 15$ tens

c. There are 3 groups of 5 tens. Count by tens. There are 15 tens.

There are 150 stamps in all.

■ **Talk About Math** Look at Example B. Tell how to show 150 with the least number of place-value pieces.

Check Understanding

For another example, see Set A, pages 464–465.

Use the picture to help you find

1. how many groups.

2. how many in each group.

3. how many in all. Write your answer in standard form.

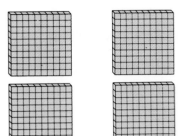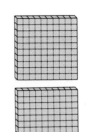

Practice

For More Practice, see Set A, pages 466–467.

Give the standard form for each exercise.
Use place-value materials if you need them.

4. 5 tens

5. 18 tens

6. 10 tens

7. 4 hundreds

8. 12 hundreds

9. 10 hundreds

10. 2 forties

11. 2 thirties

12. 2 nineties

13. 3 groups of 5 hundreds

14. 5 groups of 3 hundreds

15. 6 groups of twenty

16. 6 groups of 2 hundreds

17. **Mental Math** How could you use mental math to find the answers in Exercises 4–16?

Problem Solving

Solve each problem.

18. Each page of Myrna's stamp book holds 20 stamps. How many stamps are on 8 full pages?

19. Myrna bought 3 sheets of stamps with 100 stamps on each sheet. She sold 53 stamps to Jules. How many does she have left?

441

Multiples of 10 and 100: Mental Math

Build Understanding

A. Jennifer sells hand puppets to stores. There are 70 hand puppets in each box she sells. How many puppets are in 3 boxes?

The boxes all have the same number, so you can multiply. Find 3×70.

Think: 70 is a multiple of 10, so 70 = 7 tens.

Think about the largest puppet you have ever seen.

Show: 3 groups of 7 tens

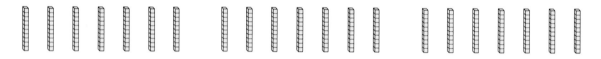

$$3 \times 7 \text{ tens} = 21 \text{ tens}$$
$$3 \times 70 = 210$$

There are 210 hand puppets in 3 boxes.

B. Find 2×500.

Think: 500 is a multiple of 100, so 500 is 5 hundreds.

Show: 2 groups of 5 hundreds

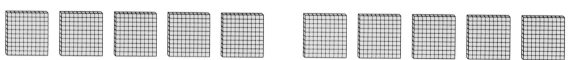

$$2 \times 5 \text{ hundreds} = 10 \text{ hundreds}$$
$$2 \times 500 = 1,000$$

■ **Talk About Math**   How could you use addition to find the answers to Examples A and B?

Check Understanding

For another example, see Set B, pages 464–465.

Find each product.

1. 6×10 **2.** 6×100 **3.** 6×30 **4.** 6×300

5. Look at Exercises 1 and 2. Describe how they are alike and how they are different.

6. Look at Exercises 3 and 4. Do you see the same patterns that you found in Exercises 1 and 2? Explain your answer.

Practice

For More Practice, see Set B, pages 466–467.

Mental Math   Find each product mentally.

7. 4×10 **8.** 15×10 **9.** 26×10 **10.** 10×8

11. 6×100 **12.** 7×100 **13.** 100×36 **14.** 100×22

15. 8×20 **16.** 5×70 **17.** 40×4 **18.** 80×5

19. 4×900 **20.** 7×300 **21.** 600×8 **22.** 500×5

Number Sense   Give each answer.

23. Look at Exercises 7–14. What rule can you give for multiplying by 10? By 100?

24. Look at Exercises 15–22. What rule can you give for multiplying by a multiple of 10? By a multiple of 100?

Problem Solving

Critical Thinking   Solve each problem.

25. How many boxes of puppets would the store manager buy if she needed 700 puppets?

26. How many boxes of puppets would the store manager buy if she needed 7,000 puppets?

Estimating Products

Build Understanding

A. Mr. Banks drives a school bus. Each day, he drives 42 miles. Estimate the number of miles he drives his bus in 5 days.

Because Mr. Banks drives the same distance each day, you can multiply.

Estimate 5×42.
Round 42 to the nearest 10, and use mental math to estimate the product.

42 is closer to 40 than it is to 50.

$5 \times 40 = 200$ $5 \times 4 = 20$

Mr. Banks drives about 200 miles in 5 days.

B. Estimate 6×267.
Round 267 to the nearest hundred. 267 is closer to 300 than to 200.

$6 \times 300 = 1,800$ $6 \times 3 = 18$

■ **Talk About Math** In Example A, does Mr. Banks drive more than or fewer than 200 miles in 5 days? Tell how you know.

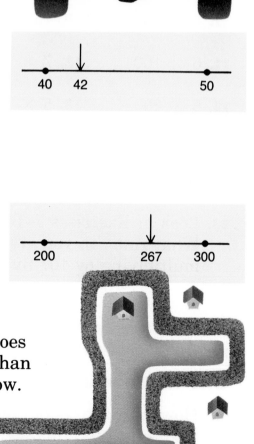

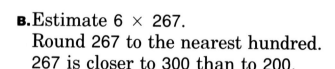

School

Bus Route "A"
42 miles

444

Check Understanding

For another example, see Set C, pages 464–465.

1. Estimate 7 × 38.

2. Would 7 × 38 be greater than 7 × 40? Tell how you know.

3. Estimate 4 × 523.

4. Would 4 × 523 be greater or less than 4 × 500? Why?

Practice

For More Practice, see Set C, pages 466–467.

Estimate each product.

5. 4 × 17   **6.** 24 × 3   **7.** 62 × 7   **8.** 9 × 88

9. 8 × 382   **10.** 832 × 3   **11.** 5 × 741   **12.** 936 × 4

13. 8 × 26   **14.** 44 × 4   **15.** 430 × 4   **16.** 2 × 580

17. 9 × 347   **18.** 73 × 5   **19.** 8 × 92   **20.** 713 × 3

Number Sense   Give each answer.

21. In which of Exercises 5–20 do you think your estimated product will be less than the actual product?

22. In which of Exercises 5–20 do you think your estimated product will be greater than the actual product?

23. How can you decide if the actual product will be greater or less than the estimate?

Skills ____ **Review**   pages 372–373

Which is greater?

1. $\frac{2}{3}$ or $\frac{1}{3}$ **2.** $\frac{3}{4}$ or $\frac{1}{4}$ **3.** $\frac{1}{5}$ or $\frac{1}{6}$ **4.** $\frac{3}{5}$ or $\frac{2}{5}$

Exploring Multiplication Further

Build Understanding

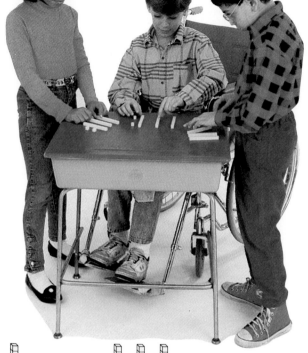

A Class Act
Materials: Place-value materials
Groups: 3–5 students

A. Parkview Elementary School has 3 classes of third graders. Each class has 32 students. In all, how many third-grade students attend Parkview Elementary School?

How many are there in 3 groups of 32?

You can use your place-value materials to find the answer.

a. Think: Make 3 groups of 32.

Show:

b. Think: Combine the 3 groups.

Show:

c. Think: Count the tens: 9 tens
Count the ones: 6 ones

Write the answer in standard form: **96**

There are 96 third-grade students in all.

B. Find four groups of 23. Use your place-value materials.

a. Think: 4 groups of 23

Show:

b. Combine the groups.

c. Trade 10 ones for 1 ten.

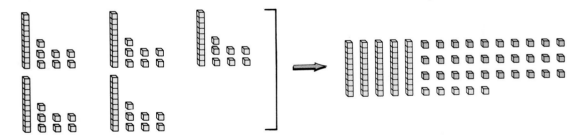

4 groups of 23 is 92.

c. Find five groups of 17.

a. Make 5 groups of 17. Then combine the groups.

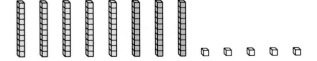

b. Trade ones for tens.

5 groups of 17 is 85.

Talk About Math How could you find
the answer to Example B by adding? Explain.

Check Understanding

For another example, see Set D, pages 464–465.

Use place-value materials to help you find how many are in

1. 2 groups of 34.   **2.** 3 groups of 25.   **3.** 3 rows of 17.

Practice

For More Practice, see Set D, pages 466–467.

Use place-value materials to help you find how many are in

4. 2 groups of 24.   **5.** 4 groups of 12.   **6.** 5 rows of 11.

7. 3 rows of 31.   **8.** 4 groups of 19.   **9.** 3 groups of 26.

10. 5 rows of 18.   **11.** 2 rows of 48.   **12.** 6 groups of 16.

13. 2 groups of 33.   **14.** 3 rows of 62.   **15.** 4 rows of 22.

Problem Solving

Solve each problem.

16. At Parkview School, there are 3 fourth-grade classes. Each class has 22 fourth-grade students. How many fourth-grade students are there in all?

17. Parkview School has bike racks for 80 bikes. There are 67 bikes in the racks. How many more bikes can be put in the racks?

18. There are 26 players on the third-grade soccer team, 31 players on the fourth-grade team, and 39 players on the fifth-grade team. How many players in all are on the 3 teams?

19. Write a story problem about 3×24. Use place-value materials to solve your problem.

20. Show how you would solve Problem 16 using paper and pencil.

21. **Calculator** Write a story problem using 15×24. Solve your problem using a calculator.

Brainstorm to get started—one idea will lead to another.

Explore ——— Math

Calculator Each of the squares has been cut from a multiplication table like the one on page 246.

In each square, find the product of the numbers on each diagonal.

22.

2	3
4	6

23.

2	3	4
4	6	8
6	9	12

24.

3	6	9	12
4	8	12	16
5	10	15	20
6	12	18	24

$2 \times 6 = 12$
$3 \times 4 = \blacksquare$

$2 \times 6 \times 12 = \blacksquare$
$4 \times 6 \times 6 = \blacksquare$

25. Describe the pattern you see.

26. Use Data Do you think the pattern will be the same for a 5-by-5 square on the multiplication table? Choose a 5-by-5 square from the table on page 246. Find the products of the numbers on each of its diagonals to see if you are right.

Multiplication: Renaming Ones

Build Understanding

A video store has 4 shelves of cartoon videos. Each shelf has 18 cartoon videos. How many cartoon videos does the store have?

Since the rows are all the same size, you can multiply. Find 4 × 18.

Estimate the answer first: 18 is close to 20. So your answer should be close to 4 × 20, or 80.

With Place-Value Materials	**With Paper and Pencil**

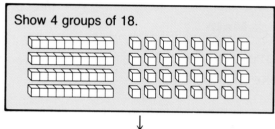

Write the problem.

$$\begin{array}{r} 18 \\ \times\ 4 \\ \hline \end{array}$$

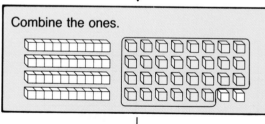

Multiply the ones.

$$\begin{array}{r} 18 \\ \times\ 4 \\ \hline \end{array}$$ 4 × 8 ones = 32 ones

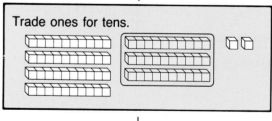

Write the ones. Write the tens.

$$\begin{array}{r} {}^{3}\ \\ 18 \\ \times\ 4 \\ \hline 2 \end{array}$$ 32 = 3 tens 2 ones

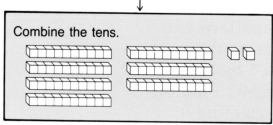

Multiply the tens. Add the extra tens. Write the tens.

$$\begin{array}{r} {}^{3}\ \\ 18 \\ \times\ 4 \\ \hline 72 \end{array}$$ 4 × 1 ten = 4 tens

4 tens + 3 tens = 7 tens

There are 72 cartoon videos.

■ **Talk About Math** Explain how you can use your estimate to see if your answer for the example is reasonable.

Check Understanding

For another example, see Set E, pages 464–465.

Find each answer.

1. Estimate 2 × 37.

2. Use place-value materials to find the actual answer.

3. Record your work.

Practice

For More Practice, see Set E, pages 466–467.

Multiply. Use place-value materials if you need them.

4. 29	**5.** 24	**6.** 12	**7.** 18	**8.** 38
× 3	× 4	× 7	× 5	× 2

9. 19	**10.** 39	**11.** 12	**12.** 13	**13.** 36
× 5	× 2	× 8	× 7	× 2

14. 26 × 3 **15.** 47 × 2 **16.** 13 × 4 **17.** 16 × 2 **18.** 28 × 3

Midchapter ———— Checkup

Find each answer.

1. How much is 27 tens? Give your answer in standard form.

2. How much is 11 hundreds? Give your answer in standard form.

3. Mental Math Find 10 × 6.

4. Estimation Estimate 4 × 96.

5. How many are in 6 groups of 12?

6. Find 3 × 26.

Explore as a Team

Estimate how many beans are on the grid paper.

1. A small jar of beans was emptied onto the grid paper. Choose one of the squares. Record how many beans are in that square.

2. Choose 3 other squares. Record how many beans are in each of these squares.

3. Decide how many beans are usually in a square.

4. Discuss how you could use the grid paper to estimate the number of beans in all. Compare your new estimates with your original estimates.

Visual Thinking Activity

1. How many cubes are in the bottom layer?

2. How many cubes are there in all?

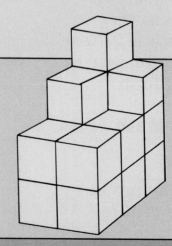

Number-Sense Project

Look back at pages 438-439.
One class recorded these results.

AGE	Choice of Tree					
	Apple	**Maple**	**Oak**	**Palm**	**Pine**	**Weeping Willow**
Pre-Teen	4	6	10	4	18	10
Teen	8	8	10	14	6	4
Adult	8	8	20	4	9	1

1. How many adults in all were asked to make a choice?

2. If 100 adults were asked, how many would probably pick the oak tree?

3. Write a sentence telling how popular the oak tree was with the different age groups.

Real-Life Decision Making

You are helping to give a birthday party for your sister. The party will be from 2:00 to 4:00 P.M. on Saturday.

1. How much time is planned for the party?

2. How long should you plan for games?

3. About what time should you plan to eat?

4. About what time should your sister open the presents?

Too Much Information

Build Understanding

There are 16 crayons in a box, in 2 rows of 8 each. A box is at each of 6 tables in the room. How many crayons are there in all?

PROBLEM SOLVING
GUIDE

Understand
QUESTION
FACTS
KEY IDEA

Plan and Solve
STRATEGY
ANSWER

Look Back
SENSIBLE ANSWER
ALTERNATE APPROACH

Understand   QUESTION   What is the total number of crayons?

FACTS   Each box has 16 crayons. There are 6 tables. Each table has a box. You do not need to know that there are 2 rows of 8 crayons in each box.

KEY IDEA   You know there are 6 tables, so there must be 6 boxes. Since each box has the same number of crayons, you can multiply.

Plan and Solve

$$\begin{array}{r} \overset{3}{1\,6} \\ \times\ \ 6 \\ \hline 9\,6 \end{array}$$

There are 96 crayons in all.

Look Back   16 is close to 20. $6 \times 20 = 120$ Because 16 is less than 20, 96 is a reasonable answer.

■ **Talk About Math**   How could you solve the problem if you did not know the total number of crayons in each box?

Next time you use crayons, think about how many colors there are.

Check Understanding

Solve this problem by answering Questions 1–7.

Pencils come in packages of 10. Each pencil costs 9¢. How many pencils are in 7 packages?

1. What does the problem ask you to find?

2. What facts are you given?

3. What information is not needed?

4. How many groups of 10 pencils are there?

5. What operation would you use to solve the problem?

6. Solve the problem.

7. Is your answer to Problem 6 reasonable?

Practice

Solve each problem.

8. Construction paper comes in packages of 200 sheets. Each sheet costs 5¢. How many sheets are in 5 packages?

9. A large box of crayons has 4 sections. Each section has 2 rows of 8 crayons. How many crayons are in a box?

10. Erasers come in packages of 5 each. Each student is to get 3 erasers. How many erasers are there in 18 packages?

11. There are 24 students at 6 tables. On each table is 16 ounces of clay. How many ounces of clay are there in all?

Reading ———— Math

Identifying Unneeded Information List the information that you did not need in order to solve Problems 8–11.

Multiplication: Renaming Ones and Tens

Build Understanding

Linda works on an automobile assembly line. The line puts together 34 cars every hour. How many cars can the line put together in 4 hours?

The same number of cars are put together every hour, so you can multiply. Find 4 × 34.

Estimation Estimate first. 34 is close to 30. Since 4 × 30 = 120, your answer should be close to 120.

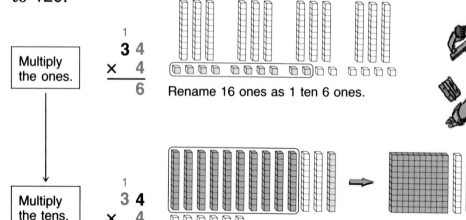

Multiply the ones.	$\begin{array}{r} 1 \\ 3\,4 \\ \times\ \ 4 \\ \hline 6 \end{array}$

Rename 16 ones as 1 ten 6 ones.

Multiply the tens.	$\begin{array}{r} 1 \\ 3\,4 \\ \times\ \ 4 \\ \hline 1\,3\,6 \end{array}$

4 × 3 tens = 12 tens
12 tens + 1 ten = 13 tens
13 tens = 1 hundred + 3 tens

one hundred thirty-six
136

Linda's assembly line puts together 136 cars in 4 hours.

■ **Talk About Math** How can you tell that your estimate in the example will be less than the actual answer?

Check Understanding

For another example, see Set F, pages 464–465.

For each exercise, tell whether you need
to rename the ones. Then multiply.

1. 56
   × 3

2. 24
   × 2

3. 72
   × 5

4. 61
   × 9

5. 47
   × 8

Practice

For More Practice, see Set F, pages 466–467.

Multiply. **Remember** to estimate first.

6. 32
   × 4

7. 53
   × 7

8. 11
   × 3

9. 46
   × 6

10. 38
    × 7

11. 74
    × 9

12. 91
    × 8

13. 38
    × 5

14. 52
    × 2

15. 47
    × 3

16. 3 × 83

17. 4 × 71

18. 9 × 338

19. 6 × 47

Mixed Practice   Use paper and pencil or mental math
to find each answer. Tell which method you used.

20. 7 × 30

21. 98 × 2

22. 120 + 6

23. 80 − 43

24. 32 ÷ 8

25. 39 × 4

26. 9 × 17

27. 52 + 9

Problem Solving

Solve each problem.

28. If the assembly line for
    trucks can make 23 trucks
    an hour, how many trucks
    can it make in an 8-hour
    shift?

29. The factory runs two 8-hour
    shifts each day. How many
    hours does it operate in a
    5-day work week?

Choose an Operation

PROBLEM SOLVING

GUIDE

Build Understanding

Disneyland in California is 1,577 miles from the Thompsons' home. Walt Disney World in Florida is 1,245 miles away. Which is closer? How much closer?

Understand

QUESTION
FACTS
KEY IDEA

Plan and Solve
STRATEGY
ANSWER

Look Back
SENSIBLE ANSWER
ALTERNATE APPROACH

Understand   You need to find which Disney attraction is closer to the Thompsons' home. Then you need to find how much closer.

 **Plan and Solve**   STRATEGY   Compare. Since 1,245 is less than 1,577, the family lives closer to Walt Disney World. To find how much closer, subtract the shorter distance from the longer distance.

$$\begin{array}{r} 1{,}5\,7\,7 \\ -\,1{,}2\,4\,5 \\ \hline 3\,3\,2 \end{array}$$

ANSWER   Walt Disney World is 332 miles closer to the Thompsons' home than Disneyland is.

Look Back   Estimate to see if your answer is reasonable. Since 332 is close to 400, the answer is reasonable.

$$\begin{array}{ccc} 1{,}577 & - & 1{,}245 \\ \downarrow & & \downarrow \\ 1{,}600 & - & 1{,}200 = 400 \end{array}$$

■ **Talk About Math**   How can you use addition to check your answer?

WALT DISNEY WORLD

DISNEYLAND

HOME

Check Understanding

The Thompsons drive about 55 miles each hour. They drive 8 hours each day. How many miles do they drive in one day?

1. What is the question?

2. What are the two key facts?

3. Which operation should you use to solve the problem?

4. What is the answer? How do you know it makes sense?

Practice

Tell whether you would *add, subtract, multiply,* or *divide.* Then find each answer.

5. Each of the 3 children was allowed to bring 12 toys. How many toys did they have in all?

6. Each of the 3 children bought an identical T-shirt. The total cost was $21. How much did each T-shirt cost?

7. The speedometer showed 3,258 miles in the morning and 3,639 miles that night. How many miles did the Thompsons travel that day?

8. Use Data Look at the map on page 124. The Thompsons made a trip from Detroit to Independence and back. How many miles did they travel?

Choose a _____ Strategy

An Apple Puzzle
9. Janice had some apples. Her mother gave her 3 more. She gave 1 to her teacher and 2 to each of 4 friends. She then had 5 apples left. How many apples did she have in the beginning?

PROBLEM SOLVING STRATEGIES

Choose an Operation
Find a Pattern
Use Logical Reasoning
Make a Table
Draw a Picture
Try and Check
Write a Number Sentence
Work Backward
Make a Graph

Multiplication with Hundreds

Build Understanding

The third-grade class in Talbot School used 3 medium-sized boxes of building blocks to build a play area for their gerbils. How many blocks did they use in all?

Building Blocks		
Small Box	96 blocks	$ 6.95
Medium Box	152 blocks	$ 9.89
Large Box	328 blocks	$13.99

Since the 3 boxes have the same number of blocks, you can multiply. Find 3×152.

Estimation You can find a range to estimate the answer. The product is between 300 and 600.

Round 152 down.
3×152
↓
$3 \times 100 = 300$

Round 152 up.
3×152
↓
$3 \times 200 = 600$

Multiply to find the actual answer.

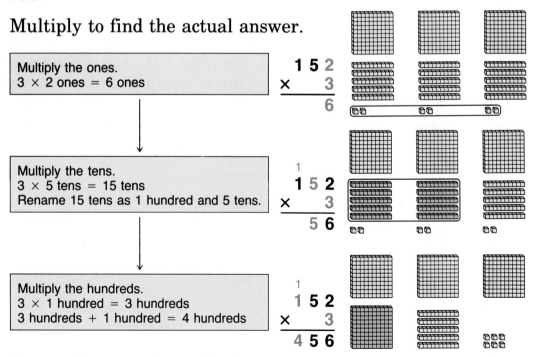

Multiply the ones.
3×2 ones $= 6$ ones

$$\begin{array}{r} 1\,5\,2 \\ \times\quad 3 \\ \hline 6 \end{array}$$

Multiply the tens.
3×5 tens $= 15$ tens
Rename 15 tens as 1 hundred and 5 tens.

$$\begin{array}{r} \overset{1}{1}\,5\,2 \\ \times\quad 3 \\ \hline 5\,6 \end{array}$$

Multiply the hundreds.
3×1 hundred $= 3$ hundreds
3 hundreds + 1 hundred = 4 hundreds

$$\begin{array}{r} \overset{1}{1}\,5\,2 \\ \times\quad 3 \\ \hline 4\,5\,6 \end{array}$$

The students used 456 blocks.

■ **Talk About Math** How do you know your answer is reasonable?

460

Check Understanding

For another example, see Set G, pages 464–465.

Find each product. In which exercise do you need
to rename ones as tens? Tens as hundreds?

1. 142
    × 4

2. 308
    × 5

3. 417 × 2

4. 821 × 6

Practice

For More Practice, see Set G, pages 466–467.

Find each product. **Remember** to find an estimate first.

5. 119
   × 3

6. 351
   × 5

7. 115
   × 6

8. 106
   × 7

9. 454
   × 4

10. 2 × 239

11. 4 × 562

12. 5 × 250

13. 7 × 614

Mixed Practice Use paper and pencil or mental math to find
each answer. Tell which method you used.

14. 34 + 50

15. 124 × 4

16. 198 − 49

17. 16 × 8

Problem Solving

Use the chart on page 460 to solve Problems 18 and 19.

18. How many blocks would
you have if you had one box
of each size?

19. Estimation How many
small boxes would have
about the same number of
blocks as in a large box?

■ Calculator Solve each problem.

20. Arrange the digits 2, 5, 8,
and 9 to make a 3-digit and
a 1-digit number that will
give you the greatest
product when you multiply.

21. The product of a 1-digit
number and a 2-digit
number is 228. Their sum is
44. What are the two
numbers?

Problem Solving REVIEW

Solve each problem.

1. A package of paper plates holds 36 plates. How many plates are in 3 packages?

2. The cost of a one-way bus ticket is $56. A round-trip ticket is $98. How much do you save by buying a round-trip ticket rather than 2 one-way tickets?

3. How can you make a dollar from quarters and nickels using 12 coins in all?

4. Write a number with 4 in the tens place and 4 in the tenths place.

5. If Mrs. Juliano types 62 words per minute, how many words can she type in 5 minutes?

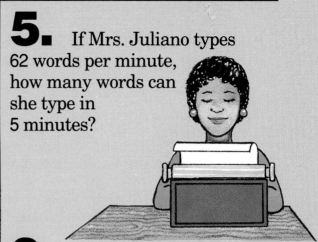

6. The middle digits of these ticket stubs are missing. The missing digits are a 0 and a 1. Sonia remembers that the two numbers were less than 100 apart. What must the two numbers be?

7. **Data File** Use data from pages 532-533. Tell which trains you could take from San Francisco after 6:15 A.M. to get to Menlo Park by 9:00 A.M. How long is the trip?

8. **Make a Data File** Most flowers have petals in multiples of 3 or 5. Find at least 2 flowers that have petals in multiples of 3, and two with petals in multiples of 5. Draw a picture of each and label.

Explore with a Calculator

Egg Farm Multiplication

Select from these digits: 2, 4, 5, 6, 9. Complete the sequences.

1. Find the greatest possible products.

   a. ▦ ▦ ☒ ▦ ☐

   b. ▦ ▦ ▦ ☒ ▦ ☐

2. Find the least possible products.

   a. ▦ ▦ ☒ ▦ ☐

   b. ▦ ▦ ▦ ☒ ▦ ☐

3. Solve each problem. Answers and other information in some problems may be used in later problems.

a. At Kenmark Egg Farm, they have 3 hen barns. Each barn has 75 chickens. How many chickens do they have in all?

b. If every hen lays an egg a day, how many eggs would they lay in one week?

c. They use eight bags of chicken feed per week. Each bag weighs 55 pounds. How many pounds of chicken feed is that? How many pounds do they use in 4 weeks?

d. If the Kenmark family wants to double the size of their egg farm, how many barns will they have? How many chickens? How many eggs per week?

Reteaching

Set A   pages 440–441

Give the standard form for
4 forties.

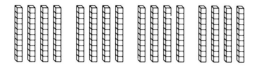

4×4 tens $= 16$ tens $= 160$

Show 160 with fewer pieces.
Replace 10 ten-strips with a
hundred square.

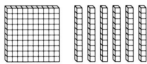

1 hundred 6 tens $= 160 \leftarrow$ Standard form

Remember that a hundred
square equals 10 ten-strips.

Give the standard form for each
exercise. Use place-value
materials to help you.

1. 7 tens   **2.** 14 tens

3. 16 tens   **4.** 5 hundreds

5. 4 thirties   **6.** 3 sixties

Set B   pages 442–443

Find 3×300.
Think: 300 is a multiple of 100, so
          300 is 3 hundreds.
Show: 3 groups of 300.

3×3 hundreds $= 9$ hundreds
$3 \times 300 = 900$

Remember that you can also use
addition to solve a multiplication
problem.

Mental Math   Find each
product mentally.

1. 6×10 **2.** 13×10

3. 25×10 **4.** 8×100

Set C   pages 444–445

Estimate 4×475. Round
475 to the nearest hundred.

```
|----●--------------●------●------●----|
   400          450   475    500
```

475 is closer to 500 than 400.

To find 4×500,
think: $4 \times 5 = 20$
So $4 \times 500 = 2,000$.

Remember that the actual
product will be greater than the
estimate if you round down.
Estimate each product.

1. 5×18 **2.** 6×21

3. 8×72 **4.** 3×225

5. 9×512 **6.** 640×4

Set D   pages 446–449

Find 3 groups of 34.
Make 3 groups of 34.

Combine the groups.
Trade 10 ones for 1 ten.

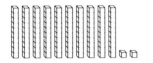

3 groups of 34 is 102.

Remember that you can find the answer to the example at the left by adding 3 groups of 34.

Use place-value materials to help you find how many are in

1. 2 groups of 31.

2. 4 groups of 14.

3. 5 groups of 12.

4. 6 groups of 17.

Set E   pages 450–451

Find 6 × 14.

6 × 4 ones = 24 ones   6 × 1 ten = 6 tens

$$\begin{array}{r} 2 \leftarrow 2\ \text{tens} \\ 14 \\ \times\ 6 \\ \hline 4 \leftarrow 4\ \text{ones} \end{array} \qquad \begin{array}{r} 2 \\ 14 \\ \times\ 6 \\ \hline 84 \quad 6\,\text{tens} + 2\,\text{tens} \end{array}$$

Remember to add the extra tens after you multiply the tens.

Multiply.

1. 17   **2.** 14
     × 3   × 8

Set F   pages 456–457

Find 7 × 48.

7 × 8 ones = 56 ones   7 × 4 tens = 28 tens

$$\begin{array}{r} 5 \leftarrow 5\ \text{tens} \\ 48 \\ \times\ 7 \\ \hline 6 \end{array} \qquad \begin{array}{r} 5 \\ 48 \\ \times\ 7 \\ \hline 336 \quad 28\,\text{tens} + 5\,\text{tens} \end{array}$$

Remember to estimate first in order to see if the answer is reasonable.

Multiply.

1. 37   **2.** 43
     × 6   × 5

Set G   pages 460–461

Find 4 × 176.

4 × 6 ones   4 × 7 tens   4 × 1 hundred

$$\begin{array}{r} 2 \\ 176 \\ \times\ 4 \\ \hline 4 \end{array} \qquad \begin{array}{r} 3\,2 \\ 176 \\ \times\ 4 \\ \hline 04 \end{array} \qquad \begin{array}{r} 3\,2 \\ 176 \\ \times\ 4 \\ \hline 704 \end{array}$$

Remember to add the extra hundreds after you multiply the hundreds. Find each product.

1. 271   **2.** 318
    × 5   × 8

More Practice

Set A   pages 440–441

Give the standard form for each exercise. Use place-value materials to help you.

1. 8 tens   **2.** 17 tens   **3.** 11 tens   **4.** 3 fifties   **5.** 11 hundreds

6. 3 groups of six hundreds   **7.** 4 groups of four hundreds

8. 5 groups of thirty   **9.** 5 groups of sixty

10. 6 groups of forty   **11.** 5 groups of two hundreds

Set B   pages 442–443

Mental Math   Find each product mentally.

1. 3×10 **2.** 12×10 **3.** 24×10 **4.** 10×9

5. 4×100 **6.** 8×100 **7.** 100×32 **8.** 100×41

9. 7×30 **10.** 4×60 **11.** 20×4 **12.** 70×6

13. 5×800 **14.** 9×300 **15.** 400×5 **16.** 600×6

Set C   pages 444–445

Estimate each product.

1. 3×11 **2.** 4×22 **3.** 59×6 **4.** 8×44

5. 7×412 **6.** 564×5 **7.** 8×390 **8.** 842×6

9. 9×32 **10.** 4×46 **11.** 687×3 **12.** 4×726

13. 5×639 **14.** 88×4 **15.** 7×68 **16.** 927×2

Number Sense   Give each answer.

17. In which of Exercises 1–16 do you think your estimated product will be less than the actual product?

18. In which of Exercises 1–16 do you think your estimated product will be greater than the actual product?

Set D pages 446–449

Use place-value materials to help you find
how many are in

1. 2 groups of 26.   **2.** 4 groups of 11.   **3.** 5 groups of 21.

4. 4 rows of 42.   **5.** 3 rows of 17.   **6.** 4 groups of 34.

7. 6 rows of 18.   **8.** 4 rows of 52.   **9.** 2 groups of 49.

Set E pages 450–451

Find each product.

1. 23
$\times 3$

2. 26
$\times 5$

3. 12
$\times 8$

4. 19
$\times 4$

5. 37
$\times 2$

6. 18 × 6   **7.** 11 × 9   **8.** 14 × 7   **9.** 29 × 3   **10.** 38 × 2

11. 22 × 4   **12.** 15 × 5   **13.** 12 × 6   **14.** 17 × 3   **15.** 34 × 2

Set F pages 456–457

Multiply.

1. 23
$\times 5$

2. 34
$\times 3$

3. 55
$\times 6$

4. 92
$\times 2$

5. 47
$\times 4$

6. 54 × 7   **7.** 82 × 5   **8.** 38 × 6   **9.** 26 × 8

10. 9 × 42   **11.** 6 × 51   **12.** 7 × 35   **13.** 4 × 84

Mixed Practice Use paper and pencil or mental math
to find each answer. Tell which method you used.

14. 150 + 9   **15.** 9 × 20   **16.** 62 − 34   **17.** 63 ÷ 7

Set G pages 460–461

Find each product.

1. 318
$\times 2$

2. 164
$\times 5$

3. 237
$\times 4$

4. 408
$\times 9$

5. 128
$\times 6$

6. 3 × 143   **7.** 6 × 350   **8.** 4 × 229   **9.** 8 × 508

Enrichment

Multiplication with Money

How could you find the cost of 5 pounds of apples at the Farmer's Market?

Find 5 × 43¢. Think of 43¢ as 43 ones.

Multiply the ones. Rename if needed.	Multiply the tens. Write the answer as dollars and cents.
$\begin{array}{r} 1 \\ 4\,3 \\ \times \;\; 5 \\ \hline 5 \end{array}$	$\begin{array}{r} 1 \\ 4\,3 \\ \times \;\; 5 \\ \hline 2\,1\,5 \end{array}$ **215¢** 215¢ is the same as $2.15.

Five pounds of apples cost $2.15.

Multiply. Write each answer as dollars and cents.

1. 27¢ × 5	2. 81¢ × 5	3. 33¢ × 6	4. 60¢ × 5	5. 23¢ × 4

6. 4 × 74¢   **7.** 2 × 15¢   **8.** 36¢ × 7   **9.** 51¢ × 8

Find the cost of each of the following.

10. 3 pounds of pears   **11.** 4 pounds of oranges

12. 5 pounds of bananas   **13.** 6 kiwi fruit

Chapter 13 Review/Test

1. Give the standard form for 6 groups of 3 hundreds.

Find each product mentally.

2. 90×4 **3.** 60×5

Estimate each product.

4. 23×9 **5.** 4×492

6. Find how many are in 4 groups of 26.

⚏⁖⁖ ⚏⁖⁖ ⚏⁖⁖ ⚏⁖⁖

Use Exercises A and B to answer Items 7–12. Draw pictures to help you.

A. $\begin{array}{r} 24 \\ \times\ 2 \\ \hline \end{array}$ **B.** $\begin{array}{r} 37 \\ \times\ 4 \\ \hline \end{array}$

In Exercise A, how many

7. ones will there be?

8. tens will there be?

9. In Exercise A, did you need to rename any ones as tens?

In Exercise B, how many

10. ones will there be?

11. tens will there be in all?

12. did you need to rename any ones as tens?

Draw pictures to help find each product.

13. 5×14 **14.** 6×23

15. 4×91 **16.** 7×302

17. Oranges come in bags of 12. Tomatoes come in boxes of 8. How many oranges are there in 6 bags?

Read this problem. Then answer the questions below.

Each of the 3 Thompson children went on 9 rides. How many rides did they take in all?

18. Would you add, subtract, multiply, or divide to solve the problem?

19. Pat got an answer of 6 for the problem. Does this answer make sense? Why or why not?

20. Solve the problem above.

21. ■ **Write About Math** Is your estimate for Exercise 5 greater or less than the exact product? How do you know?

Statistics, Graphing, and Probability

14

Did You Know: Some large libraries receive as many as 10 different newspapers every day.

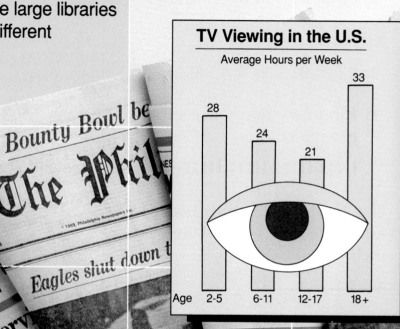

TV Viewing in the U.S.
Average Hours per Week

Age	2-5	6-11	12-17	18+
	28	24	21	33

Snowfall in Denver
Average Number of Inches per Month

Jan. Feb. Mar. Apr. May Jun. Jul. Aug. Sep. Oct. Nov. Dec.

Each ❋ equals one inch.

Estimate
Predict how many graphs will appear in the newspaper the next 5 days.

Gather Data
Check the newspaper you selected and record the number of graphs which appear.

Analyze and Report
When people are done reading the newspaper, cut out the graphs. Group them into categories. Give each category a name. Compare your categories with other students.

Median Family Income
in the United States

$30,992
$28,236
$25,948
$23,433
$21,023

$30,000
$29,000
$28,000
$27,000
$26,000
$25,000
$24,000
$23,000
$22,000
$21,000
$20,000

1980   1982   1984   1986   1988

Collecting Data

Build Understanding

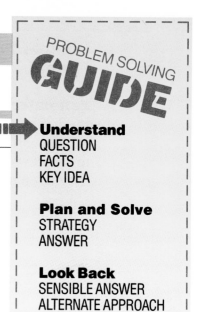
PROBLEM SOLVING
GUIDE

⦁⦁⦁➡ **Understand**
QUESTION
FACTS
KEY IDEA

Plan and Solve
STRATEGY
ANSWER

Look Back
SENSIBLE ANSWER
ALTERNATE APPROACH

There will be 10 people at Brian's birthday picnic. Brian will serve either hot dogs or hamburgers. Which should he serve?

**Understand**   QUESTION   What food should Brian serve?

FACTS   There will be 10 people at the picnic.

KEY IDEA   Brian needs a way to find out which food his guests will like.

Plan and Solve   To get the information, or **data,** Brian could ask different kinds of questions.

• He could ask each guest, "What would you like to eat at the picnic?" Then he might get 10 different answers!

• He could ask each guest, "Which would you like, hot dogs or hamburgers?" Then he might get answers that would help him.

• Because Brian likes hot dogs better, he could just ask, "Do you like hot dogs?"

Brian decided to serve hamburgers. Which question do you think he asked?

Look Back   Could Brian have done something else to get an answer?

■ **Talk About Math**   What other questions could Brian have asked? Would the results always be the same?

Check Understanding

Do you need to collect data from several people to find out

1. which colors people like?

2. how plants grow?

3. if your friend can play with you?

4. how students travel to school?

5. If you answered *no* to any of Questions 1-4, tell how you might get the information to answer those questions.

Practice

Write at least two questions you could ask your classmates to help you answer each question below.

6. The class will take sandwiches on a trip. The lunchroom can make cheese, chicken, tuna, ham, and egg salad sandwiches. How many sandwiches of each kind should the class order?

7. You are ordering 4 pizzas for a class party. A pizza can have 1 topping or no toppings. A topping can be sausage, peppers, or mushrooms. How many pizzas should have toppings?

8. You ask classmates about their favorite animals. What kinds of animals do your friends like?

9. Which of your questions for Problems 6-8 do you think would give you more helpful data?

10. **Estimation** Helen brought paper plates on a picnic. She used 32 plates for sandwiches, 27 for salads, and 18 for desserts. She had 43 plates left. About how many plates did she bring in all?

Collecting and Organizing Data

Build Understanding

A. My Favorite Things
Materials: Tally charts
Groups: 3–6 students

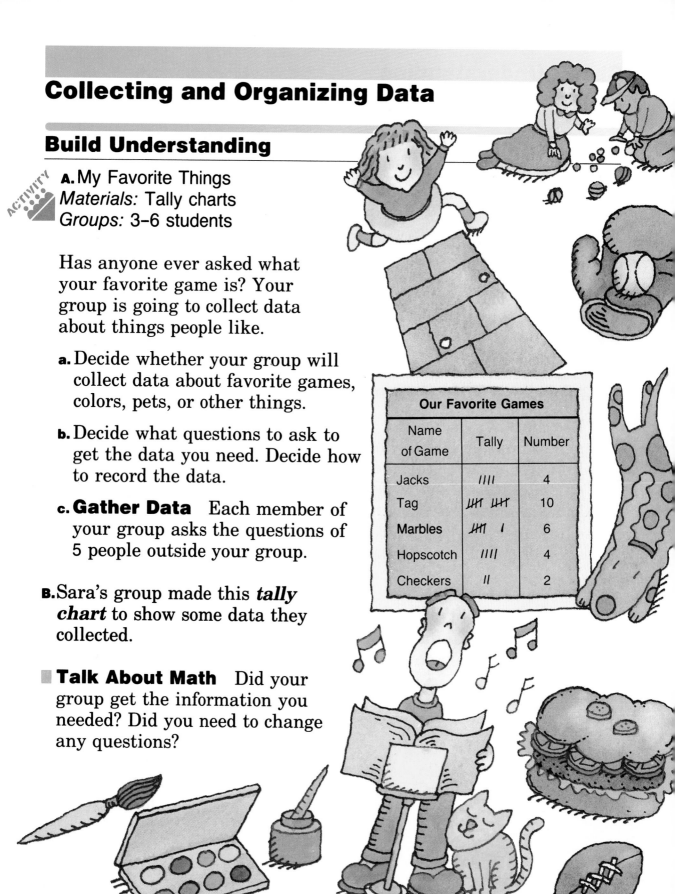

Has anyone ever asked what your favorite game is? Your group is going to collect data about things people like.

a. Decide whether your group will collect data about favorite games, colors, pets, or other things.

b. Decide what questions to ask to get the data you need. Decide how to record the data.

c. Gather Data Each member of your group asks the questions of 5 people outside your group.

Our Favorite Games

Name of Game	Tally	Number
Jacks	////	4
Tag	ЖНТ ЖНТ	10
Marbles	ЖНТ /	6
Hopscotch	////	4
Checkers	//	2

B. Sara's group made this *tally chart* to show some data they collected.

Talk About Math Did your group get the information you needed? Did you need to change any questions?

Check Understanding

For another example, see Set A, pages 498–499.

In a tally chart what does

1. each / mean?

2. //// mean?

3. What questions do you think Sara's group asked to get the results in the tally chart?

4. Can you tell from the tally chart how many children played tag last Saturday?

5. Make a tally chart to show the results of your questions.

Practice

For More Practice, see Set A, pages 500–501.

Record data about the dolls shown.
Copy and complete each tally chart.

6.

Scarf	Tallies	Number
yes		
no		

7.

Color of Clothes	Tallies	Number

8.

Snow Shovel	Tallies	Number

Problem Solving

9. Critical Thinking If there were 30 dolls, can you tell how many would be wearing a scarf? Explain.

Pictographs

Build Understanding

Pinetree School students asked 50 children what their favorite kinds of movies are. Students worked in groups to make pictographs from their data.

Each group wrote a title.

Then each group listed the kinds of movies.

Each group used a face to stand for a certain number of children. They wrote that at the bottom.

They drew faces in the graph for the numbers on the tally chart.

Below are pictographs made by the groups of students. Think about how each group showed the same data.

■ **Talk About Math** Do you think a pictograph is more helpful than a tally chart in showing this kind of information? Why or why not?

Type of Movie	Tally	Number
Westerns	IIII	5
Space	IIII IIII IIII IIII	20
Comedy	IIII IIII IIII	15
Adventure	IIII IIII	10

Favorite Movies of Children	
Westerns	
Space	
Comedy	
Adventure	
Each ☺ stands for 5 children.	

A.

Favorite Movies of Children	
Westerns	☺
Space	☺ ☺ ☺ ☺
Comedy	☺ ☺ ☺
Adventure	☺ ☺
Each ☺ stands for 5 children.	

B.

Favorite Movies	
Westerns	◖
Adventure	☺
Comedy	☺ ◖
Space	☺ ☺
Each ☺ stands for 10 children.	

476

Check Understanding

Look at Graphs A, B, C, and D to answer Exercises 1–6.

1. Which title is better? Why?

2. Do you think it matters in what order movies are listed? Why?

3. What does ☺ stand for in Graphs A, C, and D?

4. What does ☺ stand for in Graph B?

5. Did the group that made Graph B make a good decision about the number of children shown by ☺? Why?

6. Would you use one ☺ for one child? Why or why not?

For Exercises 7–11, suppose you used this tally chart to make a pictograph.

7. What title would you use?

8. How would you list the choices?

Where would you like to see a new movie?		
Place	Tally	Number
Theater	ⅢⅢ ⅢⅢ	10
Drive-in	////	4
Home on TV	ⅢⅢ ///	8

9. What picture would you use?

10. How many tally marks would each picture stand for?

11. How many pictures would you show in each row?

C.

Our Favorite Movies	
Westerns	☺
Adventure	☺ ☺
Comedy	☺ ☺ ☺
Space	☺ ☺ ☺ ☺
Each ☺ stands for 5 children.	

D.

50 Children's Favorite Movies	
Space	☺ ☺ ☺ ☺
Comedy	☺ ☺ ☺
Adventure	☺ ☺
Westerns	☺
Each ☺ stands for 5 children.	

Practice

For More Practice, see Set B, pages 500–501.

Copy and complete the pictograph, using the tally chart for the data you need. Then complete Exercise 12.

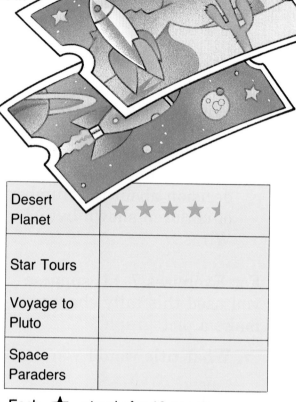

The Space Movie Most People Liked		
Name of Movie	Tally	Number
Desert Planet	ЖН ЖН ЖН ЖН ЖН ЖН ЖН ЖН ЖН	45
Star Tours	ЖН ЖН ЖН ЖН ЖН ЖН ЖН ЖН ЖН ЖН ЖН	55
Voyage to Pluto	ЖН ЖН ЖН ЖН ЖН ЖН ЖН ЖН	40
Space Paraders	ЖН ЖН ЖН ЖН ЖН ЖН ЖН ЖН ЖН ЖН	50

Desert Planet	★ ★ ★ ★ ⭐
Star Tours	
Voyage to Pluto	
Space Paraders	

Each ★ stands for 10 people.

12. Is one movie much more popular or unpopular than the others? Describe what your graph shows without using numbers.

Use Data Make your own pictograph. Use the tally chart on page 474 and complete Exercises 13–17.

13. Write a title for your graph.

14. List the games at the left.

15. Decide what picture you will use to stand for people.

16. Decide how many people each picture will stand for.

17. Draw pictures in your graph next to each game.

Mixed Practice   Study the pictograph at the right. Then answer the questions. How many people like

18. adventure films?

19. musicals?

Favorite Kinds of Movies	
Musicals	☺ ☺ ☺
Adventure	☺ ☺ ☺ ☺
History	☺ ☺
Comedy	☺ ☺ ☺ ☺ ☺

Each ☺ stands for 16 people.

Problem Solving

Calculator   Use the pictograph above to solve this problem.

20. Suppose each person picked only one kind of movie as a favorite. How many people were asked?

Reading ——— Math

Copy each sentence. Fill in the blank with the word that makes sense. Do not use any word more than once.

tally chart   bar graph
pictograph   data

1. Betty used ☺ to show information in her ___?___.

2. Bob asked many friends about their favorite color. He was collecting ___?___.

3. Luis had to keep track of answers while he questioned 25 people. He used a ___?___.

Bar Graphs

Build Understanding

Mrs. Ruiz manages the Shirt Boutique. One of her jobs is to record the sales of different styles of clothing on a bar graph.

Sales of Shirts Week of April 3		
Type of Shirt	Tally	Number
No Sleeves	LHT LHT	10
Short Sleeves	LHT LHT LHT LHT	20
Long Sleeves	LHT	5
Tank Top	LHT	5

A. To help her draw the bar graph, Mrs. Ruiz first collected data using a tally chart.

B. Mrs. Ruiz wrote a title for her bar graph. Along the bottom of the graph, she wrote the name of each style of shirt. At the left, Mrs. Ruiz wrote the numbers that would help her draw the bars.

Sales of Shirts Week of April 3

480

c. In a different color, Mrs. Ruiz added to the bars on her graph for the week of April 10.

■ **Talk About Math** Why is the bar graph more useful to Mrs. Ruiz than just her weekly tallies?

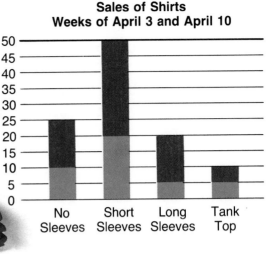

Sales of Shirts
Weeks of April 3 and April 10

Check Understanding

For another example, see Set C, pages 498–499.

1. When Mrs. Ruiz orders T-shirts for May, which kind should she buy the most of?

2. If you were Mrs. Ruiz, would you order more tank tops for May? Why?

3. **Number Sense** Why did Mrs. Ruiz count by 5s on the side of her graph instead of by 2s?

4. Why does Mrs. Ruiz use a new color for each different week of sales?

5. How many shirts of each kind were sold the week of April 10?

Practice

For More Practice, see Set C, pages 500–501.

Mrs. Ruiz also keeps track of when her store is the busiest. Use the tally sheet and answer the questions to complete the graph.

6. Copy the unfinished graph on page 482 and write a title that explains the data it will show.

Number of People in Store		
Time	Tally	Number
9 to noon	₶₶ ₶₶ ₶₶ ₶₶	20
noon to 3	₶₶ ₶₶ ₶₶ ₶₶ ₶₶ ₶₶ ₶₶ ₶₶ ₶₶ ₶₶ ₶₶ ₶₶ ₶₶ ₶₶ ₶₶ ₶₶	80
3 to 6	₶₶ ₶₶ ₶₶ ₶₶ ₶₶ ₶₶	30
6 to 9	₶₶ ₶₶ ₶₶ ₶₶ ₶₶ ₶₶ ₶₶ ₶₶	40

7. Decide what numbers you will use and write them along the bottom of your graph.

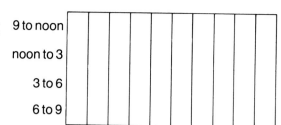

8. Draw your bars in the graph. Your bars will go from left to right instead of bottom to top.

9. Write a summary of your finished graph without using numbers.

Problem Solving

Explore ———— Math

You are going to collect data about a topic that interests you and then make a pictograph. Work in groups.

10. Decide on a question to ask your classmates. Give three or four answer choices. Example: How many hours of TV do you watch each day—1 hour, 2 hours, 3 hours, or more than 3 hours?

11. Have each person in your group question one or more students. Make sure everyone in your class, including the people in your group, answers the question. Use tally marks to record results.

12. Find the number for each choice.

13. Make a pictograph for your data.

14. Write a report describing your data. Example: Most students watch TV for 1 or 2 hours a day. Only a few watch for 3 hours. No one watches for more than 3 hours.

Midchapter Checkup

1. Suppose you are planning to serve 7 people at a party. Which question would help you best to know what to buy? Why?

   a. What drink do you like best?

   b. Which drink do you like best—orange juice, lemonade, or grape juice?

2. A ___?___ is a way of recording data.

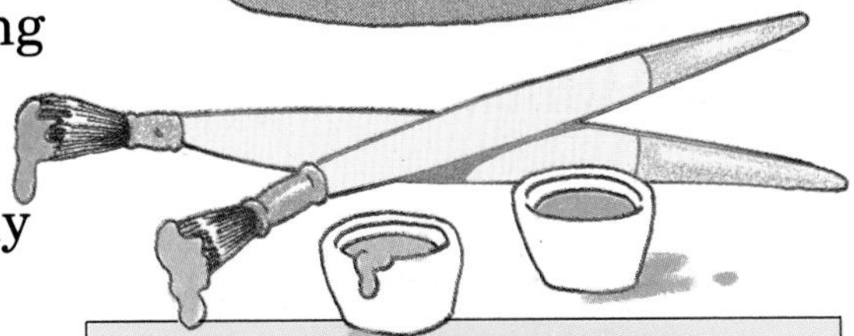

3. In recording data, how many does 𝍸 represent?

4. Study this tally chart made by the third graders at Zane School. Then complete the chart and make a pictograph from the data. **Remember** to decide how many people each picture should stand for.

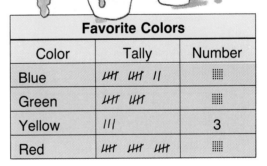

Favorite Colors

Color	Tally	Number
Blue	𝍸 𝍸 //	
Green	𝍸 𝍸	
Yellow	///	3
Red	𝍸 𝍸 𝍸	

Favorite Flowers

Flower	Tally	Number
Lilac	𝍸 𝍸	10
Tulip	𝍸 𝍸 𝍸	15
Buttercup	𝍸	5
Iris	𝍸 𝍸	10

Use the tally chart at the left to answer Questions 5 and 6.

5. What flower was more popular than the iris?

6. Make a bar graph to show the data in the table.

Problem-Solving Workshop

Real-Life Decision Making

Do you need an increase in your allowance? How much is your present allowance? What do you use it for? How much of an increase do you need? List 3 reasons why you would need to have it increased.

Could this graph help you convince your parents? It shows the allowance for 42 eight-year-olds.

Number-Sense Project

Look back at pages 470-471.

1. How many pictographs do you see?

2. How many bar graphs do you see?

3. Tell how you could make a bar graph into a pictograph or a pictograph into a bar graph.

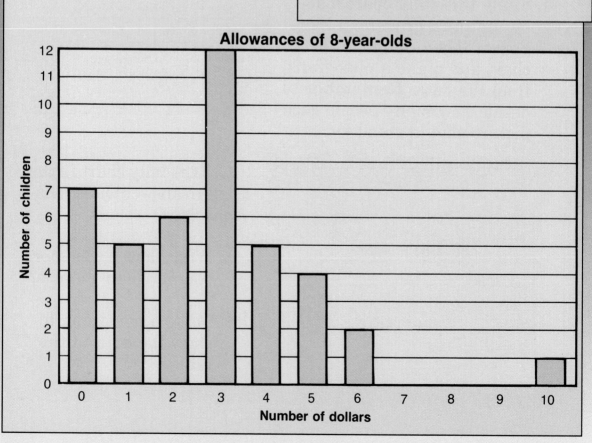

Allowances of 8-year-olds

484

Explore with a Computer

Use the *Graphing and Probability Workshop Project* for this activity.

1. At the computer, use the **Toss coin** option to do an experiment.

2. Toss 3 coins twenty times.

3. Record the results in the table.

4. View the data in the table as a **Bar graph**.

5. Repeat the experiment, tossing the coins 100 times.

6. Create your own experiment using up to 4 coins.

Math-at-Home Activity

Play *Odd or Even* with someone at home. Each player makes a fist. Put out 1-5 fingers on the count of *three*. One player calls *odd* or *even* just before the fingers are shown.

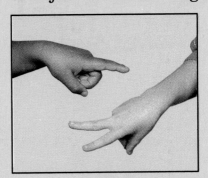

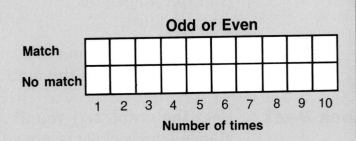

Odd or Even

Match										
No match										

1 2 3 4 5 6 7 8 9 10

Number of times

If the sum of the number of fingers matches the *odd* or *even* called, you have a *match*. Predict how many times your call and finger sum will match if you do the activity 18 times. Record the results on a bar graph.

Make a Graph

Build Understanding

The slips of paper show the number of cans collected each week for recycling. The first class to collect 50 cans wins a prize. What is the best way to keep track of the contest?

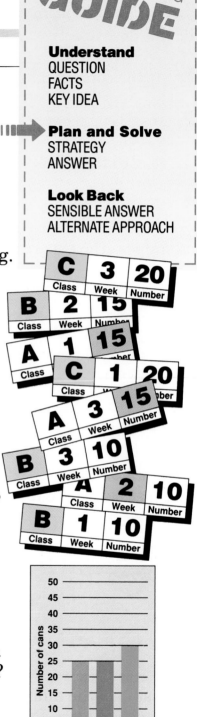

PROBLEM SOLVING
GUIDE

Understand
QUESTION
FACTS
KEY IDEA

Plan and Solve
STRATEGY
ANSWER

Look Back
SENSIBLE ANSWER
ALTERNATE APPROACH

Understand   All the facts are on slips of paper. You can record data to see which class is winning.

Plan and Solve   STRATEGY   You could make a table.

	Week 1	Week 2
Class A	15	10
Class B	10	15
Class C	20	10

Is it easy to see which class has collected the most cans?

A graph helps you compare data.

ANSWER   You can make a bar graph to show the data.

Look Back   Does the graph tell you at a glance which class is ahead? Could you use a pictograph to show the data?

■ **Talk About Math**   Why is it better to use a graph than a table for the Example?

Check Understanding

Use the slips of paper, table, and graph on page 486 to help answer Problems 1–4.

1. **Number Sense** Why did the person who made this graph count by 5s?

2. When reading the graph, do you need the numbers to know which class is ahead? Why?

3. Do you need the numbers to put data on the graph? Why?

4. Copy and complete the graph. Use the data for Week 3.

Practice

The three third-grade classes in Pia's school collected bottles for recycling. The data at the right show the numbers of bottles collected for two weeks. Make a table or a graph to help you with each problem.

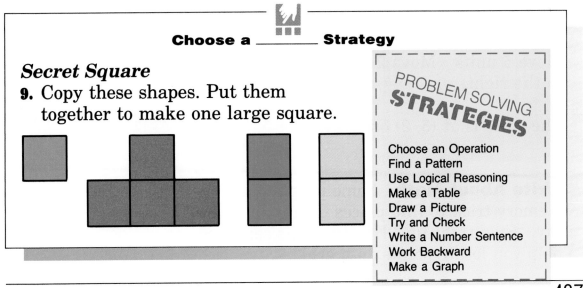

Class	Week	Number
1	1	20

Class	Week	Number
1	2	20

Class	Week	Number
2	1	25

Class	Week	Number
2	2	15

Class	Week	Number
3	1	25

Class	Week	Number
3	2	20

5. Which class collected the most bottles?

6. **Mental Math** How many bottles did Class 2 collect?

7. Which two classes collected the same number of bottles?

8. Explain why you chose to make a graph or a table.

Choose a _____ Strategy

Secret Square

9. Copy these shapes. Put them together to make one large square.

PROBLEM SOLVING STRATEGIES

Choose an Operation
Find a Pattern
Use Logical Reasoning
Make a Table
Draw a Picture
Try and Check
Write a Number Sentence
Work Backward
Make a Graph

Locating Points on a Grid

Build Understanding

Maps and graphs are very much alike. They are both drawn on a grid.

A. Start at the town square. Walk 3 blocks east on Main Street. Where are you? Are you at the corner of Main Street and Park Avenue?

Now walk 3 blocks north on Park Avenue. Where are you? What is at the corner of Park Avenue and Sunset Road?

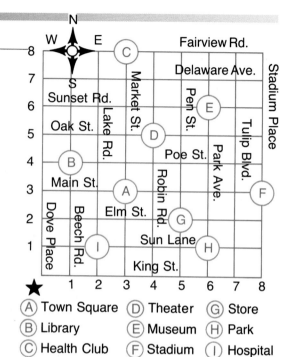

A) Town Square D) Theater G) Store
B) Library E) Museum H) Park
C) Health Club F) Stadium I) Hospital

B. You can use **number pairs** to find places on a map. Use the numbers at the side and bottom. What will you find at (5, 2) on the map?

Begin at the star.

(5, 2)

Move 5 units to the right.   Move 2 units up.

The store is at (5, 2) on the map.

C. What number pair tells where the theater is on the map?

Start at the theater. Follow the street down to the number on the bottom. The theater is 4 units to the right of the star.

Now start at the theater and follow the street to the number on the side. The theater is 5 units up from the star.

The theater is at (4, 5) on the map.

■ **Write About Math**   Some people use a memory trick to find places on a map. They say, "Step right up." How can this sentence help you locate points on a grid?

Check Understanding

For another example, see Set D, pages 498–499.

Locate the number pair (8, 3) on the map.

1. Where on the map do you begin?

2. How many units do you move to the right?

3. How many units do you move up?

4. What will you find at (8, 3)?

Practice

For More Practice, see Set D, pages 500–501.

Name the building located at each number pair.

5. (3, 8)   **6.** (1, 4)   **7.** (6, 6)   **8.** (2, 1)   **9.** (4, 5)

Write the number pair for each corner.

10. Lake Rd., Oak St.   **11.** King St., Dove Place

Problem Solving

Use grid paper to solve the problem.

12. On a grid find the point for the number pairs. Connect the points in order. Name the figure.

(1, 2) (2, 3) (4, 3) (4, 1) (2, 1) (1, 2)

Visualize the problem in your mind to help you understand it better.

Skills ———— Review   pages 314–315

Tell whether you would use paper and pencil, mental math, or a calculator. Then find each answer.

1. 4 × 6   **2.** 12 + 10   **3.** 25 ÷ 5   **4.** 2 × 7

5. 69 − 39   **6.** 3,278 + 847   **7.** 400 + 125   **8.** 900 − 98

Probabilities

Build Understanding

AUGUST 15

71

78

80

82

"It will be sunny and 85 degrees tomorrow."

Do you know if it will snow tomorrow? What would a Kansas City weather forecaster say about the *chance* of snow on August 15?

Would he say he is *certain* it will snow? That snow is *possible?* That it is *impossible* to have snow on that date?

The forecaster does not even talk about a chance of snow on August 15. If asked, he would say snow is impossible because it is too warm.

In February, Kansas City often has snow. The chance, or **probability,** of snow is greater in February than in August.

■ **Talk About Math** Have you ever heard a weather forecaster say, "There is a slight chance of rain"? What do you think this means?

Check Understanding

For another example, see Set E, pages 498–499.

1. Would you say it is certain, possible, or impossible for you to become a weather forecaster?

2. What kinds of weather is it possible for you to have tomorrow?

3. What kinds of weather would be impossible for you to have tomorrow?

4. Can you be certain about the weather you will have tomorrow? Explain.

Practice

For More Practice, see Set E, pages 500–501.

You can be a forecaster right now. Tell whether you think each event is *certain, possible,* or *impossible.*

5. You will grow taller during the next year.

6. When you phone a friend, the line will be busy.

7. You will grow to 100 feet tall.

8. Humans will travel to Mars.

9. You will watch TV tonight.

10. Tomorrow will have 24 hours.

Problem Solving

Lila is 8 years old. She says, "I want to be a weather forecaster." Tell whether each statement is *certain, possible,* or *impossible.*

11. Lila will be a weather forecaster.

12. Lila will talk about the weather on television.

13. Lila will be 12 years old tomorrow.

14. Lila likes to look at maps.

15. **Gather Data** Record the weather forecast and the actual weather for three days. Use a chart like the one shown. How many of the forecasts were correct?

Weather Forecast	Actual Weather
sunny	cloudy

Critical Thinking Answer each question. Then explain your reasoning for each answer.

16. Do you think that every student gave the same answers to Exercises 5–10?

17. If Exercises 5–10 have different answers, can all the answers be correct?

Outcomes

Build Understanding

What is your favorite animal?

Without looking, Alison picks one animal card from the box. What are the possible *outcomes?*

Alison could get an elephant card, a lion card, or a giraffe card.

Is Alison more likely to get an elephant card or a lion card?

It is *more likely* that Alison will get an elephant card. There are more elephant cards in the box.

Is Alison more likely to get a lion card or a giraffe card when she picks from the box? Why?

Alison has an equal chance of getting a lion or a giraffe card because there are two lion cards and two giraffe cards. Getting a lion card and getting a giraffe card are *equally likely.*

■ **Talk About Math**   What fraction of the cards have elephants? lions? giraffes?

Check Understanding

For another example, see Set F, pages 498–499.

1. Which is less likely, that Alison will pick an elephant card or a lion card from the box without looking?

2. How many more lion and giraffe cards would you put in the box to make all the outcomes equally likely?

492

Practice

For More Practice, see Set F, pages 500–501.

List all the possible outcomes.

3.

4.

5.

Use the pictures in Exercises 3–5 to answer Exercises 6–13.
Are the outcomes equally likely?
If not, which is more likely?

6. To pick a green marble or to pick a blue marble

7. To pick a red marble or to pick a green marble

8. To spin a 1 or to spin a 5

9. To spin a 5 or to spin a 7

10. To pick a circle or to pick a triangle

11. To pick a square or to pick a triangle

12. To pick a blue marble or to pick a red marble

13. To spin a 4 or to spin a 6

Problem Solving

Choose a ———— Strategy

Yellow, White, and Blue

14. Ramon has a bag of marbles. There are more yellow than white marbles. There are more white than blue marbles. If Ramon picks a marble without looking, is he less likely to pick a yellow or a blue marble?

Experiments

Build Understanding

ACTIVITY

Chances Are
Materials: Spinner, tally charts,
colored paper, paper bags
Groups: Partners

a. Make a spinner like the one shown.

b. List all the possible outcomes. Which
outcomes are equally likely? Is any
outcome more likely than red? Is any
outcome less likely than yellow?

c. Each partner predicts how often the
spinner will land on red in 8 spins.

d. Do the experiment. Record the results.

e. Compare the results to your predictions.

■ **Talk About Math**   Do you think you could
predict the results better if the spinner were
spun 40 or 100 times? Why or why not?

Check Understanding

For another example, see Set G, pages 498–499.

Do the experiment in the example 3 more times.
Record the results of the 4 experiments in 4 tally charts.

1. Did the spinner land on red
the same number of times in
each experiment?

2. In all 32 spins that you
made, how many times did
the spinner land on red?

3. If you spun 32 times in a
row, how many times do you
think the spinner would land
on red?

4. Do 32 spins in a row. How
many times did you get red?
Was the result close to your
prediction?

Practice

For More Practice, see Set G, pages 500–501.

Answer the following questions. You may want to do one of these activities with your partner.

Experiment A

a. Pick one card from the bag without looking.

b. Record the number. Return the card to the bag.

5. Is it possible to get an 8?

6. Is it possible to get a 12?

7. Do you have an equal chance to get a 3 or a 5?

8. Are you more likely to get a 4 than an 8?

9. How many times do you think you would get a 6 in 8 picks?

10. How many times do you think you would get a 6 in 80 picks?

Experiment B

a. Pick a marble from the jar without looking.

b. Record the color. Return the marble to the jar.

11. Do you have an equal chance to get a blue or a red marble?

12. Are you more likely to get a green marble than a red one?

13. How many blue marbles do you think you would get in 8 picks?

14. How many blue marbles do you think you would get in 80 picks?

Solve each problem.

1. In Squaretown, the streets are laid out on a 5 by 5 grid. Mr. Triangle lives at (2, 2), and Mr. Round lives at (1, 4). How many blocks does Mr. Round have to walk to Mr. Triangle's house?

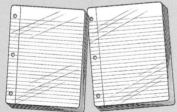

2. Lined notebook paper comes in packages of 300 sheets. A package that usually costs $2.19 has been reduced to $1.49. How much will you save if you buy 2 packages?

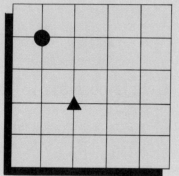

3. What division fact can help you find $\frac{1}{4}$ of 36?

4. I am a decimal in hundredths. I am greater than 0.6. I am less than 0.65. The sum of my digits is 9. Who am I?

5. These are the answers some children gave when asked "What do you like to do best in the summer?" Make a tally chart to show the results.

SWIM
PICNIC
SWIMMING
BIKE RIDING
BOAT RIDE
BOATING
SWIMMING
BIKE RIDE
SWIM AT THE LAKE
GO SWIMMING
RIDE MY BIKE
PICNICS
SAIL ON MY BOAT

6. **Data File** Use data from pages 532-533. What days do people go to the movies most often? Which are the two least busy days at the movies? Do you have a favorite day of the week to go to the movies?

7. **Make a Data File** Find 1 pictograph and 3 bar graphs in newspapers or magazines. Make a display and write a sentence that tells about each graph.

Explore with a Calculator

Math and Memory Keys

The memory keys on a calculator permit you to store numbers for later use.

1. Here is a sample of how memory keys work. (Note, do not use the $=$ key for any of these sequences.)

Use the memory keys to help you solve each problem.

Press:

MRC MRC	Clears the memory
16 M+	16 appears in the display and is *added to the memory*.
8 M−	8 appears in the display and is *subtracted from the memory*.
2 × 2 M−	4 appears in the display and is *subtracted from the memory*.
15 ÷ 3 M+	5 appears in the display and is *added to the memory*.
MRC	9 appears in the display.

2. Chris bought 3 packages with 4 cards in each, and 9 packages with 6 cards in each. How many cards did she buy in all?
(Hint: 3 × 4 M+ 9 × 6 M+ MRC)

3. Kevin has two binders of baseball cards with 25 cards in each binder and 3 displays with 15 cards in each display. How many baseball cards does he have?

4. The cost for each of 2 complete sets of cards is $19.95. Tim has a coupon for $3.50 on each set. How much will Tim have to pay for both sets?

Reteaching

Set A   pages 474–475

You can use a tally chart to show how many leaves there are of each color. For each leaf, mark / in your chart next to its color. To be sure you record every leaf, you can work from left to right.

Remember that / in a tally chart means 1 and //// means 5.

1. The first 3 leaves from left to right are recorded in this chart. Copy and complete the chart.

Bill's Leaf Collection

Color	Tally	Number
Green	/	
Red		
Yellow	//	

Set B   pages 476–479

You can make a pictograph from the data in this tally chart.

Favorite Fruits of Our Class

Fruit	Tally	Number
Apple	//// //// //// ////	20
Pear	////	5
Peach	//// //// ////	15
Orange	//// ////	10

Let ☺ stand for 5 students.
4 × 5 = 20, so 4 faces will show the 20 students who like apples.

Remember that each picture in a pictograph stands for some number.

Let ☺ stand for 5 students.

1. How many faces will stand for the 10 students who like oranges?

2. Make a pictograph to show the data in the tally chart.

Set C   pages 480–482

The bar graph at the right shows the data from Set B.

Remember that it doesn't matter whether the bars on a graph go up and down or from left to right.

Use the graph. Which fruit is

1. most popular?

2. least popular?

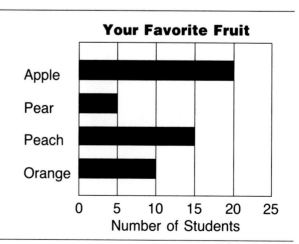

Your Favorite Fruit

Set D   pages 488–489

On the graph, the number pair for the school is (4, 3).

Remember that the first number in a number pair is the number of units to the right of the star. Name the building located at

1. (5, 1).   **2.** (3, 5).

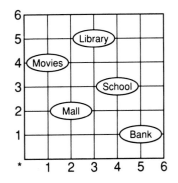

Set E   pages 490–491

Some events are certain to happen. "The sun will rise in the east."

Some events are impossible. "It will snow in Hawaii."

Some events are possible. "The Cubs will win the pennant."

Remember that the chance of an event happening is called probability.

Do you think each event is certain, possible, or impossible?

1. You will sleep 8 hours tonight.

2. You will be 200 years old.

Set F   pages 492–493

If you spin this spinner, the four possible outcomes are A, B, C, and D. **Remember** that outcomes are not always equally likely.

1. Are you more likely to spin an A or a C?

2. Are A and B equally likely?

3. Which outcomes are less likely than spinning a B?

Set G   pages 494–495

On this spinner, there is an equal chance of getting any of the 5 numbers. However, there is a greater chance of getting an odd number than of getting an even number.

Remember that you can predict the results better the more times the spinner is spun.

1. Why is there a greater chance of getting an odd number than of getting an even number?

More Practice

Set A pages 474–75

Record data about the figures shown.
Copy and complete each tally chart.

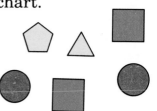
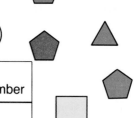

1.

Shape of Figures	Tallies	Number
Curved		
Not curved		

2.

Color of Figures	Tallies	Number

3.

Number of Straight Sides	Tallies	Number

Set B pages 476–479

For Exercises 1–3, suppose you used the tally chart to make a pictograph.

1. What title would you use?

2. How would you list the choices?

What is Your Favorite Hamburger?

Type	Tally	Number
Regular burger	//// //// //// ///	18
Cheeseburger	//// //// //	12
Pizzaburger	//// /	6

3. How many tally marks would each picture stand for?

Set C pages 480–482

This tally sheet shows the sizes of shoes sold on Tuesday.

1. Copy the unfinished graph.

2. What numbers will you use? Write them below the graph.

3. Draw the bars in the graph.

Number of Shoes Sold

Size	Tally	Number
$5-5\frac{1}{2}$	//// //// //// ////	20
$6-6\frac{1}{2}$	//// //// //// //// //// //// //// //// //// //// //// ////	60
$7-7\frac{1}{2}$	//// //// //// //// //// //// //// ////	40
$8-8\frac{1}{2}$	//// //// //// //// //// //// //// //// //// ////	50

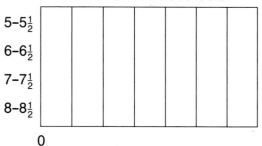

Number of Shoes Sold

500

Set D pages 488–489

Name the building located at
each number pair.

1. (2, 2)   **2.** (1, 4)   **3.** (4, 1)

Write the number pair for each
corner.

4. Ash Rd., Oak St.   **5.** Elm St.,
                                        Red Rd.

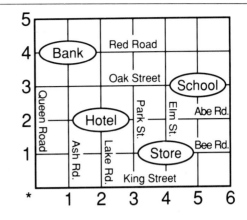

Set E pages 490–491

Tell whether you think each event is
certain, possible, or impossible.

1. The sun will set in the west.

2. You will grow to 6 feet tall.

3. It will snow in Chicago on
February 12.

4. The sun will set in the east.

Set F pages 492–493

Use the spinner at the right.

1. List all the possible outcomes
for the spinner.

2. Are the outcomes equally likely?

Which is more likely,
3. to spin a 1 or a 2?   **4.** to spin a 3 or a 4?

Set G pages 494–495

Use the spinner at the right.

1. Do you have an equal chance to
spin a 4 or a 2?

2. Are you more likely to spin a 3 than a 1?

3. How many times do you think
you would get a 4 in 8 spins?

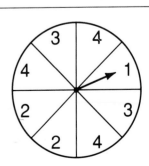

Enrichment

Number Cube Game

Each cube has the numbers from 1 to
6. Roll two number cubes like these.
Add the numbers you get.

What is the least sum you could get?
What is the greatest sum you could get?

If you rolled the cubes 40 times, what sum
do you think you would get most often?

Do the experiment. Record the sums
in a grid like the one shown. Every
time you get a sum, put an X in a
box above that number. This kind
of graph is called a **line plot.**

Sums from Two Number Cubes

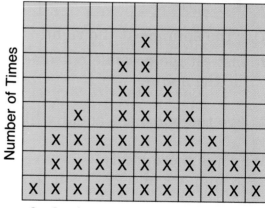

Number of Times

Sums of Numbers

1. What sum is shown
most often in the line
plot?
2. What sum is shown
least often in the line
plot?
3. What sums did you
get most often in
your 40 rolls?

4. What sums did you get
least often in your
40 rolls?

5. List all the combinations of
numbers that could give a
sum of 2.

6. List all the combinations of
numbers that could give a
sum of 7.

7. Explain why certain sums
come up more often than
others.

Chapter 14 Review/Test

Write two questions to help you gather the necessary data.

1. Your class is going on a roller-skating party. How many pairs of skates will the class need to rent?

Weather in April

Sunny	☼ ☼ ☼ ☼ ☼
Rainy	☁ ☁ ☁
Cloudy	☁ ☁

Each picture means 3 days.

2. How many more sunny days than cloudy days were there in April?

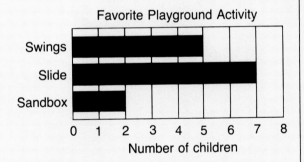

Favorite Playground Activity

Swings · Slide · Sandbox

0 1 2 3 4 5 6 7 8
Number of children

3. How many more children chose the swings than the sandbox as their favorite?

4. What letter is at (3, 2)?

5. Give the number pair for A.

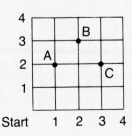

6. Tell whether it is certain, possible, or impossible for you to be 25 years old next year.

7. A jar of nuts contains many more almonds than peanuts. Which outcome is more likely?

   a. To pick an almond
   b. To pick a peanut
   c. To pick a raisin

8. Suppose a jar has 5 pink plastic chips in it, 2 orange, and 7 purple. If you pick one chip, are you more likely to get a purple chip or an orange chip?

9. Make a tally chart for the information in Item 8.

10. Look at the graph in Item 3. The seesaw was the favorite activity of 4 other children. How could you show this on the graph?

    a. Change the numbers to read 0–16.
    b. Draw 4 seesaws.
    c. Add a bar for seesaw.

11. ■ **Write About Math**
    Explain how you found the number pair for Item 5.

Division Computation

15

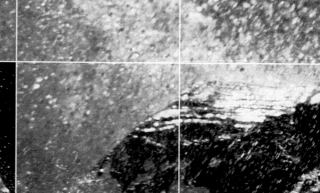
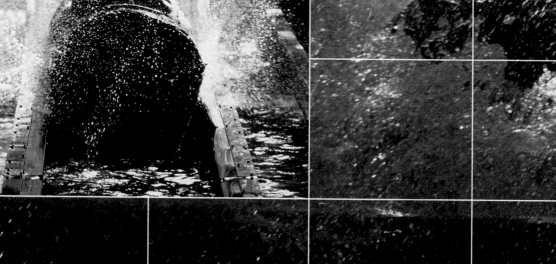

Number-Sense Project

Estimate
Predict how many in your class would want to ride the Log Ride.

Gather Data
Take a poll in your class to see how many would like to ride the Log Ride.

Analyze and Report
Total the results. Then compare the results to your prediction.

Sharing Money

Build Understanding

Dividing It Up
Materials: Play money
Groups: 3–5 students

Frank, Juan, and Ted received $42. They want to share the money equally. How much money will each boy get?

a. Use your play money to show how much the boys received.

b. Put the ten-dollar bills into three groups.

c. How many ten-dollar bills are in each group? Are there any left over? Trade the extra ten-dollar bill for 10 one-dollar bills.

d. How many dollar bills are there to share? Divide the dollar bills among the three groups.

e. Count the money in each group. There are 1 ten-dollar bill and 4 dollar bills in each group.

Each boy will get $14.

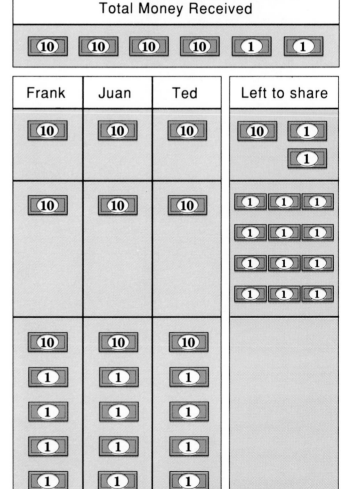

Total Money Received			
(10) (10) (10) (10) (1) (1)			

Frank	Juan	Ted	Left to share
(10)	(10)	(10)	(10) (1) (1)
(10)	(10)	(10)	(1)(1)(1) (1)(1)(1) (1)(1)(1) (1)(1)(1)
(10) (1) (1) (1) (1)	(10) (1) (1) (1) (1)	(10) (1) (1) (1) (1)	

■ **Talk About Math**   Why is it necessary to trade
the leftover ten-dollar bill for dollar bills?

Check Understanding

For another example, see Set A, pages 526–527.

Use play money to divide $48 into 4 equal groups.

1. How many $10 bills and $1 bills will you use?

2. How many equal groups will you make?

3. Divide the play money into equal groups. How much money is in each group?

4. Was a trade necessary to solve this problem? Why or why not?

Practice

For More Practice, see Set A, pages 528–529.

Use play money to divide each amount of money into equal groups. Draw a picture to show your answer. Then write how much is in each group.

5. $28 into 2 equal groups

6. $60 into 5 equal groups

7. $63 into 3 equal groups

8. $75 into 5 equal groups

9. $56 into 4 equal groups

10. $39 into 3 equal groups

11. $55 into 5 equal groups

12. $64 into 4 equal groups

Problem Solving

Solve each problem.

13. The 3 boys decided to buy a croquet set for $45. Each boy will pay the same amount. How much will each boy pay?

14. Together, the boys earned $14 on Monday, $12 on Thursday, and $25 on Saturday. How much did they earn in all?

Missing Factors

Build Understanding

The Fit-N-Fun Club is buying oranges.
Each basket has 6 oranges. How many
baskets must they buy to have 66 oranges?

Missing Factor		Factor		Product
▦	×	**6**	=	**66**
Baskets		Oranges in each basket		Oranges in all

Think about related multiplication and
division sentences for ▦ × 6 = 66.

▦ × 6 = 66   66 ÷ ▦ = 6

6 × ▦ = 66   66 ÷ 6 = ▦

Find 66 ÷ 6. You can use repeated
subtraction to find the missing factor.

As each basket is put into the cart,
you can subtract 6 from the number
still needed.

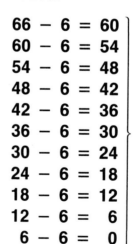

$$66 - 6 = 60$$
$$60 - 6 = 54$$
$$54 - 6 = 48$$
$$48 - 6 = 42$$
$$42 - 6 = 36$$
$$36 - 6 = 30$$
$$30 - 6 = 24$$
$$24 - 6 = 18$$
$$18 - 6 = 12$$
$$12 - 6 = 6$$
$$6 - 6 = 0$$

Since you subtracted
six 11 times, 11 is the
missing factor.
6 × 11 = 66 and
66 ÷ 6 = 11

A 9-year-old should be able to run a mile
in less than 10 minutes.

The club should buy 11 baskets
of oranges.

■ **Talk About Math**   Tell how you can use multiplication to check division.

Check Understanding

For another example, see Set B, pages 526–527.

Match each multiplication sentence with the related division sentence. Then give each missing factor.

1. ▦ × 4 = 72   **2.** 6 × ▦ = 78

a. 78 ÷ 6 = 13	**b.** 72 ÷ 4 = 18

Practice

For More Practice, see Set B, pages 528–529.

Match each multiplication sentence with the related division sentence. Then give the missing factor.

3. ▦ × 9 = 144   **4.** 4 × ▦ = 160

5. 5 × ▦ = 160   **6.** 3 × ▦ = 144

7. ▦ × 4 = 144   **8.** 2 × ▦ = 160

9. 7 × ▦ = 448   **10.** ▦ × 8 = 448

a. 144 ÷ 3 = 48	**b.** 144 ÷ 4 = 36
c. 144 ÷ 9 = 16	**d.** 160 ÷ 2 = 80
e. 160 ÷ 4 = 40	**f.** 160 ÷ 5 = 32
g. 448 ÷ 7 = 64	**h.** 448 ÷ 8 = 56

Problem Solving

Solve the problem.

11. The club is going to spend $60 for jump ropes. One kind costs $3, and another kind costs $4. How many more $3 jump ropes can they buy than $4 jump ropes?

TIPS FOR PROBLEM SOLVERS

Be flexible. If you get stuck, try another idea.

$4.00

$3.00

509

Remainders When Sharing Money

Build Understanding

What's Left?
Materials: Play money
Groups: 3–5 students

Joy, Mary, and Barbara want to share $40 equally.
How much money should each receive?

Use play money to find $40 ÷ 3.

a. Divide the $10 bills.

b. Trade the leftover $10 bill for ten $1 bills.

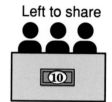

c. Divide the $1 bills.

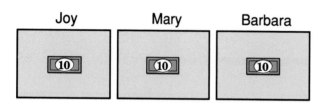

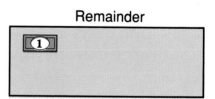

Each girl should get $13. There is $1 left over.

■ **Talk About Math** What might the girls do
with the leftover $1?

Check Understanding

For another example, see Set C, pages 526–527.

Find $59 ÷ 4. Use play money to help you.

1. How many $10 bills and $1 bills will you use?

2. How many equal groups will you make?

3. How many $10 bills will there be in each of the 4 groups?

4. Do you need to make a trade? Why or why not?

5. How many $1 bills will be in each of the 4 groups?

6. Do you have any $1 bills left over? If so, how many?

7. What answer did you record?

Practice

For More Practice, see Set C, pages 528–529.

Tell how much money is in each group and how much is left over. Use play money.

8. $46 into 4 equal groups

9. $35 into 3 equal groups

10. $68 into 6 equal groups

11. $33 into 2 equal groups

12. $56 into 5 equal groups

13. $52 into 4 equal groups

14. $53 into 4 equal groups

15. $54 into 4 equal groups

16. $55 into 4 equal groups

Problem Solving

Number Sense Find a pattern in the quotients and remainders for Exercises 13–16. Use the pattern to tell what the quotient and remainders will be.

17. $56 \div 4$ **18.** $57 \div 4$ **19.** $58 \div 4$ **20.** $59 \div 4$ **21.** $60 \div 4$

22. Each of the 3 girls paid $15 to buy tickets to a professional baseball game. How much did they pay in all?

23. Critical Thinking Joy and Mary put some $1 bills into stacks of 2. How many dollar bills could they have left over?

Explore ———— Math

For each of Exercises 24–28, find the sum of the digits of each dollar amount.

24. $24   **25.** $75   **26.** $45   **27.** $78   **28.** $30

29. By what one number can you evenly divide each of the sums in Exercises 24–28?

30. Use your play money to divide each amount of money in Exercises 24–28 by the number you found in Exercise 29.

31. When the sum of the digits of a number can be divided evenly by 3, by what number can you divide the entire number?

Tell which numbers can be evenly divided by 3. Do not actually divide.

32. 174   **33.** 255   **34.** 93   **35.** 1,792   **36.** 455

37. 1,796   **38.** 1,782   **39.** 3,875   **40.** 4,944   **41.** 8,145

In all answers when needed, R will be used to stand for remainder.

Find each answer. **Remember** to rename if necessary.

1. 41 × 5   **2.** 81 + 97   **3.** 64 ÷ 8   **4.** 28 − 19

5. 0 ÷ 3   **6.** 2,076 + 1,348   **7.** 160 − 74   **8.** 4 × 3

9. 12 × 5   **10.** 15 + 8   **11.** 101 − 40   **12.** 56 ÷ 7

13. 9 − 9   **14.** 35 × 2   **15.** 24 ÷ 3   **16.** 6,019 + 7,834

17. 182 − 97   **18.** 36 ÷ 4   **19.** 4 + 5   **20.** 1 × 38

Tell what fraction of the

21. birds are yellow.

22. plants have flowers.

23. cars are blue.

24. girls have red hair.

What fraction names the shaded part?

25.

26.

27.

513

Interpret the Remainder

Build Understanding

PROBLEM SOLVING
GUIDE

Understand
QUESTION
FACTS
KEY IDEA

Plan and Solve
STRATEGY
ANSWER

Look Back
SENSIBLE ANSWER
ALTERNATE APPROACH

Jani runs the Super Looper. If each car holds 4 riders, how many cars will be needed to be sure that all 54 people get to ride?

Understand   One car is needed for each group of 4 or fewer riders.

Plan and Solve   STRATEGY   Divide 54 by 4 by making groups of 4. If there is a remainder, there will be one more group.

There are 13 groups of 4 with a remainder of 2. $54 \div 4 = 13$, remainder 2

ANSWER   For every person to ride, there must be 14 cars.

Look Back   Use multiplication.
$13 \times 4 = 52$
$14 \times 4 = 56$
Since there are 54 people, 14 cars are needed.

■ **Talk About Math**   Do you always use the remainder? For example, how many $2 tickets could a person buy if she has $25?
$25 \div 2 = 12$, remainder 1

Check Understanding

To solve Problems 1–2, you need to divide 56 by 3. Use the fact that 56 ÷ 3 = 18, remainder 2 to tell whether the answer is 18 or 19 for each problem. Explain why you chose the number you did.

1. How many $3 rides can Angela buy for $56?

2. How many 3-packs of tickets should Mariel buy if she needs 56 tickets?

Practice

Solve each problem.

3. Some students want to buy balloons for $5 each. How many can they buy if they have $56? [56 ÷ 5 = 11, remainder 1]

4. How much money will the students in Problem 3 have left over? [56 ÷ 5 = 11, remainder 1]

5. There is a guide for every 7 students at the amusement park. How many guides are there for the 93 students?
[93 ÷ 7 = 13, remainder 2]

6. The ticket office offers 1 free ticket with every 5 you buy. LaToya bought 32 tickets. How many free tickets did she get? [32 ÷ 5 = 6, remainder 2]

Midchapter  Checkup

Draw pictures to help you find each answer.
1. 22 ÷ 2   **2.** 42 ÷ 3   **3.** 31 ÷ 2   **4.** 34 ÷ 3

Mental Math   Use the chart to help find each missing factor.
5. ▦ × 4 = 64   **6.** 5 × ▦ = 50

| **a.** 64 ÷ 4 = 16   **b.** 50 ÷ 5 = 10 |

Solve the problem.
7. How many $4 books can Leigh buy for $62?
[62 ÷ 4 = 15, remainder 2]

Problem Solving WORKSHOP

Math-at-Home Activity

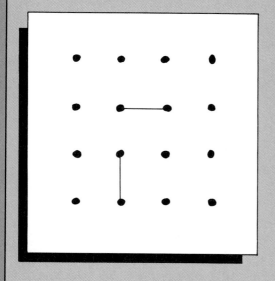

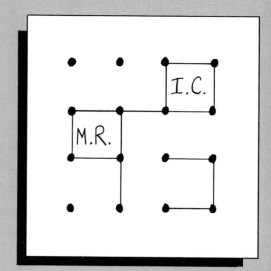

Play *Complete the Most Squares* with someone at home. Draw 16 dots; 4 rows with 4 dots in each row. The first player connects two dots drawing straight up or across. Take turns drawing a line segment to connect two dots.

When your line segment completes a square, write your initials in the square.

After all line segments have been drawn, count your initialed squares. The winner is the player who completes the most squares.

Math Laugh
If you take 3 apples from 12 apples what do you have?

ANSWER: You have three apples.

Number-Sense Project

Look back at pages 504-505.
A book of ride tickets costs $40.00. A class of students bought 6 books.

1. How much did 6 books cost?

2. If 5 students shared one book equally, how much did each student pay?

3. If there were 40 tickets in each book, how much did each ticket cost? On how many rides could each student go?

4. How many students were in the class?

Explore as a Team

1. Make a rectangle with 24 squares.

2. How many rectangles can you make with an area of 24 squares? Record them on square grid paper.

3. Is the perimeter always the same?

Remember: Perimeter is the distance around.

TIPS FOR
WORKING TOGETHER

Involve your whole group.
Help everyone to participate.

Recording Division

Build Understanding

Planning Purchases
Materials: Play money
Groups: 3–5 students

A. Todd wants to spend the same amount of money for each of 3 birthday presents. He has saved $42. How much can he spend for each present? Divide 42 into 3 equal groups.

a. Divide the $10 bills.

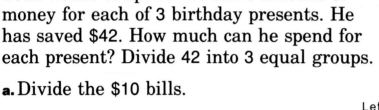

Left to share

b. Record what you did.

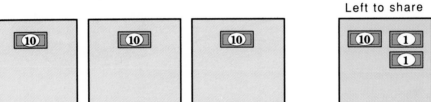

$10 bills | $1 bills

  1
3)4 | 2

1 $10 bill each

3 $10 bills shared

1 $10 bill left

c. Trade the leftover $10 bill for ten $1 bills and record.

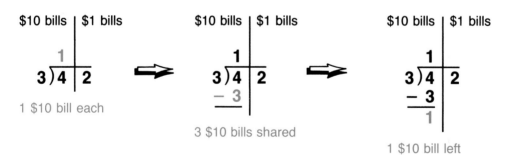

Left to share

$10 bills | $1 bills

  1
3)4 | 2
− 3
  1 | 2

12 $1 bills to share

d. Divide the $1 bills.

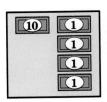

e. Record what you did.

$10 bills | $1 bills

```
      1 | 4
  3)4 | 2
  - 3 |
      1 | 2
```

⟹

$10 bills | $1 bills

```
      1 | 4
  3)4 | 2
  - 3 |
      1 | 2
      - 1 | 2
          | 0
```

4 $1 bills each

12 $1 bills shared

Todd can spend $14 for each birthday present.

B. Use play money to divide 51 into 4 equal groups and record.

Remainder

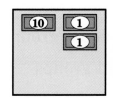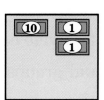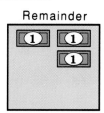

a. Divide the $10 bills.

b. Trade the leftover $10 bill.

c. Divide the $1 bills.

d. Tell the number of $1 bills left over.

$10 bills | $1 bills

```
      1 | 2
  4)5 | 1
  - 4 |
      1 | 1
  - 0 | 8
      | 3
```

12 in each group, remainder 3

■ **Talk About Math** When you divide a two-digit number by a one-digit number, how can you tell if your quotient will be less than or greater than $10?

519

Check Understanding

For another example, see Set D, pages 526–527.

Find $72 ÷ 3. You can use play money. Record each step.

1. How many $10 bills and $1 bills will you use?

2. How many equal groups will you make?

3. How many $10 bills will there be in each of the 3 groups?

4. Do you need to make a trade before you can find how many $1 bills will be in each of the 3 groups? Explain.

5. How many $1 bills will be in each of the 3 groups?

6. What answer did you record?

Use play money to divide each amount of money into equal groups. Record your work.

7. $34 into 3 equal groups

8. $52 into 4 equal groups

9. $72 ÷ 6   **10.** $67 ÷ 5   **11.** $92 ÷ 4   **12.** $25 ÷ 2

Practice

For More Practice, see Set D, pages 528–529.

Use play money to divide each amount of money into equal groups.

13. $56 into 4 equal groups

14. $56 into 5 equal groups

15. $66 into 3 equal groups

16. $66 into 4 equal groups

17. $75 ÷ 5   **18.** $43 ÷ 2   **19.** $78 ÷ 6   **20.** $82 ÷ 7

21. $41 ÷ 5   **22.** $91 ÷ 7   **23.** $54 ÷ 2   **24.** $83 ÷ 4

Mixed Practice Use paper and pencil or mental math to find each answer. Tell which method you used.

25. 3 × 9   **26.** 53 ÷ 6   **27.** 16 × 8   **28.** 18 ÷ 3   **29.** 22 ÷ 4

30. 12 ÷ 2   **31.** 7 × 48   **32.** 22 ÷ 5   **33.** 3 × 27   **34.** 72 ÷ 8

Problem Solving

Solve each problem.

35. Sela spent an equal amount of money on each of 4 presents. She had $92 to spend. How much money did she spend for each present?

36.  **Calculator** Suppose you went to the bank to get quarters for 375 pennies. How many quarters would you get?

37. Critical Thinking Find amounts less than $20 that cannot be shared equally among 4 students. Describe the pattern you see.

38. Estimation Look at Exercises 17–24. Without dividing, how can you tell when a quotient will be greater than 10?

39. Use Data Ms. Sarat can pay for the dress shown on page 89 in equal monthly payments. How much will Ms. Sarat have to pay each month if she wants to pay it off in 2 months? 3 months? 4 months? 5 months? 6 months?

Reading ———— Math

Numbers and Symbols Match the number sentence with its description.

1. The divisor is 7 and the dividend is 28.

2. One factor is 4 and the product is 28.

3. One addend is 7 and the sum is 28.

a. 7 + 21 = 28
b. 7 × 4 = 28
c. 28 − 7 = 21
d. 28 ÷ 7 = 4

Choose an Operation

PROBLEM SOLVING
GUIDE

Understand
QUESTION
FACTS
KEY IDEA

▶ **Plan and Solve**
STRATEGY
ANSWER

Look Back
SENSIBLE ANSWER
ALTERNATE APPROACH

Build Understanding

Ramona gave $64 to the
4 workers who did her gardening.
They shared the money equally.
How much did each worker get?

Understand   The workers needed to
divide the money into
4 equal groups.

 **Plan
and Solve**

STRATEGY   Divide 64 by 4.

```
$10 bills | $1 bills
       1  |  6
   4 ) 6  |  4
     - 4  |
       2  |  4
     - 2  |  4
          |  0
```

ANSWER   Each worker
received $16.

Look Back $4 \times 16 = 64$, so $64 \div 4 = 16$.
$16 is correct.

■ **Talk About Math**   How could drawing a
picture help you decide whether to use
addition, subtraction, multiplication, or
division?

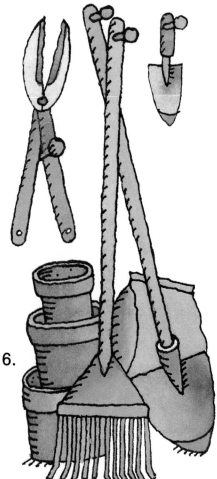

What would you grow
in a garden?

Check Understanding

Solve this problem by answering Questions 1–4.

The workers were paid $64 each week for 5 weeks. How much did they earn in all?

1. How much do the workers make each week?

2. How many weeks did they work?

3. What operation helps you find how much they made in all?

4. How much did the workers make in 5 weeks?

Practice

Tell whether you should *add, subtract, multiply,* or *divide.* Then find the answer.

5. The workers made $64 in 2 hours. How much were they paid for each hour?

6. If 54 flowers were planted equally in 6 beds, how many were planted in each bed?

7. Of 32 bushes, the workers were able to trim 16 of them on Monday. How many were left to trim?

8. Ramona paid $3.49 for each of 3 rose bushes and $7.98 for each of 2 lilac bushes. How much did she pay in all?

 Choose a _____ Strategy

9. ***Baseball Puzzler*** Fred gave Tom half of his baseball cards. Tom gave Nan half of the cards that he got from Fred. Nan gave Sam half of the cards that she got from Tom. Sam got 6 cards. How many cards did Fred have at the start?

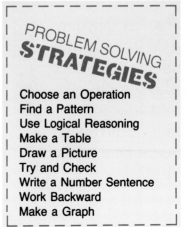

PROBLEM SOLVING STRATEGIES

Choose an Operation
Find a Pattern
Use Logical Reasoning
Make a Table
Draw a Picture
Try and Check
Write a Number Sentence
Work Backward
Make a Graph

Solve each problem.

1. If you have 2 blue pencils and 2 red pencils in a drawer, do you have an equal chance of getting either color if you grab one without looking?

2. Find the cost of 6 T-shirts.

3. Find the cost of 2 hats, 3 pins, and 1 T-shirt.

4. One hundred packs of stickers are on each rack. There are 13 racks. How many packs are there in all?

5. A teacher hid 75 items. Nine students took part in the search. About how many items would each student be expected to find?

6. It's moving day at the Mendoza's house. A special packing box can hold 8 glasses or cups. How many boxes are needed for 72 glasses and cups?

7. **Data File** Use data from pages 532-533. Karen wants to make half of the party cocoa recipe. Find the number of cups of milk and the number of marshmallows she needs.

8. **Make a Data File** Find 5 different types of numerical data about a newspaper, such as cost, number of sections, year it was founded, date of issue, and so on. Make a list to compare with your classmates.

Explore with a Calculator

Divide and Conquer!

To be a good detective, you need to make sense out of clues. Sometimes you need to work backward or do things in different order.

1. Working backward should help you find the starting number for each of these exercises.

a. ■ ÷ 6 = 5   b. ■ ÷ 7 = 7

c. ■ ÷ 3 = 12   d. ■ ÷ 8 = 10

e. ■ ÷ 8 = 40   f. ■ ÷ 4 = 15

g. ■ ÷ 2 = 11   h. ■ ÷ 9 = 12

2. Working backward and putting things in different order may help you find the mystery numbers.

CLUE CARD

a. We are two numbers. When you add us, the sum is 24. Divide one of us by the other, the quotient is 7. Who are we?

CLUE CARD

b. We are two numbers. Our sum is 30. Divide one of us by the other, the quotient is 4. Who are we?

CLUE CARD

c. We are two numbers. Our product is 75. Divide one of us by the other, the quotient is 3. Who are we?

Reteaching

Set A   pages 506–507

Divide $45 into 3 equal groups.

| $10 | $10 | $1 | $1 | $1 |
| $10 | $10 | $1 | $1 |

Put the ten-dollar bills into
3 groups.

| $10 | $10 | $10 | Left over: | $10 |

Trade the leftover $10 for
10 one-dollar bills. There are
now 15 dollar bills to share.
Divide the dollar bills among the
3 groups.

$10	$1		$10	$1		$10	$1
$1		$1		$1
$1		$1		$1
$1		$1		$1
$1		$1		$1

There is $15 in each group.

Remember that sharing money
means dividing the money into
equal groups.

Use play money to divide each
amount of money into equal
groups. Draw a picture to show
your answer. Then write how
much is in each group.

1. $26 into 2 equal groups

2. $40 into 5 equal groups

3. $65 into 5 equal groups

4. $48 into 4 equal groups

5. $36 into 3 equal groups

Set B   pages 508–509

Find the missing factor.

$$\text{▦} \times 8 = 48$$

Think about related division
and multiplication sentences.

| $\text{▦} \times 8 = 48$ | $48 \div \text{▦} = 8$ |
| $8 \times \text{▦} = 48$ | $48 \div 8 = \text{▦}$ |

Find $48 \div 8$. To find the missing
factor use repeated subtraction.

$48 - 8 = 40$	$24 - 8 = 16$
$40 - 8 = 32$	$16 - 8 = 8$
$32 - 8 = 24$	$8 - 8 = 0$

You subtracted 6 times. So 6 is
the missing factor.

$$6 \times 8 = 48 \text{ and } 48 \div 8 = 6.$$

Remember that you can use
repeated subtraction to solve a
division problem.

Match each multiplication with
the related division sentence.
Then give the missing factor.

1. $\text{▦} \times 8 = 120$ | **a.** $144 \div 6 = 24$

2. $\text{▦} \times 6 = 144$ | **b.** $144 \div 8 = 18$

3. $5 \times \text{▦} = 120$ | **c.** $120 \div 6 = 20$

4. $6 \times \text{▦} = 120$ | **d.** $120 \div 5 = 24$

5. $\text{▦} \times 8 = 144$ | **e.** $120 \div 8 = 15$

Set C pages 510–512

Find $50 ÷ 4.
Divide $50 into 4 equal groups.

a. Divide the $10 bills.

| $10 | | $10 | | $10 | Left: | $10 |

b. Trade the leftover $10 bill for ten $1 bills.

$10 → | $1 | | $1 | | $1 | | $1 | | $1 |
| $1 | | $1 | | $1 | | $1 | | $1 |

c. Divide the $1 bills among the 4 groups.

Remainder: | $1 | | $1 |

Each group has $12. There is $2 left over.

Remember that you can trade a $1 bill for ten dimes or 100 pennies.

Tell how many in each group and how many left over. Use play money.

1. $34 into 3 equal groups

2. $38 into 3 equal groups

3. $34 into 2 equal groups

4. $38 into 2 equal groups

5. $43 into 4 equal groups

6. $43 into 3 equal groups

Set D pages 518–521

Divide $41 into 3 equal groups and record.

| $10 | | $10 | | $10 | | $10 | | $1 |

$10		$1		$10		$1		$10		$1
	$1			$1			$1
	$1			$1			$1

Remainder: | $1 | | $1 |

a. Divide the $10 bills.
b. Trade the leftover $10.
c. Divide the $1 bills.
d. Tell the number of $2 bills left over.

```
        $10 bills │ $1 bills
            1     │   3
       3)    4    │   1
           − 3    │
            1     │   1
          −       │ − 0   9
                  │   2
```

13 in each group, remainder 2

Remember that if the first digit of the dividend is greater than the divisor, the quotient will be greater than $10.

Use play money to divide each amount of money into equal groups.

1. $48 into 4 equal groups

2. $48 into 5 equal groups

3. $48 into 7 equal groups

4. $55 ÷ 5   **5.** $25 ÷ 2

6. $25 ÷ 3   **7.** $72 ÷ 8

8. $61 ÷ 5   **9.** $73 ÷ 4

More Practice

Set A pages 506–507

Use play money to divide each amount of money into equal groups. Draw a picture to show your answer. Then write how much in each group.

1. $24 into 2 equal groups

2. $24 into 3 equal groups

3. $24 into 4 equal groups

4. $24 into 6 equal groups

5. $21 into 3 equal groups

6. $21 into 7 equal groups

7. $70 into 5 equal groups

8. $36 into 4 equal groups

9. $36 into 3 equal groups

10. $48 into 3 equal groups

11. $48 into 4 equal groups

12. $48 into 6 equal groups

13. $60 into 4 equal groups

14. $60 into 6 equal groups

Set B pages 508–509

Match each multiplication with the related division sentence. Then give the missing factor. Match Exercises 1–8 with a–h. Match Exercises 9–14 with i–n.

1. ▦ × 9 = 180

2. 5 × ▦ = 180

3. 4 × ▦ = 156

4. ▦ × 6 = 156

5. 6 × ▦ = 180

6. ▦ × 4 = 180

7. 3 × ▦ = 156

8. 2 × ▦ = 156

a. 180 ÷ 6 = 30 **b.** 180 ÷ 4 = 45

c. 156 ÷ 3 = 52 **d.** 180 ÷ 9 = 20

e. 156 ÷ 4 = 39 **f.** 156 ÷ 2 = 78

g. 180 ÷ 5 = 36 **h.** 156 ÷ 6 = 26

9. ▦ × 6 = 216

10. 2 × ▦ = 180

11. 3 × ▦ = 180

12. 3 × ▦ = 216

13. ▦ × 4 = 216

14. ▦ × 8 = 216

i. 180 ÷ 3 = 60 **j.** 216 ÷ 3 = 72

k. 216 ÷ 6 = 36 **l.** 180 ÷ 2 = 90

m. 216 ÷ 8 = 27 **n.** 216 ÷ 4 = 54

Set C pages 510–512

Tell how many in each group and how many
left over. Use play money.

1. $32 into 3 equal groups

2. $37 into 3 equal groups

3. $37 into 2 equal groups

4. $64 into 6 equal groups

5. $59 into 5 equal groups

6. $59 into 4 equal groups

7. $57 into 4 equal groups

8. $64 into 5 equal groups

9. $63 into 5 equal groups

10. $23 into 2 equal groups

11. $47 into 3 equal groups

12. $46 into 5 equal groups

13. $39 into 2 equal groups

14. $31 into 6 equal groups

15. $64 into 5 equal groups

16. $28 into 3 equal groups

17. $52 into 3 equal groups

18. $69 into 6 equal groups

Set D pages 518–521

Use play money to divide each amount of
money into equal groups.

1. $52 into 4 equal groups

2. $52 into 5 equal groups

3. $63 into 3 equal groups

4. $63 into 4 equal groups

5. $65 ÷ 5

6. $31 ÷ 2

7. $72 ÷ 6

8. $78 ÷ 7

9. $65 ÷ 4

10. $47 ÷ 5

11. $97 ÷ 7

12. $87 ÷ 4

Mixed Practice Use paper and pencil or
mental math to find each answer. Tell which
method you used.

13. 4×7

14. $44 \div 7$

15. 15×9

16. $42 \div 6$

17. $31 \div 5$

18. $18 \div 3$

19. 8×43

20. $27 \div 4$

21. 4×29

22. $63 \div 9$

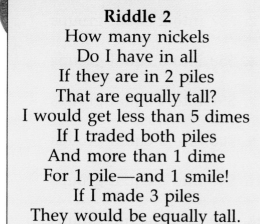

Enrichment

Riddle Rhyme

Riddle 1
Less than sixty pennies
I have in all.
They are in 5 piles
That are equally tall.
I can trade in one pile
And get less than a dime.
But more than a nickel
All of the time.
If I now made 7 piles
They would be equally tall.
Tell me how many pennies
Do I really have in all?

Riddle 2
How many nickels
Do I have in all
If they are in 2 piles
That are equally tall?
I would get less than 5 dimes
If I traded both piles
And more than 1 dime
For 1 pile—and 1 smile!
If I made 3 piles
They would be equally tall.
Tell me how many nickels
Do I have in all?

Answer Questions 1–4 to find the solution
to Riddle 1.

1. Read the first four lines of
   the riddle. Which amounts of
   money are possible?

2. Which amounts of money can
   you eliminate after reading
   the fifth and sixth lines?

3. Which amounts of money can
   you eliminate after reading
   the seventh and eighth lines?

4. Read the rest of the lines
   and solve the riddle. Give
   your answer.

5. Use a similar procedure to solve
   Riddle 2. Give your answer.

Chapter 15 Review/Test

Draw a picture to show how to divide.

1. $36 into 3 equal groups

2. $50 into 5 equal groups

Choose the division sentence for each multiplication sentence. Then give the missing factor.

3. $7 \times \text{▦} = 84$
  a. $84 \div 6 = 14$
  b. $84 \div 7 = 12$

4. $\text{▦} \times 32 = 96$
  a. $96 \div 3 = 32$
  b. $96 \div 6 = 13$

5. $8 \times \text{▦} = 128$
  a. $128 \div 8 = 16$
  b. $128 \div 4 = 32$

Tell how many are in each group and how many are left over. Draw pictures to help you.

6. $80 into 7 equal groups

7. $74 into 4 equal groups

8. $57 into 2 equal groups

9. Each ride at the carnival uses 4 tickets. A ticket book has 50 tickets. How many rides can the Lee family take with 1 book of tickets?

Use this exercise to answer Items 10–13. Draw pictures to help you.

$10 bills	$1 bills
6$\overline{)9}$	3

When $93 is divided into 6 equal groups, how many

10. $10 bills will there be?

11. $1 bills will there be?

12. $1 bills will be left over?

13. Did you need to trade any $10 bills for $1 bills?

14. Draw pictures to divide $75 into 3 equal groups.

Read this problem. Then answer the questions below.

Stan collected 18 tree leaves. He mounted 2 leaves on each page of an album. How many pages did he use?

15. Would you multiply or divide to solve the problem?

16. Solve the problem.

17. ■ **Write About Math** Explain what it means to divide.

1. Train Schedule
Find the city in which you start. Look across the row to find the time you want to leave. Look down that column to find the time the train arrives at the station you want.

2. Menu
This is the children's menu.

3. Bar Graph
The graph shows how many people attend the movies each day.

4. Recipe
Be careful when using the stove.

5. Toll Charges
The chart tells how long each toll road is and the cost to travel on each.

	Train 022	Train 026	Train 028	Train 034	Train 036
	AM	AM	AM	AM	AM
San Francisco	4:50	6:00	6:30	8:00	10:00
San Bruno	5:11	6:21	6:51	8:21	10:19
Broadway	5:18	6:28	6:58	8:28	10:26
Hillsdale	5:30	6:39	7:09	8:39	10:37
Redwood City	5:39	6:49	7:19	8:49	10:47
Menlo Park	5:46	6:57	7:26	8:56	10:53
Sunnyvale	6:02	7:13	7:43	9:12	11:09
San Jose	6:18	7:30	8:00	9:28	11:25

1. Train Schedule

2. Restaurant Menu

MENU

BURGER
Served with fries.
$3.50

GRILLED CHEESE
Served with fries.
$2.95

SPAGHETTI
Served with bread.
$2.95

JR. TURKEY OR HAM SANDWICH
Served with fries.
$3.65

CHICKEN FINGERS
Served with fries.
$4.50

JR. SALAD
$2.95

ROAST CHICKEN
Served with veggies and fries.
$4.50

BBQ RIBS
Served with veggies and fries.
$4.50

A bakery treat will be served with each meal, as well.

BEVERAGES 50¢

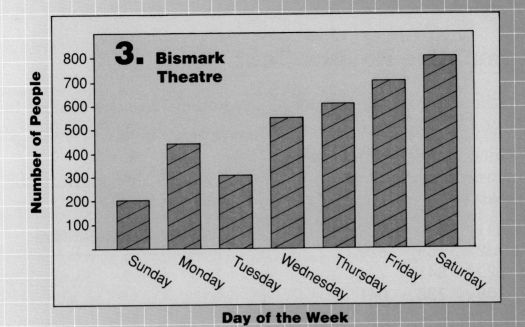

3. Bismark Theatre

(Bar graph: Number of People vs. Day of the Week)

Sunday, Monday, Tuesday, Wednesday, Thursday, Friday, Saturday

---

Party Cocoa

4. Recipe for Making Party Cocoa

18 servings

1 cup cocoa	2 cups water
1 cup sugar	12 cups milk
pinch of salt	18 marshmallows

1. Measure cocoa, sugar, salt, and water into saucepan.
2. Bring to a boil over medium heat.
3. Boil 2 minutes, stirring constantly.
4. Then pour in milk and heat again. *Do not boil.*
5. Pour into cups and top with a marshmallow before serving.

---

5. Kentucky Toll Road Information

Road Name	Miles	Auto Toll	Auto with Trailer
Audubon Parkway	23	$0.50	$1.10
Blue Grass Parkway	72	$1.30	$2.90
Cumberland Parkway	88.2	$2.00	$4.00
Daniel Boone Parkway	59.4	$1.40	$2.80
Green River Parkway	69.7	$1.50	$3.00
Pennyrile Parkway	60	$1.00	$2.30
Purchase Parkway	49	$0.90	$2.00

Cumulative Review/Test, Chapters 1–15

Give the letter for the correct answer.

1. Which numbers are written in order from least to greatest?

   A 641   629   758
   B 732   758   629
   C 629   641   732
   D 758   732   641

2. Add.

      672
    +187

  A 759
  B 859
  C 869
  D 485

3. Subtract.

      725
    −139

  A 616
  B 696
  C 694
  D 586

4. There are 8 dishes in each stack. There are 4 stacks. How many dishes are there in all?

   A 4   **B** 12   **C** 23   **D** 32

5. Multiply.

      13
    × 5

  A 55
  B 65
  C 18
  D 63

6. Multiply.

     137
   × 3

  A 391
  B 140
  C 411
  D 311

7. Round 73 to the nearest ten.

  A 70   **B** 80   **C** 75   **D** 60

8. What is the length to the nearest inch?

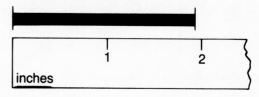

  A 1 inch   **C** 3 inches
  B 4 inches   **D** 2 inches

9. Which item should be measured in pounds?

  A a pencil   **C** a dog
  B a flower   **D** a spoon

10. Divide.

    20 ÷ 5

  A 7
  B 15
  C 25
  D 4

11. What fraction of the circles are shaded?

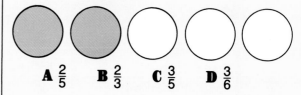

  A $\frac{2}{5}$ **B** $\frac{2}{3}$ **C** $\frac{3}{5}$ **D** $\frac{3}{6}$

12. Which decimal means the same as $\frac{39}{100}$?

  A 0.039   **C** 0.39
  B 39.0   **D** 3.9

13. What time is shown?

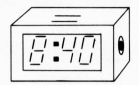

A 20 minutes after 8
B 20 minutes after 9
C 20 minutes before 8
D 20 minutes before 9

14. Find the amount of money.

2 quarters, 3 dimes, 6 pennies.

A $0.56   C $0.71
B $0.86   D $1.36

Study the graph. Then answer the question.

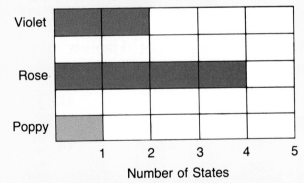

State Flowers

Number of States

15. How many states have the rose as the state flower?

A 1   B 2   C 3   D 4

16. How many 3-packs of tickets should Trina buy if she needs 47 tickets?

A 15   B 16   C 14   D 17

17. Decide whether you should *add, subtract, multiply,* or *divide.* Then find the answer.

Gardeners made $93 in 3 weeks. How much were they paid for each week?

A Add; $96
B Subtract; $90
C Multiply; $279
D Divide; $31

Read the problem. Then answer the question.

There are 20 students at 5 tables. On each table there are 10 pounds of clay. How many pounds of clay are there in all?

18. What is the key idea?

A There are 20 students at 5 tables, so you can divide.

B There are 10 pounds of clay on each of the 5 tables, so you can multiply.

C There are 10 pounds of clay for 20 students, so you can divide.

D There is a greater number of students than pounds of clay, so you can subtract.

Ordinal Numbers

Review

Ordinal numbers tell order and position.

A. Tell the position of B in ABLE. Use an ordinal number.

B is the 2nd letter in ABLE.

B. Ten people are in line ahead of Kaye. Use an ordinal number to tell Kaye's position in line.

Kaye is 11th in line.

Practice

Tell the position of the given letter in each word. Use an ordinal number.

1. E in END   **2.** M in ARM   **3.** I in MILK

4. B in NUMBER   **5.** H in MONTH   **6.** T in COMPUTER

Tell the position of the given letter in the alphabet. Use an ordinal number.

7. C   **8.** G   **9.** H   **10.** L   **11.** M   **12.** X

13. P   **14.** Z   **15.** U   **16.** A   **17.** R   **18.** T

19. D   **20.** N

Tell Ed's position in line. Use an ordinal number.

21. There are 3 people ahead of Ed.   **22.** There are 6 people ahead of Ed.

23. There are 9 people ahead of Ed.   **24.** There are 13 people ahead of Ed.

Addition Basic Facts

Review

Find 3 + 4.

Start with 3 objects.

Add 4 more.

4 5 6 7

$$3 + 4 = 7 \quad \text{or} \quad \begin{array}{r} 3 \leftarrow Addend \\ +4 \leftarrow Addend \\ \hline 7 \leftarrow Sum \end{array}$$

Practice

Add.

1. 8 +2	**2.** 5 +1	**3.** 5 +8	**4.** 7 +5	**5.** 9 +6	**6.** 6 +0
7. 2 +7	**8.** 6 +8	**9.** 7 +6	**10.** 4 +6	**11.** 4 +4	**12.** 9 +2
13. 3 +9	**14.** 8 +8	**15.** 1 +3	**16.** 6 +3	**17.** 7 +8	**18.** 8 +4

19. 6 + 5   **20.** 7 + 4   **21.** 3 + 5   **22.** 6 + 1

23. 9 + 4   **24.** 7 + 9   **25.** 2 + 4   **26.** 4 + 0

27. 5 + 2   **28.** 6 + 6   **29.** 5 + 6   **30.** 2 + 8

31. 7 + 5   **32.** 3 + 6   **33.** 1 + 4   **34.** 3 + 7

35. 6 + 7   **36.** 8 + 7   **37.** 3 + 7   **38.** 9 + 7

Subtraction Basic Facts

Review

Find 10 − 7.

Start with 10 objects.

Take away 7.

$$10 - 7 = 3 \quad \text{or} \quad \begin{array}{r} 10 \\ -7 \\ \hline 3 \end{array} \leftarrow \textit{Difference}$$

Practice

Subtract.

1. $\begin{array}{r} 7 \\ -6 \\ \hline \end{array}$	**2.** $\begin{array}{r} 9 \\ -3 \\ \hline \end{array}$	**3.** $\begin{array}{r} 14 \\ -7 \\ \hline \end{array}$	**4.** $\begin{array}{r} 12 \\ -4 \\ \hline \end{array}$	**5.** $\begin{array}{r} 11 \\ -6 \\ \hline \end{array}$	**6.** $\begin{array}{r} 5 \\ -3 \\ \hline \end{array}$
7. $\begin{array}{r} 6 \\ -5 \\ \hline \end{array}$	**8.** $\begin{array}{r} 9 \\ -4 \\ \hline \end{array}$	**9.** $\begin{array}{r} 10 \\ -8 \\ \hline \end{array}$	**10.** $\begin{array}{r} 18 \\ -9 \\ \hline \end{array}$	**11.** $\begin{array}{r} 11 \\ -6 \\ \hline \end{array}$	**12.** $\begin{array}{r} 16 \\ -7 \\ \hline \end{array}$
13. $\begin{array}{r} 10 \\ -2 \\ \hline \end{array}$	**14.** $\begin{array}{r} 9 \\ -8 \\ \hline \end{array}$	**15.** $\begin{array}{r} 8 \\ -0 \\ \hline \end{array}$	**16.** $\begin{array}{r} 10 \\ -9 \\ \hline \end{array}$	**17.** $\begin{array}{r} 6 \\ -6 \\ \hline \end{array}$	**18.** $\begin{array}{r} 12 \\ -7 \\ \hline \end{array}$

19. $11 - 4$ **20.** $11 - 7$ **21.** $5 - 2$ **22.** $10 - 1$

23. $12 - 9$ **24.** $7 - 7$ **25.** $12 - 3$ **26.** $13 - 6$

27. $8 - 5$ **28.** $9 - 1$ **29.** $9 - 5$ **30.** $8 - 6$

31. $6 - 0$ **32.** $10 - 4$ **33.** $17 - 8$ **34.** $15 - 9$

35. $9 - 8$ **36.** $4 - 4$ **37.** $9 - 7$ **38.** $16 - 9$

Whole Numbers Through Hundreds

Review

The standard form of the number three hundred fifty-seven is 357. The number has 3 digits.

hundreds	tens	ones
3	5	7

3 is the hundreds digit. 5 is the tens digit. 7 is the ones digit.

Practice

Write each number in standard form.

1. ninety-two

2. fourteen

3. forty-one

4. eighty-five

5. seven hundred twenty

6. four hundred fifty-six

7. one hundred sixty-three

8. five hundred fifty

Tell which digit is the hundreds digit.

9. 473 **10.** 216 **11.** 500 **12.** 795 **13.** 340 **14.** 827

15. 122 **16.** 601 **17.** 230 **18.** 961 **19.** 134 **20.** 785

Tell which digit is the tens digit.

21. 367 **22.** 710 **23.** 925 **24.** 846 **25.** 691 **26.** 182

Tell which digit is the ones digit.

27. 831 **28.** 547 **29.** 268 **30.** 674 **31.** 492 **32.** 920

Comparing Two-Digit Numbers

Review

A. Which number is greater, 27 or 46?
To compare two-digit numbers, first look at the tens digits.

    27   The tens digit is 2.
    46   The tens digit is 4.

4 tens is more than 2 tens, so 46 is greater than 27.

B. Compare 84 and 81. Use > or <.

The tens digits are the same, so look at the ones digits.

    84   The ones digit is 4.
    81   The ones digit is 1.

Write 84 > 81   84 **is greater than** 81.
  or 81 < 84   81 **is less than** 84.

Practice

Tell which is the greater number.

1. 35, 61   **2.** 52, 12   **3.** 44, 47   **4.** 17, 71

Tell which number is less.

5. 53, 13   **6.** 8, 32   **7.** 97, 90   **8.** 25, 30

Replace ▦ with < or >.

9. 79 ▦ 46   **10.** 88 ▦ 98   **11.** 61 ▦ 8   **12.** 40 ▦ 45

13. 6 ▦ 2   **14.** 77 ▦ 33   **15.** 14 ▦ 19   **16.** 12 ▦ 25

Ordering Two-Digit Numbers

Review

Write 69, 35, 42, and 67 in order from least to greatest.
First look at the tens digits.

3 tens	4 tens	6 tens
3 5	**4** 2	**6** 9
		6 7

The tens digits are the same in 69 and 67.
So compare the ones.

9 > **7**   so   **6 9** > **6 7**.

The numbers in order from least to greatest
are 35, 42, 67, and 69.

Practice

Write these numbers in order from least to greatest.

1. 37   31   45   **2.** 68   59   65   **3.** 72   23   95

4. 53   37   56   **5.** 49   33   11   **6.** 36   92   97

7. 23   12   26   **8.** 46   51   15   **9.** 89   33   45

Write these numbers in order from greatest to least.

10. 56   52   63   **11.** 68   59   65   **12.** 10   97   89

13. 47   61   68   **14.** 72   96   93   **15.** 64   13   95

16. 70   94   21   **17.** 88   77   71   **18.** 58   28   32

Two-Digit Addition

Review

Find 57 + 26.

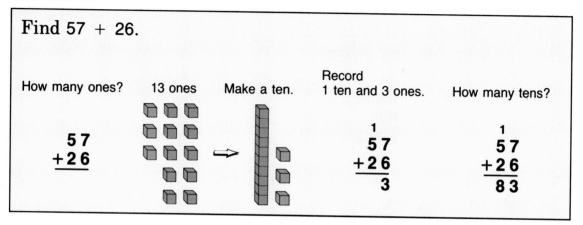

How many ones?   13 ones   Make a ten.   Record 1 ten and 3 ones.   How many tens?

$$\begin{array}{r} 5\,7 \\ +2\,6 \\ \hline \end{array} \qquad \begin{array}{r} 1 \\ 5\,7 \\ +2\,6 \\ \hline 3 \end{array} \qquad \begin{array}{r} 1 \\ 5\,7 \\ +2\,6 \\ \hline 8\,3 \end{array}$$

Practice

Add.

1. $\begin{array}{r} 13 \\ +59 \\ \hline \end{array}$
2. $\begin{array}{r} 64 \\ +27 \\ \hline \end{array}$
3. $\begin{array}{r} 22 \\ +68 \\ \hline \end{array}$
4. $\begin{array}{r} 71 \\ +\ 3 \\ \hline \end{array}$
5. $\begin{array}{r} 50 \\ +44 \\ \hline \end{array}$

6. $\begin{array}{r} 25 \\ +37 \\ \hline \end{array}$
7. $\begin{array}{r} 42 \\ +19 \\ \hline \end{array}$
8. $\begin{array}{r} 31 \\ +66 \\ \hline \end{array}$
9. $\begin{array}{r} 87 \\ +\ 7 \\ \hline \end{array}$
10. $\begin{array}{r} 18 \\ +\ 6 \\ \hline \end{array}$

11. $\begin{array}{r} 77 \\ +19 \\ \hline \end{array}$
12. $\begin{array}{r} 53 \\ +40 \\ \hline \end{array}$
13. $\begin{array}{r} 94 \\ +\ 2 \\ \hline \end{array}$
14. $\begin{array}{r} 68 \\ +17 \\ \hline \end{array}$
15. $\begin{array}{r} 55 \\ +33 \\ \hline \end{array}$

16. $\begin{array}{r} 73 \\ +17 \\ \hline \end{array}$
17. $\begin{array}{r} 42 \\ +51 \\ \hline \end{array}$
18. $\begin{array}{r} 31 \\ +60 \\ \hline \end{array}$
19. $\begin{array}{r} 75 \\ +21 \\ \hline \end{array}$
20. $\begin{array}{r} 69 \\ +29 \\ \hline \end{array}$

21. 36 + 25
22. 67 + 31
23. 82 + 8
24. 19 + 15

25. 6 + 18
26. 88 + 9
27. 48 + 43
28. 5 + 15

29. 22 + 71
30. 51 + 30
31. 64 + 26
32. 43 + 39

33. 63 + 17
34. 74 + 8
35. 4 + 34
36. 57 + 34

Three Addends

Review

Find 8 + 6 + 9.

You can add down.

$$\begin{array}{r} 8 \\ 6 \\ +9 \end{array} \Big\rangle \begin{array}{r} 14 \\ +\ 9 \\ \hline 23 \end{array}$$

Or you can add up.

$$\begin{array}{r} 8 \longrightarrow 8 \\ 6 \\ +9 \end{array} \Big\rangle \begin{array}{r} \\ +15 \\ \hline 23 \end{array}$$

Practice

Find these sums.

1. $\begin{array}{r} 9 \\ 7 \\ +1 \end{array}$
2. $\begin{array}{r} 8 \\ 4 \\ +9 \end{array}$
3. $\begin{array}{r} 7 \\ 3 \\ +5 \end{array}$
4. $\begin{array}{r} 6 \\ 8 \\ +9 \end{array}$
5. $\begin{array}{r} 9 \\ 1 \\ +4 \end{array}$
6. $\begin{array}{r} 5 \\ 6 \\ +7 \end{array}$

7. $\begin{array}{r} 2 \\ 7 \\ +6 \end{array}$
8. $\begin{array}{r} 4 \\ 5 \\ +9 \end{array}$
9. $\begin{array}{r} 3 \\ 7 \\ +8 \end{array}$
10. $\begin{array}{r} 5 \\ 2 \\ +6 \end{array}$
11. $\begin{array}{r} 9 \\ 4 \\ +3 \end{array}$
12. $\begin{array}{r} 8 \\ 6 \\ +5 \end{array}$

13. 4 + 5 + 3
14. 6 + 7 + 2
15. 9 + 7 + 5

16. 3 + 9 + 2
17. 7 + 3 + 5
18. 6 + 5 + 6

19. 8 + 4 + 5
20. 5 + 7 + 8
21. 4 + 5 + 9

22. 9 + 6 + 5
23. 5 + 6 + 5
24. 7 + 2 + 8

25. 4 + 8 + 3
26. 8 + 6 + 1
27. 8 + 9 + 8

28. 2 + 7 + 7
29. 5 + 1 + 9
30. 4 + 9 + 7

31. 3 + 6 + 7
32. 7 + 4 + 8
33. 2 + 8 + 7

Two-Digit Subtraction

Review

Find 54 − 28.

Think: Are there enough ones in 54? No.

Trade a ten for 10 more ones.

Rename 54. Subtract the ones. Subtract the tens.

$$\begin{array}{r} 5\,4 \\ -2\,8 \\ \hline \end{array}$$

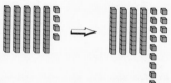

$$\begin{array}{r} \overset{4\ \ 14}{5\,\cancel{4}} \\ -2\,8 \\ \hline 2\,6 \end{array}$$

Practice

Find each difference.

1. 46 −28	**2.** 31 − 3	**3.** 57 −39	**4.** 62 −38	**5.** 81 −29
6. 50 −37	**7.** 92 −76	**8.** 95 −48	**9.** 54 −49	**10.** 44 − 8
11. 71 −68	**12.** 83 −76	**13.** 52 −26	**14.** 91 −34	**15.** 63 − 9
16. 62 −57	**17.** 80 −31	**18.** 72 −49	**19.** 75 −69	**20.** 81 −39

21. 75 − 29   **22.** 82 − 57   **23.** 45 − 17   **24.** 90 − 77

25. 62 − 14   **26.** 83 − 24   **27.** 75 − 48   **28.** 98 − 59

29. 72 − 6   **30.** 52 − 39   **31.** 96 − 18   **32.** 33 − 17

33. 20 − 14   **34.** 66 − 29   **35.** 53 − 5   **36.** 63 − 46

Time: Hour and Half-Hour

Review

A. One hour is 60 minutes. The *hour hand* on a clock moves from one number to the next in 60 minutes or 1 hour.

The *minute hand* moves from one small mark to the next in 1 minute.

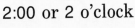

2:00 or 2 o'clock

B. A half-hour is 30 minutes. The minute hand on a clock moves through 30 small marks in a half-hour.

2:30 or
30 minutes after 2

Practice

Write the time in two ways.

1.

2.

3.

4.

5.

6.

7.

8.

9.

Time: Quarter Hour

Review

A quarter of an hour is 15 minutes. The minute hand on a clock moves through 15 small marks in a quarter of an hour.

Write each time in two ways.

A.

9:15
or
15 minutes after 9

B.

9:45
or
45 minutes after 9

Practice

Write each time in two ways.

1.

2.

3.

4.

5.
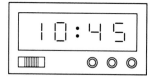

6.

7.

8.

9.

Measuring to the Nearest Inch

Review

A. Measure the line segment to the nearest inch.

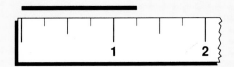

The end of the line segment is closer to 1 inch than 2 inches. The length to the nearest inch is 1 inch.

B. Measure the length of the pencil to the nearest inch.

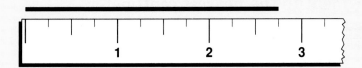

The end of the pencil is closer to 3 inches than 2 inches. The length to the nearest inch is 3 inches.

Practice

Measure each line segment to the nearest inch.

1. —————————

2. ———————————

3. ————————————————

4. ——————————————

5. ———————————————————

6. ——————————

7. ———————————————————

Measuring to the Nearest Centimeter

Review

A. Measure the line segment to the nearest centimeter.

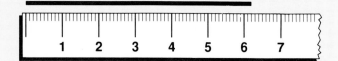

The end of the line segment is closer to 6 centimeters than 7 centimeters.
The length to the nearest centimeter is 6 centimeters.

B. Measure the line segment to the nearest centimeter.

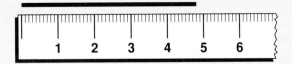

The end of the line segment is closer to 5 centimeters than 4 centimeters.
The length to the nearest centimeter is 5 centimeters.

Practice

Measure each line segment to the nearest centimeter.

1. _____   **2.** _____

3. _____   **4.** _____

5. _____

6. _____

7. _____

Counting to $0.99

Review

Write the amount of money.

| $0.25 | $0.50 | $0.60 | $0.70 | $0.71 | $0.72 |

The amount of money shown is $0.72.

Practice

Use $ and . to write each amount of money.

1.

2.

3.

4.

5.

6.

7.

8.

9.

10.

11.

12.

Independent Study Handbook

Contents

How to Use a Calculator

Calculators are used in everyday life at home and at work. They save time when solving problems with large numbers or problems with many numbers. *Remember*:

▶ **Do** estimate to check whether you pushed the correct buttons.

▶ **Don't** use a calculator when paper and pencil or mental math is faster.

Calculator displays

▶ **Number of digits** What is the greatest number you can display on your calculator? If you press 99,999 × 99,999, you get a number with more digits than the calculator display can show. Most calculators will show some kind of an "error" message.

▶ **Unnecessary zeros** If you add $2.10 and $3.20, you do not enter the "$" on your calculator. Most calculators will display 5.3 for the answer. Calculators usually drop unnecessary zeros. You write the answer as $5.30. A zero always precedes a decimal less than one.

Calculator keys

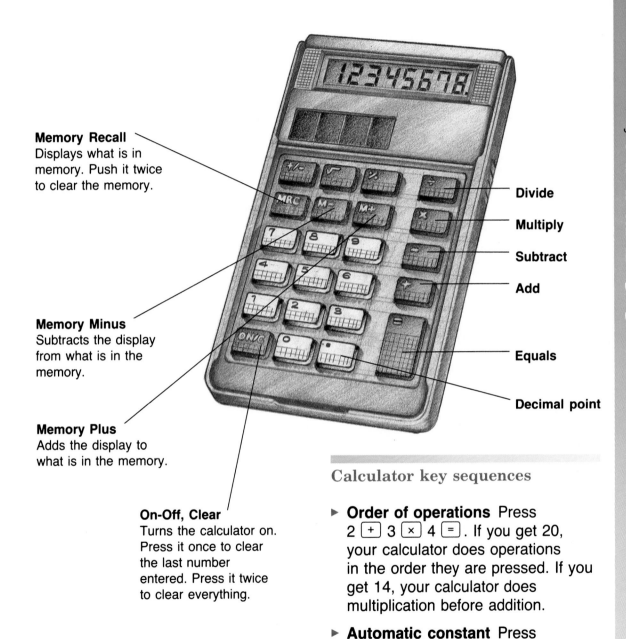

Memory Recall
Displays what is in memory. Push it twice to clear the memory.

Memory Minus
Subtracts the display from what is in the memory.

Memory Plus
Adds the display to what is in the memory.

On-Off, Clear
Turns the calculator on. Press it once to clear the last number entered. Press it twice to clear everything.

Divide

Multiply

Subtract

Add

Equals

Decimal point

Calculator key sequences

▶ **Order of operations** Press 2 [+] 3 [×] 4 [=]. If you get 20, your calculator does operations in the order they are pressed. If you get 14, your calculator does multiplication before addition.

▶ **Automatic constant** Press 2 [+] 3 [=] [=] [=] [=]. Then press 2 [×] 3 [=] [=] [=] [=]. If your calculator keeps adding 3 or multiplying by 2, your calculator has an automatic constant.

Problem-Solving Help File

Use these pages when you need help with problem solving.

Problem-Solving Guide

There is no recipe or magic formula for solving problems. But keeping a problem-solving guide in mind can help you become a better problem solver.

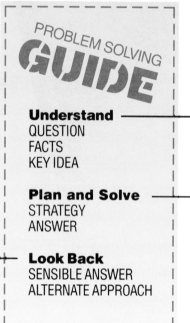

PROBLEM SOLVING GUIDE

Understand
QUESTION
FACTS
KEY IDEA

Plan and Solve
STRATEGY
ANSWER

Look Back
SENSIBLE ANSWER
ALTERNATE APPROACH

Look Back
SENSIBLE ANSWER

▶ Did you check your work?
▶ Did you use all the needed data?
▶ Does your answer have the correct labels?
▶ Is your answer close to the estimate?
▶ Is your answer reasonable for the situation?

ALTERNATE APPROACH

▶ Is there another way to get the same answer?
▶ Could you use the same strategy differently?
▶ Would another strategy be faster or simpler?

Understand
QUESTION

▶ What are you asked to find?
▶ Try to state the question in your own words.
▶ Is an exact answer needed?

FACTS

▶ What facts are given?
▶ Is there too much or too little information?
▶ Is data needed from a picture, table, or graph?
▶ Do you need to collect some data?

KEY IDEA

▶ How are the facts and the question related?
▶ Are there groups that are part of a whole?
▶ Are two groups being compared?
▶ Are there groups that are joining or separating?
▶ Are there groups of the same size?

Plan and Solve
STRATEGY

▶ What can you do to solve the problem?
▶ Can the problem be solved by computing?
▶ Estimate the answer.
▶ Choose a strategy. Try another, if needed.

ANSWER

▶ Give the answer in a sentence.
▶ Do you need to interpret a remainder?
▶ Is rounding needed?

Problem-Solving Strategies

You might think of problem-solving strategies as problem-solving tools that you own and use when needed. One or more strategies might be used for a problem. And if one strategy doesn't work, try another one.

PROBLEM SOLVING STRATEGIES

Choose an Operation
Find a Pattern
Use Logical Reasoning
Make a Table
Draw a Picture
Try and Check
Write a Number Sentence
Work Backward
Make a Graph

TIPS FOR PROBLEM SOLVERS

Don't give up. Some problems take longer than others.

Problem-Solving Behaviors and Attitudes

When you solve problems, do you give up quickly or lack confidence? Behaviors and attitudes can affect your work. So, remember these tips. They can help you become a better problem solver.

Tips for Problem Solvers

▶ **Don't give up.** Some problems take longer than others.

▶ **Be flexible.** If you get stuck, try another idea.

▶ **Be confident** so you can do your best.

▶ **Take risks.** Try your hunches. They often work.

▶ **Brainstorm to get started**—one idea will lead to another.

▶ **Visualize the problem** in your mind to help you understand it better.

▶ **Compare problems** to help you relate new problems to ones you've solved before.

▶ **Think about your thinking.** Pause to ask, "How is this going to help me solve the problem?"

▶ **Share your thinking with others.** Explaining your ideas helps you think better.

▶ **Organize your work** to help you think clearly.

Mental Math Strategies

Often the best calculator is your own mind. For simple calculations, mental math can be better than paper and pencil or a calculator. To sharpen your mental math skills, use the mental computation strategies shown on these pages.

Breaking Apart Numbers

Break apart one or more numbers to get numbers that are easier to use.

54 + 23
54 + 20 + 3   Break apart 23.
   74 + 3
      77

68 − 45
68 − 40   Break apart 45.
28 − 5   First subtract 40.
   23   Then subtract 5.

87 × 2
(80 + 7) × 2   Break apart 87.
(80 × 2) + (7 × 2)   Use the distributive
   160 + 14   property.
      174

35 + 48
(30 + 5) + (40 + 8)   Break apart 35 and 48.
(30 + 40) + (5 + 8)   Regroup the numbers.
      70 + 13
         83

Compatible Numbers

Compatible numbers are pairs of numbers that are easy to use. Look for numbers like 1, 10, 100 or 3, 30, 300 that are easy to use.

40 + 30   **28 × 10**
   70   280

2 × 9 × 5
2 × 5 × 9
  10 × 9
    90

Look for factors of 10.

When there are 3 or more numbers, look for pairs of numbers that are compatible.

3 + 48 + 7
3 + 7 + 48
  10 + 48
     58

2 × 9 × 3
2 × 3 × 9
  6 × 9
    54

Multiply the lesser factors first.

Using Equivalent Forms

Divide to find "fraction of."

$\frac{1}{3} \times 180$

$180 \div 3$

60

Change decimals or percents to fractions to get a number that is easier to use.

25% of 32

$\frac{1}{4}$ of 32

$32 \div 4$

8

Compensation

Change one number to make it easy to use. Then change the answer to compensate.

57 + 29

$57 + 30 = 87$	Add 1 to 29 to get 30.
$87 - 1 = 86$	Subtract 1 from the answer.

165 − 97

$165 - 100 = 65$	Add 3 to 97 to get 100.
$65 + 3 = 68$	Add 3 to the answer.

Change one number to make it easy to use. Then change the other number to compensate.

66 + 19

$65 + 20$

85 — Add 1 to 19 and subtract 1 from 66.

157 − 98 — Add 2 to 98 and to 157.

$159 - 100$

59

Estimation Strategies

In everyday life, an exact answer is often unnecessary. For example, you can estimate while shopping to see if you have enough money.

When you do need an exact answer, estimation helps you find possible errors. Estimation is especially important for checking whether you pushed a wrong button on a calculator.

To help you make good estimates, use the estimation strategies shown on these pages.

Front-End Digits

Use just the first digit in each number to help you make an estimate.

173	100
421	400
+348	**+300**
	800

Since 73 + 21 + 48 is about 100, you can also adjust the estimate by adding 100 to get 900.

Rounding

Round to the nearest 10 or 100.

37	40
+22	**+20**
	60

88	90
−42	**−40**
	50

425	400
× 4	**× 4**
	1,600

Round both numbers up and both numbers down to get a range.

136 + 243
$$200 + 300 = 500$$
$$100 + 200 = 300$$

136 + 243 is between 300 and 500.

Substituting Compatible Numbers

Use numbers that are close to the original numbers.

6)$\overline{27}$

6)$\overline{24}$ or 6)$\overline{30}$

6)$\overline{27}$ is about 5.

4)$\overline{77}$

4)$\overline{80}$

4)$\overline{77}$ is about 20.

23)$\overline{476}$

24)$\overline{480}$ or 23)$\overline{460}$ or 25)$\overline{500}$

23)$\overline{476}$ is about 20.

$24 \times 78 \times 4$

$25 \times 78 \times 4$

100×78

$24 \times 78 \times 4$ is about 7,800.

Clustering

Look for groups of numbers that are close to the same number.

627	Each number is
658	about 600, so the
589	sum is about 4 ×
+613	600 or 2,400.

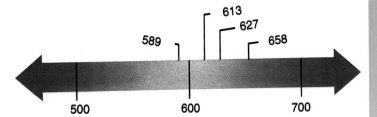

Comparing to a Reference Point

Compare the numbers to numbers you can work with easily.

346	Both numbers are less than 500, so the
+438	sum is less than 1,000.

Math Study Skills

Try these math study skills to help you do your best.

Before a Lesson

▸ **Preview the lesson.** Look over the lesson to see what it's about.

▸ **Set a purpose.** Are you about to learn a new topic or revisit a familiar one?

▸ **Recall what you know.** What have you learned about this topic previously?

Build Understanding

Reading the lesson

▸ **Read slowly.** Don't try to read a math book as fast as a story book.

▸ **Learn vocabulary and symbols.** Note new math terms and symbols. Use the glossary and index. Watch for words like "product" that have other meanings outside of math.

▸ **Read diagrams, tables, graphs.** Use a ruler to help you read rows and columns.

▸ **Do the examples.** Work the examples yourself as you go through them.

Doing Activities

▸ **Use materials.** Keep the materials organized. Use them to explore new ideas.

▸ **Work with others.** When you work with others, use the tips for working together given on page 560.

Build Understandin

A. A market gets boxes of 24 heads in each box. I heads of lettuce are in

Since each box contai same number of he

Check Understanding

Trying on your own

▶ **Note what you don't understand.** When you try some exercises, be aware of what you don't understand.

▶ **Reread the lesson.** When you don't understand, reread the "Build Understanding" section.

Preventing errors

▶ **Find another example.** When you need another example, turn to the "Reteaching" set at the back of the chapter.

▶ **Try again.** Keep trying until you feel you understand.

Practice and Problem Solving

Reading the exercises

▶ **Read directions.** Read carefully.

▶ **Read word problems.** Read slowly and reread, if needed.

Doing written work

▶ **Show your work.** Record what you did. Make your paper easy to follow and the answer easy to find.

▶ **Check your work.** Read what you write.

▶ **Find more practice.** Use the "More Practice" at the back of the chapter when needed.

After a Lesson

▶ **Look back.** Summarize the lesson. Would you be able to teach it to another student?

▶ **Connect to other lessons.** Think about how this lesson is related to other lessons.

Working in Groups

When you do math working with others, you'll learn more math, you'll learn how to work as a team, and you'll enjoy math more.

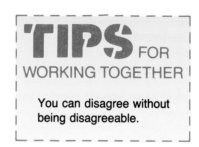

TIPS FOR
WORKING TOGETHER

You can disagree without being disagreeable.

Roles for Group Members

When you work in a group, it can be helpful for each person to have a role. Some roles are:

▶ **Reporter**—This person summarizes the group's thinking.

▶ **Encourager**—This person encourages group members to take part and to work together well.

▶ **Recorder**—This person records the group's work.

▶ **Checker**—This person asks group members to explain their thinking or may ask others if they agree.

▶ **Materials Manager**—This person gets any materials that are needed and returns them at the end of class.

Tips for Working Together

Here are some tips for working well with others in a group.

▶ Involve your whole group. Help everyone to participate.

▶ Help keep your group on task.

▶ To make sure your group understands the task or solution, have each group member say it in his or her own words, summarize the steps, or give an example.

▶ Work as a group. If you understand, help another group member. Don't work ahead of the others.

▶ Be a good tutor. Make up similar problems or easier ones to help someone understand.

▶ When you are unsure, ask someone in your group for help or say you don't understand.

▶ Tell someone when he or she does or says something that helps you.

▶ Don't decide by voting. Try to understand which might be the best solution and why.

▶ Remember, you can disagree without being disagreeable.

Tables

Metric System

Length
10 millimeters (mm) = 1 centimeter (cm)
10 centimeters
100 millimeters } = 1 decimeter (dm)
10 decimeters
100 centimeters } = 1 meter (m)
1,000 meters = 1 kilometer (km)

Area
100 square millimeters (mm^2) = 1 square centimeter (cm^2)
10,000 square centimeters = 1 square meter (m^2)
100 square meters = 1 are (a)
10,000 square meters = 1 hectare (ha)

Volume
1,000 cubic millimeters (mm^3) = 1 cubic centimeter (cm^3)
1,000 cubic centimeters = 1 cubic decimeter (dm^3)
1,000,000 cubic centimeters = 1 cubic meter (m^3)

Mass (weight)
1,000 milligrams (mg) = 1 gram (g)
1,000 grams = 1 kilogram (kg)
1,000 kilograms = 1 metric ton (t)

Capacity
1,000 milliliters (mL) = 1 liter (L)

Time

60 seconds = 1 minute
60 minutes = 1 hour
24 hours = 1 day
7 days = 1 week
365 days
52 weeks } = 1 year
12 months
366 days = 1 leap year

Addition-Subtraction Table

+	0	1	2	3	4	5	6	7	8	9
0	0	1	2	3	4	5	6	7	8	9
1	1	2	3	4	5	6	7	8	9	10
2	2	3	4	5	6	7	8	9	10	11
3	3	4	5	6	7	8	9	10	11	12
4	4	5	6	7	8	9	10	11	12	13
5	5	6	7	8	9	10	11	12	13	14
6	6	7	8	9	10	11	12	13	14	15
7	7	8	9	10	11	12	13	14	15	16
8	8	9	10	11	12	13	14	15	16	17
9	9	10	11	12	13	14	15	16	17	18

Multiplication-Division Table

×	1	2	3	4	5	6	7	8	9
1	1	2	3	4	5	6	7	8	9
2	2	4	6	8	10	12	14	16	18
3	3	6	9	12	15	18	21	24	27
4	4	8	12	16	20	24	28	32	36
5	5	10	15	20	25	30	35	40	45
6	6	12	18	24	30	36	42	48	54
7	7	14	21	28	35	42	49	56	63
8	8	16	24	32	40	48	56	64	72
9	9	18	27	36	45	54	63	72	81

Customary System

Length
12 inches (in.) = 1 foot (ft)
3 feet
36 inches } = 1 yard (yd)
1,760 yards
5,280 feet } = 1 mile (mi)
6,076 feet = 1 nautical mile

Area
144 square inches (sq in.) = 1 square foot (sq ft)
9 square feet = 1 square yard (sq yd)
4,840 square yards = 1 acre (A)

Volume
1,728 cubic inches (cu in.) = 1 cubic foot (cu ft)
27 cubic feet = 1 cubic yard (cu yd)

Weight
16 ounces (oz) = 1 pound (lb)
2,000 pounds = 1 ton (T)

Capacity
8 fluid ounces (fl oz) = 1 cup (c)
2 cups = 1 pint (pt)
2 pints = 1 quart (qt)
4 quarts = 1 gallon (gal)

Glossary

Add To find the total when putting together two or more quantities.

Addend A number that is added. In $8 + 4 = 12$, the addends are 8 and 4.

Addition property of zero The sum of zero and a number is that number.

Angle ($\angle$) The figure formed by two rays with the same endpoint.

Area A number given in square units that indicates the size of the inside of a plane figure.

Array An arrangement of objects or numbers in rows and columns.

Associative property (Grouping property) The way in which addends (or factors) are grouped does not affect the sum (or product).
$(7 + 2) + 5 = 7 + (2 + 5)$
$(7 \times 2) \times 5 = 7 \times (2 \times 5)$

Average A number obtained by dividing the sum of two or more addends by the number of addends.

Basic Fact A number sentence that has at least two one-digit numbers. The sentences below are examples of basic facts.
$7 + 2 = 9$ $16 - 7 = 9$
$5 \times 3 = 15$ $8 \div 4 = 2$

Billion The word name for 1,000,000,000.

Centimeter A unit of length in the metric system. Your little finger is about 1 centimeter wide.

Circle A plane figure with all points the same distance from a given point called the *center*.

Circumference The distance around a circle.

Clockwise The direction in which the hands of a clock move. The hands pass the numbers in order.

Clustering An estimation method used when all the numbers are close to the same number.

Column A line of objects or numbers from top to bottom in an array.

Common denominator A common multiple of two or more denominators. A common denominator for $\frac{1}{6}$ and $\frac{3}{8}$ is 48.

Common factor A number that is a factor of two or more numbers. A common factor of 6 and 12 is 3.

Common multiple A number that is a multiple of two or more numbers.

Commutative property (Order property) The order in which numbers are added (or multiplied) does not affect the sum (or product). $4 + 6 = 6 + 4$; $4 \times 6 = 6 \times 4$

Compass An instrument used for drawing circles.

Compatible number A number close to the number in the problem being solved that is used for mental computation.

Composite number A whole number, greater than 0, that has more than two factors.

Cone A solid figure formed by connecting a circle to a point not in the plane of the circle.

Congruent figures Two figures with the same size and shape.

Coordinates Integers in an ordered pair giving the location of a point in a coordinate plane.

Corner (1) The point where the 2 sides of an angle meet. (2) The point where 2 sides of a polygon meet. (3) The point where edges of a polyhedron meet.

Cube A prism with all square faces.

Cup A unit for measuring capacity in the customary system. 2 cups equals 1 pint.

Curve A line that has no straight part.

Cylinder A space figure with two circular bases that are parallel and congruent.

Data A collection of gathered information that has not been organized.

Decimal A number used to name a whole quantity and/or a fractional part. It is written in standard form with a point to separate the whole number and fraction parts.

Decimeter A unit for measuring length in the metric system.
10 decimeters equal 1 meter.

Degree (of an angle) A unit for measuring angles.

Degree Celsius A unit for measuring temperature in the metric system.

Degree Fahrenheit A unit for measuring temperature in the customary system.

Denominator The number below the line in a fraction. It names the number of equal parts or objects. In $\frac{3}{4}$, the denominator is 4.

Diagonal In a polygon, a line segment that connects corners not next to each other.

Diameter In a circle, a segment that passes through the center and that has both endpoints on the circle.

Difference The number found by subtracting one number from another. In $95 - 68 = 27$, the difference is 27.

Digit One of the symbols used for writing numbers: 0, 1, 2, 3, 4, 5, 6, 7, 8, and 9.

Distributive property When a factor is a sum, multiplying each addend before adding does not change the product. $5(3 + 4) = (5 \times 3) + (5 \times 4)$

Divide To find how a total amount can be separated into an equal number of groups, or into groups of equal size.

Dividend A number that is divided by another number.

Divisible A number is divisible by another if the remainder is zero after dividing.

Divisor The number by which another number is divided.

Edge Segment where two faces of a polyhedron meet.

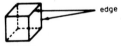

Endpoint The point at the end of a line segment or a ray.

Equal Things that are the same as each other in size or amount or value.

Equal fractions Fractions that name the same number. $\frac{2}{3}$ and $\frac{8}{12}$ are equal fractions.

Equally likely Outcomes that will happen about as often as each other.

Equation A mathematical sentence with the = symbol.

Estimate A number that is close to another number. A term used for a calculation not requiring an exact answer.

Even number A whole number that has 0, 2, 4, 6, or 8 in the ones place.

Expanded form A way to write a number to show the value of each digit.

Face Flat surface that is part of a polyhedron.

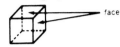

Factor (1) A number to be multiplied. (2) A number that divides evenly into a given second number is a factor of that number.

Family of facts The related number sentences for addition and subtraction (or multiplication and division) that contain all the same numbers.
$5 + 3 = 8$ $8 - 3 = 5$
$3 + 5 = 8$ $8 - 5 = 3$

Flip A change in location of a figure by flipping it over a line, creating a mirror image (reflection) of the figure.

Foot A unit for measuring length in the customary system. 1 foot equals 12 inches.

Fraction A number that names a part of a whole or of a set. It is written in the form $\frac{a}{b}$.

Frequency The number of times a certain item occurs in a set of data.

Gallon A unit for measuring capacity in the customary system. 1 gallon equals 4 quarts.

Geometric figure A closed shape made with line segments or curves in a plane.

Gram A unit for measuring weight in the metric system. A raisin weighs about 1 gram.

Graph A drawing used to show information in an organized way.

Greater than ($>$) A relation between two numbers, with the greater number given first.
$8 > 5$ $9 > 1.4$

Grouping Putting a known number of objects into each group and making as many groups as you can.

Hexagon A six-sided polygon.

Hour hand The short hand on a clock that names the number of hours.

Improper fraction A fraction whose numerator is greater than or equal to its denominator.

Inch A unit for measuring length in the customary system. A paper clip is about 1 inch long.

Integers The whole numbers and their opposites. Some integers are $+3$, -3, 0, $+16$, -16.

Intersecting lines Lines that meet at a point.

Kilogram A unit for measuring weight in the metric system. 1 kilogram equals 1,000 grams.

Kilometer A unit for measuring length in the metric system. 1 kilometer equals 1,000 meters.

Less than ($<$) A relation between two numbers, with the lesser number given first.
$5 < 8$ $1.4 < 9$

Line A set of points continuing without end in both directions.

Line plot A graph that uses Xs to show information and compare quantities.

Line of symmetry A line on which a figure can be folded into two congruent parts.

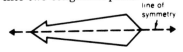

Line segment Two points and the straight path between them.

Liter A unit for measuring capacity in the metric system. 1 liter equals 1,000 milliliters.

Lowest terms A fraction for which 1 is the greatest common factor of both the numerator and the denominator.

Meter A unit for measuring length in the metric system. 1 meter equals 100 centimeters.

Mile A unit for measuring length in the customary system. 1 mile equals 5,280 feet.

Milliliter A unit for measuring capacity in the metric system. An eyedropper holds about 1 milliliter.

Million The word name for 1,000,000.

Minuend A number from which another number is subtracted. In $95 - 68 = 27$, the minuend is 95.

Minute hand The long hand on a clock that names the number of minutes.

Mixed number A number that has a whole number part and a fraction part.

More likely An outcome that will happen more often than another outcome.

Multiple A multiple of a number is the product of that number and a whole number.

Multiplicand A number that is multiplied by another number. In $27 \times 3 = 81$, the multiplicand is 27.

Multiplication property of one The product of one and a number is that number.

Multiplication property of zero The product of zero and a number is zero.

Multiplier A number that multiplies another number. In $27 \times 3 = 81$, the multiplier is 3.

Multiply To find the total when putting together groups of equal size, or to find the number that is "times as many" as another number.

Number pair *See* Ordered pair.

Number sentence A way to write a relationship between numbers.
$18 + 27 = 45$ $9 > 6$

Numerator The number above the line in a fraction. It names the number of parts or objects being thought about. In $\frac{3}{4}$, the numerator is 3.

Octagon An eight-sided polygon.

Odd number A whole number that has 1, 3, 5, 7, or 9 in the ones place.

Ordered pair A pair of numbers arranged so there is a first number and a second number, used to locate a point on a grid.

Ordinal number A number, such as *third,* used to tell order or position.

Organized list All the possibilities for a situation written in a certain order.

Ounce A unit for measuring weight in the customary system. A slice of bread weighs about 1 ounce.

Outcome A possible result of an action.

Parallel lines Lines in a plane that never meet.

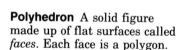

Parallelogram A quadrilateral with opposite sides parallel and congruent.

Pentagon A five-sided polygon.

Percent (%) A word meaning "hundredths" or "out of 100." 45 percent (45%) equals 0.45 or $\frac{45}{100}$.

Perimeter The sum of the lengths of the sides of a polygon.

Perpendicular lines Lines that intersect to form right angles.

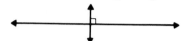

Pint A unit for measuring capacity in the customary system. 1 pint equals 2 cups.

Place value The number each digit represents is determined by the position the digit occupies.

Plane A flat surface that extends without end in all directions.

Point An exact location in space.

Polygon A plane figure made by line segments called *sides,* each side meeting two other sides, one at each of its endpoints.

Polyhedron A solid figure made up of flat surfaces called *faces.* Each face is a polygon.

Prime factor A factor that is a prime number. The prime factors of 10 are 2 and 5.

Prime number A whole number, greater than 1, that has exactly two factors: itself and 1.

Prism A polyhedron with two parallel, congruent faces, called *bases.* All other faces are parallelograms.

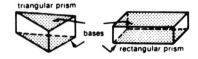

Probability A number from 0 to 1 that tells how likely it is that a given outcome will occur. The closer to 1, the *more likely* the outcome is to occur. The closer to 0, the *less likely* it is to occur.

Product The number found by multiplying numbers. In 27 × 3 = 81, the product is 81.

Protractor An instrument used to measure angles.

Pyramid A polyhedron formed by connecting points of a polygon to a point not in the plane of the polygon. The polygon and its interior is the *base*.

triangular pyramid   rectangular pyramid

Quadrilateral A four-sided polygon.

Quart A unit for measuring capacity in the customary system. 2 pints equal 1 quart.

Quotient The answer after dividing one number by another.

Radius In a circle, a segment that connects the center of the circle with a point on the circle.

Range The difference between the greatest and the least numbers in a set of data.

Ratio A pair of numbers that names a rate or a comparison.

Ray A set of points that has one endpoint and that extends without end in one direction.

Rectangle A parallelogram with four right angles.

Regular polygon A polygon with all sides congruent and all angles congruent.

Remainder The number that is left over after dividing. When 20 is divided by 6, the remainder is 2.

Repeating decimal A decimal in which one or more digits

keep repeating, such as 0.518181818. . .

Right angle An angle with a measure of 90°.

Right triangle Triangle with one right angle.

Rotation A change in location of a figure by turning it about a point.

Rounded number A number expressed to the *nearest 10, 100, 1,000,* and so on. 368 rounded to the nearest 10 is 370; rounded to the nearest 100 is 400.

Row A line of objects or numbers from left to right in an array.

Sample Part of a group upon which an experiment or survey is conducted.

Sequence A set of numbers formed by a pattern.

Sharing Putting the same number of objects into each group when you know the number of groups.

Side *See* Polygon.

Similar figures Figures with the same shape but not necessarily the same size.

Slide A change in location of a figure by moving it without turning it.

Solid figure A figure that has three dimensions—length, width, and height.

Sphere A solid figure with all points the same distance from a given point called the *center.*

Square (in geometry) A rectangle with four congruent sides.

Square (in numeration) To multiply a number by itself.

Square products A sequence of numbers that can be shown by dots arranged in the shape of a square.

Standard form The notation

for writing numbers using the digits 0–9 and each place represents a power of ten.

Statistics Numerical facts that are collected, organized, and analyzed.

Subtract To find how many are left when some are taken away, or to compare two quantities.

Subtrahend A number to be subtracted from another number. In 95 − 68 = 27, the subtrahend is 68.

Sum The number found by adding numbers. In 8 + 4 = 12, the sum is 12.

Surface The outside of a solid figure.

Symmetric figure A plane figure that can be folded in half so the two halves match.

Tally chart A table to help with counting when collecting data.

Terminating decimal A decimal with an exact number of nonzero digits, such as 0.375.

Triangle A three-sided polygon.

Triangular numbers A sequence of numbers that can be shown by dots arranged in the shape of a triangle.

Turn A change in location of a figure by moving it around a given point.

Vertex *See* Corner.

Volume A number given in cubic units that indicates the size of the inside of a solid figure.

Whole number One of the numbers 0, 1, 2, 3, and so on.

Yard A unit for measuring length in the customary system. 1 yard equals 3 feet.

Index

(Continued from page ii)
Janeart LTD. 504–505 L. A.
Lavenstein: 419 Ron Morecraft: 8, 57, 94, 116, 158, 226, 254, 255, 256, 257, 261, 263, 285, 299
Stock Boston: John Coletti 165
The Stock Market 453; Thomas Braise 438–439; Charles Krebs 149, 438–439; Eric Lawton 438–439; John Maher 438–439; Roy Morsch 438–439

Illustrations
Jacque Auger, Ron Becker, Dolores Bego, Ron Berg, Eliot Bergman, Lloyd Birmingham, Alex Bloch, Lee Lee Brazeal, Dan Bridy, David Cain, Susan Johnston Carlson, Jim Deigan, Jim Delapine, Nancy Didion, Mac Evans, Mark Fisher, Robert Frank, Janice Fried, Toni Goffe, Franklin Hammond, Fred Harsh, Steve Henry, Dave Joly, Mark

Kaplan, Andy Levine, Ron Lieberman, Kathleen Dunne McCarthy, Peter McMahon, Kimble Mead, James Needham, Julie Pace, Charles Peale, Bob Pepper, Brenda Pepper, Nikolai Punin, Claudia Sargent, Susan Skoorka, Kirsten Soderlind, Randy South, Barton Stabler, Susan Swan, John Trotta, Paul Vaccarello, Rhonda Voo